Praise for Tom Porter's
And Grandma Said . . . Iroquois Teachings

" . . . The book is equal in importance to Arthur C. Parker's *Parker on the Iroquois* or William Fenton's *The Great Law and the Longhouse*. It may be their superior since it is the product of someone who has experienced Mohawk life in all of its dimensions, by a person who has devoted his life to preserving the heritage of his Nation.
—*Award-winning journalist, Douglas M. George-Kanentiio, Bear Clan Mohawk*

" . . . If you can only read one book this year, there's no better choice than this, the story of a beloved elder who has never failed to honor and uphold the wisdom of his ancestors."
—*Award-winning author Joseph Bruchac, Abenaki*

"Tom Porter . . . has inspired many young people to become role models for the coming generations."
—*Tekaronianeken Jake Swamp, Wolf Clan Mohawk*

" . . . Porter offers a clear view of the many cultural elements of one man's struggle to maintain tradition."
—*John Kahionhes Fadden, Turtle Clan Mohawk*

"I couldn't put it down . . . This book will be a classic. It will become as important to Native people as the Bible is to Christians."
—*Karen Suydam, artist and student of Native culture*

More detailed acclaim from author and award-winning journalist, *Douglas M. George-Kanentiio, Bear Clan Mohawk*

"I have known Tom Porter (Sakokweniónkwas) for most of my life; he is a cousin, a blood relative from the Akwesasne Mohawk Territory astride the St. Lawrence River 100 km southwest of Montreal. He has, over the past four decades, become one of the most respected cultural teachers among the Iroquois, a spiritual leader welcome across the continent for his sincerity, wit and knowledge. In *And Grandma Said* he summarizes the ancient customs and traditions of the Mohawk people using his distinctive teaching style which blends together charm, humor and a remarkable command of aboriginal culture.

Tom Porter began his teaching career as a member of the touring group "The White Roots of Peace." Organized under the authority of the Mohawk Nation Council, the group crisscrossed the continent providing its audience with unfiltered insights into the history, culture and concerns of Native people. It enabled young Mohawks like Tom to channel their energy into a highly demanding occupation as cultural ambassadors while igniting the fires of contemporary Native political activism. Tom was selected as a spokesperson because he was not only an excellent public speaker but had the trust of the Mohawk Nation Council. He could be expected to represent Akwesasne with honor and to set an example for his peer group as to personal conduct. Tom encouraged his Native audiences to take pride in their heritage and to look into their history for the strength they needed to remove the shackles of generations of active suppression by Canada and the USA. The response was immediate, passionate and enduring as Natives began to organize formal resistance to destructive policies aimed at obliterating indigenous people as distinct political and cultural entities.

Tom absorbed as much as he taught. His growing wisdom and inherent leadership qualities were acknowledged by the traditional leaders of the Mohawk Nation when he was asked to serve on its governing council while still a very young man. While there he enhanced his knowledge about Mohawk history and spiritual beliefs. He was accorded great respect for his sensitivity and the respect he gave to all people, even those who became adversaries to the Nation. I was privileged to travel with Tom on many trips and to listen to his lectures before many audiences. Whether it was before a small circle of Native inmates or a skeptical class of post graduate college students, Tom never wavered from his basic message: Mohawks were good human beings in possession of a way of thinking important to the world.

As the years rolled by I came to realize how important it was for our leaders such as Tom to establish a written legacy as to their knowledge. I also knew it would be vital to preserve the flow of Tom's speaking which is uniquely Mohawk. Fortunately, the editor of *And Grandma Said* has proven to be the best person possible for collecting and editing a portion of Tom's teachings, leaving intact the rhythm of Tom's thoughts. Lesley Forrester has done a tremendous service to contemporary aboriginal literature by having Tom address the most important elements of Iroquois history and culture. Together, Tom and Lesley have produced a book which is, without exception, the best summation of what it means to be a traditional Mohawk in modern times. It covers the creation of the world, the formation of the Iroquois Confederacy, the importance of clans and the role of leaders. It does so without being bound by technical language but by using words which are direct from the heart. As the reader is enlightened about ceremony and society they are also entertained by stories of deep personal significance to Tom and his family. The book is equal in importance to Arthur C. Parker's *Parker on the Iroquois* or William Fenton's *The Great Law and the Longhouse*. It may be their superior since it is the product of someone who has experienced Mohawk life in all of its dimensions, by a person who has devoted his life to preserving the heritage of his Nation."

—*Douglas M. George-Kanentiio, Bear Clan Mohawk*
Author of *Iroquois on Fire*
(Praeger Publishers: 2006) ISBN: 0-275-98384-6.
Winner of the Wassaja Award for Journalism Excellence
by the Native American Journalists Association in 1994
Former Member of the Board of Trustees
for the National Museum of the American Indian

And Grandma Said . . .

Iroquois Teachings

as passed down through the oral tradition

TOM PORTER
(Sakokweniónkwas)
Bear Clan Elder of the Mohawk Nation

Transcribed and edited
by Lesley Forrester

With drawings by
John Kahionhes Fadden

Library of Congress Control Number: 2008903517
ISBN: Hardcover   978-1-4363-3566-9
            Softcover   978-1-4363-3565-2

Porter, Tom, 1944–
1. Mohawk Indians 2. Iroquois Indians 3. Indians of North America
4. Native North Americans 5. Oral Tradition   I. Title
299.POR

The speeches of respected elder Thomas R. Porter (Sakokweniónkwas), a member of
the Bear Clan of the Mohawk Nation at Akwesasne, were recorded, transcribed and
edited to form a book. Collected together in print for the first time, these traditional
teachings about the history, culture and earth-based spirituality of the Haudenosaunee
(Iroquois) are now offered to Native and non-Native people alike. Porter describes the
tragic effects of colonization on his people and shares the teachings passed down to him
through the oral tradition by the grandmother who raised him in these traditional values.

Care has been taken to trace ownership of copyright material contained in this book.
The editor will gladly receive any information that will enable her to rectify any
reference or credit line in subsequent additions.

Rev. date: 06/14/2022

To order additional copies of this book, contact:
Xlibris
844-714-8691
www.Xlibris.com
Orders@Xlibris.com
562044
For information about discounts for bulk purchases, please contact the editor at
lesleyforrester28@gmail.com

Dedication

To Grandma
Konwanataha
Agatha Harriet David Chubb
"Hattie"
March 22, 1889-May 29, 1978

When the Lilacs Bloom
By Roy Hurd

I was taught not to brag
or boast of the gifts I've been given.
But this one time, I'm gonna cross that line
in the hope that I'll be forgiven.
I had the best grandma
that anyone could know.
In early June, when the lilacs bloom,
that's when I miss her so.

She left when the lilacs were bloomin'.
She took her last walk in the spring.
The very last sound that she ever heard
was the song that the robin sings.
Her eyes still shine in my memory.
I can see her smile in the moon.
I look to the sky with tears in my eyes
every year when the lilacs bloom.

I know she's right here with me
when that winter wind gets colder.
When times get tough and the road gets rough
I can feel her hand on my shoulder.
She visits when I'm dreamin'.
She's in everything I do.
Her spirit sings with the breath of spring
every year when the lilacs bloom.

She left when the lilacs were bloomin'.
She took her last walk in the spring.
The very last sound that she ever heard
was the song that the robin sings.
Her eyes still shine in my memory.
I can see her smile in the moon.
I look to the sky with tears in my eyes
every year when the lilacs bloom.

Contents

Illustrations/Images (and Credits)

Longhouse, page 199
Top: drawing of a Longhouse made of elm bark (John Kahionhes Fadden)
Bottom: Akwesasne Longhouse, photographed in 2008 (Lesley Forrester)

Grandma, page 200
Top left: "Grandma" in her apron (courtesy of Marcella David)
Top right: Grandma's rocker (Lesley Forrester)
Middle right: Corncob pipe (Lesley Forrester)
Bottom: Grandma's house at Akwesasne (Lesley Forrester)

Grandma and Grandpa, page 201
Left: Hattie and Louis Chubb as a young couple (family archives)
Right: Louis Chubb in later years (courtesy of Marcella David)

Ahkwesáhsne Freedom School/Grandchildren, page 202
Top: Students/staff, many in traditional clothing (Kahentanoron, 2007)
Middle: Tom's grandkids currently attending:
   Left: Konwahonkarawi Porter (family archives)
   Middle: Rowennaskats Porter (family archives)
   Right: Iakokwenienstha Porter (family archives)
Bottom: photo of school, March 2008 (Lesley Forrester)

Water Drums, page 203
Left top and bottom: water drums (Lesley Forrester)
Right: drawing "Singers" (John Kahionhes Fadden)

Wampum, page 204
Top: replicas of the Wampum Strings for each nation (Lesley Forrester)
Bottom left: pump drill (Lesley Forrester)
Bottom right: quahog shell (Lesley Forrester)

Examples of Wampum Belts, page 205
Top: replica of the Hiawatha belt (Lesley Forrester)
Bottom: replica of the Two Row Wampum belt (Lesley Forrester)

White Corn, page 206
Top left: braided white corn (Lesley Forrester)
Right: field of white corn (Kanatsioharè:ke archives)
Bottom: Atenaha/The Seed Game (Lesley Forrester)

Tom and Alice's Wedding, page 207
Top: Tom and Alice's Wedding, November 7, 1970 (family archives)
Middle: another example of a wedding basket (Lesley Forrester)
Bottom: Tom (Sakokweniónkwas) and Alice in 2007 (family archives)

Tom's Six Children, page 208
Left: Aronienens Porter and Yvette Ashinawey (Sherri Watenonsiiostha Porter)
Right: Katsitsiahawi Perkins, Kanastatsi Porter,
Tewasontahawitha Porter and Katsitsiakwas Lazore (family archives)

Wedding of Aronienens and Watenonsiiostha Porter, page 209
Top left: Aronienens, Tom's son, and Watenonsiiostha/Sherri (family archives)
Top right: Aronienens and Tom (Donna Olson)
Bottom: Watenonsiiostha with Aronienens, his parents, and his siblings (family archives)

Tobacco, page 210
Top: old-style Chief's tobacco bag (Lesley Forrester)
Bottom: oien'kwa'ón:we/Indian tobacco (Lesley Forrester)

Haudenosaunee (Iroquois) Chiefs, page 211
Top left: condolence cane (Lesley Forrester)
Top right: drawing of a Mohawk Chief's kahstowa (John Kahionhes Fadden)
Bottom left: drawing of the Circle Wampum (John Kahionhes Fadden)
Bottom right: a deer antler such as those used on a Chief's kahstowa (Lesley Forrester)

Tekáhstia'ks/Grandchildren, page 212
Top left: Tekáhstia'ks, Tom's parrot (Karen Suydam)
Grandchildren:
> Top right: Rahnienhawi Burns (family archives)
> Next to top right: Rahente Perkins (family archives)
> Center left: Tsioweriio Lazore (Lesley Forrester)
> Center right: Roweren Lazore (Lesley Forrester)
> Bottom left: Konwanontiio Lazore (family archives)
> Bottom next: Karhatiron Perkins (family archives)
> Bottom next: Ronatiio Perkins (Lesley Forrester)
> Bottom right: Karonhiate Lazore (family archives)

Carlisle Indian Industrial School, 1879-1918, page 213
Top left: main entrance (photo courtesy of Barbara Landis)
Top right: student body assembled on the grounds, circa 1900 (The Carlisle Indian Industrial School Photograph Collection, U. S. Army Military History Institute, Carlisle Barracks, PA.)
Bottom right and left: Chiricahua Apaches on arrival and four months after (Arizona Historical Foundation, Barry Goldwater Historic Photograph Collection FP FPC #1, Carlisle Indian School)

Kanatsioharè:ke, page 214
Top left: the West Wing and the Bed and Breakfast (Kanatsioharè:ke archives)
Center left: horses grazing (Kanastatsi Porter)
Center right: the "clean pot" for which Kanatsioharè:ke is named (Dr. Robert Phillips)
Bottom: recent restoration of the barn (L. Braxton Ratcliff)

Foreword

Getting the book on paper

One day, Sakokweniónkwas (Tom Porter) commented that he just wasn't finding the time to get to work on a book he wanted to write.

I had had the good fortune to hear this Mohawk Bear Clan elder speak on many occasions. He spoke about Mohawk culture, traditions, spirituality, language revitalization, and the effects of colonization. He also spoke of leaving his home in the Mohawk territory of Akwesasne in order to reestablish a Mohawk community called Kanatsioharè:ke in the Mohawk Valley, west of Fonda, New York. That move was the fulfillment of a prophecy that someday, traditional Mohawks would return to the home of their ancestors.

By the time I met him, I already had many friends and acquaintances in the Mohawk territory of Tyendinaga, located near my home. The experience of hearing Tom Porter speak, and of personally visiting Kanatsioharè:ke and the Mohawk Valley combined to influence my life in a very profound way.

Tom's desire to write came about as the result of a dream. In this dream, his grandmother told him to write down everything that she had taught him. Tom said that everything he talked about in his presentations, he had learned directly or indirectly from her. All he needed to do was get it all written down on paper. But that was no small task as he had given hundreds of presentations—some of which were days long.

Due to some medical problems, I had some spare time and an adequate disability pension. So I offered to follow him around and tape his speeches and presentations. I would then transcribe them—including as much of the Mohawk as I could. That might get a lot of what he wanted to say written down on paper. It would be a beginning. And it was a pleasure to be able to offer to do this without any thought of financial gain.

To begin recording, I purchased a body mic for Tom. For the next year or so, I taped him as often as I could. I pored through every audio and videotape that I could find, in the office at Kanatsioharè:ke and even in the back cupboards of Tom and his wife Alice's apartment. I also contacted other people in the First Nations communities where Tom had spoken and asked to borrow and transcribe tapes they had made of his speeches. Tom and Ionataiewas (Kay Olan)—the director of the community at the time—were very helpful in paving the way, introducing me and explaining what the project was about.

Although Tom and I are very close in age, I had always had the kind of respect for his knowledge of traditional ways, as well as his charismatic speaking ability, that I would have for an elder. I couldn't remember a time when I had heard him speak, that I hadn't both laughed and cried—and I don't normally consider myself someone who cries easily. It was also evident to me how highly respected he was throughout the Haudenosaunee Confederacy (the traditional political entity that the Mohawk are a part of).

After lots of taping and transcribing, he asked me to begin editing the transcripts—to take out the repetition and to make them grammatically correct. I was totally intimidated. At the beginning, I really could not bear to change a single word. First, what if I were to inadvertently change the meaning; and of almost equal concern, what if I lost the poetry and charisma that give his words such power and impact?

After much thought and discussion, I made the decision to produce two versions. The first would be an archival version, containing a completely verbatim transcript of every word. The other would be a book in a format that, while not compromising meaning, would be very readable—hopefully, something that people of all ages might find both informative and enjoyable. And one that is clear enough that even non-Natives and Iroquois unfamiliar with traditional ways, would easily understand. In that way, anyone in doubt about the accuracy of even minor points, could access the source documents. I decided that once the transcribing was done, I would make at least two copies of the transcripts as well as two copies of the recordings to be held in at least two different locations.

Then I began ever, ever so slowly to edit. Looking back, I realize that it was actually over a period of about two years that I gradually came to an awareness of Tom's unique syntax, and the ways in which it needed changing, to become more readable. What was eloquent and charming orally was actually cumbersome and often confusing in writing.

Although the examples that follow may sound concrete and perhaps dispassionate, most of this process came out of a kind of unconscious familiarity I gained from the many hours of transcribing his words.

As one example, he has a habit of putting the adverb at the beginning of a statement. While this is the correct word order in Mohawk, it is often confusing in English. He will say, for instance, "Even it got dimmer" rather than "It got even dimmer." So the edited versions will almost always include moving the adverbs into their more usual English position.

Another example is a tendency I notice among other Mohawks as well. It is the tendency to put the subject at the end of the sentence. For example, "He is a scroungy little guy with a pencil tail, the muskrat." This part I struggled with much longer because to me it is part of the poetry of his syntax. I finally compromised by leaving the subject at the end when the meaning stayed clear. In other more complex statements, I used the English convention of putting the full subject at the beginning.

My goal was to maintain Tom's "voice," the unique flavor of his way of speaking without losing the readability of the material.

From the beginning, I nurtured my fear of changing the meaning in any way. This has resulted in frequently leaving a lack of subject-verb agreement. The resulting ambiguity often reflects my own lack of certainty as to his real meaning. Instead, I leave it to the reader. Mohawk is said to have something like nine thousand pronouns. While Tom may be clear in his own language about all these pronouns, he plays rather fast and loose with the English ones. So where it is not clear in surrounding text, whether he means the singular or the plural, I have preferred to leave his own words.

He does a similar thing with the definite and indefinite article. In Mohawk, speakers use "ne ne" without needing to distinguish between the two kinds of articles. Where Tom's usage clearly conflicts with the rest of the meaning in a statement, I have changed from "a" to "the" and vice versa. Where the meaning is ambiguous, I have again left it to the reader.

I have also left untouched most of the wonderful words he has invented, finding them often more expressive and refreshing than the "correct" English terms. For example, he describes a nun's habit as one of those "face-sticking-out" dresses. And he talks about Sky Woman's curious searching as "nosying around."

I have often even left the repetition is in its original redundant form, with its poetry and charm, such as his description of the "miraculous wonders" of the Creator.

Anyone who has heard Tom speak will know how often the event is full of laughter—both his own and that of the audience. Since it is not always evident from the written word when he is joking or being playful, I have used exclamation marks to indicate this. The points he emphasizes are generally in italics.

One dilemma was the challenge of incorporating Mohawk without losing readers who are not speakers or who have not studied it in its written form. Tom has committed much of his life and energy to supporting the continued use and revitalization of the language. Mohawk, using the method of transcription that includes diacritics (accents, pauses, and glottal sound markers), requires lots of accent marks, colons, and apostrophes. Adding quotation marks would only have complicated things further—especially if I had used quotation marks for both the Mohawk and the English translations. In order to give the language the importance it deserves and make it as readable as possible, I have chosen instead to omit the quotation marks wherever possible, and used italics for the direct English translations.

Another issue was the problem of what to capitalize. The goal was to capitalize in a way which best captured the notions of respect, as held in traditional culture. As much as possible, common English usage was followed for words unrelated to the culture. Major events, ceremonies, and some objects sacred to the Iroquois were capitalized.

In the Thanksgiving Address and Tobacco Burning, after much discussion, it was decided to capitalize only the parts of Creation whose spirits were being directly addressed, much as one would capitalize "Mother" as a name, rather than "mother" as a reference to that particular relative. So when Tom is directly thanking the "Waters of the World" for the job that they do the phrase is capitalized, but not when he refers indirectly to the rain, the creek, etc. This principle was simpler in theory than in practice, but I have attempted to be as consistent as possible.

In contrast to English, where a person's title is often spoken, Iroquois titles do not appear to be used in direct address. Nevertheless, to indicate respect for the roles that these titles represent, words like "Clan Mother," "Faithkeeper," and "Sub-Chief" have been capitalized in general usage, as well as "Chief." (This appears to be consistent with the American tendency to capitalize words like "Senator" in general usage.) Names of the clans are also capitalized, as in, "She is a member of the Bear Clan."

Perhaps the biggest challenge has been ensuring, insofar as possible, the accuracy of the Mohawk words and passages he uses, for future generations. One example is the crucial speech of Tom's ancestor about the role the Iroquois played in the development of the American Constitution. There are also situations where clearly the Mohawk he uses carries more information than the English. For example, at one point Tom talks about there being two words in Mohawk and only one in English for a particular spiritual concept. To me, these are prime examples of how the language carries the culture and therefore accuracy is extremely important.

Tom reports that his Mohawk is almost as "fractured" as his English. In addition, he was never trained to write in Mohawk. In his words, "I'm not really a writer of our language, just a little. But I don't know if I'm writing right. I don't know where to put the dots, the emphasis. I never learned that."

For the purposes of the book, he asked to have Karihwénhawe (Dorothy Lazore) correct his written Mohawk. Yet since she was raised as a Catholic and not raised as a traditional Longhouse woman, there are spiritual references and ceremonial language that she might not be familiar with. In contrast, those more steeped in the traditional culture and the old language have not necessarily learned to write it. Where possible, I requested both speakers educated in written Mohawk and those practicing traditional ways to give me feedback.

I have also relied on the many hours that I have spent studying this eloquent language myself to ensure that wherever possible, any corrections that have been made to Tom's Mohawk retain the same root words and are as true to his pronouns as possible. For example, commonly the Mohawk word "*Shonkwa*ia'tíson" is used when referring to the Creator. The pronoun at the beginning means "our." Tom, however, frequently uses "*Tak*ia'tíson," the pronoun which is usually translated as "you to me." Literally, he is saying, "You who made my body."

Tom's spoken language often contains some Onondaga, and is also influenced by his growing up in the Snye area of Akwesasne. That is the part of the reservation where members of other Iroquois nations came to live, following the American Revolution. And being as creative in his mother tongue as he is in English, his speech at times contains words he has invented as Mohawk versions of Onondaga words!

Thus the written Mohawk in the book is the best effort of several minds coming together, but is not always exactly as spoken by Tom.

In order to reconcile some issues in which it was challenging to reach a consensus, a glossary was created, containing two modern linguistic versions of the spelling—one usually closer to the Akwesasne dialect, and the other closer to that of Tyendinaga.

Throughout the book itself, the diacritic versions are generally used, and *i* rather than *y* is used as a consonant. An exception was made for the Mohawk names of people and places. In those cases, preference has been given to how individuals have chosen to spell their own names throughout their lives or to how people have grown accustomed to spelling certain place names. Thus Akwesasne is written as it has been commonly spelled for years, whereas a more modern linguistic spelling would be Ahkwesáhshne. In the glossary, however, those words have been transcribed as they would be according to current linguistic understanding.

Thanks to extensive work by Karihwénhawe (Dorothy Lazore) and Thoná: wayen (Stephen Green), the longer passages are also transcribed in an appendix, in both dialects.

There is one word that is spelled the English way, simply for ease of understanding. That is the Mohawk word for "yes," normally written as "hen," but pronounced more or less like a nasalized version of the English "huh." Tom has a habit of sprinkling his speech with a final "huh?" much as we would say "right?" or "you know?" Regardless of whether he means it as the Mohawk word for "yes" or the English "huh," I have chosen, for the sake of readability, to spell it "huh" rather than "hen." I hope this is clear, huh?

As well, after each part of the Ohén:ton Karihwatéhkwen (the Thanksgiving Address), listeners often respond to affirm their agreement that they are of one mind. Some of the older speakers use "tho" (pronounced like the English "toe"). Others use the Mohawk affirmation "hen" or even the more English "uh-huh." I have again used the English spelling "huh" for the benefit of readers unfamiliar with Mohawk phonetics.

One of the dilemmas in organizing the book has been how to divide things up into chapters—or even whether to do that. The average reader is accustomed to these breaks. Since we were already deviating from the traditional concept of an oral culture even to write any of this down, it did not seem to be too big a stretch to make separate chapters, especially for the major topic changes, such as the Creation story and the Great Law. As it evolved, it made more sense to create separate chapters with material from varied sources than to ask Tom to artificially link blocks of material together.

The concern that remains is that the reader may take the chapter titles too seriously and assume that everything Tom has to say on a topic is in the chapter of that name, or conversely, that everything in the chapter of that name is closely related to that topic. To open the book, for example, to the "Clan System" and presume the words in that chapter are all he has to say about it would be to misunderstand that clans are a fundamental part of a traditional way of life and therefore affect, and are affected by, everything else that is important to a traditional person.

Tom himself frequently makes reference to the numerous diversions and seeming tangents he takes when speaking. His genius and his genuineness, in my humble opinion, come from the fact that he always speaks from the heart, from whatever arises in the moment. Thus he and his "uncles" never do the Opening Address in the same words twice. It arises from moment to moment as it's spoken. He emphasizes the importance of approaching it that way when he teaches others how to do an Opening.

Tom talks about the ancestors not using time references as we know them. When a story is told, it is as if it is being relived in the present moment, reinspirited or reenergized as it is retold. Thus the retention of the speeches as given, rather than reworking them to fit the present "facts," seemed to be the approach most suited to the culture. Where events might be confusing to the reader if understood as happening in the present, I have simply footnoted the approximate dates of the speeches.

In closing, then, I would like to thank the many people who have spent time discussing these issues with me, those who have pored over the manuscript and given valuable suggestions and all those who have supported Tom's desire to bring this book into a printed form.

Thanks for work on the language is therefore due not only to Karihwénhawe (Dorothy Lazore) of Akwesasne and Thoná:wayen (Stephen Green) of Tyendinaga but also to Kawén:nase (Anna Lazore) of Akwesasne and Tehawennahkhwa (Wes Miller) of Six Nations. Karihwaienhne (Delia Cook) and Tom's aunt, Karonhiako:he (Marcella David) of Akwesasne, also helped with feedback on Grandma's Mohawk name.

With general editing and suggestions, Ionataiewas (Kay Olan) and my stepsister, Susan Lorimer, put in incalculable hours. John Fadden, Joe Bruchac, and Stephen Green each provided very valuable feedback; and John Fadden generously offered the use of his many wonderful sketches to illustrate aspects of the culture that might be unfamiliar to readers.

Gratitude also needs to be expressed to the people who assisted with the photos in the book—hunting down photographs, loaning them to the project, allowing photos to be taken in their homes, loaning cultural artifacts and replicas to be photographed, searching through attics and basements to locate Grandma's original rocking chair, and downloading the photos on a laptop to make sure they were what Tom wanted. A great big thanks/nia:wen therefore goes to the following people: Ionataiewas (Kay Olan), L. Braxton Ratcliff, Tami Mitchell, Karonhiako:he (Marcella David), Watenonsiiostha (Sherri Porter), Katsitsiakwas Lazore, Katsitsiahawi Perkins, and Kanastatsi Porter.

Thanks also goes to Tom's great friends and supporters, Kamala and Tom Buckner who, not only taped, but also transcribed one of the two versions that were used in the chapters on the Great Law.

I have done this work with my whole heart and to the best of my ability. If there are inaccuracies, especially in the Mohawk, these are much more likely to be due to my own copying errors than to those of the linguists who worked so hard to make it accurate. If there are any omissions, inaccuracies, or distortions, they are not my intention. However, I take full responsibility for them.

Edited and transcribed in the Creator's time,

Lesley Forrester
Stirling, Ontario, Canada

Chapter 1

The Dream

Grandma said, "Try to write it all down and make a book."

We're sorta clannish people, us Iroquois. We kinda keep to ourselves. We don't open up much to the outside world. And the reason why is because years ago, if you believed in the Indian way or the Longhouse way or anything like that, people made fun of you. Even our own Indians, our own cousins, who had given up the Longhouse ways could be kinda abusive.

But that has mostly stopped now since about thirty years ago. A couple of years ago I was talking to a 102-year-old woman from my reservation. She told me, "I've always loved the traditional people, the Longhouse people, even though I wasn't raised in that." She said, "Because after all, before the European came here, that's all we were, was traditional Longhouse Indians. We weren't nothing else. And so that's the reason why I always salute them. And I always respected them even though other people's opinions were so different from mine."

That was nice, hearing it from a 102-year-old lady.

There are about twelve thousand or thirteen Mohawks living in our reservation. And she said, "If you were to go ask all the people, I think over half will tell you that they belong to the Longhouse, they're traditional now, although they may not be. But they will *tell* you that."

So that means there's a big change from thirty years ago. 'Cause thirty years ago, "Oh you Longhouse, you're the bottom of the barrel." It wasn't good, see? So the Longhouse has been the subject of ridicule a lot of times in the past. And it's just now, in recent years, there's a movement that has brought it into the light, I would say. The wind and the air touch it now. It's been like a cut that never got air—it couldn't heal. And so in these last years now, the Longhouse and what they stand for, and the principles that they have, are starting to be exposed a little bit here and there.

And now they speak all over the world from the Longhouse. They've sent people to Geneva and to the United Nations there in New York City, Manhattan. And I know that it's true because I was with them.

So now there's becoming an appreciation for it. And so now I'm also caught somewhat because when I was growing, we sorta weren't allowed to talk about this stuff outside of our Longhouse. Everything stayed right in there. We didn't even talk to other Mohawks who weren't Longhouse. It was almost like we had to make our own world.

And so it's taken me a little bit of getting used to over the years, to sorta walk out the door and start to talk about this. When I started, a few years ago, some of the old, old Indian people were somewhat offended because I was talking about it. Because they were coming from that world where you're gonna get beaten up or you're gonna get ridiculed if you do. So they didn't want any trouble. Some of them had begun to become so protective of it that if anybody came from outside, everything stopped. They'd just stop. So their attitude was "Don't say nothing to nobody. Just, we do our Longhouse stuff, and that's it. And don't tell nobody *nothin'*."

But it's changed now, quite a bit. Most of those people who were very critical like that, because they were afraid or whatever, have passed away. I've studied this a long time, and I see nothing in it that's a big secret. Because this stuff is the same as the sun. And the sun hides from nobody except when it's cloudy. And even then it still makes light in the day for us. So that's why I want to share this with you.

And so lately I've been wearing a microphone on me because there are these friends that are following me around different places. And they're recording what I say so that it can be transcribed into a book, in case myself and others that know a little bit about this, if we die or something, well, there'll be something left here for the younger generations and others. And all through the years, I've never done this before. Others have, just by taking notes. You'll see some books they wrote that I didn't even know about. But this is the first time I've really known about what's going on. And so we're gonna attempt to do that.

I should have done it way before, but I never have time for it, and I'm not that orderly either, about things. But I certainly do a lot of talking all over the place. So then finally we came to the idea, well, why don't we just record what is said when I talk to people? And that way, we'll try to feed about ten birds with one corn. And so that's what's sort of going on right here.

And the reason why is because my grandmother came to see me a few years ago, in a dream. She's been passed away for twenty-eight years.[1] And she said to me, "What I'd like you to do is to try to sit down and remember everything that Grandma said, that all your grandmas said, and your elders. What I want you to do is start writing it down. Write it down on the book or paper." (We call a book "paper" in our language.) And she said, "Whatever we told you over the years since you were born—our beliefs and our way of looking at the world, our way of walking in the world—write it down. And put it together.

"And that will be for our people. Our young people need grandmas. Our younger generation, they need to know things, and nobody's telling them. Even the older people that are even older than you, they don't know a lot of things. So could you do that? Try to write it down and make a book," she said. "And then when you've put it all together, you put my picture in it, the way you remember me."

And I didn't know what she meant. Now I do. But I didn't know at the time if there was a picture that she favored or what. And then she said, "On that

---

[1] Tom made this comment in 2004.

book, on the front of the cover, you put *And Grandma Said*. That's gonna be the name of it." She even told me what the title would be!

The way I remember her is, whenever there was some kind of problem or something, she would always go upstairs in her house. And she had an old rocking chair. My grandfather is the one that put the weaving on the chair part of it. And that was her favorite rocking chair. She always wore an apron, you know, for cooking. She'd go up there on that chair. And she'd have her pipe, just a regular pipe like you buy in the store. She'd put Indian tobacco in there. And that's what she used to pray with. And then that rocking chair would start rocking, and that smoke would go up—fast too. That meant she was *really* praying. The faster that rocking chair was going, the more praying she was doing!

That's the way I remember her. So I found a picture of Grandma, with her apron on, and we took a picture of that rocking chair—we still have it in our family. And then I put them in the book, 'cause that's the image I have of her.

My name is Sakokweniónkwas. My English name is Tom Porter. And I'm a person who comes from the Mohawk Nation, the reservation called Akwesasne.[2] It's in the northern part of the state of New York. In 1993, we left the reservation and we went back to our homeland, which is about an hour from Albany, New York, near Fonda.

It was prophesied by our great-grandmothers about 230 years ago that one day our grandchildren would return home. And that's what we have done. We have fulfilled that prophecy.

If there is one thing I could accomplish here in this book, it would be to give a true picture, a true image of the Native people, both bad and good. So that when people talk about us, they could do it justice. And our Great Law tells both the good and the bad of its history, which is very important to do.

The way I usually like to do this is in chronological order. And if I'm teaching at a university somewhere, like a Native Studies program, I always start with the beginning of the world and follow the different events that

---

[2.]   Throughout the book, the most common spelling of Akwesasne has been used. See the glossary for contemporary linguistic spelling options.

happen according to their order. And that way, by the time they finish the term, they have completed a journey.

Here I have listed what I think of as a chronological order of our existence since the beginning of time on this world.

1. Creation (Thanksgiving)
2. Clan System
3. Four Sacred Rituals
4. Great Law (Constitution)
5. Karihwí:io (Handsome Lake)
6. modern disarray (colonization, foreign political system)

And we need to talk about the future too; what we are leaving on the shoulders of our young people. And of course, everything that Grandma said.

We should start with Creation. Creation starts prior to the human's existence on this earth. It goes back earlier than that when we weren't even here yet. It gives us a glimpse of that.

We're probably talking about millions of years. Probably, who knows? The Creation story is the origin of the first instruction we were given. It's the source of what I call the Thanksgiving Address, which is the most important prayer—if you want to call it a prayer—that we, the Iroquois, have. It includes the essence of all our existence. It includes all the relationships to the earth that we are in. That's what it does.

I often refer to it as the skeleton key. You know, in the older days when they used to refer to the key that could open every door? Well that Thanksgiving Address is for our Six Nations, our human people, it's our skeleton key to the world that we live in. And it'll open up all things for us. I say that is the number one chronological event, so that's where we can start, where we'll begin.

Then the second thing that happened was the Clan System was devised and given to us. And that was a whole structure, a whole social system, both spiritual and political.

And then after that, the next big chronological thing that happened in the history is that we were given the Four Sacred Rituals. These are the origin of what makes all Longhouse ceremonies we do, operate. And so we'll look at the history of that. And so that's the third one.

After hundreds of years of that, then another thing happened, another disastrous thing in the history of mankind. That was when the Great Law became a necessity. So it was sent here by the Creator. And there's a whole epic, a whole history to that. The Great Law takes ten days to recite, maybe eleven or twelve days.

The Great Law became the inspiration to the whole world. I believe that it is where America got its ideas for becoming a country. It was supposedly based on the democracy of our people. America's idea of democracy may seem silly or cartoonish to us Iroquois, when we look at it because although it's better than kings and queens, it's still lacking in terms of what the Iroquois and what the Creator meant for it to be.

And so that would be the fourth big event.

And then later on, after hundreds and hundreds of years went by, finally we get to the Europeans coming here, the white brothers. This is a time when our demise, the demise of all the Iroquois Indians, almost became reality. Had there not been intervention by the Creator and the Four Sacred Beings and Handsome Lake (who was the one that received their message), we would probably not be here today. We would be long gone through drunkenness, through the diseases, through the wars and through all that stuff.

But Handsome Lake received these spiritual messages. It takes four days to recite the messages, from early in the morning until noon or one o'clock. We refer to them as the Karihwí:io.[3] The Karihwí:io was important to get us back on the road to our recovery and to landing us on our feet.

---

3.   Karihwí:io, usually referred to in English as the Code of Handsome Lake, might be more literally translated as "the good business" or "it is a good business/affair/thing." Tom refers to the adoption of the Karihwí:io as one of the major chronological events in the history of the Iroquois, but it is not a topic that he generally lectures on, possibly because of the Baptist influences on it. For more detail on it, see Chief Jacob Thomas, *Teachings from the Longhouse* (Toronto: Stoddart Publishing Co. Ltd., 1994). Currently out of print, it is to be reprinted by the Jake Thomas Learning Centre.

And that was one of the roughest times, perhaps, of our history—or else at least equal to when the Great Law came. Maybe events at the time of the Great Law were rougher, though. That would need discussion because here, at the time of Handsome Lake, people en masse had become insane because of drink: rum, whisky and things like that. Whereas at the time of the Great Law, they became insane with power and manipulation. And that was the equivalent of the alcohol. So I'm not sure which is worse.

And then after that, we try to end up on our feet.

So now we come to the modern times—our sixth topic. Canada brings in the Indian Act. America brings in the Bureau of Indian Affairs. There are elected systems of this kind, elected systems of this other kind. This is when the political systems are all designed to get rid of the traditional system of the Six Nations and to make it disappear forevermore. So this may be the worst one. Because now, physically, literally, we may stop. We may not be able to continue on—our concepts, our spiritual things, our biological bloodlines, if that's important. And to some it is and to some it isn't. And so all of that is bringing situations where it causes dissent. It causes dispute. It causes unrest between families and communities.

But they never give up. Every reservation is always struggling between the traditional political systems and the American-imposed elective systems. And that's where we are presently, trying to make sense out of it.

By the time we finish all this, somebody reading this should be able to give a pretty good summary to anybody in the world about our image—good and bad—our struggle as we have walked, our scars and our wounds, and our hurts and our happinesses as well.

So then after all of that, what does it sum up to be, at the end? Well, this is the Indian today. And this is why the Indian is as he is today. At least we can start from that basis. And so to me, that's bridge building. To me, if we are going to survive as Indian people in the world, then we're going to need allies. And if we're not going to survive, then, it's because of all of these things.

So I'm giving you the outline of what I would hope to cover if there was room. We may not be able to even come close to that, but that would be the hope if it was ideal, if you see what I mean.

Chapter 2

The Opening Address

What we say before we do anything that's important, a skeleton key.

We always begin with the Thanksgiving Address, which is this first one here on the list. The Iroquois nations, when they have meetings or they have ceremonies or they have social dances or any big thing, always do what they call Ohén:ton Karihwatéhkwen. That's what *we* call it. In English, some people call it the Opening Prayer, probably for lack of a better way to say it. Some people call it the Thanksgiving Address. Others call it the Greetings. But in my language, Mohawk, this is what we call it—Ohén:ton Karihwatéhkwen. A more literal translation would be *what we say before we do anything important*.

I always admired the ability of our people to recite the Opening, the Ohén: ton Karihwatéhkwen, before meetings, and I wanted to do that some day in my life when I grew up. I wanted to emulate them because they never used a book; they never used a tape recorder. They always came from the heart. Not one of them ever said it exactly word-for-word, the same as the other, and yet it *was* exactly the same.

It's like if you were to take a beautiful rose with drops of dew on its petals and then you were to describe that to us. And then let's say we didn't hear that. And so then another person is there and is going to describe what he has seen. And yet another. Well, we are all talking about the very same thing, but it would be much different words from each of us as we describe the beauty and everything about that rose. And that's the same way with all the prayers that we, the Iroquois people do; it's always the same, but it's never word-for-word. It's always living in the moment.

And I guess that's one thing about our spirituality that's probably different. None of the prayers we ever do is the same as yesterday. It's always forever changing. It changes at the moment, for the moment.

One of my uncles said, "If tradition does not bend or change, it dies." It *dies*. So if we keep everything exactly the same as yesterday and never move it, never change it a single word, that means it's gonna get arthritic. It's gonna become like cement, and it's going to be of no use. Only if it changes, and it can move and it can bend, is it going to be useful and is it going to live tomorrow. And so that's the way I look at it.

I often ask someone to volunteer, to do this Opening. Without fear or anything 'cause there's no test. There's no right, and there's no wrong. And one of the things my uncles told me is that whenever somebody asks you to do it, you do the best you can. And that will be just as great as could be. There is no such thing as, "Did I do it right?" or "Did I make a mistake?" So if anybody wants to volunteer, if anybody feels comfortable to do it, that's often how we begin.

I'll give you an example of it myself this time. And then we'll go to the Creation story. I'm gonna do it in English for you because I know you're not gonna understand my language, although I wish you could. But I'm gonna try to get as close as I can.

And first in my own language, I ask the Creator for permission to use a language that he didn't give to me.

> Ne ká:ti Takia'tíson entehsatahonhsiiohste. Ne ká:ti wi wahi kenh niionkwè:take. Kenh nón:wa iakwaia'taié:ri nón:wa wenhniserá: te. Á:ienhre ne akwé:kon aionkwata'karí:teke ta ká:ti wi ne Takia'tíson ne ká:ti enkate'nién:ten ne enkerihwaké:ron. Ne ne wi wahi ionkwanonhsión:ni ne tsi ní:ioht kionkwehtáhkwen. Ne ká:ti wi wahi enkate'nienton enkhe'nikonhraientáhten ne ká:ti ne

wi wahi tóhsa thé:nen thaiawén:'en ne sa'nikòn:ra. Ne ká:ti ne tsi nihatiwennò:ten nitenatatekon renhnarà:ken. Ne ká:ti enkatste. Ta eh ká:ti niiohtonhak onkwa'nikòn:ra.

I said, "Today is a special day on which I'm going to attempt to explain the spiritual worldview of the Iroquois, so that's why I'm gonna use English." So I told the Creator, "Don't run away on me 'cause you're hearing me talk a different language!" (Whenever I pray, Mohawk always comes out because that's what I am.)

It starts this way:

Our Creator made the whole world, the whole universe. And he made everything that grows. And every animal and every bird and every kind of water—everything. And when he finished that, then the last ones he made were the human beings. In fact, of all of the human beings, our elder people say the Indian was the very last one to get made, the Indian people, Native people. And then he put us here on this earth. And then when he put us here, he didn't just throw us here and say, "You're on your own. You do what you can do." He didn't do that.

When he let us be here at the beginning of the world, when it was new, he instructed us about how the world goes, how it operates, and how you live here. He told us that. And that's what we call Ohén:ton Karihwatéhkwen. It's *what we say before we do anything important*, what you have to observe before any important events. And our Creator gave us this miraculous life from ever since we are born until wherever we are traveling today in our life's path. And so we say to our Creator, "Thank you for the privilege that I can walk again today. And our mind is agreed." And if it is, you will say, "Huh."[1]

And then the Creator said that whenever you come together—little meeting, big meeting, medium meeting—the first thing you have to recognize is the different *human* life: your family, your village, your community. And so as I look around, I see the ladies. They're nice ladies—pretty ladies,

---

[1.] The English affirmation "huh" has more or less the same pronunciation as the Mohawk "hen" meaning *yes*.

young ones, middle-aged and my age—but they're all pretty, and they all have dignity. Good-looking women, I see. And I see it looks like they have relatively good health, maybe not perfect, but enough to still go yet.

And then when I look around, I see the menfolk. Oh, how distinguished looking they all are. Some are young and handsome, looking like movie stars. Some are a little bit older, and they look like they know what they are doing. Some are my age, and they look like they've been around! But when you look at 'em altogether, what a fine, good-looking group of people we are.

And so what we do is we give our kindness and our love to one another and we say thank you that we will share these moments today with each other. And our mind again is agreed.

(Response: "tho" [2] or "huh.")

The Creator made the earth. And when he made the earth, the Creator said that the earth is gonna be a woman. And not just any woman, she's gonna be the mother of *all* women. Or *all* life forms. And she will have the power to give life to the trees and the birds, to the bears, to the deer, to the humans. That's why she's exceptional.

And when our Mother Earth has given life and birth, then the big job begins. Now she has to nourish us from her body with the food that we need to live. And so yesterday, every food that you and I ate, and our kids and our relatives ate, came from her, the one we call our Mother, the Earth. And what we will eat today, will have come from her. And look how many there are of us. And if you multiply that by the towns from where we came, that's a big group of people, every day, she has to feed. What a job that woman does. And that's our Mother, the Earth.

And as my elders suggest to us, she has never thrown us away, discarded us or abandoned us since the beginning of time. And so what we're gonna

---

[2.] Tom adds: the formal way the old Mohawks say it, when they agree, is they say "Tho" (pronounced *toe*). Then the Mohawks that are not so old-fashioned, they'll say, "Uh-huh." Editor's note: other affirmations used include "yeah," "yes," and "huh."

do because of that is we will bring our minds together as *one*. What you and I will do is we will put our thankfulness one layer after another layer, here. And then we will take our greetings and make layers of it. And then you and I, who are the children of our Mother the Earth, will pick it up, and we'll carry it. And we say, "Mother Earth, today, we who are your children, salute you with love." And we say, "Thank you. Because our life is nourished again. Mother Earth, thank you, with love." And our mind is agreed.

(Response: "tho" or "huh.")

And then the next thing that happened after our Creator made Mother Earth is that he made the water that's in the creeks and the streams and the lakes. And when he did this, he said that water isn't just water, it is sacred. Every water is sacred. *Every* water is holy everywhere in the whole world. He said, "The water has spirit, it's got a soul, it's got life in it."

And he talked to the water. He said, "And your job, Water, is to move, to look for the humans, look for the birds, look for the bears, look for the deer." And that's why the water's moving in the stream out here. It's doing its job, going looking around for the life. And then it goes into the big river and then into the big ocean and then back into the clouds. Around and around, refreshing because it's alive. It's refreshing because it gives life.

And so that's why every day you and I have to drink water. And when we drink that cold glass of water, specially at the Fourth of July time, how refreshing that tastes. There's hope, there's a good chance that I'm gonna go on living. Just from that cold glass of water. There's nothing better.

And then when you work hard every day and you sweat and there's grime gathered upon your body and you don't feel too good because of it, you just jump in the river and take a good swim. And by golly, you feel good again. Or just take a shower. And you feel refreshed and healthy. And so that's what the rivers do. The streams of water. They quench our thirst and they clean and purify our body so that we may have a healthy, good life.

And then when you listen to the oceans and the big lakes, you hear the heartbeat of the water. You see that it is living. The big waves come, and they hit Mother Earth. It's the same thing as what's going on right here, in your heart. It's beating with a rhythm because it's living. And so what we will do, you and I, again we put layers of thank-yous, greetings and love right here. And we send it to the Spirit of the Waters of the World. And we say, "We, who are your human relatives, thank you for the quenching of our thirst yesterday. And today." And on behalf of our children, we say, with love, thank you to the Water. And our mind is agreed.

(Response: "tho" or "huh.")

And then another thing that our Creator did is he put in the water, the fish, and all kinds of water creatures. And he told those fish what their job is gonna be. It's that whenever the bear or the human needs nourishment, they will sacrifice their life for us. But only when we are hungry. No more. And also he said, if anything falls in the water, the fish are gonna grab it, eat it up right away, keep it clean—that water. And so those fish are doing their job. Even if it's hard nowadays, 'cause of pollution, those fish never give up. They just keep on trying to fulfill what the Creator told them to do.

And so what we will do is with one mind, we send our thank-you, greetings, and our love to all the Fish and the Water Life of the Waters of the World. And our mind, again, is agreed.

(Response: "tho" or "huh.")

And then our Creator, what he did after that is he planted medicine next to the river and next to the ponds and next to the lakes. And then he planted medicine in the big hills and the valleys and in the big fields. And he said, "For every sickness that there is known to the animals and the humans and the birds, there's a medicine or two or three that can jointly or singularly take away all the sickness."

And those truths were given to our grandfathers long ago. And the unfortunate thing is many grandfathers have lost that knowledge. But those medicines are not at fault for that. It is us that are the forgetful ones and the ones who have become ignorant. But Grandma said those medicines are still there. And when you go see them and you ask for them to heal your sick, they smile from ear to ear to be of service to us, to the birds and to the bears. 'Cause that's what the Creator wants them to do.

And so to the Medicines of the World who patiently wait for us to doctor our sick, we say thank you for staying with us and for doctoring those of us that you do doctor. To the Medicines of the World, with love, we thank you today. And our mind is agreed.

(Response: "tho" or "huh.")

And then our Creator did another thing. He gave us the food that's in the garden. There are all kinds of foods in there, but he chose three to be the leaders. Those ones are the corn and the beans and the squash. We, the Iroquois, call them the *Three Sisters*. The turnips, the carrots—they're all under their leadership. So this summer, they grew *good*. We've got food now that's hanging on the wall different places.[3] So when the wind and snow comes, we won't get hungry. When ceremony comes, we've got food, to celebrate. And all last summer, those gardens, led by the Three Sisters, did their job.

And so I ask that us people who reap the benefit of their work last summer, that we put in front of us our thank-yous and greetings and love. And then we send it to that Corn and to the Beans and to the Squashes and all the Vegetables that grew on vines and to *all* the other things that grew. 'Cause their seeds are put away so that when the big snow goes away and Mother Earth becomes warm, they will grow again. There will be more life. And so to the Gardens of the World, we say thank you with love. And our mind is agreed.

(Response: "tho" or "huh.")

And then what our Creator did is he made berries. And when he made the berries, he made lots of different kinds of them. For instance, the leader of them all is the strawberry because once the snow from winter goes away, it's the first berry to flower. And because it's the first one to wake up, it was chosen to become the leader of all the berry world. And we call the strawberry, because it looks like a heart, the Big Medicine.

---

3.   Tom is referring to the braided white corn hanging around the room in which he's talking.

And whenever there's a real ceremony throughout the year, they have to use strawberry drink in it. And so it is after the strawberry's done then the raspberries come. Then the blueberries. Then the blackberries. Then all kinda gooseberries. Right until snow comes, there are still berries on some of those bushes. So you see, the Creator really took care of us through the whole summer. The store that we have has fresh produce, one kind after another, from our Mother Earth. And so I ask that all of us put our minds together as one, and we send our thank-yous and our greetings and our love to the Strawberries and to *all* of the Berry World because they sweeten our life. They taste so good. We say thank you to them. And our mind is agreed.

(Response: "tho" or "huh.")

And then our Creator did another thing. He made the trees, all kinda trees. And then he chose one—they call it the maple tree. In my language we say, wáhta. And he said, "Once the snow starts to melt, that maple tree is the first one that's gonna wake up. Its blood is gonna start to flow. And that sap of the maple tree, you can drink that. It too becomes a great medicine for you. And then you can cook it, that sap, and it turns into a sweet syrup. You can even make sugar out of it. And then throughout the year, you will use that sweetness of the maple to put in the other food, to make it all nice and sweet and good."

And so this last year, that maple tree did do its job. And we did save the sap, and we did cook it. And then shortly after, all the other trees began to follow and wake up. And they gave us apples, here. They gave us peaches. Right here, between the houses, we've got trees with peaches. They gave us pears; we've got them too. Gave us apples; we've got 'em back there. They gave us cherries; we've got 'em in here too. All kinds of things, we've got them here from the trees. And they all did their job. And then from those trees also we use fallen limbs, and we cut 'em up. Then when it gets so cold, we can make warm fires in every woodstove in here.

And then those trees make the oxygen in the air we breathe, the oxygen that you and I need every day. And the buffalo need it, and the deer need it, and the birds need it. And if those trees were to stop being trees, they would no longer make oxygen. And then you and I and all life would suffocate, there would be no more life.

So you see, the tree is not just a tree. The tree is one of the sources of our life. And we need to stand by them. And we need to watch over them and protect them as much as we can. For they do that for us.

And so we shall become of one mind, and what we do is put many thank-yous and greetings and love again in front of us. As it piles up in a big heap, you and I will grab its perimeters, and we will throw it to the east, to the north and the west and to the south so that every tree will hear and feel our hello and feel our thankfulness and feel our compassion. And then they will be so touched by that that they will grow again another year. And we and our families will live again. And so to the Trees of the World, and their leader the Maple, with love, we say thank you. And our mind is agreed.

(Response: "tho" or "huh.")

And then in those trees, in that forest there, our Creator put the animals. Some of them are little ones, some are medium, and some of them are big: moose and elk. But here where we live, in the Rotinonhsón:ni[4] country, the Creator chose the deer to be the leader of all those animals. Because we needed those deer. All through the West, where the plains are, and the Lakota, he chose the buffalo to be the leader over there. In different parts of the world, there are different ones that are the leaders. But here, it's the deer, in this Northeast.

And so, those deer, when we need food for our ceremonies, they will give their lives. From them, from the skin of their hides, we can make shoes. And from those deer, there are medicine societies that help to heal the sick.

Even from that deer, our leaders of the Rotinonhsón:ni wear those horns on their sacred hats so that they will be alert to any dangers that come to our people. And so the deer and the animals, they help us all the time. They're still living.

Even the ones that are next to the barn, the ones they call domesticated. By the houses, they are roaming, the domesticated ones. And we include

---

4.   Literally, *the People of the Longhouse* (the Iroquois)

them in there. And the dogs and the cats. Every one. All the Animals. And so to them we say thank you. And our mind is agreed.

(Response: "tho" or "huh.")

And then next are the ones that I really like a lot. These are the ones they call the birds. After everything was done, and the Creator made us, he didn't want us to be sad in our life. The Creator didn't want boredom or lonesomeness to come into our lives, although it will now and then. But not to find a home in our minds. The Creator likes to see us smile. He likes it when we joke. That's why when you go into Iroquois country, you hear a lot of laughing going on. The more traditional the people, the more laughing you hear! It's really something; it's called "a big medicine."

And to guarantee that that should be the way it is—laughter and dance and song—the Creator made the robins and the chickadees, the sparrows and the mourning dove, every kind of bird. And he put beautiful colored feathers on their bodies. So they look pretty. And then he took those birds, and he threw them everywhere in the air. And he said to them, "You will zoom by where the men and women walk on the earth, with all your bright, beautiful colors. It will be so nice to see."

And then he gathered them together, and he had a big meeting with them. And he gave them their songs and the rhythms of them, the way they are. And when he finished, he said, "Now your job is to make sure that the deer and the bears and the moose and the elks and the humans don't get lonesome, and don't get bored with life. So every morning before the sun shows his face, just when the dawn light comes and it's still a little dark, I want all of you birds to get up. And start to sing the songs that bring the miraculous new day, every day." He said, "You will welcome the miraculous day and *life*."

And then he said, "Amongst all of you, I have selected the Eagle to be the chief or the leader of the Bird Life. And that eagle will be our protector." That's why it's right here on our hat, the eagle's feather.[5]

---

5.   The eagle feather is part of the Iroquois men's headdress, the kahstówa.

And so every day, even this morning, those birds were flying and those birds were singing the songs of joy of life. And so what we'll do, the people, is we shall become of one mind, and we'll put thank-yous, greetings, love, and kindness together in one big pile. And then we'll grab it at the edges and throw it to the north and the west and the south and east, so that *every* Bird that sang this morning will hear our thank-you. They will hear our kindness. And they will sing again tomorrow 'cause they know we're gonna say thank you to them. And they're so happy to do it because we said thank you. And so to the Birds of the World, for the songs that they sang this morning, with love, we salute you. And our mind is agreed.

(Response: "tho" or "huh.")

And then there are four winds in the universe. And they're coming from the north, south, east, and west. And those winds, some elders say, are two sets of twins. It's nice to hear it that way. It's a nice story. They say that Mother Earth got tired from giving birth. And nobody that has had children before can say that's not tiring. I mean, talk about *tired*. And I don't even know. But me and my wife, we've got six kids. So I have some idea.

But you know, Mother Earth is not just giving birth to one or to twins. She's giving hundreds of multiple births, almost simultaneously all the time. So think how much more tired she must get, our Mother Earth.

And so when our Mother Earth gets tired, they say that the wind of the north and the wind of the east together, they try to help. They bring a white blanket of snow, and they cover her body so she can rest. And when she has rested sufficiently, the other two brothers from the south and the west, they take the white blanket of snow off. And the next thing you know there's a wall-to-wall, green carpet of grass all over Mother Earth. And flowers are popping up here and there of every color imaginable. And life is reborn.

And so the four sacred winds, they keep the balance so that life can go on with energy. If there's no air, they come and blow the strong breezes. They carry the stagnant air away and revitalize it so that it is fresh, what we breathe. And so those winds never rest. They're doing the job that the

Creator told them to do. So we shall become of one mind again, and we'll put thank-yous, greetings, and love right there. And we'll throw it to the east, to the north, to the west, to the south. And we say, "Four Winds, thank you for bringing the changing of the seasons so that there will be life." And our mind again is agreed.

(Response: "tho" or "huh.")

And then what our Creator did, this time up in the sky in the west, he put what they call, in Mohawk, Ionkhisothokon:'a Ratiwé:ras. That means *our Grandfathers, the Thunderers*. And the Iroquois, they say the Thunderers, are only little tiny people. They would come up higher than your ankle, but not higher than your knee. But Grandma said, "You know that dynamite is only that big of a stick? But it can blow up a whole house. A big, big thing, it can blow it up. But it's only a little one. That's the same as them Thunderers. They're all little, but they can work thundrous things."

And so the Creator said to the Thunderers, "Your job will be to be the grandpa. And the people are gonna be your grandchildren. And a good grandfather periodically comes to see his grandchildren. But when you go see your grandchildren, don't just go abruptly there. Always hit your big drums, send your big thunder voice across the sky. Let 'em know you're coming so they can get ready to receive you."

And so usually, you'll see the blackening of the clouds first. Then you'll hear the distant drum of their voices. And you know you can get your tobacco ready. You get your prayer stuff ready to welcome them where you live every time. Almost every Iroquois traditional family, they've got special little pipes just for them. Every time the Thunderers come, they send beautiful smoke to them.

This past summer they came to visit us quite frequently. And our corn shot right up. And all the other foods in our garden, they shot right up. Lots of beans in there, lots of corn. Took care of us. And the lightning burned all the impurities in the sky. After they left, the air smelled sweet, so fresh and clean. And they put down brand new water as they passed through into our Mohawk River here and into the little Kanakare Creek right here so that we will have a fresh supply of water. Because we're their grandchildren.

We are so lucky we have such good grandparents. And so with oneness of mind, we who are the grandchildren today, we put many thank-yous and many greetings and much love and compassion and kindness right in front of us. And then you and I, the grandchildren, will pick it up, all around the edges, and we'll throw it high into the sky, especially to the west.

And we'll say, "Grandpa Thunderer, thank you for all the work you did last summer. Thank you, we've got food. Thank you, we've got water to drink. Thank you, we can have water to bathe in to clean our bodies. Thank you that the horses have water to drink. Grandpa Thunderer, with love, we thank you." And again, our mind is agreed.

(Response: "tho" or "huh.")

And then there is another thing that our Creator did. They say he made two suns in the sky. And the one sun we call, in my language Kiohkehnékha Karáhkwa. Kiohkehnékha means *in the daytime*. Then karáhkwa means *sun*. They call him the Big Man. Some elders even say that the rays of the sun are like the hands of the Creator. And so you see how sacred it is, our life. And how privileged we are that the Creator touches each one of us. No matter that there are hundreds of us, that light surrounds every one of us simultaneously. And such is the power of our Creator.

And you know the reason he shines the light? Because if he didn't, there would be total darkness. And if I walk in total darkness, I can't see. I'll bump into things, and I might cut myself, and blood would come. Or if I walk, I might bump into my sister. Her head and my head will collide, and there will be blood again. And she will hurt, and I will hurt. So the Creator shines the light so that when I see that column there, I won't bump into it. I'll go around it. And when I see my sister, I don't have to bump into her. I go around and she goes around me. And thus there will be peace.

And so because the sun shines all over the world, the Creator wants there to be peace, not war. He wants us to learn how to be in harmony, how to respect the sacred life of all. So there will be no war. And that can only happen if we're willing to share everything. Nobody rich. Nobody poor. Just like the Christian world says, "He breaks the bread, everybody eats it." And just like the Indian says, "You've got corn, fix the soup, and everybody's gonna eat it." *Everybody*. Specially the children, they start first. And with that kindness, how is there gonna be war?

The sun is shining beautifully today so that we may see our path. He warms us up with our miraculous, wonderful day. And so to the Sun, our Eldest Brother, we say thank you with love. And our mind is agreed.

(Response: "tho" or "huh.")

And then there's a nighttime sun. We call it Ionkhihsótha Ahsonhthenhnéhkha Karáhkwa. That means our *Grandmother, the Nighttime Sun*. And her, she walks twenty-eight to thirty days on a single predictable path in the universe. That's what we see. And as she does this, they say, she orchestrates all the women of every nation.

She regulates their bodies, so every month, the old blood of the woman goes away and new blood is made. That new blood is just like a comfortable, quilted, soft blanket where a little tiny human being can begin its journey to life. Grandma Moon regulates that. And the reason we call her Grandma is because she's the grandest of all the mothers in the world. She's the *leader*. And that's why we have children. And that's why we have grandchildren. And some of you have great-grandchildren. It's because Grandma is still working her miraculous wonders.

And so, on behalf of all the children that were born yesterday and last night and today, Grandma Moon, we say, thank you for allowing this good life. And our mind is agreed.

(Response: "tho" or "huh.")

And now the one that I always tell people I like the most. I used to hear the elders in our Longhouse, specially my grandparents. They used to say that Grandmother Moon is a woman, and so she likes to get dolled up when she goes out at night. Every night, she has beautiful diamond earrings on her ears, hanging way down. And she's got a diamond necklace right here, every night. And she's got all over her body beautiful diamonds. And you know what those diamonds are? Those are the stars in the sky that surround her where she walks. I loved it when I heard the old people say that "Grandma's all dolled up tonight, doing her job."

And so to the Stars that beautify our Grandma Moon, we say thank you, and our mind is agreed.

(Response: "tho" or "huh.")

And then of course as I've already said before, we the humans were the last ones to be made of all Creation. We are last. And that's why Grandma and other elders have suggested—they didn't say this is a *fact*, but they made a strong suggestion—that because we were the last of thousands and thousands of millions of creations, the Creator might have been exhausted and *tired* by the time he came to making us.

And so they say, "We think that when he put us together, he musta not exactly put one of the wires together right. And so we have a little handicap more than all other living things. For the robin is always gonna be robin. And the buffalo is always gonna be buffalo. Eagle will always be eagle. But humans, we always try to be somebody we're not. Always got a mask on."

We don't really know each other. We don't even know *ourselves* sometimes 'cause we always try to be something we aren't. And humans always tend to exaggerate too.

"How big was that deer you went hunting and caught?"
"Ahhhh, got ten horns."
And they have *no* horns really!

"How big was that fish you caught?"
Caught a little thing like that and by the time he got home, it was *that* big!

"Oh your kids did good in school?"
"Yeah, they're on the principal's list."
It's almost all red marks!

So we never tell the truth. It's hard to tell the truth. We always add an extra leg, add an extra thing to it. That's why the Creator doesn't trust us with our life. And that's why he keeps it a secret when we're gonna leave this world. He knew when we were born; it was already predestined. But he doesn't dare show us the maps of our individual lives because we're gonna add something extra on it. We exaggerate. That's why we're handicapped, humans. And that's why we're the ones that can get in trouble more than any other life form on this earth. So we are sorta like the dangerous ones. We are like the baby ones that all other life needs to take care of. And look at everything else in the world. If all we humans died, everything else would keep going! So we are the ones that are the most in need of help.

And for that reason, the Creator made what we call Kaié:ri Niionkwè:take, the *Four Beings*. We also call them Ratironhiakehró:non, the *Sky Dweller Beings* or sometimes we refer to them as the Four Mysterious Beings. And these beings don't have faces. And they don't have bodies like you and I. They are four powers of the Sky World, of the universe world. Their job is to help the Creator keep the world going, keep life going. They've been assigned especially to babysit us because of that one fault we have, of not being able to tell the truth for what it is. We always put that extra leg on it. Their job is to make sure we don't put *ten* legs on it.

And so, at various times in history, in various parts of the world, the different races have forgotten their teachings, neglected them. And when they have, fights have begun, and disruptions have come, and they have begun to kill each other in wars. They have thrown away the Creator's instructions for peace. They have thrown away the sun, and that's why there has been war.

And so what our elders say to us is that whenever that happened, he would summon these Four Sacred Beings, these four powers, and one of them or jointly (usually one of them) would volunteer to be born as a human. He would be born as the Peacemaker for that region or for that particular people. He'd remind them to go back and recover what they had given up that caused their wars and their disarray.

And so probably one of those was born as a Buddha. Probably one was born as Confucius. Probably one was born as Jesus Christ. That's what our elders have suggested to us. And I know for sure that one of them was born as the Teacher that brought us our Four Sacred Rituals that we're gonna talk about here. And then when we really had war here, about two thousand years ago, one of them was born as the Peacemaker who brought the Constitution of the

Five Nations to us, the Great Peace. And he was one of our Huron people. We don't say the name of the Peacemaker. I'll explain why later on.

So they're the ones that have been sent here to bring peace, to stop the wars and turmoil. And that's why we always mention them in our thanksgivings, all the time without fail. Because we have children that are being born, grandchildren that are being born, yet. And we need their help to intervene, to keep us on the road of peace and thankfulness. And so to those Four Sacred Powers, the Peace Prophets of the World, we say thank you to you now on behalf of our people. And our mind is agreed.

(Response: "tho" or "huh.")

And then there's our Creator, the one we also say doesn't have a real face or body. When the Western world came here, they told us that "man was made in the image of God." And we don't say that's not true. We say, of course, that's true, providing that you understand that when the buffalo talks about God, that the buffalo was also made in the image of God. And when the eagle talks about God, God is an eagle; he's the image of them. And when the frogs talk about God, they were made in the image of God. It's not exclusive to us, it's not just *us* that have the right to life. Everything that's in the world that lives has the right, and it's made in the image of God.

And so that's why in this lady's body, God is in her body. In her body, God is in there; the Creator's in there. In your body, everyone here, even the horses out there, God is in there. And every tree that grows, God is in there. So you count it all, every life form in the universe, and then you draw a line at the bottom. Now you get to add it up. What your sum totals, that's what we call God. It isn't just a little old thing. It's something *big, unimaginable, powerful, in all life.* That's the one that made us.

And so when our Creator finished all of this, he put the man and the woman side by side together. And he said, kanonronkhwáhtshera. *Compassion and love* you will have. And from that man and woman's compassion and love, there will be replicas of them born. Those are the generations. And the Iroquois always say seven generations. So that when we think, we are supposed to be thinking seven generations. So that what we are doing today is not gonna hurt those seven generations when they come. The decisions we make have to touch them. They have to go that far. And I'm saying this because in our daily life, all the things we do are not just for you and me. They're just as much for the ones that are not born yet.

And when the Creator finished everything, he said, "I didn't make a coliseum for you or an archival institute, a building for you to put all the philosophical or spiritual doctrines in. I didn't write it in books or anything."

He said, "The only thing I did is let you live on your Mother Earth. And everything you need is at your fingertips. Just don't be a pig about it. Don't be greedy. Share. And if you do this, your life will be everlasting. But I want you to know, I wait every day for every woman, every man, and every kid to take just a couple of minutes, a couple seconds and face me every day. And just say, 'My Creator, I thank you for this miraculous life. Thank you, Mother Earth.'"

And that's all that's necessary for us. There's no big cathedral. There's no Library of Congress that holds our knowledge. Just a simple word, thank you, a true word to the Creator, and there will be everlasting life. And so that's why we say the Ohén:ton Karihwatéhkwen. That's what comes before any important things. Then we will be grounded in life.

And so to our Creator . . . I ask you and I to simultaneously spin out many layers of thankfulness and many layers of hellos and greetings and much kindness and love 'til it touches the ceiling and it wants to seep out the windows of this room. And then what we'll do is stand back at its perimeters, you and I, and grab it all at the edges, and throw it high into the universe. And say, "Creator, our Maker, thank you for this wonderful life." And our mind is agreed.

(Response: "tho" or "huh.")

And that is a reader's digest form of the spiritual key of the ceremonial world of the Iroquois: the Mohawk and the Oneida, the Onondaga, the Cayuga, the Seneca, and the Tuscarora. And I would even dare to say further than that, of all the nations in North America and South America.

If you want to step back a couple of thousand years, it is probably the same words that the Irish had at one time. Africa has some of it yet. All the world's people used to have it. They call it universal truth. *That's* what we have to get back to.[6]

---

6. Tom added: while we're at this, we do have in the craft store, a book that's got the Opening Prayer, the Opening Address, in it. It's a little one too, pocket size. And it's in Spanish, it's in Japanese, it's in Chinese, it's in Portuguese, it's in French, it's in Italian, it's in I don't know. They keep on translating it into different languages. It's a wonderful thing. And I think the more that that book goes all over the world, it becomes a skeleton key for all humans to see if they can find their path again, and stuff like that. (Editor's note: *Thanksgiving Address, Ohén:ton Karihwatéhkwen* [Corrales, New Mexico: Native Self-Sufficiency Center, Six Nations Indian Museum Tracking Project, Tree of Peace Society, 1993, ISBN 0-9643214-0-8]. In the craft store at Kanatsioharè:ke, there is also a CD of Tom reciting the Opening Address in both Mohawk and English.)

Chapter 3

Colonialism

They tried to teach us that us Indians don't count for nothing.

Once you're colonized or brainwashed, it's like being on a track—it's hard to get off. I'm one of the ones who can attest to that. It's been a struggle and a *half*, let me tell you. *Ah*, it's been a struggle.

I was talking about that 102-year-old lady before. At the time she was raised, they were almost devoid of knowledge of the traditions. You might wonder, how could that be that she's a 102-year-old lady and yet she wouldn't be able to tell about these things. But it's because she wasn't raised traditionally. Hardly anybody was. So these days you can find a fifteen-year-old that can tell you way more than that old lady can tell you about tradition and about history. Those people at that time, the majority of them, were just totally like putty in the hand of the colonizer. So that's kinda unique in a sense to hear her talk about loving and respecting the traditional people.

When I tell the old stories, I've always tried to make them relevant or true in my life. I've found myself rationalizing them. I have done this not because I wanted to, but because of the memories of my childhood, being a kid and going to school. I remember that they used to hit us. In fact my generation was the last of the Mohawks of Akwesasne to be physically punished for speaking our language.

I'm gonna give my best guess, that about 75 percent, if not more, of my generation were fluent Mohawks and were *not* fluent in English when I was a little boy. And I believe we were the last ones to get hit on our hands by a ruler, to get our ears pulled, to get our hair pulled because we couldn't understand *English*. I'm probably the last generation of all the Iroquois too. Because I think Akwesasne is the one place that has really used the language the most, of any of the reservations.

I attended a government school. It was organized by the federal and the state governments together through some kind of an agreement. But the Christians—the Catholic and the Protestant religions—were the only two religions that were allowed to instruct the kids. And if you were Longhouse, you went with the Catholics. The nuns taught you. And every Monday, the Catholics or the Protestants came to get the kids out of class. There was no other choice.

So even though we were Longhouse, we were not permitted to go to the Longhouse. There was no such thing as the Longhouse having a religious day. If you were strong enough, you got to stay behind in the class. But nobody had enough gumption to argue the system, so we just went with the Catholics. Our parents didn't want to make trouble. They were afraid of the system, afraid of the white people. So we just went with the flow.

And in a way that helped me because it made me understand. You know what helped me the most so I didn't become like them? The nuns gave us big books, and they sat there. In those days they wore those just-face-sticking-out clothes, the long dress, and everything. Well, I used to be afraid of them because of the stories I had heard of superstitious stuff, medicines, and witchcraft. And then in my mind, that was mixed with the Europeans' witchcraft and their black clothes.

So I associated the nuns with the witches. That's what I thought they were! I really used to be afraid of them 'cause what I was hearing came just at that age, I guess. So I was afraid of them from the beginning and all the while I was there.

They gave us big books that had beautiful colored pictures in them. *Colored.* And at that time, colored pictures were *something.* Almost everything else was in black and white. And they had desert scenes with men in them. I think there was Moses and people like that. They had sandals on their feet, and they wore white clothes, like gowns or something, way to the ground. They carried long sticks. And they had big beards.

And I looked at them. And they were saying that was God's army; those were God's helpers and messengers. And they told us that was our leader. So I looked at those pictures. It was a big book too. The faces were almost life-sized to me because I was little.

And I said, "That don't look like *my* uncle. That don't look like *my* Chiefs. That don't look like anybody of my people." So I just rejected it. I said, "That's not mine. It doesn't even look like us *at all.*"

So fortunately for me, since I didn't identify with their appearance, I didn't listen. That's why I can't even compare it to our Longhouse ways now. All I did was just sit there, just to be present, 'cause we *had* to attend. That's my experience. Someone else's could be different depending on what they were told and depending on who was affecting their family and their life.

Mine was always getting hit with the ruler. Mine was always hearing them saying, "Don't talk Mohawk." And so everything for me was like hardball! That's why I grew up sort of like a fighter—to defend who I am. Because I was attacked all the time. My language was attacked in school, year after year, and I was punished for it. There was no place there for the things in the Longhouse that I have. When we tried it, we were reprimanded for it.

Our music, our art, our baskets, or anything we did that was artistic was forbidden in there. Even our story, our history. In the curriculum of the State of New York, in the late 1960s, all the schools had this book called *The Great Tree and the Longhouse.* It's quite a book. And all the schools used that.

But the St. Regis Mohawk School where I went did not have access to that book. They didn't have that in our school. It wasn't even a subject. Malone, Massena, Brushton—every town, every other school in the state had it as part of their curriculum. But not where the Mohawks went to school. I don't know about the Onondagas, but the St. Regis Mohawks did not. So anything that was Mohawk, in nature or content, we didn't study it, *at all*.

Fortunately for us, we did have Ray Fadden for many years. He was my science teacher when I was in grade 5, and I believe he taught my mother as well. As part of a reward system when we got our work finished, he would talk to us, inspire us, and make us proud to be Onkwehón:we. His presence was very important. He influenced a lot of people, and I believe a lot of them wouldn't have done as good as they did, without him. We could spend a long time talking about all the things that Ray taught us as well. But that was not part of the curriculum. The school didn't really want him doing that. And they made it difficult for him, even painting over the Native images that he put over the doors of the classrooms.

Well, one must question the rationale behind that. And that's in my lifetime. So you see what I mean when I say hardball? I've been told over and over that to be an Indian, to believe the way an Indian believes, to dress like an Indian, to behave like an Indian is all hocus-pocus, nonsense, and you'd best straighten up and start accepting the Western world: the language, the religion, the everything. Being told that over and over since I was little is what made me a rebel, in a sense. And I mean not a *rebel* rebel, but a rebel deep inside, *way* deep inside.

But, I'm not immune to colonization either, 'cause I was just a kid. So one of the things that hurts me so bad I still can't even deal with it is . . . I had good teachers, *good teachers*: Grandma and Grandpa and all of them. And I can name all of them for you. And they told me things, and then the school told me not to believe in them because they weren't "documented."

"They're only myths, it's only . . ."

What I'm saying to you is that no white man, nobody foreign is there anymore twisting my arm or kicking my butt as they did when I was a kid. Not *anymore*.

Because now the image of that person is in here, in my head, way subconsciously kicking my butt every day. *I'm kicking my own butt*. So no physical American or Canadian man has to do it to me anymore. He's already inside here where I can't get him out. That's what they call the colonization process. That's how effective it is. It's deadly.

So while I was growing up, I was rebelling from everything that I'm supposed to be as an Indian too because I was told, "It's fantasy. It's superstitious. It's witchcraft. It's not even real." It was reinforced over and over. Every little corner I turned was always like that.

So the reason why I have a hard time talking about it is because my own grandmother tried not to let me go to school. She didn't want me to go to school, *ever*, because she said, "You're gonna turn into that kinda people. You will abandon who you are. And who you're supposed to be." She almost got arrested by the State of New York because there's a law that says when you get to be six, or whatever, you're supposed to go to school. So I almost put her in jail that one time in my life. But she was trying to protect me.

My grandpa used to talk about the clans, how the Clan System runs. And I'll share with you what he told me too, in a moment. He was a product of the Carlisle Indian School in Pennsylvania. And I've got documentation showing that Grandpa Bero was the leader of the runaways, of the Indians of Carlisle. He led the pack of everybody that ran away from that place. Grandpa Paul Bero was my grandmother's uncle, my mother's mother's uncle—so he would be like my great-grandfather.[1]

When he was only seven or eight years old, he ran away from Carlisle, in the winter months. In those days, there was no Thruway; there was no interstate. He made it all the way through the Allegheny Mountains and all the way through the Adirondacks, in the winter, as a seven-, eight-year-old boy. All the way to Akwesasne. That's over six hundred miles, in dead winter. And he got home.

So to me, he was like a hero, a *hero*. And he used to tell me these things. And even though he was educated, he could speak English, he used to like to say, "Sebenteen pifty pour."[2] That's how he said it. He used to say that

---

1. The way family is determined will become clear later on. At this point, the simplest way to look at it is that any relative of a grandparent's generation or older is thought of as a grandparent.
2. 1754.

all the time. He'd be talking Mohawk, but he'd say in English, "Sebenteen pifty pour." I don't know if it was 'cause he didn't have teeth or he didn't know how to say it right or what it was. But when I was growing up, I was even saying that, "Sebenteen pifty pour" myself, because I thought that was the way you said it!

Why I'm telling you this is that *I never really believed him*. Because where I went to school, when I tried to share this, they got mad. Whenever I would tell them something at school about a treaty or something, 'cause I grew up there where they talked about it, "No place for that." No room, *always*.

So I always listened to my grandmother and the Chiefs and the old people, like Grandpa Bero; I always listened 'cause he was my Grandpa. But I didn't really take it as if it was *really* true because I had learned not to believe it. It was no use hearing it. It was useless until the 1960s when we had the White Roots of Peace.

The White Roots of Peace was created as a renaissance movement of the tradition. The name was taken from the old Great Law. It was a group of Iroquois. Sometimes Sioux traveled with us, sometimes Choctaw, sometimes Cree, but it was primarily Iroquois. The others just came with us to learn. We went to different reservations and urban centers in Chicago; Los Angeles; San Francisco; Vancouver; Florida; Atlanta, Georgia; Boston—all over—to revitalize the Indian people. It was a contemporary effort to revitalize the whole Indian world.

And some people say that it was that group that turned around the way Indians were. It was sorta like the lightning rod that grounded the movement of Indians in terms of tradition. Because at that time our Indians didn't wanna be Indians. Whatever they knew about Indians was bad, so they thought it was bad to be an Indian.

And the White Roots of Peace kinda showed them and taught them that to think that way is not right. And it was very effective in showing that. And from there, that's where Wounded Knee started, and the Alcatraz Island takeover after that. And some scholars say that it was that small White Roots of Peace group that woke up the consciousness of the Indian people.

In fact, I think if somebody wanted to do the research a little bit about the White Roots of Peace, they would find that in various places, they still talk about it even though that was forty years ago. There are still Indians out West who talk about it. And once in a while, I get letters.[3]

So anyway, when we had the White Roots of Peace, they took us over to Albany. And they said, "Come and see where all the wampum belts are." In this education building in Albany, in the cellar, there are big vaults. And they had all the wampum belts in there for the Six Nations that they had taken from us. I used to hear about this, even as a little kid, that the government took our belts so we would forget our stories, see?[4] That's why they did it. And that we were gonna try to get them back. And that's all I heard, but I'd never seen them.

So when we were with the White Roots of Peace, and we had an engagement over there, whoever it was said, "We're gonna take these White Roots of Peace Indian guys down cellar, and they're gonna see those wampum belts."

Wow!

We—these White Roots of Peace Indian guys—were planning how we were gonna knock those guards down, knock 'em out, then how we were

---

3.   As Tom was telling me this, he reached into his pile of mail for the day and handed me just such a letter. It was from a woman who had been only ten years old when the White Roots of Peace came to her community. In the letter, she told Tom that she had been wanting to find him for years to tell him personally what an impact he had on her life and how he had helped her to feel good about who she was. Forty years later. Her moving letter brought tears to my eyes, he had meant so much to her.

4.   Major events and agreements, such as treaties, used to be recorded pictorially and in symbols in long belts made of wampum. (For more about the making of wampum, see Chapter 18, "The Four Sacred Rituals Part 3.") Wampum keepers and others memorized the agreements and memorized details about the events commemorated in these belts. Then they used the belts as mnemonic devices to recall the details. (Although referred to as "belts," they were not a form of clothing.)

gonna get away and how we were gonna take all those belts with us that they wouldn't give back to our people because that was the least that we could do. We almost did it. And you know if we had done it, we'd be behind bars yet today. But if you understand it from our point of view, we'd be serving our people, the greatness of them.

We didn't do it because there were too many guards there at that time, specially for us.

But that's not all.

After that, they took us upstairs. I don't know if it was the second or the third floor of that place. And, of course, I used to hear Grandpa. He used to say, "Ne ne tsi nikahá:wi *sebenteen pifty pour.*"

He used to say that:
Né:'e onkwahsóhtshera'kénha tsi nón:we niiakwahwatsiratákie. Ne éh tho wahontkennnísa Skahnéhtati. Eh né:'e éh tho ne ratihá: wi ne Onekohrha'shón:'a akia'tahnha'shón:'a. Kwah o'tokén:'en kaienton ohswen'karà:ke tsi ní:wa thi akia'táhnha. Né:'e ne éh tho wahonwatirihónnien Ratihnarà:ken. Ne ne tsi ní:ioht ionkwe'tahkwen ionkwaianerénhsera.

What he was saying was,
Our grandfather's time, they were gone to a meeting in Albany.

Skahnéhtati we call Albany. He said,
And there for the first time they took the great wampum belts, they even touched the floor, how big they were. And there they were telling the white people about our Constitution, our Great Law, of how to make government.

And he said,
Ne' éh tho théntsko:te. Benjamin Franklin ne Thomas Jefferson.
They're sitting there, Benjamin Franklin and Thomas Jefferson.

He said their names.

We were learning about them in school. And I didn't know who they were at the time Grandpa Bero said their names. But I remembered them; he said them so many times. So this image was in my head. But when I tried to talk about it at school, none of the teachers would hear me. "There's no such thing," they said. It was a complete denial.

And I always remembered. I *still* remember it word-for-word. But I didn't really believe it. I thought it was just a story.

So when they took us to that second or third floor, we went into a big room. The ceilings were twelve foot, I think, ten foot at least. And there were paintings on the wall.

I don't remember if it was right on the wall itself, or if it was on something that was on the wall. But there was one scene—we have it in the craft store. And at the bottom of it, there were Indians, standing up in front of the white people. And the Indians had those wampum belts around their arms, and they were even touching the floor. And at the bottom of this big picture that was painted on the wall, in gold, was *1754.*

And when I saw it, *I cried* because I hadn't believed my grandparents, my teachers in my family. I wasted all those years 'cause I thought it wasn't true, that it was just a fairy tale.

So that's what changed my life a little bit there, and I started to have faith in my leaders and my Clan Mothers and my elders. Even if people say what they're talking about is bullshit, I say those are still my grandmothers; that's my grandfather. So I changed my opinion. I decided I was gonna listen now and make sense of it. And that's what I've been doing ever since.

And I've since tried to find that building. I've since tried to take a picture of it myself. But nobody has told me, even today, where that building is. It almost feels like they're hiding it.

There were other pictures on the other walls. At the bottom of this one in big letters was 1754. I'd like to spend a couple of days there, just looking for that.

The wampum belts have been returned, through litigation, but it took many, *many* years. But most of them have been returned, I believe. And Onondaga's got 'em now, in the vault in Syracuse.

But wherever that building is, I'd like to see it again. I'd like to.

Even though I went through all *this*, it's not over. Even when I'm doing the Creation story, you'll see. I never fully accepted whatever I learned from my people because in the back of my mind, there is still that person that's telling me, "That's not true." In my subconscious: "That's not true. There's no truth to that. It's not real." *Still.*

If I do beadwork, or if I make a moccasin, or maybe if I write a book (which I wrote once or twice), or if I make a basket or do something that's creative or whatever, I'm never satisfied, I find. And I didn't know I was doing this until I reflected one time and I caught myself. I forget how come I came to that consciousness, but I caught myself.

I didn't know I was doing this, but whenever I accomplish something, I'm always looking to see where the first white woman or man is. Any one will do. And I show them what I did. And if that white man looks at it and he says, "Tom, that's pretty. That's good," I think *God* said it's okay. Because I've been taught that us Indians "don't count for *nothing*. The white man is the only one that's God's cousin, his close relative, not us. We don't know nothing about it."

So in my subconscious, I'm always looking for a white man to hold me, to touch me, to give me what you call it? Validation. To confirm my existence. I *know that's not right*. But in here, inside, I've been trained to do that. And when you talk about how to free yourself from colonization, I think you can never do it. You're always gonna have those scars, forever. And you'll remember it.

It never finishes for me. Probably I'm gonna die like that, huh? I'm going on sixty years,[5] and I'm still dragging that, *still* dragging that.

[5.] Tom made this speech in 2004.

But how our young people . . . I don't think they even know this, huh? And I don't think they're gonna realize this. *At least I realized it.* You know what I mean? So that's always like a consolation to me 'cause at least I know now why. But you still have to deal with that. Your memory doesn't forget. Every once in a while, something reminds you of a time, and you relive it again, and you remember it.

Oh, I remember a time when I was young. It was the darkest time in my life. I was going to try to kill myself. With a rope. 'Cause I was taught to fight and then I was taught not to fight. And I didn't know what to do. Yeah, I was gonna fight.

And the hardest thing of it is . . . is that Grandpa Bero is dead. He died about thirty-five years ago. And there are things that he taught and talked about that now have come to light and understanding. And he didn't know that because he was not in that time yet where . . . He didn't know.

My grandmother died some twenty-seven years ago. And whenever I talk about how we came back here to the Mohawk Valley, to Kanatsioharè: ke and how she used to say things about coming here, I'm reminded; she never knew that we *did* come back. The older people suffered a lot. And they took it with them to their graves. They were never relieved of that stress and that heavy burden they carried.

And I guess that's what makes me cry. I've been relieved of many of the burdens and stresses that they carried. I'm more liberated, you might say, in a sense.

So you'll notice that as we do this story, there will be times that I keep trying to make a comparison with whatever I know about the Western world because I'm still trying to prove that all of it's true, to myself. And you'll see where that is 'cause it's *very* obvious.

Even one of the old Chiefs in Onondaga, a most respected Chief, his opinion of the Creation story was "That story is only a myth. It's just like those stories of the Europeans, like Cinderella. It's only just a 'Three Bears' story. This story of Creation we have is not really true." He said this.

At the time, I looked at him. That Chief was very old. He's passed on since, and a very good Chief he was. He was a good man, and he had a good family. But when he said that, he might as well have taken a big club and hit me on the head with it. If he was a Chief and he had this kind of an opinion, where was he gonna lead us?

Here was one of my own elders saying this to me. At the time, I thought I was finished with that, and that's why he hurt me . . . because it's not a myth to me. To *me*. I still love the Chief. And I still honor him. But . . . and so a lot of times older people hurt the young people. And I don't know if they realize it sometimes. So we have to always be careful of that too.

My experience has been whenever I've told any parts of our history where it's somewhat similar to the Christians', whenever I've told any of that in universities, right away the intellectuals in the world of academia say, "Oh, that's *our* story. You're telling *our* story." Even though it may also be similar to the Africans and the Chinese.

For example, when I talk about the twelve teachers, which I'll talk about later,[6] right away they say, "You must have been influenced by the Jesuits."

It's like we don't have a world of our own. We don't have any way to have our very own history. 'Cause we were taught that by the missionaries. We were taught that by the school or somebody, see? So every time we find something that's good or whatever, it's "Oh, we taught you that." (So "how lucky you are," you know?)

That's why after hearing that, growing up, you subconsciously feel inferior to everyone, and you're always looking for a way to grow up, to be real. At least I am. But I'm not as bad as I used to be. Now that I realize it, it's a lot better.

And so my answer to them is *this*: look, you may be right, and you may be wrong. Because we all have to drink water. Whether you're Irish, Polish, Egyptian, Black, Indian, Mohawk, or Seneca. Even if you're a deer or a

---

6.   See chapter 16, "The Four Sacred Rituals Part 1: The Teacher."

bear, you've gotta drink water. Did *you* teach *us* that? Did *we* teach *you* that? Or is that just the truth of the universe?

The wind that blows, the air that blows, all over the world, is the same air that blows on each of us, whether it blows in New York City or Seneca country. Because we all have to breathe. Did you give it to me? Or did somebody else, or the universal truth do it? So we have the same wind and the same sun who's our brother. He shines the light that makes our corn grow into food, makes every food grow that we eat. And if that sun goes out, then you and I don't exist any more. Regardless of how much money we've got, or what our status is, or what our labels are, if the sun goes out, the richest person dies too, with us. Wealth has no significance because we're all equal in that regard. It's an original truth.

So a lot of things about our creation, our worldviews, and concepts will be very similar because we all have the same mother, the same sun, and the same air that we breathe. *Of course,* there are gonna be similarities. We came from the same earth.

And they have a hard time understanding that. Because there's a notion that only one has the truth. All you've got to do is listen to any missionary who knocks on your door, saying, "*I* bear the truth." But there are many of them. And that's the experience we had when we were growing up too. Everybody was looking to take our soul. Because they had "the light." So that's part of our reality. And we have to deal with that too.

Anyway, that's my answer to them—is that there's truth that we have in common. So naturally, there are gonna be a lot of parallels when we talk about our world. Not because anyone has a copyright on it. It's because water is water.

Chapter 4

Creation Story Part 1:
Sky Woman and Turtle Island

*I think the Creation story is the most important of the events I am recounting
'cause it's so fundamental.*

Now the Creation story is the story that impacts our people and our
concepts of the world perhaps more than any Iroquois realizes. This story
is fragmented in the minds of most Iroquois people today. Even when I
was a kid, it was fragmented. I never heard this story, the way I'm gonna
tell it to you, when I was a boy. I heard it in bits and pieces—over here,
over there. A couple of years down the road, I heard another part. I never
heard it from *A* to *Z*. It was never whole. It took me over thirty years to
put these pieces together. And I didn't just hear it in Akwesasne either.
I heard the parts in different places. And I had all kinds of responses.

It begins in a place called Karonhià:ke. Karonhià:ke simply means
the place in the sky. It was the name of that planet or that earth that
we came from before we were on this earth. So it seems like it's
somewhere in the solar system. And then, of course, I've always tried
to rationalize it.

In this world called Karonhià:ke, somewhere in the solar system were our people, our ancestors. They had a sophistication there, in that world. They had what today they call ESP—extrasensory perception. It was common practice amongst them. It wasn't foreign, it wasn't rare, it wasn't odd. It was *normal* for them to do this.

Some elders say that their ESP was such that, say I wanted to drink some water a ways away, I wouldn't have to physically go there to get it. That water would just come to me. And I would drink it. People like Daisy Thomas and those different seers like my grandmother was, they carry that thing that came from Karonhià:ke. That's what seers are; they're still just being what they were from the other world.

And so that's why it exists in most Indian country. And it also exists in Africa; it exists in China; it exists in white people; it exists in every race of the world, wherever there are people, and it's even in the animals. But you find it amongst the people in the world who still possess the closest knowledge of their *original* teachings before they were boxed into religions, back when there were original truths that bound everybody in the world.

But now that religions have come into it, there are dozens and dozens of them competing for all of us. And they're not being spiritual, they're religions. They have memberships and stuff like that. These become the priorities, somewhat.

But when you go back to those people in Africa and China or in white Europe, wherever you can find some of the original teachings left, there are universal truths. It's like they're automatically understood. I don't need much talking to understand them, and they don't need much talking to understand me because we come from the same truth. You see what I mean?

So the less religion we have, the more unity we have already existing. And it's from the original teachings. It's *real*, so it doesn't really need much propping up. I've found this to be very true. Aboriginal peoples across the world have seers—people who have the ability to see. And they depend on them a lot too.

But here in America, they don't hold much credence in them. I talked to a priest, an orthodox Greek priest, and they don't have any use for seers *at all*. He was almost offended that I even brought it up. And he almost said they were the work of the devil. *And he's a priest!* He's a wonderful man, but his concept of the world and the spiritual is just such and such. If you don't do things a certain way, you don't even stand a chance of being on that road of life. And I didn't really realize that it was *that* bad, at least not in these modern days.

I told him, "The Iroquois, we have that all over. It's *abundant*. We all go by our dreams. We go by the things that the Creator sends us, all the time. We've always done it."

So these people in Karonhià:ke were able to do that, on a common day-to-day basis there. They could almost read each other's minds.

And often you'll see a man and a woman who are married that were meant to be together. They don't have to say much, 'cause they can read each other's minds. They pick things up without either of them saying anything because it's meant to be. They have this kind of power.

A lot of our Indian nations didn't change from their original truths until just a couple of hundred years ago, really. So they still have a close connection, even people who didn't grow up or weren't born in Indian country. It is still in the membrane of our society so much that it transcends our colonization somewhat. It's hard to understand, but it's *there*. And it wouldn't be hard to make it come back again, make it real.

Of all the people in the world, we are probably the ones that could do it the fastest because we haven't been removed from it that long, actually. So we have a lot of advantage in a way.

But on the other hand, we have a disadvantage because our heart was just recently raped and ripped apart. And so it's going to take healing in order for that to go to the next step.

And I think that's what my problem is. I've gotta get over that yet. I've still got to go through that.

But anyway, that's how they were in Karonhià:ke. And so that validates in my mind why we have Grandma like she was, why we had Daisy Thomas, and why we've had all those people that have the ability to see. Providing they're real. There are a lot of seers that are only there to make money. They're not real. But when you see a real one, you know. You know for *sure*.

This woman, if I remember right, and if the old people were right . . . (See, here I go again, "if," did you catch that? I just caught myself.) This lady from the sky, if I remember—and I'm going back 50 years—is Atsi'tsiaká: ion. Her name was Atsi'tsiaká:ion. And translated into English, it means *the flower that has matured*, or you could say *the old flower*. Either one, but it sounds better if you say *the matured flower*!

And in this world, there was this tree. And it was dark there. There was no sun over there in that solar system or wherever they were in that part of the Sky World. This tree grew in the middle.

And here in this world of Karonhià:ke, this tree had everything growing on it. It had apples, it had peaches, it had plums, it had cherries, it had pears, it had everything you can think of in terms of fruit.

And when I was little, I used to wonder about that. I thought that was foolish 'cause I'd never seen that before. But later on, when I got a little older, I found out that the white brother, he can make peaches, pears, and plums grow on one tree. They call it grafting. And it reinforced that story, and it made it valid, 'cause now somebody had proved it could be done. But then it also said that the white man did it. They told me the white man did it, so he's the one that's "godly" 'cause he can do that. And we can't. You know what I mean?

So everything had two sides to it, an effect emotionally for *me* as well, you know. And for you it would be different maybe, depending on where you're coming from at the moment.

Since this was the thing that grew everything, it had a *power*, this tree. They called it the Life Tree. 'Cause it produced the thing that made everything *live*. They talked about this tree being such a powerful life-giving source that it *glowed*. It had a radiance to it. And in that world where there was no sun, it was that tree whose glow gave them some light in the darkness.

And they were told, whatever's on that tree, whatever grows on there, it's for the people. *But* you can't do anything with that tree: you can't climb on that tree; you can't swing on that tree; nor can you go there and pull the peaches, the apricots or the pears off of it. It's for *you*, the people and the animals and the birds. But you've gotta wait until the pear finishes ripening and it falls to the ground. Then you can go get it.

Once the peaches come off, they're yours. But you can't go over there and pick them 'cause they might not be ready. Nobody can climb on there 'cause they might break the branches. And then it'll interfere with the energy and the source of the power for the world. That tree. That's the teaching.

So there's some similarity there, right? To the other story, the white brother's? But a little bit different too.

Now this woman got pregnant. 'Course you know, being pregnant there is the same as being pregnant today. When a woman gets pregnant, a new life begins to form in her body. And all the thousands of connections—mechanisms of the brain and things that cause you to be able to move, to see, to understand, to perceive things—all hook to this new baby to give it the same. And so it effects changes in the woman who's going through this. Radical changes.

So sometimes she's in a good mood, a happy mood. And then the next minute or the next half hour, she's ready to cut your head off. A minute later she wants to do something. It's impossible to do that, but she's convinced she's going to. There are mood swings going on in her because this new human being is taking those powers and touching those nerves. That's what causes this erratic, moody behavior. And my grandmother said that's the way it happens to most women.

My wife and I have lots of kids. That's the way we saw it too. During that time, that's what happened to her. And so this pregnant woman in the Sky World says to her husband:

Enhhh tsi wa'kahskane'ke thí:ken tsi nón:we nikakwirò:ten
ahsén:nen tsi nó:nwe iawanákere, ohtè:ra ni tewakatohontsión:
ni tókat asekhnekónnien onerahtákeri. Ahh tsi skén:nen
enkanontónnion.

That means she told her husband:
*In the middle of where we live, there's that tree. And I would have
no greater pleasure, my husband, than if you were to go over to
that tree, and get some of its small tender fresh roots. And its bark,
its skin. Make a tea for me to drink. I would be so satisfied, and I
would have such great peace.*

And the husband says to her:
Sesa'nikónhrhen ken í:iah teió:wen's aiakwatsté:riste thi okwi:re?

He says:
Did you forget that we're not supposed to touch that tree?

And she says,
Hánio wá:s tsi a'é:ren niahá:se.

That means,
*DOGGONE IT! GET OVER THERE AND DO WHAT I SAID,
INSTEAD OF TALKING ABOUT STUFF LIKE THAT.*

And of course he jumped. Some women are like that, you know. I don't
know if he was more afraid of the Creator's creation or her! But he was
afraid of her more, I guess. Or maybe he loved her so much; I don't know
what it was. But he went. Reluctantly. And so he got over there where the
big tree was, the beautiful big tree with all of its fruit. He looked at the
tree, and he was still reluctant. He didn't wanna do it.

But he was in a dilemma. 'Cause if he were to go back . . .

So he looked at that tree, and he went a little bit closer, but he didn't touch
it. He looked. And right close to the base of the tree, there was a hole that
appeared from nowhere, from nothing. It just appeared. And he looked at
that. And "Geez," he says, "you can't see the bottom of it."

And he wasn't gonna get any closer. *That's enough*, he thought. It was enough for him. And he backed off. So he went back home, back to his house or his lodge or whatever.

And she says:
>Hátskwi. Shá:wi ken thí:ken ohtè:ra? Shá:wi ken thì:ken onónhkwa?
>*You got that medicine or that root?*

And he says:
>Í:iah teiotón:'on. *I couldn't do it.*

And she hollers at him, "What's wrong wit' you?" She says, "I shoulda known not to send you over there. You got no backbone. You got no courage. You're *lazy*." She said that to him, made him feel bad. She wouldn't give him a chance to explain anything, either.

She says:
>Ah sháthi tsi iohá:te.[1] *Get out of the way.* I'll go do it. I should have done it myself in the first place.

And so she went over there after scolding and making him feel like *nothing*. She didn't even give him a chance to finish talking. She went over there 'cause she didn't believe him, and she saw that hole in the ground next to the tree.

She said, "Gee, that's true, what he said. That part. I wonder what did that?" She went closer and she looked at the hole. "Gee, I can't even see how far down it is."

So she got on her hands and knees and she put her nose right to it and looked at it really hard. And that wasn't enough. This time she stuck her head *in* there. And she said, "Wow. I never seen that before."

Some elders, I've heard them say that the husband was angry with her and pushed her down into the hole. But my family said they didn't ever hear

---

1. Tom is using a rude (impolite) way of expressing this to show how Sky Woman behaved when pregnant.

that because she was *pregnant*. And in the Indian world, a woman that's pregnant is the most sacred. So whether you are mad or not, you're not supposed to do away with the most precious thing, this little baby that's not born yet.

So you know right there that all Iroquois are against abortions. It's not permitted. But on the other hand, there are medicines that grow that can cause abortions. Well, we still know about those medicines. So it's up to you and me as individuals what our choice is, whether we want to be a killer or not. So as an Iroquois, I'm on the for-life side, and I'm also on the other one that's for abortions—although *I* will never do an abortion—because that person has to have the freedom to make that choice. So I'm on both sides, 100 percent. Iroquois cannot be otherwise, 'cause you can't take away someone's freedom or their decision to choose whatever route they want to take.

So do you see that a lot of this is a help to us today in our life's decisions and things? Clarifies things really well. So I'm telling you both of these versions so that you too will be dogged by it! Which one is right or wrong? Doesn't matter. So I'm telling you both of them. *You* decide what you like best.

Anyway, as she was busy nosying around in that hole, she didn't notice, but did you ever see the sands in the hourglass when you tip it over, how they go down? Well, that's what was happening here. But she was so busy looking down the hole, she didn't notice that the grains of dirt were falling. And by this time, the hole was getting bigger. The next thing you know she started to fall.

Once she realized that she was falling, she started frantically trying to grab anything she could reach. And they say, because this was the Tree of Life, there were all kinda seeds, things that fell around those roots onto the ground below, at the base of the tree. And as she tried to avoid falling, she grabbed the strawberry plant that was growing near there. And she grabbed peach seeds, cherry seeds, and different kinds of seeds in her hands.

And she began to fall down through the sky, through the atmosphere, tumbling, head over heels. And as she was falling down, you have to remember that on this earth where we live, there was no land—no mountains, no valleys. The complete planet was surrounded by water. There was no kinda land anywhere.

The only ones that lived here were turtles, fish, beavers, otters, ducks, geese, and herons. And all these creatures had webbed toes and fingers in order to survive in the water. But deer didn't live here or any of those kinds of things that didn't have webbed feet. We're all Johnny-come-latelies. We're all the new ones.

"As she came falling down there," my grandmother used to tell us, "there was a flock of blue herons." That's what she used to say, "Blue herons. Flying in the sky." And then other elders in my family, they say it was geese. You know how geese fly in formation? Well, it doesn't make any difference; we can just say "water birds." Then it satisfies both versions. But it depends on who's telling you, huh? When I tell people, I always tell all the versions I've heard so that you can make your own judgment. I won't deprive you of anything.

And so, as she was tumbling down through the atmosphere, these birds happened to take a peek up there. And they said, "What in the *heck is that* coming down here?" They'd never seen such a creature. They didn't know what it was.

You know how a horse is when you're going somewhere? That horse always comes and looks at you. Or if a deer sees you somewhere and you keep quiet, he comes over. He's looking, and he's trying to find out what you are about. Same thing with a dog or any kind of bird. They'll look at you. And it was the same thing with these guys that were flying. They'd never seen this strange thing. They wanted to know "what is that?"

So they flew over close to where she was falling. And they examined her with a fine-tooth comb. They looked at her skin, and they noticed it wasn't like the skin they've got for water. And they looked at her toes and fingers, and they noticed there was nothing between them; they weren't webbed to help her swim. So they gathered that she wasn't from their world—the world of water. And if she was going there, she would not survive.

They felt sorry for her, and they tried to intervene. So what they said was, "Let's all fly together. We'll hook our wings together and make a soft feathery place so she can gently fall on our bodies. We'll catch her. Then she won't get hurt. And we'll try to take her back where she came from 'cause we don't think she can survive in this water where we live."

So they caught her gently on their feathery backs, and they began to go in an orchestrated way. They flew her way up high, as far as they could go. Pretty soon they became totally exhausted. They just didn't have the energy to go any farther up. And they came to the realization that they just couldn't get her back up there. It was too far, too high. They had run out of power.

So they said quickly in their little council of birds, "Well, we'll have to take her to where we live. We don't know what we're gonna do when we get there, though. She's in trouble. We can't fix that. But that's the only choice we've got, so we better find something to help us."

So they said, "Okay, we'll go down with her on our backs, but we're gonna glide around on the air currents and go just as slow as we can."

And one of them said, "You go down first. Dive down there and tell all the different life in the water there that there's a great emergency. Tell them what's happening. Maybe together they can find a way or think of a plan to help this lady."

So that one heron or goose or whatever he was, he said, "Okay."

And he dove down as fast as he could. When he got near the water, Né:'e wa'thohén:rehte. *He began to scream at the top of his lungs.*

And he got the attention of all the different animals that were in the water. They all came over.

So he said, "Something's happened to us. We've never seen it before. *Ever.* Some kind of strange creature is falling from the sky. We don't know where she came from. Somewhere up there.

And we caught her, and we saved her. Now we have to bring her down here because we couldn't take her back up where she came from. But she don't have nothing like us to survive in the water world. So how will she survive? Maybe she's gonna drown on us, die, whatever."

So all the animals of the water world had a meeting. And they didn't know what to do at all. They were completely befuddled about it. Just as they were ready to quit, since they didn't have any options, *finally* the big turtle spoke up.

And that turtle said, "I don't really have an answer, either. But I might have a temporary answer. How about if when they get down here, you tell them to put that woman right in the middle of my back. I'll stay afloat up on top of the big water, and I'll hold her up. And then we can try to keep thinking about what we might do to help her."

So when they got down, they put her on that turtle. And she stood there. And all the animals came from every direction, of all sizes and shapes and forms. They were all nosy; they were all curious to see what this creature was, this monster, or whatever it was. And they looked at her. And they came to the same conclusion as the birds did—that she had to have land so she wouldn't drown in the water.

And then she opened up her hands. She showed them that she had a strawberry plant.

And that's why you've gotta have a strawberry drink every time Longhouse has a ceremony. And in summer, you dry them with the sun, and then you save them so you can use them later. 'Cause before, we didn't have refrigerators or freezers. And that drink can almost taste like water, but it still has to have strawberries, *every* time, in order to be a real ceremony. That came from the Creation story, see.

So she had all of these seeds in her hand, which were to be her food source. But there was no dirt to plant them.

So the beaver said, "Dirt. I think I remember my grandfather and great-grandfathers talking one time when I was just a young kid. I heard that below this big water somewhere, way down, there's dirt down there. But we've never seen it. We've never been down to there."

Then the otter said, "I seem to have heard that too, from our grandpa, and elders. They said that there was dirt."

And they all came to the same conclusion. They had heard it. But none of them had ever been there. So finally the beaver said, "Well, I have a big tail, you know. And it can push me, and I can go fast, and I'm a good swimmer. And I can hold my breath a long time. I could go and try to retrieve that dirt. And if I do, then I'll bring it for her, and she can plant those seeds, and she will have food."

So he took a run and a jump and he dove. He splashed into the water, and down he went. And he was gone a long time, a *long* time. And all of a sudden, his body *popped* out of the water. (It reminds me of when you put a balloon under the water. When you hold it and then you let it go, it just jumps out of the water. And that's what happened to him.)

And everybody saw him. He was lifeless. He was not moving at all. It appeared that he had drowned; he had died. And so they pulled his body up there. And sure enough, he had drowned. He had never made it to the bottom of the big water.

So then the otter tried it. And then different ones tried it. They all took turns, but they *all* died. Finally, a little tiny one, the smallest one—they call him anò:kien in my language, and in English that's *muskrat*—he came forward. He doesn't have anything to help him to be great. He's just a little tiny scroungy thing, not like the beaver, not like the otter with their streamlined bodies that make them swift as an arrow. He's just a scroungy little old muskrat.

But all the other kinda creatures had tried it, and they couldn't do it, so now he was their last chance. So they were looking at him. And if there was a place to hide, I suppose he woulda hid. But there was no place. So he felt he had to be brave; he had to do his share.

He said, "Well, I'm not a good swimmer. I don't have a big tail like the beaver to propel me down in the water. All I am is just a little old muskrat. And if they didn't make it, probably I'm not gonna make it either. But at least I'm *gonna try*."

So they said okay. And so he ran along on top of that turtle's back. And he jumped and he dove in. *Splash*, the water came up. And down he went. Geez, he was gone longer than *every one* of those animals.

All of a sudden, his little old scroungy body came popping up on top. His eyes were closed. And there was no movement in his body whatsoever. And he, it appeared, had gone as well. He didn't make it.

So the other animals, they went over there and grabbed him. They dragged him up on top of the turtle's back to examine him, to see if he was dead. They touched him all over, and he was cold as ice. Every indication that he was dead. But finally when they touched around his chest, they felt a little warmth and a little movement. A movement *so* faint . . . but he was living. So they pushed on his stomach, and water came up. And they pushed on his stomach, and more water came up.

As they revived him, his eyes opened up, and he started to blink. And when they opened his little tiny black hand, there were some little granules of the dirt there, from the big water. And not only there, but in his little tiny mouth, the way you would carry snuff, there was some more of that dirt.

And so when he came to, he went over there to the woman, Atsi'tsiaká: ion. And he gave it to her, that dirt. *Everybody* was happy. All the animals were so elated, so joyous, 'cause they were able to do it in their combined efforts, through great sacrifice. Life could begin, see?

And so the woman took the dirt. And she put it right there in the middle of the turtle's back. And then she started a kind of sideways shuffle walk in a circle where that dirt was in the middle. And as she started to move she started chanting the language of Karonhià:ke, for that's where she was from. My great-grandfather told me that what she was saying is contained in the Great Feather Dance.[2] When they use the big turtle rattle and they sing in the Longhouse, the chants they use contain the original words she was saying as she went around.

And as she went around there, the miracle of birth began. And the granules of dirt began to multiply and grow. Instead of a little speckle, it had become a pile. And as she continued to sing or to chant that song, it began to multiply even more. And not only that, but the turtle began to grow

---

2. See the section on the Great Feather Dance in chapter 17, "The Four Sacred Rituals Part 2: Three of the Rituals."

bigger in accordance with the growth of that dirt. And as she continued to go around in an even-bigger circle, the turtle grew and grew 'til it became bigger than this room. And there was wall-to-wall dirt covering it now. That was the miracle of birth.

If you were to take our Indian tobacco, you could look at one seed from that seed ball. It's just like when a fly goes to the bathroom on a wall. You can hardly see it. That's how tiny those seeds are. And yet that seed can grow into a beautiful lush plant from that one little thing. That's the miracle of birth. It started there.

So she went on dancing like that. And that's why Senecas, Mohawks, Cayugas, Oneidas, Tuscaroras, Cherokees, Navajos, and Hopis, when we have ceremony, always go in what you might call a counterclockwise direction, still today, in every Longhouse. The same direction she went.

The only time that we go the other way is when there's a death. Then we serve the food clockwise. So only at Ohkí:we,[3] they always start their dance clockwise for at least one complete circle. And then, even if there's a death, they turn around and they go counterclockwise, back to the regular way of life, back to the power of life at the end.

And that night at Ohkí:we, everybody who does the social dance, always goes clockwise, and then when they're finished one circle, they turn and they go back the proper way, counterclockwise. That's the way it's done. It's connected to that, see? It's separate but it's hooked there too.

So this turtle got bigger and bigger until it became what they call Turtle Island. That's why the Lakota, the Blackfoot, the Mohawks, most all of the original people, when they refer to the earth, call it *Turtle Island*. Even in the deepest part of Africa, you will still hear the real original black people say Turtle Island the same as we do. That's what we call this earth where we live. And it came from this story.

---

3.   For more about Ohkí:we, see chapter 21, "Three Souls or Spirits and Ohkí:we."

Chapter 5

Creation Story Part 2:
Mother Earth and Her Twins

"You're going to give birth to two. And these two that will be born will each be given half the power of the world."

Now, as she was doing that, she was pregnant already, remember? By this time, she was big. And now she was gonna give birth. And she gave birth to one girl. And then what happened is that her daughter began to grow.

Sky Woman,[1] Atsi'tsiaká:ion, raised her little baby daughter. She grew fast. And the only people that were here on Turtle Island were the mother and the little girl. There were no other human beings here. Just the water animals and the water birds.

As this young girl became a young woman, every once in a while, the mother would dance and sing. And as she did this, the turtle kept on growing, and the land became bigger too.

[1.] Sky Woman is a nickname for Atsi'tsiaká:ion (*Mature Flower*).

They were always in the middle of the land. So one time the daughter said to her mother, "Gee, I can't even see it, where the land goes like that. I don't know where it goes. I've never been over there. I wonder what it looks like way down that way."

So the mother said, "Well, why don't you go see? Go take a walk and take your time."

And so one day the daughter said, "Okay, I'm gonna go."

Early in the morning, she left. And by that time, the world had become big; that turtle had grown big. She walked, and she walked, and she walked. And she looked at this, and she looked at that. For the most part, there were rolling hills. And finally when she got to her destination, she came to the edge of the turtle's back.

And that's where she saw the big waves of the ocean, coming in and hitting on the shore of the turtle. If you were to go to the ocean right now, you would hear the particular sound that the waves make, coming in like that.

The young daughter saw all that and she appreciated the vastness of this new land, this new world. And as she was ready to come home, just as she turned around, she noticed something in the sky that she'd never seen before.

And what was in the sky was the clouds. But there was a particular cloud hanging lower than the other clouds. And that caught her attention; it made her curious. So she kinda stared at it. And the cloud started to approach her, where she was standing. And when it came close enough to her, she could see that it was in the form of a man.

Some of our older people said he had on leather clothes with fringes—you know when you tan a deerskin and it turns as soft and as white as cotton? And that's why at first he looked like a cloud 'cause he was all dressed in white.

And of course this young woman had never seen a man before, had never seen another human except for her mother. So anyone would make her nervous or anxious, I would imagine. So in her anxiety or whatever about seeing this man, she fell down on the ground. Passed out right there.

And remember I was saying earlier, that I always try to justify these things because I was forever being told they weren't true? So here is how I used to make it real to myself. I remember in the fifties when Elvis Presley was starting to sing and be in the world of entertainment. I used to see it on the TV and in the news. Thousands and thousands of people would go to hear him sing. And hundreds of women would pass out, right there, just from his presence. And I said to myself, well, "And that's just Elvis!" So can you imagine what happened to this woman?

Anyway, when this man dressed in white leather clothes with long fringes came to her, and she passed out, they say he had two arrows with him. One arrow was very well made, with a sharp arrowhead on it. And the other arrow was somewhat warped, not as straight as a really good arrow. And even the arrowhead on it was blunt. But it was still an arrow.

He took those arrows, and he crossed them. And he placed them on her body. And when he did that, that's when the wind began to blow from the north and east and the west and the south. Now they say the Four Sacred Winds began to function as we know them today. That's when the changing of the seasons started to happen in the four directions of this world as we know it.

And when he put those arrows on her body, what she didn't know, as she laid there, is that she had become pregnant. So it was like a spiritual conception. Even in the Western world, when they talk about the different religious messiahs—such as Jesus, or Buddha, or even the black ones—when they had their messiahs, they always claim that it was a person born from a virgin. Well, it wasn't really a virgin. Because even though that woman didn't have intercourse physically with the man, there was an intercourse on a spiritual level. That's what caused the pregnancy. And that's more powerful even than the physical.

After a while, she started to come home not knowing what had happened to her 'cause she had passed out. But she did find these arrows. And after that she began to dream. And messages used to come to her in dreams or in what you might call a *vision*.

This voice spoke to her. And it said, "You have been chosen to give birth. But you're not going to give birth to one. You're going to give birth to two. And these two that will be born will each be given half the power of the world. One will have half the world's power. And the other one will have the other half of the world's power.

"And with this power, these two are going to bring identity and character to the world where you live. They're gonna make lots of things to dress it up, to make it nice. So you're gonna be their mother. And when these twins are born, the first one that'll be born, you will call him Teharonhiawá:kon." And that's how she knew what kinda name to use.

And then he said, "The second one of these twins that will be born will be called Shawískara."

And that's how she knew how to tell the names to her mother.

During her pregnancy, the young woman found that she had a very hard time carrying these twins. She noticed that there was a lot of kicking going on, a lot of movement going on. She was often being hit hard. And it was because though they were brothers, the one brother didn't like his other brother, even while he was inside his mother.

So as they were being formed, they would have arguments or they would push each other to make room in there. It was this one brother in particular who initiated all of this stuff. He would kick his brother. And sometimes he would miss, and he would kick his mother. Sometimes he pushed his fist at him, and he'd miss, and he'd hit his mother.

Sometimes he scratched. And it really took its toll on the mother. She barely made it, they say, to give birth, 'cause of this situation.

When it came time to be born, Teharonhiawá:kon was the first one. He came down the birth canal, and he was born just the way all babies are. And he's the one they call Teharonhiawá:kon.

But the other brother, who was always picking on him, he said, "I'm not gonna go the same way my brother did. I'm not gonna follow him." He decided that he was gonna come out of her side. So he began to kick and scratch and bite and do everything he could until his mother's side ruptured. And that's where he came out, how he was born. And he's the one they call Shawískara.

And so because that one decided to be born out of his mother's side, it killed her. She died; she hemorrhaged to death, I guess. So they didn't know what to do. The babies' grandmother felt really bad about it. She got very upset and she went into mourning.

But there was nobody to help her, so she had to help herself. And she not only had to help herself, but she had two babies that were brand new. She had to figure out how to raise them and nourish them and do whatever. And so she took care of them.

And her daughter was laying there on the ground. So the mother took a container—I don't know if it was a clay pot or a basket or whatever—and she went and got dirt. She carried it back and she began to put the dirt on her daughter. She began to cover her body. And then she got some more. She kept on doing that until the dirt piled up over top of the daughter. She didn't bury her under the ground. She put dirt on top, like a mound. That's *different*.

This is when we began calling it "our Mother, the Earth" because this is the first time these people became part of the earth. And it's the first time that anyone had babies from *this* earth. And that's how she became the Mother of the Earth—Mother Earth. It started then. And yet today, after all these years, we still call her that, *Mother Earth.*

And where her head was in the mound, there appeared above it one plant. It grew there. That was the corn. And right next to it came what they call squash—pumpkins, watermelon, cantaloupes, and those kinds of things. They have vines on them. And a third one that started growing right there could wrap itself around the corn. And that was the beans.

In Iroquois country you'll always hear those three called the *Three Sisters*. Áhsen Nikontatenò:sen. That's how you say it in my language. And so that was the Creator's gift and our Mother's gift to give sustenance to future generations who would be coming from there. And they would keep those seeds that came from our Mother's head, from Mother Earth's grave. And those three kinds of food are what were going to be the main foundation of our diet, our fundamental sustenance for the future.

Directly above where her heart was in this mound grew another plant. We call that plant oien'kwa'ón:we. That's *sacred tobacco*. And the Creator said, "I give that to you as a special gift through your Mother." That's why it came from her heart. And that's where prayer has to come from—is the heart.

In this universe that we're in, there are thousands and millions of things going on; it's so busy.

And so the Creator said to us when the world was new, "No matter how busy I am in running this universe, as vast and big as it is, I have given you this tobacco. Anytime you are walking the earth that you need some kind of special attention, that you need a hand, or you simply want to say thank you, you will have this tobacco. And then I give you fire with it, and the power of this fire. And you will put this tobacco on the fire, and when the smoke goes up, I will *stop* what I'm doing, running the universe, the business of the world. No matter how busy it is, when you make that smoke go up, I will stop and I will listen, and I will pay attention to *you*, to what it is that you have to say to me. And that's why I give you this tobacco."

And then the other parts of Mother Earth's body grow wild turnips, wild onions, wild cabbage, and all kinds of things that we can use to eat. So that's why even the milkweed that grows out there, when they're young, they're good to cook up. Different things out there that people think are weeds are good food for you. Because they came from her body.

Some anthropologists say that we didn't have corn and we didn't have beans. They say there's no proof that we had those because they checked the graveyards and they checked the old sites. And they even try to say when it came here. But you see what they're failing to understand is that we came from Central America, us Iroquois. We didn't always live over here, where we're living now. We're from way in the southwest somewhere.

And there are stories that back that up, in *our* legends, about how the five different nations came to be six nations and whatever. There are *stories*. It's a long time ago, but not really that long ago. So okay, they might not find corn here. But they're gonna find it where we came from. And that's down in the Central American area. So we're first cousins with the Mayans and the Aztecs and all those people, us Mohawk/Iroquois people. We're the first cousins to them over there. That's the way I heard the old people tell it.

So that's their problem because they're trying to prove that we don't exist. That's what they're trying to do. But they don't know *our* story. So, you know, let them have the headache. We know what we did.

In Montreal, there's a record of this Creation story I'm telling you here, from the year 1600 and something. I believe it was recorded by Franciscan priests. The Mohawks were telling it to them. And there are even paintings of it that were made in the 1600s that exist in the archives there. They depict this lady and men riding the birds. But they had a bridle on those birds as if they were being ridden like horses. And the people that are supposed to be Indians look like Roman people, look like European people.

And so the artists of the day heard the story and tried to put it on canvas. But they used their own figures, the way they were used to drawing, see? Yet the concepts are in there. About 1610 or 1620, these paintings were done. And they're still in existence. So this Creation story has been told since then, for sure, without much change. Because it's verified by those European artists.

But anyway, back to this again. And so that's how we've come to know our Mother, the Earth.

After that, the two boys began to grow. And as they grew, the one brother always shunned his other brother. It was always one way, like that. The other brother never reacted in an adverse kind of way. He tried to protect himself, that's all. But he never even tried to get even with him.

He put up with a lot. And then one time, the grandmother happened to be grooming them. She had the one little boy, Shawískara, kneeling in between her legs while she was fixing his long hair. I don't know if she was braiding it or taking snarls or burdocks out or what.

And all of a sudden he said, "My grandmother, do you remember what happened?"

And she said, "What are you talking about?"

He said, "Remember that time when me and my brother were born?"

She said, "Yeah. That's when I lost my daughter. The one I love so much."

So the little boy Shawískara said, "Yeah. That's right. And did you know that it was my brother, Teharonhiawá:kon? He's the one who hit and scratched and bit until he broke my mother's side. And that's where he came out. That's why my mother died."

That's what he said. He blamed it on his brother even though he himself was the one who did that.

And then his grandmother said, "I didn't ever think about that. I didn't know that. Oh . . . So that's what happened." And right away, she got really mad. And you know from that day on, she never ever fixed Teharonhiawá:kon's hair again. She never groomed him. She never bathed him anymore like she did the other one. She didn't take care of him. And whenever she had food, it was like you give a dog food. She put it in a dish and that was that. "Eat it."

The other boy, she would talk to him and visit him, and they would eat together. But her one grandson, the one that got the blame, she just shunned him. She had no more kind words for him; she stopped behaving in any grandmotherly way towards him. And so his life began to be kind of a misery at that time.

Her grandson, Shawískara, was the apple of her eye from then on, and she favored him in every way. She loved him, and she held him. And there wasn't anything he could say or do that was wrong. Do you know some grandmothers and some mothers like that? Their grandsons can be little devils, but it's all right, "They're good." That's what happened.

And so that little boy, Teharonhiawá:kon, had a hard time growing up because of all this. Every time that Shawískara would go by his brother, no matter if he had to go out of his way, he would knock his glasses off of his brother (you know, if he had glasses) or pull his ear. Or he'd yank on his hair. Or he'd give him a shove. Or he'd put out his foot so he'd trip over it. Anything to be a nuisance. He was always doing things to his brother.

And whenever Teharonhiawá:kon tried to defend himself, the grandmother would yell at him, "Leave your brother alone." He always got the blame. He never started anything. But he took the full brunt of the ridicule, everything. So you must bear that in mind when I tell you what happened later.

As they got a little bigger, Teharonhiawá:kon made the nice onennó:ron. They call it *sweet flag*. It grows in damp ground, by the water, near ponds, and such. Singers use it when they sing so their voices won't get harsh. And speakers use it. Sometimes people use it just as a breath freshener. And if you've got a cold, you can use it. You can grind it up and make tea. You can put it on your windows to keep witchcraft away from your house. It's a multipurpose root.

Onennó:ron means *the root that's rare*. Or very expensive. Not expensive in terms of money, but an *invaluable* root because it does so many things. Bad medicine doesn't like it. People who do witchcraft don't like to be around it either. So it also protects you from evil people. It's a very friendly medicine all the time, no matter what time of the day. And so Teharonhiawá: kon made that.

But then Shawískara, he got jealous. And he made some other medicine that looks like it, but it can make you sick.

And then they say that Teharonhiawá:kon made beautiful roses and blackberries and raspberries. And in those days, when he made them, the stems didn't have any thorns on them. But Shawískara also became jealous because his brother had made these beautiful things.

Shawískara said, "Well, I'll fix him." He put thorns on the raspberries and blackberries and the roses and things, so even though they're good, they can hurt you. And so can the medicines he made.

That's how the medicine world is; there are two sets of medicine. The ones made by Teharonhiawá:kon, you can pick in the morning. Its feelings are not hurt easily. The medicines made by Shawískara are the ones you pick in the afternoon, or even in the dark.

Shawískara's answer to the onennó:ron, the sweet flag, was a medicine that he made, they call onennoron'kó:wa. It's like sweet flag root except it grows right *in* water. And the roots on that are like the roots on sweet flag, except they're big, and they're long. And they call it the *big sweet flag*.

If you want that one at the most powerful time, they say to pick that around midnight. To pick it, you have to dive in the water. You've gotta go under the water and grab it. And when you grab it, it's like a big snake—it starts to wiggle in your hands. You've gotta have a lot of nerve to do it 'cause you don't know if you're grabbing an eel or a real snake or what. Only certain people can pick it. Most people are too afraid. I know people who used to go at midnight and get it. They use that one as a big medicine; it can do lots of things, *both* bad and good. A lot of the people who do witchcraft use that. But it can also do good. It's up to you what you want to do with it. It has a lot of power. And it grows wherever there's water.

So Shawískara made that; that's his medicine.

And another one is what they call ginseng. It looks like a human being, the roots. You can tell from the root if it's a woman or a man. It's hard to find it 'cause it hides like most medicine does. When you pick ginseng, you can pick it in the morning, or you can pick it at night. It doesn't matter, but usually at night towards sunset 'cause that was also made by Shawískara.

But you're not supposed to bring that in your house because it's too temperamental, the mind of the medicine's power. It's so temperamental that any little thing can make it mad. And if something makes it mad, it can attack you. It can get after you.

That's why people keep ginseng in a shed behind their house. A lot of the old people used to have sheds in the back where they put their medicine. And some of them had hollow trees out back somewhere. They used to keep medicine in there. They didn't bring it into the house or anywhere near it 'cause they were afraid that it might jump on them.

Anything that Shawískara made is very temperamental. That's why you're not allowed to keep it in your house. Whereas sweet flag and other regular medicines that Teharonhiawá:kon made, you can put them in the house and put them in a bag, and they're alright; they don't attack you. They help you. But the ones Shawískara made, if you say the wrong thing, you do the wrong thing, they can jump on you, see?

They use ginseng too as part of a love formula medicine. You're not supposed to do that. It's not right. But people have a choice to do it or not do it. And I used to have one relative, an older guy like a grandfather, who made a love formula. And he used ginseng as part of it.

You put the juice of that medicine on a feather, like a fluff, and you'd wear it in your hat. Or maybe when men used to dress up, they'd put it on a silk scarf. Or they'd put on a bandana, and they'd put the juice on it. Whatever you wanted to put it on. You could put it on your shirt, if you wanted to.

Someone might go a dance. And if he saw a woman he liked, even if she didn't like him, as soon as that feather or scarf touched her skin, she'd follow him all night long. And he almost couldn't get rid of her 'cause she would be stuck; she'd follow him like a dog. Men used it, and women used it. And it wasn't supposed to be used every day. I don't know what they called it.

Menominees and Chippewas used to come from Wisconsin all the way to Akwesasne just to get that. One of them was an old man whose name was Baker. He used to *swear* by that. He was a drummer for powwow singers for the Chippewa in the Bad River Reservation. He used to give my grandfather Union Leader tobacco as a part of his present for that medicine. He's dead now; but when I used to go out there, he used to recognize me, and he used to say, "Geez, your Grandpa makes the good medicine." He was an old man, and he had a young girlfriend all the time!

But nobody makes it now, that I know of. I know some of the ingredients, but I've never tried it. I never really learned. I just know *about* it. And if somebody knew that formula, they could just about get rich on it!

Anyway, my point is that the medicines that are growing are either made by one or the other of the twin brothers, and you have to know which one in order to take the most advantage of it.

After that, Teharonhiawá:kon made the deer and Shawískara got jealous and angry about it. So he made the wolf to go after the deer. Teharonhiawá: kon made the moose. And again, the coyotes and mountain lions, those kinda animals, Shawískara made them, to go after the moose and the elk and different ones. So whatever the one did, the other one always did something to ruin it or to make it a problem.

And it went on like that, a lot of it. And my grandmother even used to say, unbelievable as it is, "At the beginning when the world was new, the rivers were the way modern highways are today. On the one side, all the traffic goes one way. But on the other side of the same road, it goes the other way."

And she said, "Whenever you wanted to go and visit somebody that lived down the river, you got on the river and you went on that side with your canoe or dugout or whatever, and you didn't have to paddle. All you had to do was steer it, and the current would take you there.

"And when you were done visiting over there in that village, and you wanted to come home, you just went *across* the river, and the current was going the other way. Again you didn't have to work. All you had to do was steer. And that's the way they navigated the rivers when the world was new."

But when Shawískara came along and saw beautiful rivers like that, so nice and smooth and everything, he punched those rivers, and he kicked them. And that's what caused them to stop being straight and calm. Now they're turbulent. That's when Niagara Falls came to be, and the Lachine Rapids and the Akwesasne Rapids where we live. And look at the Grand Canyon—Shawískara's the one who did that.

Well, because of that action of Shawískara, at that point, the Creator interceded. At that point of their doings.

And he said, "Beginning now, and in the future, for the birds, for the bears, for the deer, for the humans, all that lives," he said, "from now on, because Shawískara did that when you go visiting down the river, it'll be easy to go there because the water flows that way. All you have to do is steer. But when you're done visiting at that village down the river, when you come home, you can't cross that river anymore. He broke that. Now the river only flows one way.

"So now when you go back home, it will take a lot of work and a lot of sweat to paddle your canoe against the river's current. It will still be easy to get there, but it will be hard to get back. And so your life will be this way, like that river. Half of your life will be easy, enjoyable, and pleasant. And the other half of your life will be sweat and hard work to survive. And that's going to be true for all humans, all the birds, all the bears, the deer, and everything that lives. Half of your life is gonna be easy, and the other half is going to be hard. Because he broke that river."

And my grandfather used to say to us kids, "Whatever you do, don't you go down to Cornwall or Cornwall Island, anywhere down around that way. Don't you go over there," he'd say, "because that big man lives over there—Shawískara. And he's a giant. And his brother is a giant too. And even the biggest trees around our reservation here, only come up as far as his knees. That's how big he is."

My grandfather, my mother's father, his name was Louis Chubb. He was a product of the Carlisle School. That's where he went all his childhood. And so my grandfather was a Christian man, not Longhouse, 'cause of that and the family he came from.

Grandpa was twenty-one years old when he got home from Carlisle. And when he got back to the Akwesasne reservation, he didn't know how to talk or understand Mohawk anymore. But he musta had it when he was little. They took him there when he was four, so he forgot almost all of it. And since he couldn't talk it when he came home, he had to relearn it.

And then he married my grandmother who was a Longhouse woman. Well, she was actually both 'cause she had to appease the world she lived in. But she was our Longhouse lady. So even though my grandfather wasn't traditional, he talked only Mohawk all the time when I was a little boy growing up 'cause that's all my grandmother understood. But he spoke it so well that I never suspected that he had ever lost it. And I didn't know he lost it until probably fifteen years ago when one of my aunts told me.

And even though he was not Longhouse in the least, he wasn't *against* it, but he didn't want to go there. He didn't want to belong to it, and he didn't validate it in any way. But he didn't tell us to go against it either; he just never gave any indication that it was alright to go there. And yet he didn't stop us from going there.

But he used to say to us kids, "Now yous guys stay around here, around the house where we live. Don't be going no running around way over there in the woods somewheres." He used to talk about the little people living there and stuff. And how they could take us and make us get lost. Even though he wasn't traditional, he used to say that to us.

And sometimes they say one of them would see Shawískara. There's a Christian church in St. Regis with a big steeple that goes way up. He'd be standing with his elbow on top of the steeple. And sometime, they would see him cross the river, St. Regis River. That's quite a ways. He would only take two or three steps, and he'd be in Snye[2]. And the people would report seeing him doing that.

And so Grandpa used to say, "Well, that one, the brother, Shawískara is over there in Cornwall. And he's the one that broke the river over there." He'd say, "He's the one kicked that river. And because he was so big, big boulders went all over, and that's what made those rapids. So you couldn't even ever get a boat there without tipping over, see? And he's the one did it."

"And that guy there is *merciless*. He has no pity on anybody. If he catch *you*, you're in *trouble*." He'd say, "He kick you on your butt end, and you'll fly from Cornwall all the way to Fort Covington." (That's about fifteen miles). "That's where you'll land if he catches you!" he'd say.

So that's why we never went away from where we lived. Because there were all these things, that if they caught us would give us trouble. So we didn't need babysitters. We were watching ourselves 'cause we didn't want to get caught by those little people or by the giants.

So the point is my grandfather wasn't even a traditional person, but in our society, I guess it must have been so ingrained yet at the time that it still came through even though he didn't acknowledge it. He *was* acknowledging it, whether he knew it or not. And so that's why I always remembered this story because we were always afraid to go over there. Every time we saw the rapids, we knew. (Since the seaway went through, you can't see the rapids anymore though. They aren't there now.)

---

2. Snye is a section of Akwesasne.

But these two brothers from the Creation, no matter what colonization happens, the story still seems to transcend all that and still remain somewhat intact.

So that's how we got the mountains and valleys and all those things. They made it, those two boys.

Chapter 6

Creation Story Part 3:
Human Beings and Grandmother Moon

"My Creator, I thank you for this miraculous world that you have allowed me to be a part of . . . Every need I have is here, at my fingertips with my Mother."

And finally, this is the part I didn't used to like to tell. But this is what my grandmother used to say. I used to think she was being unfair, racist. And I never appreciated that part of the story, although I listened intently, until I heard a black man, right from Africa, speaking at the Centre on St. Urbain Street, in Montréal.[1]

He was talking about their spirituality and stuff. And he recited this same section that I didn't like to hear my grandmother say. And that's when I changed my mind. Now I don't mind saying it. But I watch where I say it because some people immediately get mad, and then they don't listen. They react without really investigating it. Now I'm gonna tell you how it goes.

---

1. Tom is referring to the Intercultural Institute of Montreal.

So they made the animals and everything and the good medicine, the bad medicine, and so on. And it wasn't so much good and bad medicine; it was medicine that will help you and medicine that'll make you sick—or it won't heal you. And even the twins—we don't like to refer to them as good and evil. We just say one was the Teharonhiawá:kon twin, and he made all these nice things that help us; and Shawískara was the one that always made the mischievous things, the one that was always like a prankster, rather than say "the evil one." So when we tell the story, we have to be careful that we don't do that too much. And there are reasons for it.

And so finally, after making all Creation, now they were gonna make the human beings. So the first one they made, Grandma said, Shawískara took the dirt; he's the one that started it. And he said, "This time I'm gonna show my brother . . ." (Whereas before, the other one was making everything, and then Shawískara was ruining it.) But this time, Shawískara was gonna do it first. So he did. He took the dirt and different elements of nature. And he used his brother, Teharonhiawá:kon, as his pattern. He was going to make it in the image of his brother.

So he kinda studied him, and he began to mold his dirt and the stuff. And he made a woman and a man out of this stuff, using the same process for both. Then he knew that he had to put life in them. And so he put them in a fire. And Grandma said, "Because they had never done this before, ever, they didn't have the formula, they didn't have the recipe, and they didn't have the timing. None of it was given to them."

So he waited for them to cook. And when he pulled them out, they were burnt. Even their hair was all singed up, burnt. And so Grandma said, "The first humans that were made from this earth were the black people, because they kept them in there too long, and they burnt."

So Shawískara opened up their mouths, the black ones, and he blew in there three times. And those dolls that were made out of the earth wouldn't come alive. And so after blowing in there and blowing in there and not being successful in making them live, Shawískara finally said to his brother, whom he despised and whom he always made trouble with and who should never respond, he said, "My brother, can you help me? I made these dolls, and I've tried and tried to put life in them, in their mouths. And it won't work."

So he said, "My brother, could you help me and make them live?"

And the brother looked at him. And he didn't hesitate too long, and he said, "I'll try to help you." So Teharonhiawá:kon took the dolls. He opened their mouths and he blew in there three times. And after the third breath, the eyes began to move, and the arms moved. And they came alive, the dolls. And so he stood 'em up. And that was the black people.

So then Shawískara said, "Well, I'm gonna make another pair. But this time I'm not gonna leave them in the fire that long." So what he did is he went to the ocean. And you know when you go to the ocean, there's big foam from the waves? He took that foam and he took elements from nature and the ground. And he used that foam as the basis of existence of that pair. And out of it, he again formed a male and a female. And then again he used his brother as the image or the pattern for his creation. And then he took them and put them in the fire. And this time he said, "I'm not gonna put them in there as long. And that way, they won't burn."

So he took them out. And this time they weren't cooked. It was the white man who was born this time. And Grandma said, Í:iah teió:ri. *They weren't cooked right, not all the way cooked.* But it wasn't a mistake; it cannot be a mistake 'cause they were made like that. And so then again he blew in them, and he couldn't make them live. So he had to ask his brother *again.* "Can you help me?"

And without too much reluctance, Teharonhiawá:kon did. He blew in there, and then *their* eyes blinked, and they began to move. And so they came alive. And so the next oldest one to be living on earth is the white man. The oldest is the black man, then the white man. From the one extreme to the other extreme because they had no formula; they didn't know what they were doing. And that's why it's that way.

Then finally, he made another pair. And he put them in the fire. And this time when he pulled them out, they weren't black and they weren't white. The only thing is their eyes were slanted, like Chinese or Asian people. They were *nice* though. But their eyes were like that. And again when he blew on them, he couldn't make them breathe either. So he asked Teharonhiawá:kon again, "Can you help me?" And he did. And they breathed. So the third one is the Asian people.

And then finally, Teharonhiawá:kon said, "I've seen all of it now, and I'm gonna do it too." So he did. He took the ground from the Mother Earth. And he did like his brother did. And *he* put them in the fire. And he left them for a length of time that was in between those others. And this is where I laugh at my grandmother 'cause she says, "When he pulled them out, there were the perfect human beings, not too black, not too white. Just *right*."

And so he blew in their mouths, Teharonhiawá:kon did. And that's where our Grandma and Grandpa came from.

So now you have four. So the black and the yellow and the Indian, they're the *older* brothers. And the white one is gonna be the baby brother, forever. That happens because they say, when he took the white one out of the fire, it didn't cook all the way. It didn't mature, it never grew up, never finished. And that's why the white one is always like a little boy, like a little girl.

When you say to little kids, "Don't do this, it's gonna hurt you," turn your back and they do it. "Don't swing in the barn on that rope, you might fall and break your neck." They'll do it. "Don't play with the fire, it's gonna burn you." *They'll* do it. That's mostly what little kids do. If you say "Don't," that's what they're gonna *do*, generally speaking.

And so it is with the European people, the one that's the white race. Whenever our elders in the past have told them stuff, they didn't follow it. And nowadays, a lot of our old religious leaders have told them, "Don't pollute the river." And they keep doing it. They said, "Don't pollute the air." They've made proclamations about it. Even in Rio de Janeiro, at that big meeting they had, that summit. They told them there in the world body, "Don't do this, don't ruin the air, don't ruin the water, don't ruin the Mother Earth 'cause all those belong to our kids. And that's what's gonna sustain our life and our generations."

And they don't stop their factories. They don't stop the things that are ruining our life. They won't listen. If you say, "Don't do it," they'll do it. And so my grandmother used to say, "Our white brothers have to be babysitted, them, because they always do what you tell them not to do. That's their makeup. That's the way they're made. They're always nosy and curious, like little kids."

Our spiritual focus takes in seven generations. So when the leaders have a council, we're always told that we're counciling so that what we do today doesn't hurt the seventh generation that's gonna be born, our great-grandchildren.[2] Whatever we do today, if it would hurt them, it's *wrong*.

And right now, there is no regard for all the natural elements of the universe by the big corporations, by the big countries, by the Rockefellers, by anybody. They have no regard for it at our expense, their expense, at the expense of their kids and ours. They're gonna take us all with them, see? We can't control them; they won't listen. And that's what we were told to be aware of.

The world those two boys shaped and affected and created, it beautified what was already there. It was all one big land. And even though they argued and they had a hard time, still the result of all their efforts was awesome, absolutely awesome. All you've gotta do is go look at Niagara Falls. All you've gotta do is go to the Grand Canyon. All you've gotta do is go see the gorgeous natural world all over New York State. All you've gotta do is just go up this hill, here at Kanatsiohare:ke, and you will see how awesome it is.

They did it. Every river, they're the ones that touched that.

Shonkwaia'tison, the Creator, was so proud of what they did, without judgment. You know what I mean? There could have been a lot of judgments made here 'cause that one guy was not such a hot, nice guy. But still, the Creator said to them, "Even though you two argued and you fought every now and then, what you did, *oh,* it's awesome. What a *magnificent* job. I'm so pleased."

And so the Creator said to them, "Because you two did such a wonderful job, I'm going to do whatever it is that you request of me. You ask me for something you need or something that you want and as a reward, I will do it for you."

The first one, Shawiskara, he *jumped* up there and he said, "My Creator, my Father, I want you to do something *right away.*" He wasted no time. "I want

---

2.   Tom is counting here the generations in living memory from his great-grandparents to his great-grandchildren, making a total of seven generations.

you to put a barrier between me and my brother because my brother always pulls my hair when he gets next to me. He always trips me up with his foot so I'll fall on my face. I make a river, he ruins the river and everything. He messes me up. He's forever bothering me. He's a *nuisance*. So, Creator, my wish to you is to put something between me and my brother so he can't pull my hair anymore. And he can't ruin the things I do. And he can't bother me anymore. That's what I want." So that was what *he* wished.

And now it was the turn of Teharonhiawá:kon, the Skyholder, the Embracer of the Sky And the whole day went by and the Skyholder twin, he just looked around. And he walked casually. And he looked at this. Then he looked at that. He looked it over, up and down, every which way. Then he went on; he looked some more, and pretty soon the sun went down. And he hadn't finished. He hadn't come up with an answer. Then he walked some more, and he walked some more, looking at everything. He walked some more another place, and he looked some more. And here, the Creator was waiting for his response.

And the second day went by. So the third day, all day went by, and he looked again at everything, checked it out. And the sun was about ready to go down again. Finally, he stood up, and he stopped walking, the Teharonhiawá:kon twin. And he said, "My Father, my Creator, my Maker, I stand before you today at this moment because you asked if there's something I want, to reward me for the good things that my brother and I did. And my brother has answered you right away, very clearly. But me, I apologize to you that I took so long.

"But because you have asked me this question, I thought that I should really think seriously and give you a proper, well-thought-out answer. I don't want to answer you in a foolish or frivolous way. So I ask your forgiveness for my long delay in responding. And now, my Creator, I ask you to continue to listen to me as it is true that me and my brother, we did these things, different things. You know everything that happened."

And so Teharonhiawá:kon continued to talk to the Creator. And he said, "What we did, we did with the power you gave to me and my brother. And with that power, if I feel the pains of hunger in my stomach, all I need to do is to go to the strawberries, the raspberry bush, the blueberry bush, the blackberry bush. All I've gotta do is go pick the wild potatoes, the wild turnips, and wild carrots, or whatever. And I eat them. And my hunger pains go away. They're all around, the things that will take away my hunger.

"If I should become ill or sick, and I have no peace in my mind or in my body, I can go to any woods, any valley, any swamp, any river's edge. And I can pick the medicine, and the sickness can go away. And health and peace will come back to my mind and my body. And I will be happy and comfortable again.

"If I become thirsty and dry in my throat, all I have to do is to go to any creek, any river, any stream. And I can drink. And my thirst will be quenched. And I will have hope that I can go on living.

"My Creator, I have walked for these three days to make sure that I am telling you the truth, because of this great thing you have offered me and my brother. And so my response is that I ask nothing. Everything you gave me and my brother is sufficient. It's already right here at my fingertips. I have no request to make at all.

"But, my Creator, I stand before you 'cause you're my father, and I say thank you for this miraculous world that you have allowed me to be a part of. Thank you, for every need I have is here, at my fingertips, with my Mother. Thank you. And that is my answer."

And his brother got *so envious* and *so* mad and angry at that civilized, well-thought-out response that he *immediately* jumped up and he grabbed a spear. And he came, and he was gonna end his brother's life. He tried to stab him, but the Embracer of the Sky, Teharonhiawá:kon, fell down.

You know how the deer shed their horns and they get new ones? One had fallen there on the ground. And it just happened that where Teharonhiawá:kon got knocked down, his hand accidentally hit that deer's horn.

Teharonhiawá:kon grabbed that deer's horn and he held it in front of himself and it broke the spear's lunge into his heart. Then he pushed it and he knocked his brother down. Then he pounced on him and straddled him on his belly, and he held that deer's horn against his chest, his heart area. And you could see the indentation it was making there. It was sharp, huh? And he held it there, so that it was almost piercing the skin of Shawískara.

Teharonhiawá:kon said, "I could push this just once and end your life forever. And if I added up all the things you did to me since even before we were born . . . when we were still inside our mother's belly, you were attacking me and making my life miserable. You're even the one who killed our mother.

"And then after that you poisoned our grandmother's mind about me, saying I killed my mother. And ever since I was a little boy my grandmother quit being a grandma to me. She never gave me any nourishment. She never gave me any attention, any love, or compassion or kindness. She was only a figure of an old lady for me. Even though she was my grandma. And she bestowed kindness on you because you lied to her, and she believed you.

"And adding all those things up, it would be easy to push this right through your heart. But," he said, "my brother, you *are* my brother. You are my flesh and blood, and I can't do it to you, even though you did all these things to me."

And so he got off. He let him live. And just then his grandmother came onto the scene, in time to see the part where he was on top of Shawískara. She didn't see all of it; she only saw the last part. And she went over there, the grandmother, 'cause she was very angry now from what she'd seen.

She went over where he was and she grabbed him and she pulled him. And she said, "Why are you bothering your brother? You're *always* bothering him all this time, all his life." And she shook him up and she really laid into him. And here Shawískara was the one trying to kill *him*. And Teharonhiawá:kon got the blame again.

So for the first time, they say, Teharonhiawá:kon became *so* angry that he grabbed his grandmother by her long hair. In his fit of anger. And he swung her by the hair. And swung her and swung her and swung her, fast as he could go and angry as he was. And he threw her up in the sky. And that's why the Iroquois, we all call the moon Ionkhihsótha *our Grandma*. Because she was the grandmother. And she was the one that came from the other place to here that began this life. And so now Grandma is the moon. She became that.

So the Creator said, "You requested a barrier, something between you two. So therefore it shall be."

Teharonhiawá:kon said, "Yes, that's what he requested. We cannot be together in the same place. There does need to be a barrier. And so we're gonna cut this world in half. And my brother can stay over there in the darkness. That's where he will be, Shawískara. He's the one who controls the night. And I will be the one that brings the light to the earth. I will be the sun."

When Teharonhiawá:kon became the sun, we began to call him Shonkwahtsí:'a. It means *our Eldest Brother* because he is the oldest of us all.

And so there has to be half that's night and half that's day. Those are the two brothers. So there has to be death and there has to be birth. There has to be happiness, joy, and laughter. And there has to be tears and crying. And so it is that everything is balanced like that. And that's their job.

And it is said that all the humans—that's the black ones, the white ones, the red ones, yellow—were all here on the big turtle. And the Creator started to do what Shawískara and the other one requested.

He came and he took a chunk from here, of that turtle. And he pulled it a long way away so it was surrounded by water. And then he took the black ones and he put them over there. And then the Creator took another big chunk from here, and he pulled it way over too. And when he did, he put all the white ones that were over here, *there*. And then he took another big chunk off of it. And he put all of the yellow ones over there.

And he didn't move us Indians. We stayed here. We're at the original place.

When he did this, he gave us the drum to use. He gave us the rattle—it used to be the gourd rattle—at the beginning. And that's why, in the big medicine societies, they use gourds and not horn rattles. Because that's the oldest one. And they say that when you use the gourd rattle for the big medicine, that's the same sound that she heard when she fell through the sky to this earth.

And he gave them their instructions, how they were to be. And they were all the same instructions, how to behave and how to live on this earth, our *original* instructions. And we were to follow those in each of those respective lands "as long as the sun will shine, as long as grass grows, and as long as the rivers flow." That's why in the treaties the Indians made with the American or European, you will see that terminology in there; it comes from the Creation. It means forever. As long as there's a world.

Then what our Creator did is, in between these lands, he put salt in that water.

Now in Iroquois country, especially where I grew up, on my reservation, Akwesasne/St. Regis,[3] sometimes I used to see this, that somebody who lived not far from where we lived was practicing witchcraft or bad medicine. Although we didn't discuss it openly, we sorta knew who was doing this, who the witches were, man or woman.

And whenever those kinda people would come to our house, what Grandma used to do is take coarse salt, rock salt, or pickling salt. If you don't have that, even regular salt will do. And if she saw that lady or that man (who does bad medicine) coming down that road, if she saw that they might come here, she'd take that salt, and she'd sprinkle it on the chairs or on the couch, wherever anybody might sit.

Because if that person sits on that chair, they can sit there, but they can't sit still. The salt goes against what they do. It's like that onennó:ron too, but salt is the one that's used the most.

My uncle told me that the reason the traditional people didn't want the babies to be taken by the Christians, especially the Catholics, was because the Catholic priests used to put salt on the babies' tongues when they would baptize them. I don't know if they still do it, but they used to.

They say when that salt is put on someone's tongue, it kills their spirit. And their spirit is now controlled by the Catholics. They couldn't ever

---

[3.] This territory goes by several names because it lies on the border of New York State in the United States and on the borders of both Ontario and Quebec provinces in Canada.

have a free spirit. They would always be obligated. And that was at birth; that's when they were only a few days old, they started it, see? And I don't know if that's really true, but that's what my uncle told me. He said, "You can't tell our other people that 'cause they trust the priest too much." But he said, "That's why *we* don't wanna do that. We have to try to protect our kids, their freedom, and their life."

And it's the same idea as in this Creation story. The Creator put salt in the water to fulfill Shawískara's request. And that's why when I was growing up, it was *pounded* into my head by my great-grandfather, and by my grandmother, that we have *no* business, us Indians, to go to France, Italy, Austria, anywhere across the big water. We're not allowed to do that. Otherwise, we will break that promise. Because if we go there and we die in France or England, our spirit can't come back across that salty water. It can't come across that barrier.

We would have to stay there forever until the new world and the new order of the universe is done. We would go through this for many years if we died there. That's the reason why they told us not to do that. So I never went anywhere until about twenty-some years ago, in '79 and '80. The Italian delegation came here to help us in our civil war that one time, when they were having the Winter Olympics in Lake Placid. They saved our lives—that delegation from the Italian government. They stopped the United States from killing us. Mario Capanna, Luciano Neri, and those guys.

They were public government officials, but they came to intercede. If they hadn't, they would have had a blackout on us. And if they woulda killed us, nobody would have known, really.

They were trying to kill the Longhouse people, people who believe in our treaties and stuff. And they were trying to bring New York State governance onto our land. So we had a big fight. And people were in jail, whatever. They came and helped us by exposing it to the world, huh? So they couldn't do it.

So that's why when *I* was invited to Italy, that was one of the most tragic dilemmas of my life. Because I wanted to repay them for saving the lives of our people. And yet not break my teachings. How could I not make just a simple visit? So Alice and I did go there. But all the time we were there, we were always worried about it. "I hope nobody shoots us. I hope we don't get in a car wreck 'cause I don't want to be stuck over here!" That's what we were thinking.

So that's why they tell you, when you're cooking for a feast, never put salt in your food, in what you are cooking. When the feast is done, and you serve the dead people, there's no salt in there. But if *I* want to put salt in *my* plate that I'm eating, I'm free to do that and you are too. But the one that's for the dead, you can't put salt in there. So that means anything you have prepared, you can't use salt in the process.

Except I often wondered about salt pork because the old Indians really used to like salt pork. It became part of the diet in older days, when colonists first came, I guess. The European, he's the one that brought that salt pork. And it became a big delicacy for lots of the Indians. And so when we have feasts, a lot of older people say, "Make salt pork and biscuit for the feast." 'Cause they like it. Well, that's naturally with salt, so I guess because it was that, it's okay, I guess. I don't know. I don't know what to say about that. But I know *I* love salt pork with a biscuit!

They tell us not to go across the saltwater. When they made the soldiers go, a lot of the time, what they would do is take this earth in their shoe. But I think that's a new thing. It was an *idea* that they had that it would help them, the best thing they could think of doing if they had no choice. But I don't know if they knew that for a fact.

When they were being sent over there, what could have happened is probably a seer saw that and told them to do that. See? Because it was a dilemma for them, a *big* dilemma. It was for *me*. I was *really* caught 'cause I wanted to honor them for what they did for us as a nation. And at the same time, I didn't want to break the teachings from my grandmother and those people that taught me what my morals and values should be. It was really a hard time for me.

Chapter 7

Creation Story Part 4:
Counting from One to Ten

When we count, we are recounting the Creation story.

By the time we finish the Creation story, we've counted from one to ten. And this counting from one to ten for the Iroquois is our chronological telling of the major events of our Creation. So every time we count from one to ten, we are telling the major events of the Creation story. And that's wonderful for kids, for people to know that never did. A lot of people haven't heard that before.

Now as Sky Woman, Atsi'tsiaká:ion, was falling, she was pregnant already, remember? By this time, she's big. And now she's gonna give birth. And this is the one where we call it enska. That means *one*. So number one is attributed to her. And the Senecas and Onondagas, they call it ska.

And also there are a lot of songs the Iroquois do. Every year, they create songs they call Otsiskanie songs. That's what the Six Nations sing. They're all women's songs. They do them at Grand River, at Cattaraugus, Allegheny, Onondaga, Seneca, Akwesasne—all over—every Easter whenever there's a white man's holiday. (They don't do it because it's a white man's holiday; they do it because nobody works, and they have the opportunity to do it.)

They sing dozens and dozens of brand new songs for women. They call those kind of songs Otsiskanie. So in Otsi*ska*nie, you can see the root word: ska. That's what *I* think; I hear it. So when you say *one*, it came from this lady who fell. So number one is attributed to her. The beginning of life; that's why we begin, when we count, with her. Enska.

Once she made the world grow like that, she became bigger and bigger until she gave birth. And when she gave birth, she gave birth to one girl. And that's where, again, the number *one* or enska or ska is reaffirmed. The one, the beginning of life. It took two of them to do that.

When we say in Mohawk, tékeni, that word comes from the word tehníkhen. Tehníkhen means *twins, two*. And that's what that young girl, when she was pregnant, had—twins. And so our word that we use for two, tékeni, comes from the word twin because of those two boys that were gonna be born.

Áhsen means *three,* and it comes from the root word ahsén:nen *in the middle* or *in the center of.* You could add tsi nón and say ahsén:nen tsi nón, which gives us a location. If you say tsi nón:we, it means of a particular thing or place, *the middle of that.*

When they placed the woman who fell from Karonhià:ke, the animals put her in the middle of the turtle's back. So the words ahsén:nen tsi nón mean *in the center, in the middle of.* Hence our word for *three* is ahsén:nen, which means in the middle of the turtle's back. That's *three.*

Now remember, Teharonhiawá:kon took the dolls. He opened their mouths, and he blew in there three times. And after the third breath, the eyes began to move, and the arms moved. And they came alive. And that's where the number three again is important.

And so now there are the four—the black, the white, the yellow, and us Indians. This is where our word for *four* comes from. The root word means *that's done now.* So if you're making a basket, and you did it well, you're done. Tkaié:ri. Or you're making a beautiful anything—beaded moccasins—and you finish. And you look at it, and you say, Tkaié:ri. That means it's complete; it's *done*.[1]

So the word *four* is kaié:ri. It comes from tkaié:ri. It refers to these humans and all life because we were the last to be created, of all Creation. Now everything is done. So he said tkaié:ri. Now they have life. So that's where four comes from. *It's proper, it's complete, it's living.* It comes from the word tkaié:ri. Follow it? That's four. So that refers to the human beings. All of life, in its totality, is now complete.

In the Mohawk language, for number *five*, we say *wísk*. It comes from the root word in Sha*wísk*ara. Do you see where the root word is? *Five*, wísk, Sha*wísk*ara.

And it's shortened like my name. In the Akwesasne Longhouse, my name is Sakokweniónkwas. But when I walk in the Longhouse, you will hear elders as well as youth, they will say Sako. They don't say Sakokweniónkwas. They have abbreviated it. And it's the same with a lot of names. Like my granddaughter. Her name is Iakokwen*iensta*. And they'll just say, Iensta. They shorten it.

We're told *not* to do that by our elders, but even the elders do it. So they're not walking their talk either. But I understand what they're getting at 'cause we're gonna get lost if we keep on shortening things. But we still do it anyway. And we've been doing it since the beginning of time, as this proves. This is the beginning of the world, and *five* is already wísk instead of Shawískara.

It's not as easy to translate his name as his brother's name. Teharonhiawá:kon means, *he who embraces or holds up the sky.* But this one, I've asked many of the older people, "What does that mean? How do you translate Shawískara?" And none of them know. Or some people say it has to do with ice, cold ice, in this wísk part.[2] It has something to do with that.

---

1.   Literally: It's correct.
2.   The Mohawk word for ice is "ó:wise."

And some people say it means like when you come real quickly into something, like a bird dives and then just swerves off and goes another place. Some people say it's like that. Or like you're rushing in somewhere, and you don't even . . . you just go, just rush in and go right away, something like that. It's like his visit is so short and gone. He's just there momentarily, and then he's gone. It implies that in there too.

It bothered me for a number of years 'cause nobody could tell me what it meant. So one time, I burned tobacco and I asked the Creator, "Nobody tells me what this means, that name. So can you let me know? Is there a way you can let me know what it means?" And then I dreamt about it. So I have an answer that I've been using ever since. Now when people ask me what it means, I tell them it came from a dream because I asked.

Whether that dream is correct or not, it came to me, so here's what it told me: Shawískara means that it's like a tornado or a big wind or hurricane comes. All of a sudden it comes there, and it comes so fast that everything not tied down starts flying around: the dust, the papers, everything. Even your hair goes around when that comes. And that's him. He comes so fast that it just causes everything that's not tied down to be in disarray. And that's what the dream said he is, what his name means. And if you think about it, that's the nature of him too. But that's from a dream.

But that's where five comes from.

So then when we say *six*, we say ià:ia'k. If you say wa'kie*ià:ia'k*e it means *she crossed over*. You can hear the root ià:ia'k meaning *cross over*.

And so ià:ia'k means *six*. So wa'kieià:ia'ke refers to the woman when she came from the other world to this world, and she crossed over there to get here. So whenever we say *six*, we're referring to the original woman that crossed over from Karonhià:ke to the earth planet.

Anything that crosses over, we use ià:ia'k. Like in the council of the nation, whenever they make laws in council in the Longhouse, they have to cross it over the fire. So they say tenkatsienhì:*ia'k*e, *it will cross over the fire*. If it doesn't cross over, it's not a law. So it has to go over it and then back over and then over there and then back over again. So the three party system in the nations, it has to go over those. In this instance in law, it has to do with a fire, crossing over a fire.[3] But it's *crossing over* from one point to another point.

And that's the six.

Okay now, number *seven* is tsià:ta and the root word of that one is, oià:ta. Oià:ta is a *body*. Saià:ta is *your body*. Kaia'ton:ni means *a doll*. Akoià:ta *her body*, onkwaià:ta *our body*. And so *seven* is tsià:ta, referring to layers of generations, of existence.

And so the seventh son of a seventh son usually is a powerful medicine. The seventh daughter of a seventh daughter is a very powerful power, medicine, to heal people. Just by touching, if you're a seventh son of a seventh son, usually you can touch a sick person, and they'll get better. It's the same among all races of people. They're always pretty much of one mind even though they don't know each other.

And those people were very much evident in Mohawk country until not too long ago. There was even one in my family. I knew him. He was what you would call my grandmother's sort of nephew, but he was almost as old as she was. And he was a seventh son of a seventh son. People used to give him a *lot* of gifts 'cause he healed people. Not just Indians, but even in New York City. He had a limousine when he was a little *kid*.

But he ruined his medicine because he used alcohol, and he womanized later. And all that depletes your strength and your power, any unnatural kind of stuff, alcohol or womanizing—stuff like that. It takes away that power. So he was that.

So *seven*, tsià:ta comes from the word oià:ta, the sacredness of the body. And that manifests over generations in the strength of the human body.

---

3.   This will be clearer after the section on the Leadership. Briefly, the clans or parties sit on opposite sides of the Longhouse with a fire between them. The proposed law is passed across the fire (both literally and symbolically) by the party that introduced it, to the party on the other side of the Longhouse, for their input. It gets passed back and forth, until there is consensus amongst all the clans.

The seventh son of the seventh son is the ultimate product of it. It holds the power.

So that's seven.

And sha'té:kon is *eight*. It comes from the word *sha'té:*ioht.

Suppose I were to take a round globe, a perfectly round globe, and I were to bisect it completely in the center. And then suppose you were asking me to describe that act. I look at the globe that's split in half exactly, and then I look at one side, and I look at the other side, and I'll say, *sha'té:*ioht, sha'té:ioht. They're the same. One side looks the same as the other side.

So sha'té:kon comes from the word sha'té:ioht, *the same on one side as the other side.*

So that means the balance of your life's journey or your world. The world: one half is night, but the other half is day. And then the other part of it, when it turns around, it's the *same*. Except one is dark and one is light; it alternates. So when it's dark here, the other side is daylight. When the other side is dark again, it's light here. So sha'té:ioht.

When we come to number *nine*, we say kióhton. Or tióhton. (That's how it used to be before the linguists came, a couple of years ago.)

The root word for number *nine* is tsi ni*kiohtón*:ne. And so you say number *nine*: kióhton. Tsi nikiohtón:ne is saying literally *the way it was* (at the beginning, referring to the beginning). *The way it was.* So that refers to what you might call a review of our history or of our life. Tsi nikiohtón: ne, *the way it was, where we came from.*

So if we do that review of all these things, it puts us in a knowing place. We are informed where we are. We will know why we're here, why we are at this point in our life. Because you know all of this stuff, you now know where you stand. Tsi nikiohtón:ne.

And then when you get to number *ten*, we say, oié:ri. It comes back to the word we get four from, tka*ié:ri*. Now it's *complete*. Your world, your journey is complete. It has made a full circle. That's why we say *oié:ri*, tka*ié:ri*. *It's proper, it's true, it's correct.*

When I was a little boy, I can vaguely remember that there was a bouncy tune that my grandmother would sing, counting all the way from one to ten. It was a chant, like the Stomp Dance. But it was for little babies, to bounce them. She'd put them on her lap, and she'd shake them up and down. I remember her doing it to my brothers and sisters when they were little, and I wasn't too much bigger. My grandma also used to do it to me too, but I can't remember that part. She could even sing it backwards.

And I never ever thought of recording it. My grandmother died, and I still never thought about it. It wasn't 'til later years that some of the Onondaga Clan Mothers asked me if I could sing it for them 'cause nobody sings that any more. In fact, until I talked about it, they didn't even know it existed, that song. Once they heard me talking about this, they wanted me to record it on a tape recorder. But I was too little. I don't know how to do it.

The Senecas and Cayugas didn't know it either, none that I ever heard of. I could have done something about it up to three years ago because my grandmother's younger sister, who was ninety-two, just died three years ago.[4] And she probably would have been the last one that would have known that in our family. But I was here at Kanatsioharè:ke, and she was at Akwesasne, and I didn't ask her.

What I'm telling you is probably the only thing left now . . . probably my grandmother was the only family still doing it.

So anyway, we've finished the number part of it now. So you get the gist of it anyway, huh, how the world is done?

[4.] Tom made this comment in the year 2000.

Chapter 8

Creation Story Part 5: Endnotes

Don't wait for them to die 'cause if they die, they'll take it with them.

So anyway when you hear the Creation story like that, you can understand why the grandmother is the moon. The grandmother always favored her Shawískara grandson, always took his part. That's why you always see her with him. So it's usually at night she's still with him.

Once in a while, you may go out in broad daylight when the sun is shining and you may see Grandmother Moon visiting the other grandson, Teharonhiawá:kon, our Elder Brother, the Sun.

So that's what I know and share with you about the Creation story.

And there are parts I didn't get to. For example, lacrosse came from the Creation story. The two brothers used to play lacrosse. That's where it became like a medicine. And in fact, lacrosse *is* medicine. The sport lacrosse that people play nowadays is *not* medicine, but even it has power. But when it's a lacrosse game *for* the healing of the sick, it's a very powerful game.

I've played lacrosse through the years, as medicine, not as a sport. And that has its own rules as well. But it came from the Creation story, from a part I didn't tell.

And I've interjected things in there—that's probably why it's so long—about how I think it affects my life and your life, to make it more than just a story of Creation, to make it *real*. And then if you do likewise when you tell that story, it's gonna become even longer. When you start to do that, then you open yourself to universal truths more and more.

Sometimes when I talk about things and share whatever I know, I don't even know what I'm talking about. My mouth is going, but I don't know when I'm done, what I said. It's almost like something takes over my body, takes over my mind. Many times through the years.

But I'll tell you one thing though, it's *much,* much easier to not have to refind that knowledge from dreams or from trying to make yourself sensitive to those things. It's much easier just to listen to a grandma or a grandpa who knows. Don't wait for them to die 'cause if they die, they'll take it with them. And for you to get that knowledge from them when they're six feet under is an ordeal and a *half.* For you to keep your body clean enough to get that knowledge from those who have already died requires lots of discipline, lots of sacrifice, and lots of *pain* and frustration.

And you never know if it's real or not real. So my advice is not to wait. Even though knowledge is never gone, if you don't get it from the living (who are your relatives or whatever) . . . It's easier to take a shuttle from here to San Francisco instead of walking with holes in your moccasins through the desert and the cactus. That could be painful. So it's better to take the shortcut! 'Cause if you're gonna rely on dreams and visions to regain it, it's lots of days, lots of pain. And even then, there may be other powers that may come in there that try to trick you too in the spiritual world. There always was, there always will be.

But that is the Creation story, the way I kinda remember it. And like I told you, it took me over thirty years to be able to tell you that much. It wasn't given to me in a session or two sessions or a workshop or some summer camp. It was in fragments here and there, in little pieces. I had to take that puzzle that was broken into ten thousand pieces and gather it from this floor, as it was all messed up. And see where does this fit, where does that fit. And before me, my uncles did that, and some of my grandfathers and grandmother did it too. So it helped a little more. And so now the puzzles are not in ten thousand pieces as much for our young. Now it's maybe only in a hundred pieces. It's easier to pull it together. But that took generations.

So that's all I can remember.

And I think the Creation story is the most important of the events I am recounting 'cause it's so fundamental.

Chapter 9

Language in 3-D

When you hear the language and you understand, it's like 3-D. It's in Technicolor.

Like all people of the world, we have a language. I know you're not gonna understand my language, but I wish you could. Because Mohawk is beautiful. The language that I heard my grandma and my mother talk is very poetic, but it wasn't meant to be poetry. It just was. And it just *is* yet today.

I used to listen to Grandma talk, all the old elders talk, and all the old Chiefs talk. And when they used to tell stories about long ago, I listened to the words, and I saw vivid pictures of action, of colors, of even songs in the language.

When any of my elders talk Mohawk, when they describe something, it's just as if the whole side of this building was the great big screen of an outdoor theater that has three dimensions to it. You know how you have to wear those special glasses and they make three dimensions? When you hear the language and you understand, it's like 3-D. It's in Technicolor. If you can really understand Indian, you can smell the food when it's cooking, you can smell the trees and the water when someone is speaking it. It's a living language. Yeah.

And then when it's interpreted into English, it becomes just a little six-inch black-and-white television set. English is just capitals—dark—and ends with a period, and that's all. You know what I mean? That's the way it appears—very not, you know, living. For me.

Let me give you a few examples of what I mean. For instance, I will say,
Onekwénhtara niwahsohkò:ten kí:ken akwakià:tawi.

In English that is generally translated, *This shirt* I am wearing *is colored red.* Okay? But what I really said is, *This shirt* I am wearing *is the color of the blood that flows in my body.* That's what I'm wearing. It's not just "red."

If I say my sister, who sits over there,
Oròn:ia niwahsohkò:ten thí:ken akokià:tawi.

She is wearing *a blouse or a shirt that is the color of the sky.* It's not just "blue." It's the *color of the sky.* You see?

And my other sister is wearing
Ne óhonte ne' niwahsohkò:ten akokià:tawi.

She is wearing *the blouse of the grass that grows, that color.* You can't just say "green." There's no such a thing as just "green." It's gotta be related to the grass.

Another example I wanna tell you is that one time I heard my old elders talking about something that everybody here is familiar with. And that's death. When somebody dies, you bury them. Well, in Mohawk, I listen to the old elders talk, and you know the phrase "dead and buried" seems very cold. It's kinda termination, the end. And it's not a very soothing kind . . .

But let me tell you in Mohawk what we call that. We don't just say you bury somebody. This is what we say,
Tentsitewahwawén:eke thi rón:kwe.

That means *we will take his body, and we will wrap it in the garden blanket of Mother Earth.* You see, very comforting. Very nice. It's not cold and ending. And that's what the Mohawk, Seneca, and Onondaga languages, the Ojibwa language, are about.

They say on the other planet where that first woman came from—where we the Iroquois people, the humans came from—that's the kind of language that they talk, the Mohawk language, Seneca, Onondaga. That's what we're told. That's why we're told never to forget how to speak that.

And in fact they say that the songs that they sing with the Great Feather Dance are in the language that comes from that other place. And the reason why we use that language and we use that turtle rattle is to continue to bring life and miracles.

Another example is the Ohén:ton Karihwatéhkwen. Some people call it the Thanksgiving Address, others call it the Greetings or the Opening Prayer. All these other things are good translations; they're all descriptive, but they're not *exact* translations. They're not literal translations. I'd like you to know what the literal translation is.

Ohén:ton says *in the front of it, in front,* or *before.*

The karihw part refers to *matters* or *issues,* and they're always going to be important, whatever they are. So *before anything that's important.*

Watéhkwen means it's *of the nature of, of that nature,* or *of that environment.* Téhkwen, it's like *the words of acknowledgement* to all that's important.

So the Ohén:ton Karihwatéhkwen refers to *what we say before we do anything important.* It's what we say to prepare ourselves so that we include into it, that kind of thinking. It's *of that* so that the world's going to be wrapped up in that or the environment is going to be of that. Do you see what I'm saying?

It simply indicates that *this is what's going to be happening.* That's the way the river's gonna flow. There's a river, and once you get in there, then it's gonna take you. And that's what this is gonna do. It's going to take you. It tells you that it's going to be like that. That means you're gonna talk about the Creator and the sacred life that he put us on.

So that's how you translate it in real English instead of just saying *Thanksgiving Address* or *Opening Prayer*. That doesn't really do it justice. It's kind of a rough slang for it.

People can speak Mohawk fluently, but they're not always associating the meaning with what they're really saying. The whole new Western world has taken precedence.

For example, in the Indian world where I grew up, when a real Iroquois man shakes hands with you, here's how he does it. He grasps your arm just below the elbow. He doesn't do the white brothers' handshake. The real one puts both your forearms side by side. That's the old way to shake and greet.

In my language it says, tenthshenentshakarén:ron. When you say tenthshenentshakarén:ron to Mohawk people, they will do the white handshake. And that's sufficient. But I tell them all we have to do is translate it, and it tells you, right there. Listen to what it says: onén:tsha is your arm. It means to *shake his arm*.

And then they say, "Oh yeah." The practice has become so much of a habit that they don't even think about what it's really saying. And that's true of a lot of things in our language.

So now their language is only a shadow following their actions. You know, instead of the other way around, see? And this is a perfect example. When you say to a Mohawk, tenthse*nentsha*, that means w*rap his arm*. That's our greeting. But they will grab hands instead of the arm. And yet it's so plain. There's no mistaking it, if you think onén:tsha is your *arm*. Tenthshenén:tsha means *grab his arm*. Tenthshenentshakarén:ron means *shake his arm*.

And then when you hear old people talking, they hold arms together in a circle—that wampum circle. They call it the Confederacy circle. You know that circle? It's got all those strings of wampum going towards the center. That's what they call the rontenentshanawá:kon. They're holding arms together, see? That's an example of it.

Even though I know that and I teach that, I'll still shake *hands* even though I know it's supposed to be shaking *arms*. But a lot of the students I've had don't forget, and so they embarrass me in my own teaching 'cause they're the ones who shake *arms*, the old way. And I realize, "Oh yeah, that's right, we're s'posed to do that."

Look how much I'm versed in it. I was the teacher telling them, and I'm *still* going on that old track. It's hard to derail myself from my brainwashing process.

And I know that all my old Chiefs, even when they shook hands with you, they did it gently. When they shook hands, they didn't shake arms 'cause they too were doing it the European way. But at least when they did it, you didn't even hardly feel they were touching you. It was just like a feather. They were doing it so smoothly. They didn't squeeze it at all.

And in America, if you do it like that, they frown on you. They think you're a weakling. They think you're a sissy. They think you're *nothing*, you know? This is in America. That's what *they* think.

So we've got a long of undoing to do if we're gonna find ourselves in the path we're journeying and if we're gonna be effective. We've got a lot to do. We're very lost, a lot of us.

Including myself. I'm just finding my path in *lots of things*. And mostly, I'm fortunate because I have my language. Even though I was guilty of doing what I just said, just using the examples of day-to-day rather than listening to my language, I've learned. And I'm very lucky, lucky enough to know enough of my language that I can take words apart and find their roots. That's my bridge to this past, I would say.

Not long ago, I was at a language conference in London, and the graduates were there from the immersion language school at Six Nations, the ones that graduated already. Also some of the graduates from the Freedom School. There were four of them there, and most of them are in college.

And they found out that most of these kids going to the Freedom School or to the Kawenní:io School or the immersion schools have far surpassed the other kids that go to regular public schools without immersion, without the language. They're way ahead of them in everything—in math, in grammar, in the academics. All the way round, they just fare better. And it's a *fact*. Both in Grand River as well as in Akwesasne, especially in Akwesasne, it's like that.

And a lot of those people had criticized that. But these kids that they said were gonna be dummies are way, *way* more academic. They absorb it more than the others. The others want to act foolish all the time. Whereas these kids have *purpose*. Those four kids spoke on the stage there. And they spoke probably about fifteen to twenty minutes each. Three boys and one girl. And you didn't see one of them carry a paper or notes, what they were gonna say. Not one of them. They spoke there with no "ah, um, a." None of that. I mean just like that—like a plane flying without any hesitation or reluctance or anything. They did, those four.

And every one of them said, with tears in their eyes, "Thank you, all the teachers, that you had faith in us. Thank you for giving us an identity of who we are because that's what helped me in my school is to know who I am. And there's no doubt that's what you gave me. You gave me my identity." All of them said that. Ahhhh, people were crying in there.

And that's when someone sang an Atón:wa[1] song, one that was his father's or his uncle's, he sang that. And his father said, "I'm so proud of you." And he said, "I haven't done this, and I haven't ever been able to do it." It was a real powerful thing, huh?

And everybody came and just hugged the hell out of them and shook their hands and really . . . it was great, huh? So I said if *all* our young people could turn out like that, what specimens, what specimens! And they didn't need a paper to remind them what to say either. The truth just came right out.

---

[1].   For an explanation of the Atón:wa song, see chapter 17, "The Four Sacred Rituals Part 2: Three of the Rituals."

Chapter 10

The Clan System[1]

In the human body, the bones are what give the body structure and the ability to function. The clan serves the same purpose in the societies of the Rotinonhsón:ni people.

Many thousands of years ago, the population of the humans on the earth was very small. As years passed, it increased considerably. Along with this increase, many problems began to occur. Many new villages were created, and families grew farther apart. There was a time when first cousins were considered like brother and sister, but now first cousins had become like strangers. The respect and love family members had for one another diminished, causing social problems in all the villages.

With the larger population, the number of deaths increased. During this period of history, it was customary for a family to mourn or be in grief for

---

[1.] Most of the material from this chapter came from the book written by Tom Porter, *Clanology, Clan System of the Iroquois*, ed. Joanne Swamp, Barbara Barnes, Brenda LaFrance, Delia Cook, Dora Lazore, Nancy Thompson, Audrey Thompson, Madeline David and Dawn David (Cornwall Island/ Hogansburg: Native North American Travelling College, 1993).

their loved ones for a period of one year. The human population grew so much that the people of the villages found themselves in constant grief. The one-year mourning period would not be completed before another family member died. It became a common sight to see people and families openly crying and in grief. This situation caused the people not to function properly or normally.

The elders of the villages began to notice that our ceremonies were becoming less and less attended by the people. Those who recited and conducted the ceremonies became hard to find, and those who did had difficulty remembering how to do them properly.

One day, the elders became alarmed and called a meeting of all the people of the villages. The people were told of the basic problems, and all were asked for ideas that would result in restoring peace and respect.

Many meetings were called by the elders in an attempt to find a solution or a way that could restore stability to all the people. None of the meetings were successful. After several attempts, finally there was a man who did stand up and ask for permission to respond to the request of the elders. This man was very young and had a reputation for never saying a single word to anyone.

The man said that he had been observing all the life forms made by the Creator, and from that observation came several ideas that could solve the problems of the people. He told the people that the Creator made all kinds of waters. "Some waters are known as lakes, some are known as creeks, some are known as rivers, and some are known as oceans, but they are all bodies of water."

He said, "The Creator made all the birds. Some of the birds are called the eagles, some are called the blackbirds, some are called the robins, and some are called the crows. All of these birds are birds, but each has their own way and their own name."

The man told everyone that even the wind was divided into different groups. "The cold wind comes from the north, the warm wind comes from the south, the wet wind comes from the west, and the no-planting wind from the east. All of these winds are simply wind, but each has its own job and character." The man told all the people they should follow the example of nature which the Creator made. If the people follow the ways of nature, then they too will divide themselves into manageable working groups.

The people and the elders listened very closely to what the man told them. Everyone was amazed at what the man said. It seemed to make very good sense. It was at that point the elders said they would give the man a special name. The elders chose the name Ro'nikonhrowá:nen (he who has great ideas). Ro'nikonhrowá:nen gathered the people and told them that they should all be ready to travel early the next morning.

The next day the people were ready and they did travel. As the people traveled, they followed the river. Then Ro'nikonhrowá:nen saw a grape vine hanging from a tree. He pulled the grape vine down and threw one end across the river where it got caught and hooked itself to the opposite side of the river. At this point Ro'nikonhrowá:nen began crossing the river, holding on to the grape vine. As he crossed the river, he asked the people to cross with him.

One by one the people did so, but eventually the vine let go, and not all were able to make it across the river. Now it came to be that half of the people were on one side of the river and the other half on the other side.

Ro'nikonhrowá:nen then told the people on his side of the river that in the coming morning, they should pay close attention to whatever seemed strange or abnormal.

The people on both sides of the river set up their camps. Early the next morning the eldest woman woke up and immediately gave thanks to the Creator for allowing her to pass through the night without incident. She gave thanks for the miracle of a beautiful new day. The elderly woman then went down to the river to fetch water so that she could prepare the morning meal. As she dipped water from the river, she heard a noise. Looking up, she saw a deer standing there. Later on in the day, Ro'nikonhrowá:nen asked the lady if she had seen anything unusual.

She told him that while dipping water at the river, she had seen a deer standing there, and the deer was staring at her. Ro'nikonhrowá:nen then informed her that the Deer would be the clan that she and all her offspring would belong to forevermore.

The following day, another elderly lady from one of the families gave thanks to the Creator and then went down to the river to fetch water to prepare the morning meal. When the old lady looked up, she saw a bear. Soon afterward Ro'nikonhrowá:nen approached her and asked her what she had seen that was unusual. The old lady said she saw a bear. The old lady was informed that she and all her offspring would from then on belong to the clan of the Bear.

This same occurrence was repeated twice more when the snipe and eel were seen by two other older women. This happened on one side of the river. From that day forward, the Deer, the Bear, the Snipe, and the Eel would always be together as one united group. This is what modern-day anthropologists call a moiety.

Now the young man who was given the name of Ro'nikonhrowá:nen had to cross over the river where many other families had set up their campfires. The people on the other side of the river had been anxiously waiting for him to arrive.

Ro'nikonhrowá:nen gathered all the people on that side of the river and explained to them what he expected them to do. He told the people that they should be very observant of anything that seemed unusual, especially in the early morning hours of the day. He told the women, who were the eldest of each family, to be especially watchful. He also told them that they must give thanks (prayer) to the Creator who, in fact, is the Maker of the whole universe and all its life.

The night came, and everyone retired around their campfires. The next day, very early in the morning, one of the elderly women awoke and began to give thanks to our Creator. The elderly woman then went to the river where she fetched some water to prepare the morning meal. When the old woman stood up, she heard a noise that caught her attention, and there she saw a wolf staring at her.

Ro'nikonhrowá:nen then informed her that she and all her offspring would be of the Wolf Clan. On the following days, several of the older women from big families had the very same experience. It was in this way that the people on that side of the river received the Wolf, the Beaver, the Turtle, and the Hawk Clan.

The people and the clans now existing on that side of the river became another moiety. It is because of this that all Iroquois communities who still embrace and follow their clans will be found with this dual system. In Onondaga, the two parties are known as the Longhouse people and the Mud House people.

Ro'nikonhrowá:nen told the people that when one of the parties addresses the other, they will call each other cousins. If someone dies from the Wolf, the Turtle, the Hawk, or the Beaver Clan, it is said that all the people on that side of the house will be in grief or mourning. It will then be the responsibility of the people on the other side of the house to aid those who are in grief.

The people who did not lose anyone on their side of the house are called Roti'nikonhrakáhte, *they whose minds are strong*. The people who are from the clans of the Roti'nikonhrakáhte will do all the speaking at the wake and the funeral. They will do the cooking, the digging of the grave, and whatever else it takes to respectfully put away the dead. The people called Roti'nikonhrakáhte will be obligated for a period of nine days, and on the tenth day, they will be officially released from their duties for that particular death.

The side which loses a loved one are called Roti'nikonhrakwenhtará:'on, *they whose minds have fallen to the ground*.

This history of the clans is one version, and there are probably others. This particular version is said to have occurred before the Great Law of Peace was established.

The numerous clans that our people have today were given originally by Ro'nikonhrowá:nen. Later on, I will talk about how the Clan System was revitalized, and incorporated into the new Clan System by the Peacemaker many hundreds of years after the original Clan System was introduced. The Clan System continues with a great vibrancy in all Iroquois communities today.

The Clan System is the fundamental building block of the Rotinonhsón: ni. The clans are extremely important, and in fact without the clans, we would have almost nothing as a society of people. In the human body, the bones are what give the body structure and the ability to function. The clan serves the same purpose in the societies of the Rotinonhsón:ni people.

Clans of the Mohawk People

The clans are taken from the animal, bird, or fish life. The clans are inherited from the mothers. This type of transmission of the clan is called a matrilineal system.

Spiritual, social, economic, and political life are interwoven; one without the other is not considered whole or complete. (The spiritual and political are inseparable.)

Giving of a name

Amongst the Rotinonhsón:ni nations, each of the clans have specific names that belong to each clan. A Bear Clan person must have a Bear Clan name. It is not proper for a Bear Clan person to have a Wolf or Turtle Clan name. A person begins his or her life with a name, and that name begins one's identity. A baby is born into a clan. This is another step to one's identity. Another identification is the baby's gender, a boy or a girl.

Retrieving of a name

There is a procedure to correct or retrieve a name if taken by another clan. The women of the clan whose name was taken will make a basket, and together they will go to the family that has taken their name. When the women arrive at the home of that family, they will say, "We have arrived here carrying this basket. We retrieve our name by putting it in our basket and carrying it back home. This name belongs to our clan family." The women will then leave the name in the basket, and that name will now be available to a newborn child of that specific clan.

Number of Mohawk Clans

The Mohawk people have three principal clans: the Turtle Clan, the Bear Clan, and the Wolf Clan. Today we have other clans among us. At various times in the past, people from our different nations were attacked by the people of the United States. When attacked, our people scattered with only the clothes on their backs. Many of them arrived here in Akwesasne for shelter. There was a community of Iroquois, namely Onondaga, along with some Oneidas and Cayugas, who lived in Ahswé:katsi (Ogdensburg). In 1806, the Ahswé:katsi people moved in with the Akwesasne Mohawks and for that reason, today the Akwesasne Mohawks have a large number of Snipe Clan, Deer Clan, and a few Eel Clan families.

Marriage forbidden between members of the same clan

The laws of the clans are very simple and rigidly adhered to. Since everyone in a clan is part of a large extended family, it is forbidden for a man to marry a woman of the same clan. The elders have said that a Mohawk Bear Clan man cannot marry a Bear Clan woman of any other nation. They are still considered brother and sister. The elders also spoke of the greater extended family. They said if a Bear Clan person was traveling to the Navajo or Hopi country and didn't know anyone there, he would look for the people of the Bear Clan, and that family would recognize him as part of their family. Likewise if a Hopi were visiting here, we who are of his or her clan would take care of them as a member of our family.

It is said that sometimes a man or woman finds a mate of the same clan and goes to another nation or community to get married. When they arrive there, they lie about their real clans so the leaders of the community who don't know them will marry them. The elders say about such doings, "You may not be truthful to your fellow human beings, but the Creator cannot be fooled. The children talk loud and will tell your secret." What this means is that the children of such a marriage will be born with possible mental problems or have physical deformities.

Elders would also say, "Children born of parents of the same clan should never be put in any positions of leadership within the nation." An example of this happening is a person attending a meeting and he or she seems to understand and be agreeable, but after the meeting makes an incorrect report. This is not done on purpose, but it seems to be a natural occurrence. If people who have parents of the same clan attain a leadership position, they will most likely lead our people and nation to ruin.

So that's important. Ensewarihó:wanahte sewen'tá:ra. *Announce proudly what clan you belong to* to your kids. When your men become of the proper age, before they wink at the girls or before the girls wink at the guys, first find out what clan you belong to. If they're the same clan, you save your winks. 'Cause it's forbidden. It's very bad if someone marries a member of the same clan. *Really* bad.

Descriptions of the characteristics of the various clans

I want to make it very clear in all people's minds that the descriptions of the characteristics of the various clans are not written in stone. The description of the characteristics come from years of listening to many elders speak about the clans. The elders sometimes poked fun at their own clan and the clans of others. Most of the time the elders spoke seriously about the clans. The following writings are a collection and combination of serious and not-so-serious information that I can remember hearing from those elders.

The clan of your mother usually is dominant, but the clan of your father also influences your character and behavior to various degrees. There are probably instances where an individual is completely the exception to the rule. Many newspapers publish astrology columns, and I thought it interesting to do something similar based on our own culture.

One must remember that in anything worthwhile there is always laughter. A sacred ceremony is not sacred if there is no room for laughter. So it is with these writings of the clan. I hope you will find them interesting, entertaining, and useful.

A'nó:wara *(Turtle Clan)*

The Turtle Clan is one of the principal clans of the Mohawks. The turtle is the symbol of the entire earth. We walk upon the turtle's back. The people of the Turtle Clan are the foundation of our nation. Because of this fact, the Turtle Clan people are very consistent, determined, and humbly stubborn. The Turtle Clan people are, in most cases, very shy. They tend to be somewhat middle-of-the-road between the Wolf and Bear Clan characteristics. Whenever anything occurs that is surprising or startling, the turtles immediately go back into their shells until they see things have calmed down, and so it is with the people of the Turtle Clan.

The Turtle Clan people react best in common, ordinary, and very normal day-to-day activities. They do not appreciate surprises or sensationalism. It takes a bit of an effort to personally know a Turtle Clan person. They will acknowledge you with proper greetings, but to really become a trusted friend takes much more effort than it would with people of the other clans. The Turtle Clan people are somewhat moody. They will usually shy away at first from anything new.

Rotiskaré:wake (*Bear Clan*)

Each clan of the people has certain strong traits or characteristics. If one is sensitive and observant, one can determine with some certainty what clan people belong to just by their behavior.

The Bear Clan people are somewhat on the bashful side and quiet. They tend to be very sensitive to others. They are diplomatic by nature. The people of the Bear Clan usually will walk away from trouble. They can usually take a lot of ridicule, kidding, and abuse—more than normal—but they do have their limit; and when you go beyond that limit, you have to get out of their way. They can get very fierce. Once you get them mad or angry, they will never forget. Some of them may forgive, but they will not forget. More often, they will hold a grudge for many, many years. It has even been said that their offspring will carry the grudge to the next generation.

The Bear Clan people usually are sensitive. The Bear Clan people will know the kind of medicine needed, or if they don't know, they will probably know someone who does know what can heal a sick person. The Bear Clan people are healers. It is best to say they are people of medicine. There is a story about that. We can come back to that story after we talk about each of the different clans. The Bear Clan people are also extremely fond of small children and especially newborn babies.

Rotikwáho (*Wolf Clan*)

The people of the Wolf Clan are usually aggressive. They tend to respond almost instantly to things in their life. They are a very honest and straightforward people. In this regard, most Wolf Clan people are not generally thought to possess diplomatic characteristics. The Wolf Clan will say what is on their mind without much hesitation or regard for the feelings of anyone. If you would like to have an argument—just for the sake of arguing, no matter what subject—just go see the people of the Wolf Clan, and you will instantly have your wish fulfilled.

The Wolf Clan people seem not to believe what is told to them at first. They always cross-examine, but once satisfied, they are workers and believers. They will finish the job with great determination. It is hard to be humble if you are of the Wolf Clan. This generally seems to be true. The Wolf Clan people are workers and doers. Wolf Clan people are not particularly close to one another. They seem to not really get along; but mess with one of them, and they always instantly unite.

In Akwesasne, the Wolf Clan are the most populous and strongest clan. They have many people who speak the Mohawk language, sing the songs of the Four Sacred Rituals, and can recite the spiritual speeches of the Four Sacred Rituals. If ever the Akwesasne Mohawks lose their beliefs and traditions, the Wolf Clan people will probably be the last to do so.

Roti'nehsí:io (*Snipe Clan*)

The Akwesasne people who belong to the Snipe Clan are originally either Onondagas, Cayugas, or Senecas. Most likely they are from the Onondagas.

The following is observed of the people belonging to the Snipe Clan. They are always busy or involved in something. They are usually not lazy. They are sometimes moody, but most of the time they have a more joyous nature. It is said that the Snipe Clan people are a noisy bunch. They are very alert and full of energy. They take great interest in almost all things; so much so that they have a hard time completing any one project.

If a Snipe Clan person sees a group of people busy doing something, they will enthusiastically invite themselves and become a part of it. They will put their whole heart into the project, as if there was no tomorrow. If they see someone doing something else, they will leave what they are doing and will jump into another project with great enthusiasm. They will do the same thing over and over again.

The Snipe Clan people are usually positive-thinking people. They do have a temper that is kind of quick at times, but does not last long. The Snipe Clan people are good conversationalists. They usually know enough about everything to be very interesting.

Rotinenio'thró:non (*Deer Clan*)

The Deer Clan people are originally from the Onondaga or the Cayuga nations. The people of the Deer Clan are generally on the timid and shy side. They tend to form an opinion quickly. They don't always gather all the facts on which to make a decision. The Deer Clan people are easily intimidated and somewhat athletic.

They are a people of good intentions, as long as there are people to break the ice. They tend to be followers more than bold leaders. They are generally kindhearted, but are very sensitive. Their feelings can be hurt without anyone knowing why. They have a strong trait of being unpredictable. At times when one may think that everything is hopeless, the Deer Clan will come through and save the day.

Rotihshennakéhte (*They carry the name*)

In Akwesasne, some people regard the Rotihshennakéhte as a clan, but in fact they are not a clan. They are a certain identifiable group of people who do not have a clan. They become the carriers of the name of whichever clan adopts them.

Many years ago, when our people were attacked and killed, our ancestors would go to the place where they lost people and capture women, men, and children to replace lost ones. These captives, non-Native and Native, were adopted and married into the Mohawks. They and their offspring were, and still are, called the people of the Rotihshennakéhte.

The Bear Clan and Medicine

Many years ago, before the arrival of the European people here in North America, the Creator came to visit his people. The Creator decided to check on his people to see if they were still following his teachings.

One day, the people noticed that a big chunk of the sun fell from the sky and came crashing towards the earth. It was a huge ball of flames, and when it crashed to earth, there appeared a most handsome man. This wonderful man was the Creator himself. This man prepared himself to visit his people. The first thing he did was to transform his body into that of a very tired, dirty, and shabby-looking old man. The Creator did this so no one would recognize him.

In those days our people lived in villages. Each village was inhabited by a single clan. The villages were many miles apart from one another. Usually, each village was located by a lake or some body of water. Generally, there were small trails or paths that connected these villages.

The Creator, Shonkwaia'tíson, who was now transformed into an old man, began his journey following a small path, picking up an old, crooked, and twisted stick that became his cane or walking stick. As the Creator made his way along the path, he had to go through thorn bushes and burdock patches. The thorn bushes tore his clothes, making them even more shabby looking. The burdock got stuck in his hair, and all his exposed skin was scratched by the bushes.

Finally, Shonkwaia'tíson came to a clearing alongside of a small lake and saw smoke rising from the cooking fires of that village. He was so relieved to finally find his people that he hurriedly approached.

An older woman met Shonkwaia'tíson when he reached the village, and she was very hostile to the old man. She chased him away. She ridiculed his physical appearance and called him a "lazy, stinking beggar." He was very disappointed, disillusioned, and very hurt.

He pulled himself together and continued on his way, following the dirt trail in search of another village that might welcome him.

Shonkwaia'tíson was now becoming tired, worn down, and very hungry. Mile after mile wore holes in his moccasins. His feet were beginning to ache and blister.

After many miles of walking, Shonkwaia'tíson again saw smoke rising in the distance. Upon reaching that village, he noticed the antlers of a deer affixed to the bark houses. As he entered the Deer Clan village, a small group of Deer Clan women scolded him and told him to leave because they didn't want a lazy, stinking old man hanging around their village.

Once again, the old man was disappointed and walked away ever so hurt.

Shonkwaia'tíson continued to walk and walk. Every single time he found villages, he was turned away and verbally abused. He attempted to visit the Eel Clan, the Hawk Clan, the Turtle Clan, the Beaver Clan, the Snipe Clan. All these other clans turned him away.

Now he was so hurt and so disappointed that all his people had abandoned their ways and teachings. His feet were all blistered, and his body was all scratched. He became very weak and barely able to walk because of hunger. Now the old man came to the conclusion that all his people no longer followed the sacred ways. Shonkwaia'tíson decided to return to the Sky World and, from there, would change the world forevermore.

Shonkwaia'tíson was just about to return to his home in the Sky World when he noticed smoke rising in the distance. With great pain and a last effort, he made his way to that village. He noticed that there were Bear Clan emblems hanging from the walls of the bark houses. As he approached the village, he was feeling reluctant and anxious. He was very much afraid of being rejected as he had been up until that moment. As he approached closer, he saw a very old woman who helpfully embraced him and offered warm words of welcome.

The old woman said to Shonkwaia'tíson,
          Watkonnonhwará:ton Rákhso.

This means *I give you my greetings and thankfulness together with love, Grandfather.*

Now the woman guided Shonkwaia'tíson to her house where she offered him some herb tea and whatever food she had at the moment. The old Bear Clan lady fixed water for Shonkwaia'tíson to bathe and offered him a robe to wrap himself in while she washed and mended his old clothes. The Bear Clan woman fixed a bed with blankets of fur for the old man to rest on. That evening, she prepared many types of food and puddings for him. Shonkwaia'tíson was so pleased that there still was someone on earth who remembered his teachings.

The next morning, she woke to find him in severe pain. The Bear Clan woman felt so sorry for the old man and asked what she could do to help him be more comfortable. He told her that in the forest where the hardwood trees grew, there were patches of medicine plants. He described exactly what they looked like and gave her sacred tobacco to offer to the leader of the medicine patch. He told her exactly how to wash the medicine, how many roots, how much water to use, how long and how hot to cook the medicine. The Bear Clan woman did exactly as she was told, and the old man drank the medicine. In just a short while, he was well and happy. Soon the old woman was sewing new moccasins and an entire outfit for him. The people of the village would gather at her house to sing for the old man's entertainment.

The next morning, when the old woman got up, the old man again was very sick. Again he told the Bear Clan woman where to go to find the proper medicinal plants and exactly how to prepare them. He drank the medicine and the sickness went away. Every day, he became ill with every possible sickness. Each time this happened the Bear Clan woman was told what medicine plant or plants to prepare. Every single time, the old man would become well.

Now on this particular day, the man told the woman that he had taught her and her people all the knowledge of medicine as a special gift. The Bear Clan people never forgot the ways and teachings of our Creator. From that point on, the Bear Clan people would be knowledgeable about medicine for their people. For regardless of clan, those who embrace the teachings of our Creator will be acknowledged by our Creator with a special gift.

Now on the last day of the Shonkwaia'tíson's visit, this is what happened . . .

Again, the Bear Clan woman woke up to find the old man in severe pain and very sick. She asked what she might do to help him. For the last time he instructed her where to find the medicine. When she returned she noticed that a huge flame was shining through the cracks and openings of her house. The Bear Clan woman thought that her house was on fire and rushed to save him. Just as she turned the corner of her house, she saw the old man transform himself into a handsome young man and then into a huge ball of flames. Stunned with awe, she watched as the great ball of flames shot up into the sky and then disappeared into the sun.

So it was that the people of the Bear Clan received from the Creator their knowledge of medicine.

So there are some lessons that we can learn from Shonkwaia'tíson's visit:

1. Never ridicule or make fun of someone, for this person may be the Creator.
2. When someone visits your home or community always welcome them.
3. When someone visits your home, don't ask if they are hungry. Share whatever food you have with them. Give them something to drink.
4. Don't ask if they have a place to sleep or stay. Fix a bed where they may rest.
5. Always know what the teachings of the Creator are.

The Traditional Family Structure of the Iroquois Nations[2]

The first thing that I will say about this is that we are a matrilineal society. I belong to the Bear Clan because my mother was Bear Clan and so was my mother's mother. The word for *Mother* is Istén:'a, and the word for all my *mother's sisters* is the exact same: Istén:'a. They're called "Mother" too. So that's the way they look at me, as their son.

Although I have a father, and my father can pass knowledge to me, it remains the duty of my mother's brothers to teach me the things of life that are important. My uncles are the ones responsible for making sure I have been taught the ceremonies of our nation and Longhouse. My mother and her sisters, and for sure my grandmother on my mother's side, will be really concerned that I become knowledgeable in my people's beliefs and traditions.

Whenever there is a ceremony of any kind, I will always sit on the side of the Longhouse that my mother sits on. For the Bear Clan, that is on the

---

[2.]   This section was first printed in the Kanatsioharè:ke newsletter of 2003.

south side of the house. The traditional people, because of this structure, have as many mothers as their mothers have sisters. All my first cousins are viewed as though they were my brothers and sisters. My second cousins are viewed as though they were my first cousins. Everything is much closer and more tightly knit, in the traditional family. That's why they say our relations are closer than the white man's way—a lot closer.

All elder people, the age of my biological grandparents, are addressed as grandmother or grandfather even if they are not related by blood. All the men that are my father's age are addressed as my uncles.

It is also the teaching that we can never marry someone that is the same clan as our mother, for we would be sisters and brothers even if we came from different nations. On my father's side, according to tradition, we are not allowed to marry a third cousin. We can marry our fourth cousin on our father's side, but even some elders still frown upon that.

Also the older people, in older times, didn't really use the names of the people unless there was a formal ceremony going on. They would refer to one another as uncle, grandfather, grandmother, mother, cousin, brother, sister, or lastly, my friend.

Also all the condoled[3] Chiefs of our nation should never be called by their name, but when addressing them we must say "Uncle." It is said that good parents and grandparents always tell the offspring who their relatives are and who they are related to. Even as far away as a tenth cousin. We are told by the elders to always be proud of our relatives and always be ready to greet them with fondness and compassion.

But because our culture has been attacked and disarrayed, it's not really functioning the way it's supposed to. When it's working in its prime, for example, an uncle's job is to raise his sisters' kids. Even though there's a father there, he, the uncle, is the one that's really responsible. And the father

---

3. The term "condoled" makes it clear that they are traditional Chiefs (rather than elected Chiefs from the system imposed on the people by the Canadian or American government). More about this in chapter 27, "The Great Law of Peace Part 2: the Birth of the Confederacy."

ısters' kids *and* his own. Everything is double, reinforced.
vay the kids could get wild or crazy 'cause they would get
ıforcement, if the culture were functioning.

ιo try to revive, to reintroduce all our stuff. And the more we
the more healthy we get as families; the more security there is.
ι protection there is. The more *everything* there is.

. of that is formal. All of that is like a process that we're all supposed
w in order for our society to function and to flow like a river going
ι, wherever it's going, to the ocean.

So that's the second great event in our chronological order, the Clan
System, see?

Chapter 11

Trading Eyes

Erase the blackboard . . . and see if you can understand what a Mohawk sees, feels, is happy about, and is sad about.

In this chapter I'm gonna try to see if I can help non-Natives to feel a part of what it might be to be a Native American person. That's what I will try to do.

In order that we may be most successful in this, there has to be a cooperation with you and me. That means that we have to try to erase the blackboards that each of us have in our mind right now. Maybe I'm a Dutchman, maybe I'm an Australian man, maybe I'm an Italian man or Polish man. Well, just for these few moments, I'm gonna ask you to erase the Polish, erase the Italian, erase the Dutch, and let's try and see if we can be a Mohawk, specifically. Then you can understand what a Mohawk sees, feels, is happy about, and is sad about. That's the way we can best do it. So we have to erase all our institutional trainings, all that everybody has impressed on us, I guess, in order to do this.

Remember I told you at the beginning I am what they call a "pagan" Mohawk. I'm one of those pagan Mohawks. I'm one of the ones, along with Grandma and other elders, that didn't want to get converted, you know, to Catholicism or to Protestantism or to Mormonism or to Jehovah's Witnessism or Islamism or Buddhism or anything. I just wanted to stay the way the God, the Creator, made us in the beginning.

And so I come from the Longhouse. They call us the Longhouse people. That's why I don't know much about others because I was raised in that. We have beautiful ceremonies, very beautiful ceremonies, all year around. We begin in the middle of January. Just our New Year's ceremonies take six, sometimes even seven days for the Mohawks to do it. That begins our spiritual year. And it goes on month after month, many ceremonies. There's hundreds of songs that you have to really study to know how to sing them. And there are a lot of spiritual speeches that go with those songs.

And not only that, but there are dozens and dozens of ways that you gotta make special kinds of food for that special kind of ceremony. So when you add it all up, I mean you gotta be an engineer. You know what I mean? And this is old paganism. I wouldn't take it too lightly; it's hard to be one of those. Easier to go to McDonald's!

Okay now, my grandmother was a Bear Clan woman. And you know Mohawks and all Iroquois nations—we go by a matrilineal system. My father was an Oneida Indian. And my mother is a Mohawk from Akwesasne. And so I'm not an Oneida, I'm a Mohawk 'cause my ma was Mohawk.

Just like my wife is a Choctaw. So all my kids, they're not Mohawks; they're Choctaws because we follow the mother's side. Our clans come from there. Also, in the Iroquois way, it is the women who choose which man will be the leaders of our nation. If that man doesn't do his proper job in representing our nation, it is also those women who depose him and take him out of office. And I mean like that, like I snap my fingers. Mr. Richard Nixon wouldn't have stood a chance if he was an Iroquois. You know what I mean? He got away with murder. He's lucky he wasn't Iroquois.

Now Grandma, my grandma, oh, she was the most wonderful woman in the whole world. My grandmother, her name was Konwanataha. You know what that means in English? Kanata is like a *village* or a *community*. And when you say Konwanataha, it means that she picks up the village or the whole community, and she carries it around. *The Carrier of the Village.* That was her name. She was a Bear Clan woman. She had eleven children. Yeah. And I remember her always wearing an apron.

We had lots of cows, milking cows. We made butter. And we had hogs. And we made blood sausage too. And I've seen my grandmother gut those hogs. And catch that, you know, to make the blood sausage. Tripe, and all that stuff from the cow—hay, turkeys, ducks, chickens. My grandmother had all of that where I grew up, when I was little.

When I was eleven years old was the first time that an electric pole or telephone pole was put on Mohawk land in Akwesasne. I remember that. Before that, people only had kerosene lamps and no fancy things. When we went to the town of Bombay, which was the closest town to us, or to Fort Covington, we would go with a neighbor or my grandfather. Everybody had a team of horses. You hooked on the wagon, and you took your corn to the town. They had a mill there, and they made flour out of it. That's what we used to do.

In the summertime, we hooked up the horses, and then we'd go about six or ten miles south into the foothills of the Adirondacks. And we would eat blackberries and blueberries. When we finished, we'd get back on the team of horses and come home. And they'd can all those berries for the winter. I remember that all in my youth. Grandma was the main leader of all those activities.

Grandma was also what you would call a seer. Do you know what I mean when I say a "seer"? We call it in my language teieia'taréhtha. It means that she makes judgments or she finds out something. If somebody is sick, and you don't know why you're sick, or you have a problem—emotional or spiritual or physical—and you don't know why, well, you would go to my grandma or other people like her. And you'd say, "Grandma, I need help." That's all you gotta say.

And she'll say, "Okay." And then she'll do some things. Then she'll see what's wrong with you—how come this problem started, where it came from, and what it's doing to you. Do you have a pain in here? You don't have to tell Grandma nothing. She'll come to you, and she'll touch you right here, and she'll say, "Oh, I found that's where you're having pain, right there." And then she'll tell you why you got that pain and also what you gotta do to get rid of it. That's what she was, a seer, a healer like.

Oh, she was everything, that Grandma. She could milk cows, doctor people, and she could tell stories. And anytime I needed her, she was always there. She was my best friend, my grandmother.

She passed away about twelve years ago.[1] I thought I would never ever be able to accept that day when I was growing up. I had been told by the elders that we only live here on the earth so long. And when we run out of the marks on the life stick that the Creator gave to us, nobody can avoid it. We have to face it. I was just a little boy, and I used to cry, really cry, just at the thought that someday, Grandma would run out of those marks on her life stick, and she'd have to leave. And then what was I gonna do without Grandma?

So finally I grew up. Nothing ever happened to Grandma. And then finally, when she was eighty-nine years old, she passed. She ran out of marks on her stick. And I cried, about ten minutes, fifteen minutes. And I didn't know how I was gonna go on in this world without her. I even thought, maybe I could go with her. That's how much I thought of my grandma.

But you know, I seen my grandmother laying down with her moccasins on, in her Mohawk skirt and leggings, in her beautiful smock, in her shawl; and her hair was fixed so nice, and as she lay there, she talked to me. And here's what she said to me in my sadness. She said,

> Grandson, tóhsa sa'nikonhraksen ia'tekaié:ri tsi ní:kon wa'konrihónnien tsi náhe í:se ia'satahsónteren ó:nen. Ó:nen ní:'i wa'kerihwaié:rite ne tsi iohontsiá:te ia'satahsónteron.

That means:

> *Grandson, I have done my work and my duty upon the Mother Earth. I raised all my kids and grandchildren. I taught 'em what's right. Everything I prepared for them. And now I finished all my work. Now, I have to go on the road to the Spirit World. So, Grandson, don't be sad. Lift up your eyes, roll up your sleeves. You must take over. Your turn now.*

---

[1] Tom made this speech in 1989.

And I never cried again after that.

Even as she lay dead, she still helped me to continue on. And so everything I'm talking about through this book is largely her words, her teachings, her inspirations and all.

My grandma's uncle was taken to Carlisle Indian School in Pennsylvania. He went there. His English name was Paul Bero. His Mohawk name was Oronhiatá:kon, *the Sky that Bursts*. And later on he received a nickname: Paul Bunyan. He was still living when I was ten. I imagine if he was living today, he'd be about 125, 130 years old.[2] So I had the opportunity to know him.

When he was put in Carlisle Indian School, what they did was they gathered up the Indian kids, and they put 'em on a train. And they took 'em down to Philadelphia, I guess, or Harrisburg, and then on to Carlisle. They put 'em there, all little kids. My grandpa[3] was one of the first ones. And he seen the Sioux over there and Cheyennes and Arapahos and different kinda Indians.

'Course my grandfather couldn't talk to them because he didn't understand Cheyenne. And he didn't understand Lakota or Navajo either. He talked only Mohawk and other Iroquois-kinda languages. And my grandfather said he was sad over there, *sad*. Those little kids, little boys, were crying almost every night.

They wanted to go home to see their mother, their father, their grandma, and their grandpa. They were five hundred miles away. They had to stay there, I don't know how long. So every night you could hear them crying. Sioux Indians wanna go back, Seneca wants to go back, Mohawk wants to go back. But they had to stay there.

He said, "And then they brought us into a room. And one man, he used the clippers. And he went like this."

---

[2].   As noted earlier, Tom made this speech in 1989.

[3].   As Tom explained in the section on the Traditional Family Structure of the Iroquois Nations, he follows the Iroquois convention of referring to any relative in his grandparents' generation or older as a grandpa.

And he cut off their hair, the Cheyenne and Lakota and Seneca and Mohawk too.

"And" he said, "black hair was piled up just like the old-time hay." You know, before there was rakes and stuff, you piled up the hay with pitchforks, and you put it on a wagon. He said it was human hair, Lakota hair, all piled there.

They put some kind of a grayish black or some kind of grayish-colored uniforms on all of them. And some of them, they tried to go home. They got so lonesome; some of them got sick. And they knew they got there by a train, so they tried to run away by following the tracks. They tried to go back to South Dakota or Montana or back to up where I live by following them. And they found them froze to death on the side of the tracks. They never made it; they were only six years old, seven years old.

My grandpa Paul Bero ran away too. He could only take so much, I guess. And you know, he musta been six, seven, or maybe eight at the very most when he ran away. In those days, there was no Interstate 81. There wasn't any of that. It was almost all just little old dirt roads. And there was lots of woods around yet, in those days.

Do you know that my grandpa, Paul Bero, went through the woods all the way through the Adirondack Mountains in the wintertime? And he was between six and eight years old. He made it five hundred miles through the woods and through the mountains *all* the way back to Akwesasne. It was a miracle. Not a scratch on him. And he didn't have no compass, nothin'. He just went by the stars and the sun, and he got home.

Later on, when he grew up a little bit, they used to take him to Saranac Lake and the Lake Placid area. They used to cut trees down there. So they'd take the Indians over there to work on that. And these Saranac Lake people would put a bag on his head. They would take him into the middle of the woods, somewhere in the Saranac Lake, Tupper Lake area. They'd put him in there, and then they'd tell him to take the bag off and make it back to their camp without seeing how he got there. And he'd take the bag off, and in just a little while, he'd be back in camp. That grandfather of mine, you couldn't get him lost for nothin'! And that's where he got the nickname of Paul Bunyan. That was my grandma's uncle.

Now that was way back in Carlisle days, okay? You might think, "Oh that's over. That's not gonna happen no more." Well, it did end. They didn't send them to Carlisle any more. But pretty soon they built government schools on the reservation instead of going there.

My grandpa told the story about what happened to him. And my other grandpas told the story of what happened to them. And it wasn't always very pleasant.

So my grandmother, she didn't want to go to school. And she didn't want her kids to go to school either. But they did. And so when I was born, my grandmother didn't send me to school. She couldn't talk English, you know. And I'm talking Mohawk all the time—me and Grandma.

In the middle of our reservation, there's a school called the St. Regis Mohawk School. It's a government school for the Indians. And don't be mistaken, they call it St. Regis Mohawk Indian School, but there was nothing Mohawk about that school. There was absolutely nothing Indian about that school except the fact that it was full of Mohawk kids.

So when I was about six years old, seven years old, no more Carlisle School. But finally there was this knocking on my grandmother's door during the summer months. I remember distinctly. And into the house comes this Mohawk woman who works for the government of the United States—in New York City, I guess. And she talks Mohawk to my grandma. She says, "I think that according to the records, you have a grandson that's such-and-such an age, and he's not in school. Why isn't he in school? And where is he?" Talking about me.

And my grandmother said, "Well, yes, I have a grandson. But I didn't send him to school because I don't think the school is good for him."

And so this lady from the government said to my grandmother, "Well, there's a law in New York State that every child, upon reaching the age of five or six, *has* to go to school. And if you don't send your grandson to the school, we will take you and your daughter to Franklin County Family Court where we will proclaim you unfit parents. And then we will take your grandson to the school or another boarding school somewhere," she said. (In Niagara Falls, or Lockport, New York, or wherever.)

So that lady said, "September, I want your grandson to be in the school in Hogansburg, St. Regis Mohawk School." Then she left.

And I seen my grandmother, and she was sad. 'Member I said that my grandmother used to smoke a pipe? Whenever she's got trouble, she puts sacred tobacco in that pipe. And she sits on that rocking chair and smokes that sacred smoke up. And she's really praying on that rocking chair so fast. So that's what she did.

Afterwards, I went to see my grandmother. And she said, "Did you hear what that woman said?"

I said,
> Yes. Onkwathón:te'ne.

That means:
> *Yeah, I did hear.*

I said,
> Grandma, aesathontá:ton ken aionkwateweienstá:non? Í:iah ni'té: kehre aesahnhó:ton tekanatá:ronhwe.

I said:
> *Grandma, can I go to school? Because I don't want the white people to put you in their jail in Malone, New York. You can't talk English. How you gonna talk to them? And because of me, you can go to jail.*

She said,
> You're gonna lose your Mohawk language. You're gonna lose the way you think as a Mohawk, if you go there. You will think like America people does.

I said,
> Grandma, I'll make you a promise. I don't care how many years they put me in the school. I'll never lose how to talk to you, our language. And when I finish that school, Grandma, however long it takes, I'll help you to hoe your garden, your corn, and your potatoes, the

beans in there. And I'll come back, and I'll help milk those cows.
No way they're gonna change my mind. Okay, Grandma?

And she didn't answer, just tears came down.

Come September, she still didn't answer. That woman came again in
September. And they took us in the car to the Mohawk School. They put
us in the kindergarten, about thirty or thirty-five Mohawk kids. And in my
estimate at that time, 75 percent of those kids didn't know how to speak
English. We only had Mohawk, huh?

So this lady comes in there, the one that works for the government, and
she says in our language, in Mohawk,

> You are here in this school today, all you kids, and you have to learn
> how to read and how to write, like the white people do. If you don't,
> you're gonna have a hard time in life. So you must try hard to read
> and to write. You must listen to these teachers here.

And she said,

> If you do a good job and you learn everything, you won't have to dig
> ditches. And you won't have to work with the white farmers around
> the reservation, like your grandpa does—you know, shoveling
> manure and cutting the corn for them. You won't have to. If you
> study hard and you graduate, you'll sit behind the white people's
> desk and you'll push a pen on a paper. And you're gonna wear a
> white shirt with a tie around the neck.

> And also when you get up from the desk from pushing the pen, to
> go get tea or coffee, every time you stand up, you're gonna hear
> the jingling of money in your pocket. You'll have so much money
> in there if you study hard. Now good luck to you. Good luck.

She's talking all Mohawk, huh?

She said,

> Oh, I forgot one more thing. The rule here is nobody is
> allowed to speak Mohawk in this school so that you can learn
> English better.

And there were big windows in the room.

> You see swings and the teeter-totter and the merry-go-round out there, those things? If you work hard, you get a recess, time to play. And even when you're playing on the swings out there, don't talk Mohawk, because the school doesn't like that.

And she left.

In the door, before she left, was a woman. And this woman, we learned so many things from her. She was a music teacher, an art teacher, everything. A one-woman show. And she had a longer neck than Mohawks. We'd never seen a woman have a long neck before. She was almost like a giraffe to us! And we were surprised. And so she was introduced to us, "That's your teacher."

Okay, now that Indian lady goes out and this teacher is standing up there. And she's talking, and talking to us. But 70 percent of us don't know what she's saying because we don't know how to talk English yet. We're only guessing. And we're scared. Grandma didn't like schools, and here I am. My heart is going like this, about ninety miles an hour. We didn't know what was gonna come next.

You know how kids are, they can't sit still too long—even Mohawks. So finally after about ten or fifteen minutes, I said something in Mohawk to my cousin who was sitting right in the next row to me. And that teacher started knocking on her desk really fast like this—impatiently. Everybody got quiet. As soon as she hit that desk like that, we all got scared.

I was talking to my cousin, and she saw me, and she caught me. So she says, "Come over here. C'mon over *here*."

And I could understand just a little bit of English, plus my grandmother does the same thing too—signals to me—when she wants me! So I went up there. And I didn't know what she was gonna do to me. My heart was really going fast.

She took my hand, and she opened it. And she used that big oak ruler with the iron in there and went like this—whacked me. I mean *really* hard.

And it stung, like bees stinging all over. And when she hit me . . . See, my grandmother never hit me. My Grandmother, in all my memories, never laid a hand on me. It's not the belief of our people. But here was a United States white woman. She's the first one who ever hit me.

And when that stinging sensation was going through my hand, I immediately got black in my eyes and in my ears. Like when you get mad or something, you know, angry. Everything got black. And all I could say was, "Sometime, I'm gonna get you back."

At that instant of time, I wanted revenge. Teacher, I'm gonna get you some way, somehow, pretty soon. I hated her. And what my Grandpa Bero said about Carlisle, what happened to him, what Grandma said was all confirmed when that woman hit my hand with that ruler.

I'm gonna skip that now. There are other experiences there to tell you about.

When we went to another teacher's room, that's the first time that I had seen a piano. No Mohawks had pianos, you know. If they did, it was rare in those days, huh?

We have in our Mohawk culture what we call a water drum. We put water in there. And you play it. And we have hundreds of songs: Deer Dance, Raccoon Dance, Fish Dance, Duck Dance—you name it—Women's Dance, Stomp Dance with rattles. Oh, beautiful things. A social can go on for hours and hours, even days, without repeating the same song. That's how many songs we've got, yet today.

So this teacher is in there. And I'm being very blunt with you; we thought she was a witch. You know why? You know that old kinda chair? She went like this—turned the seat on the chair and it went up.[4] The Mohawks were just looking at that. That's a mighty powerful woman, you know!

It wasn't 'til later we figured it out; there's a screw in there. 'Cause Mohawks don't have that kinda chair, you know. So we kind of listened to her 'cause

---

4. Tom is talking about wooden stools or chairs whose seats can be raised by spinning them.

we thought she was doing witchcraft or something. And that's our first remembrance of her singing.

She sat there and she says, "Children, we're gonna sing our songs today."

And we're all Mohawks, okay? And we only know Deer Dance, Round Dance, Rabbit Dance with drums.

And she sat there, and she says, "Okay, children, when I say three, we're all gonna sing." And she started hitting the piano, and then she says, "One, two, three. Yankee Doodle went to town . . ."

We finished "Yankee Doodle went to town," and then we went across the London Bridge. Or the London Bridge fell down, or something happened to the bridge. And then after that song, we went around the rose bush, or some kind of a bush. I can't really remember—blackberry bush or, I don't know, some kind of a bush, and we go around it and sing. But the point I'm getting at is none of those were Mohawk songs. None of them.

In the art department, as pagan Mohawks, Longhouse Mohawks, we don't have Christmas trees on the twenty-fifth of December. You know what I mean? But in the school, they cut down the tree, and they put the tree right in the house. And they put lights on there. And you know Mohawks and Senecas believe you never waste food. You never throw food—apple or popcorn, anything. But you know what they did in there? They took popcorn, and they put it on a string, and they played with it, and then they put it on the tree.

That's sacrilegious to us. You're not supposed to fool with food like that.

After that comes Valentine's Day. And she gave us a beautiful . . . And we love red. I mean, Mohawks love red-colored, bright colors, you know. And she gave us these nice papers, and we folded them, and then she drew on them. We had to cut with the scissors, a heart, on Valentine's Day. And she says we have to send it to every teacher in the whole school. And on the board it says, "My dear teacher, I'm thinking about you on Valentine's Day, and I love you."

No Mohawk loves their teacher! But we had to write that on there, and we had to send it.

Okay, I'm gonna skip all those years, now. My father was an iron worker and . . . did you ever hear the word "squaw"? Don't take offence at this, but squaw is a Mohawk word.[5] And it means *the reproductive organ of a woman*.

My father was an iron worker, and so he took us away from the reservation, to a city. At that time, I could speak English, but not the greatest. Sometimes, I'd get my verb and noun in the wrong place, but you know, I could basically communicate. And when I did talk English, a lot of times I would try to translate Mohawk to English, see? And a lot of times it would be backwards. So it didn't sound right. But I didn't realize that it wasn't right.

And so my father took us to that city and that's where he left us. He left my mother with five kids. My youngest brother wasn't even born yet. A Greek woman from across the ocean took him. And so we had to go to school. We had no money to go back home to our reservation. We got stuck in the city there and went to school.

I was the only Mohawk there, and I didn't talk like the other kids talked. And because of the way I talked, they were pulling my hair; they would pull my ears, or they would shove me anytime they would see me. And of course, nobody shoves me too much 'cause I'm gonna shove back. So as a consequence of that, I was always at the principal's office, getting scolded. And finally, I was on my last warning from the principal, my *last* warning.

And in those days in that city, in the playground there were big cinders, like from burning something. I don't know why they were in there. But it hurt if you fell on them. And no matter what happened, I'd get the blame from the principal.

That principal was chubby like a barrel. He seemed tall to me then, but he was probably only about 5'4" or 5'6". And he had a white shirt on all the time. And a tie. And his skin came over that. You could see the blood in there, you know, it would change colors—red to white. He was a fierce-looking guy. So I didn't wanna go there anymore. His office was on the second floor of the school.

[5.]   The full Mohawk word is otsi*skwa*.

Now these guys, these kids, fellow students, they'd seen my mother. And my mother was outside on the porch. And she had long black hair. And in the back of her hair there are two parakeets that we had. Somebody gave them to us. And every morning, early in the morning, when she makes breakfast for us, those parakeets open the gate of their cage. And they go in the back of my mother's black hair, long hair. And it's warm back there. They don't fly anywhere else until it warms up.

And when those kids all went to school, they'd seen my mother. And they said, "Lookit that squaw."

That made me mad, a little bit. I didn't even know if I should call my mother a squaw too since if I have to believe the way they do, then I would call my mother a squaw. And I said, "Yeah, my mother's a squaw." 'Cause I don't want trouble, see?

But then I knew it was wrong.

So on the way to school, we had a fight, because of my mother. And this time, about six guys grabbed me. They tore up my clothes. They dragged me in those cinders. And I really fought back hard, as hard as I could fight. The teachers come running out and broke us up. And you know who went to the office?

Not the six guys. Me.

I went up to that big man, that principal's office. And I stood there. His desk was in such a way that the door was over there and I was farthest from the door. He had a stack of books on his desk. Principals are so busy; they got lots of things on their desk. And this principal . . . you know in those barber shops they had those big old-fashioned leather straps that they sharpened razor blades with? He had one of them in there.

And he took that strap. He says, "I've had enough of you. You don't ever learn. You don't ever listen." And he took that strap, and he raised it up, and he smashed it with all his might—on the books that were piled on his desk. He didn't hit me, he hit the books—I guess to show me that I'm next. That's what I thought anyway.

And when he hit the books, they all fell down on the floor. But I couldn't get out 'cause the door was over there where he was standing. So the only way I could go, 'cause I know I'm next after the books, I'm gonna get that strap, that big thing. I got on top of the chair with all the power and the courage I had to defend myself. Then I stepped up on top of his desk while he was picking the books up off the floor.

As he stood up, I jumped like a tiger. I grabbed on his ears, and I bit his nose, and I scratched his face. And as I came down, I kicked him right between his legs as hard as I could kick.

And that man turned white. He didn't know what hit him.

And my heart was just going . . . I mean, I was dying, I was so afraid. But I knew I had to do it if I was gonna get out of there. And as soon as he went backwards, the door was free. So I ran out that door. And he went running after me. A whole bunch of teachers went running after me.

But I was faster than they were. And I went down to the first floor and down to the next floor, and I went into the cellar.

In those days, they had those big furnaces with really big pipes wrapped with asbestos. I climbed up there in between the ceiling and the big pipes. And I kept still. My breathing was so hard. And as I lay there on my belly, I could hear my heart hitting that pipe, and it sounded like a very loud noise to me.

And when that principal and all those teachers came in the dark, dark ol' cellar, they were looking for me. "Where's that Indian? Where'd that Indian go?" They're looking all over the coal. They were burning coal in those days. And they said, "That Indian is crazy."

I was listening to every word as I was lying on that pipe. And at one point, as I'm lying up there, I almost died from fright. I almost had a heart attack, I guess. And I stopped my breathing so they couldn't hear me. And at one point, that principal came right under where I was. And I started to think about whether I could jump on him. But I couldn't because there were six or seven teachers that were looking for me there too, and I wouldn't have a chance. So I didn't jump him again. I just kept still.

And pretty soon they said, "The window is open. He must be gone." And they all left.

I didn't leave that building until dark. Way after school hours. And I went out that same window that was open, and I went home. All my clothes were torn up. And my knees and my legs and my hands were all scratched from being dragged through the cinders of the schoolyard. I cried to my mother. And I said, "Ma, let's go home. Let's go back to Grandma's house, back to the reservation. These people are mean."

She says, "We don't have no money. We got nothin'. How we gonna get home? It's about 250 miles away from here."

I didn't go back to school. I didn't wanna go back. Then, my mother received a notice from them. And you know what they told her? They wanted her to sign something to put me in a special children's psychiatric hospital, because they thought I was crazy.

The next two days, my mother and all my brothers and sisters packed everything. And you know, we went back to Grandma's, at Akwesasne, so fast. And I continued school again at the reservation. And we only had to deal with that Yankee-Doodle-went-to-town teacher. And that was a great consolation to me.

I don't want to dwell too much on this part 'cause a lot of these things happened to me in school.

Now I'm gonna go to about 1956-57, when they centralized schools. That was the first time I had to go to school with the white people again. That was something I didn't want to do because I already had an experience with it. But I had to; it was the law.

In all the years that I went to school, I never made the honor roll. I always had red marks. And you know, I hardly ever went to school because every time I didn't wanna go, my grandmother, she would back me up. And my mother, too. They'd write a note, anything I wanted: stomach ache, earache, measles, broke my leg. They always backed me up. As a result, I never went to high school, but you know, I felt good about it.

So now finally I had to go to the centralization school. There's only five Mohawks and about twenty-five Frenchmen, Englishmen, and Irishmen in the class, huh? All the Mohawks, we wanna sit in the back of the class, altogether. We're afraid too.

And then finally the teacher says, "You can't . . . the Indians can't just sit by themselves. You've got to disperse among the other students."

So they seated us by alphabetical order. But when she turned to write on the blackboard, all Mohawks, back to the back of the room again. It took two weeks before we became accustomed to sitting around the room among the white people, not the Indians, 'cause of what happened to us.

In that room, there was a teacher I'm gonna call Mrs. Johnson. This woman, Mrs. Johnson, used to put red, red lipstick on. And she used to put on lots of powder and perfume. When she came close to you, you'd get a headache. That's what she was like.

She passed out these textbooks—and I never was a student, never, I was always failing. So she passed out this textbook. Every student got one. And she said, "Now this is the book that we're going to read this year. So I want you to go through it, look at the pictures, the titles, and the chapters. You know, familiarize yourself with it."

And so we did. The white people, they all listened, and you could hear the pages turning while we looked at them. I got in the middle of the book, right in the middle. I looked at that, and all of a sudden I said, "Holy cow, that's Grandpa's picture." My grandfather's picture was in there. He had long braids on, wrapped up with mink's fur with an eagle feather sticking out of his hair. And he had a beautiful shirt, that was tailor-made. That was Grandpa.

And I said, "What in the world is he doing in here? In this school I hate so much."

And millions of thoughts went through my head of things that happened since I started school. Up 'til now I rebelled at school all the time, "But yet Grandpa is in here. I must be going nuts. How can I dislike this school so much and yet Grandpa is a part of it, by being in this book?"

And then I thought, "Well, the day is coming when those Irish people, those Frenchmen and those Polish people, and those English people, students, they're gonna have to come to that part of the book, some time this year. And I'm gonna be so proud about my grandma and about my grandpa. For the first time, those white people are gonna listen about my great history, about Grandpa's greatness and truth."

And you know, that's the first year I didn't skip school. I was never even late enough to miss the bus. You know why? Because I thought if I just missed school one day, that teacher might trick me, and she'll read about Grandpa when I'm not there. And I ain't gonna have that. So I went to school every day. And then you know what happened? When the report cards came out, for the first time in my life, Tom Porter, a Mohawk Indian, made the honor roll. For the first time in my life.

And the teachers saw that. And they said, "Tom, how did you get on the honor roll?"

I said, "Nothing to it. I just came to school every day, and I was listening to what the teachers were saying."

September passed. October passed. And now comes December. And we're getting close now, finally getting close. Oh, I was so proud. You know how a rooster chases a hen, how they dance around with their feathers spread out like that? They're real proud. Well, in a way I felt like that, because that picture was coming. That part of the book was coming. And the blood went through my whole body. And I got cold chills on myself, and I felt *wonderful* that now Grandpa's story was gonna be told.

And so there I sat. We concluded the previous chapter. Everybody turned that page at the very same time. And there was Grandpa's picture. What a wonderful feeling. I can't describe to you how wonderful that feeling was. There was nothing wrong anywhere in the world. I mean the world was *perfect*.

And Mrs. Johnson says, "Students, we don't have that much time left in the school year, so I'm gonna ask that we skip over this chapter on the Indian people because we have much more important things to cover."

And I heard that, and I thought, "Gee, she can't mean that." I couldn't believe it. So finally, I wanted to make sure what I thought I heard her say. So I raised my hand. I says, "Mrs. Johnson, what did you say?"

And she says, "Skip over on the American Indian because that isn't as important a subject. We got lots of very important, vital subjects we have to cover between now and June."

I didn't wanna understand what she said. But I understood. And I said, "Teacher, what about my grandfather?"

She came over next to me, and this is what she said, "The sooner you Mohawk Indians realize that education is the only remedy to heal your ills and the sooner you Mohawk Indians realize that that Indian stuff is like water over the dam, and you must get yourself educated, the less you will be on the welfare rolls, and the less problems you will have with alcoholism amongst you. That's water over the dam." And that's what she said right next to my face.

By that time, it had completely soaked in, what she meant. And I took the book, and I just pushed it, and it fell on the floor. And right away, tears came down. I mean, like rain. I got so angry and so hopeless that everything got black. I couldn't even hear anybody, I was so disappointed. And as the tears come down, I put my head on the desk. I didn't want those Irishmen, those Englishmen, to see me crying. I hid my tears.

That teacher broke my heart. And she broke my spirit that day.

For fifteen minutes, I just gave up hope. Is this what it's about? And I don't know how long I cried. But finally the tears went away. And my hearing came back. And I sat up. My book was still on the floor. You know what they were talking about? As they were going through the aisles, they were having a review. And this is what I heard, that George Washington was born in such and such a time. And George Washington is the "Father of Our Country." And George Washington is the very first president of the United States of America. And he also used a rowboat, and he crossed the chunky ice of the Delaware River to fight for our freedom.

They finished with him, and I remember them talking about Abraham Lincoln who was dirt-poor. He never had shoes or stockings. He lived in a little log cabin somewheres in Illinois or somewhere up there. And he walked one mile to a little red schoolhouse in the ice and snow barefooted. And even though he was dirt-poor, he became the president of the United States. And he freed the black people from slavery.

And just then, as I was listening to this, all of a sudden—I kid you not—something came through the top of the big windows of that room, like a lightning, like a bluish light. It came from that window, from the outside. And it came, and it hit me on my head. And when it hit my head, it shook my whole body. And I got cold chills all over my back, and my hair just wanted to stand up. It came from that light, from the sky. And it made me feel *wonderful*. It made me feel *perfect* again. And you know what I did? I felt so good and so sure and so competent that I didn't raise my hand. I stood up, right in front of my desk.

And I said, "Mrs. Johnson," with 100 percent confidence.

She says, "You don't have permission. You sit down."

I says, "Mrs. Johnson."

"I told you to sit down. You have no permission to stand up and to talk, disrupt this class."

I says, "Mrs. Johnson. I'm not gonna sit down. And if you think you're strong enough, let me see you come here and make this Mohawk sit on that chair. I guarantee you can't do it. Mrs. Johnson, I want you to answer me a question."

"I said sit down."

I says, "No, you answer first, what I gotta ask you."

And she started to get nervous. And another Mohawk was sitting by me. He said,
    Ha'o shehrón:ri. Ha'o shehrón:ri.

That means *Cut her off, cut her off.* He's whispering. And it made me feel good.

And I said, "Mrs. Johnson, I want you to answer me now. I wanna know, George Washington and Abraham Lincoln, were they born yesterday, or last week? Or are they water over the dam too. I wanna know."

"You shut your little mouth, you Indian. And you march yourself right down to the office." And she shook, started to shake like an earthquake. And she started to cry, like a rainstorm.

And I says, "What the matter, Mrs. Johnson? Was George Washington born yesterday? Or is he water over the dam, like my grandpa?"

And she got mad. "Get to the office."

And I smiled, with the most confidence in the world. And I felt like that young rooster chasing the hen. And I walked to the front of that classroom, past her, and I said, "Mrs. Johnson, I'm going to see the president of the United States, your principal. And nobody gonna stop me."

And as I walked, I remembered the stories of my grandmother and my grandfather and the old Chiefs who talked about the cavalry coming after the Indian. I remembered that.

And I says, "I betcha somebody's gonna try to stop me from going to the principal's office 'cause I got a thing to say to him too."

And as I went out through that classroom door, the floors were shiny, and the iron lockers went down each side, far as you can see. And I imagined the United States Army coming down there to stop me from going to the principal. And I said, "Let 'em come, I'm ready, and I'm gonna hit them, and they're gonna go like a haystack. Everyone's hay is gonna fly all over. That's what I'll do to that army if they stop me."

And I went to the principal's office.

The principal—I'm gonna call him Mr. Stanley—said, "What can I do for you?"

And you know what I said to him? I said, "There isn't *nothing*, Mr. Stanley, you can do for me. You see over there that door, where it says Exit?" I says. "Soon as I get of the right age, I'm leaving here. And I'll never come back to a United States school again for the rest of my life." I said, "And if God, the Creator, gives me the good blessing to have children one day, over my dead body will I bring my children into a United States schoolhouse."

And he looks at me with big eyes. "What in the world possesses you to say such a thing?"

I says, "Mr. Stanley, let's start at the beginning. In the kindergarten, they give us the stick when we couldn't speak your language. You know what that means? The Mohawk is no good, and English is. You know what it means when they play 'Yankee Doodle Went to Town'? It means water drum, Rabbit Dance, Fish Dance is no good. Yankee Doodle Went to Town is the best. All through these years, you told me I was no good. Your teachers, your school, everybody told me I was no good. Every day since I was in kindergarten, you made me feel like I was a *nothing*, a nobody. And you wanted me to be ashamed of my own people. And I had enough, Mr. Stanley. I had enough. That's why you're not gonna do that to my kids."

And I left. I never even went to high school. Yet when I was a little boy, I had this dream that I wanted to be a doctor, a Western medical doctor. And I would mix it with my grandmother's medicine knowledge. What dynamite. Oh, then I thought, "No, I'm gonna be a lawyer. And I will fight for my people's rights that have been trampled on through these centuries because we couldn't speak English. I will be a lawyer." I had those dreams. But the teachers never gave me a chance. That's why I never went to high school.

Anyway, I quit. I quit all that, and I received my liberation. My dreams were never answered, but I had other dreams that came in their place.

Now I'm asking you to imagine what it's like in modern, contemporary times. What I'm talking about wasn't that long ago—just a little while. I'm not that old. But that's what happened to me.

You know we have ceremonies? And in these ceremonies we have songs for the garden, like the corn, so it'll grow good. We've got ceremonies for the beans so they will grow good. We have ceremonies for the thunder so the rain will come. We have Sun Dance Ceremony for the sun so there will always be sun, so we'll live. That's what we do. And so my grandmother said, "The key to success for anybody's life, be it human, animal, or bird, is this. If you wanna have health and good life, you must make that person, that little thing, feel important and wanted. And they will grow, and they will have health, and they will have success."

That, my brothers of the human race, was denied my people and many nations on this continent over the last generations. And since that time, I have a wife and children. And all my children are big now. And I never sent them to that school. Just as I said I wouldn't do. We started our own Akwesasne Freedom School. Our very own. And it's all Mohawk immersion—science, mathematics, everything. The last year goes to seventh grade. And after the seventh grade, then they go to the white man's school. So the last year they teach everything in English, so that there will be a transition to the white man's school.

And my kids all went to that. And the year before last[6] my daughter went to school in the white man's school for the first time, and she was on the honor roll. My son almost made the honor roll, missed it by a couple of points, last year. This year, all my kids will make the honor roll, I'm pretty sure. You see, all we need is to be listened to, respected for what we are, and to have the same opportunity to feel good about ourselves.

The stories I have just been telling you are mine. I'm only one Indian in North America. If you were me, and those things happened to you, maybe you'd drink too. Or maybe you'd shoot yourself in the head. Imagine if the Chinese or the Russians came here. And they said to us, "From now on, all of you here, in the next minute, I want you talking Chinese. And if you don't, I'll bust you right over the head." And then year after year, they told us that we were no good, maybe all of us would be failures too, like the American Indian.

But you know, I don't want to be negative either, you know what I mean? Please don't get me wrong. I just want to share with you that story of

---

6.   As noted earlier, Tom made this speech in 1989.

my life. It's the story of so many Indians' lives, as well as other races of people who have come here. And we can learn from those kinds of things for tomorrow. So that doesn't happen again. And we will get better. Scars will heal. You know, they'll heal, and we go on.

You see we have to laugh at ourselves. And whenever something traumatic or sad happens, we have to find something to laugh at. That's what will get us through. And the Indian people, we are professionals at making jokes about our own selves, at how crazy we are. It keeps us going.

So you know I have to recall this one. In the sixth grade, there was a teacher that came from the Midwest, the Chicago area or somewheres. This teacher, she looked like a doll. She was something else. She had red hair—I mean *red*, red hair—and it was long, almost to the middle of her back. And it had curls, ringlets in it. And I mean she was really built like a doll.

She was a very nice woman.

You know what she did? We were reading prose and poetry. She was an English teacher, so she was reading to us prose and poetry from a book. And this book, it talked about how the squaws were washing clothes by hitting them on stones—in a creek.

Squaws.

When she said "squaws" every Mohawk in that school got embarrassed. We didn't know what to do because she was good to us. You could tell that she felt with us. The feeling was there.

That night, it just happened that my grandmother said, "What did yous learn about today?"

And I didn't think about it. I said, "Oh, never mind, I'm not gonna tell you."

I said the wrong thing.

Grandma said, "What did yous learn about? How come you don't wanna tell?"

I says, "Never mind, it's not important."

"Oh no, I wanna know what was that English. I'm interested now."

And I put my foot in my mouth I guess. Well, I told my grandmother, "Grandma, I shouldn't tell you this."

She says, "You can tell me everything. It's okay."

And I didn't wanna tell her. But finally I said, "Well, the teacher was talking about squaws."

My grandma, she got mad. And she says, "Tomorrow, when you go to school, you tell that teacher she must quit, she must cease to talk about squaw. 'Cause if she don't, I'm going to school, and I'm gonna grab her by her squaw, and I'm gonna drag her all over the floor."

So I was worried!

This was the first good teacher we had. And so I went to school the next day, and I told my cousin, I says, "We got trouble."

He said, "What happened?"

I says, "Our grandmother, she knows what that teacher was talking about yesterday." And I told my cousin exactly what's gonna happen if she don't quit. "So we have to tell that teacher to quit saying that word. We're not to talk about it in class anymore 'cause it's not good."

But my cousin and I, we didn't know how to speak English. I mean we know how to speak English, but nobody ever taught us how to say "squaw" in English. We didn't know that. And so we didn't know how we were gonna tell her. So what we did is we took a piece of paper, my cousins and the rest of us. We all worked together, and we drew a picture of "squaw"—what we considered what is that. You know what I mean? We tried.

And we folded that paper up, real small. I mean you couldn't get it any smaller. No letters, just the picture. And when she went out in the hall, we put that little tiny piece of paper on her desk. But she sat in the back, and we faced the other way. So we couldn't see her. And so every Mohawk in that class in the sixth grade was completely motionless, no sound anywhere.

All of a sudden, she comes in the door. And everybody's completely quiet, girls and boys. Then we begin to hear this paper moving, unraveling. Took a long time.

And then there was no response, nothing. And we're trying to look from here to see what's going on, you know? Finally this teacher—her name was Mrs. Garvey, from the Midwest, with the beautiful red ringlet hair—she came up to the front of the classroom, and she looked at us.

Her face was redder than her hair. And she had red, red eyes. Tears were coming down her face. And this is what she said to us. She said, "My dear Mohawk students, I love you. I had no idea that I was offending you or hurting you." She says, "How many times American teachers must have really hurt you. I feel so sorry for you, my dear Mohawks. I had no intent to hurt you. And I will never say this word 'squaw' again, as long as I live."

She cried her head off. And we understood.

That was the first teacher we had that ever acknowledged us as human beings. That's one teacher that I want you also to know. She was wonderful.

Chapter 12

Funerals and Contradictions

There's a contradiction because the daughter in the Creation story died, and they made a mound. It's very explicit. But here, it says they didn't know about death.

There are some contradictions in some of these chapters. When I was younger, it bothered me; but as I got older, I realized that probably something happened a long time ago. Something got mixed up or whatever. And they did the best they could, so I should be satisfied with that.

In the Creation story, the way I was telling it and even in versions from other sources with variations, there's a statement about life and death. But when you listen to the funerals, the wakes when people die, there are special ceremonial words they use there, that differ from the Creation story, that are contrary to it. And I'm not sure where those words come from, where they fit or anything.

In those speeches, when people die, they say that it was the Creator (not the two boys) who picked up the dirt, and he made the doll or the human being. And he used his own self as his pattern. And they say, "Then what he did is he blew in its mouth three times"—the same as in the Creation story—"and it began to move." And it was a man, that he made.

So he put the man down, and the man walked around. The Creator watched his movements and what he did. After observing him for a while, the Creator said that it was not sufficient that the man should walk by himself. So he took more dirt, and he made a woman this time. And he blew in her mouth three times. And she came alive.

And he put the woman next to the man, side by side. And he said, "Now, you will have love for each other and you will work together with each other. You will be partners. And you will be man and wife, together. And through your togetherness, you will be reproducing humans like yourselves—little babies will be born. And the world will be filled with people because of this."

And so that's how it began. That's what they say in those speeches.

And so after a while, there were many people in the villages. They even had to make other villages 'cause they got too big. And then make other villages. And that's why there are different Indians all over the place. And this was when the world was new. And so in the first years this was happening, nobody knew about death. They had never experienced it before. It says in those speeches that they lived forever. They didn't know about death.

Well, there's a contradiction because the woman, the daughter in the Creation story, died, and they made a mound. It's very explicit there too. But here it says they didn't know about death. I don't know if these funeral speeches are influenced by Christian thinking. Maybe they were. I tend to think so because it says that man was made in the image of God, and that's a direct quote from the Christians. So they may have borrowed that and inserted it in there, or whatever, I'm not sure.

It used to bother me because I'm a purist, a perfectionist. I don't want to mix my stuff up. But because I've been called to do funerals, even though it bothered me, I said it the way I heard them say it. I put my dissent aside and did it, just so that they could get buried! And so over the years, I've become quite comfortable with it. But I'm not afraid to note that in my book, it still doesn't fit. I say it simply because they all say it, and nobody questions it anymore.

They had no death—this is what they say when there's a funeral—they didn't know about death *at all.* They'd never seen it. Then all of a sudden one man died. But they didn't know he died because they didn't know what death was. He fell down, it says, on the ground. And they didn't know what happened to him, so they went over there. And they noticed he wasn't breathing, or anything. His body just fell down.

So they tried to sit him up. And he fell back down. They tried to grab him by both arms and stand him up on his feet. They shook him to try to wake him up. And he wouldn't. And when they let him go, he just fell down again. That was the first time they had to deal with that, they said. And they didn't know what to do. Finally, somebody came up with the idea, "Well, maybe we'll just leave him alone and he'll wake up later, tonight, or tomorrow or whatever, on his own."

They waited for awhile, and he didn't, so they said, "Okay, we're gonna build a scaffold over there. We'll put poles across like a platform. And we'll put his body on top. That way, during the night if he wakes up, well, he can get down. Or if he wakes up tomorrow, he can get down, you see. 'Cause we've been waiting, and he doesn't wake up."

So they did. They put him on there, and he didn't get up that next day, nor the next day, nor the next day. So they just left him up there. 'Cause they didn't know what else to do. So, geez, after a few weeks, they went over there and they looked. And there was nothing left of him, except bones. And what had happened is the birds and the different animals had been eating his bare flesh 'til just the bones were left.

That was the first time.

They felt bad about it, but they couldn't do anything else. So after a while, they got over that. And after not too long again, another man fell down. The same thing, second one. And still they didn't know what the heck that was. They tried to revive him and stand him up, to no avail. He fell down again too.

And so they built another scaffold, and they put his body up there too. Again, with the same thinking that he might get up, eventually, and if he did, well he could come back to the village. But they got tired of waiting for him too, to wake up and breathe. So that was their first experience of what we call death, but they didn't know it was *that*.

Finally, after a while they got over that too 'cause there were just bones left of that second one's body. Birds and other creatures ate it all up.

The third one was a little girl. This little girl was just a tiny little thing, and she was like the sweetheart of the village. She was a beautiful and very friendly little girl, so the whole village knew her. And all of a sudden *she* had collapsed.

So this time, it impacted the people more than those guys 'cause they were already grown-up, and they had lived a long time. This little girl, with her bounciness and her freshness, she was so tiny, so little. That one really hurt them. They were in great grief over it. And they were also alarmed 'cause this little girl had passed away just like those two men.

And they dreaded putting her on a scaffold—only the bones would be left. And so they said, "There's one man that lives in our village. And when somebody needs something, we always go see him. He has the ability to see tomorrow and the future. So let's go consult with him. Perhaps he may be able to help us and find out what's going on here with these people."

So they went to see him. And he said, "Let me look into it and see. But I don't know. That's such a big thing that I don't know if I *could* find out. I don't have that kind of access to power, or knowledge. But I can *ask*."

That night, when the seer went to bed, he said to the Creator, "The people have asked me a big question about these people that collapse and can't get up. And the birds eat them all up. And now this little girl did that same thing, and we don't want that to happen to her. And we all like that little girl, and we will miss her so much. Why did this happen? The people want to know 'cause they've never seen it before." So that was the nature of his prayer.

And during the night, as he lay in his bed, a man's voice spoke to him. And it was the Creator entering his dream. And so what it says in there is, "It is good what you did. You asked about something that changed. And it's good that the people are alarmed about it. But the first thing you're gonna tell the people is, we call this death, what happened. And they will know this from here on in. And you tell them that, number one, *they're never to fear it*. They're never to fear it because the same as somebody is born, death is another stage. Born is going in and death is going out. It's like an exit.

"So it's the same thing. You become born, you become a teenager, that's another stage. You become an adult, that's another stage. You become an elder, that's another stage. And then the other stage is death. You leave and you go to another world. That's why they shouldn't fear it." That's what he said to tell the people.

Then he said, "And then when you gather the people tomorrow, then you tell them too that the human body was not made to be everlasting, like a stone or something. It's not forever."

And the other thing, they say two different ways in Mohawk. I find it hard in English to do it the way they do it. One is í:iah thaetewanákere onwe, like *we're not living forever* and the other is í:iah thakionnheke that *our soul in the present body we are in isn't everlasting*. In English, it sounds like they're the same. But there are definitely two in Mohawk.

And then he said, "That's why I gave you the clans. The people will have clans." And he said, "I put you in a house." (He's talking about the Longhouse. In our political structure, whether it's Longhouse or not, it's still considered a house. And certain clans sit on one side and certain clans sit on the other side.) And that's when he said, "When somebody dies on that side of the house, all your clans on that side are gonna be called Roti'nikonhrakwenhtará:'on." That means in English *their minds all fell on the ground*. That's because they're in grief 'cause one of their members on their side of the house, died.[1]

And then he said to tell them, "I have commissioned or I have made a power." They call this power, Ahsontowanenkó:wa. And that means the *great, great*

---

1. Since the material for this chapter came from a source and time different from the previous chapter, Tom does not address the issue of the similarity between this version of the Clan System from the Creator and the version which credits the introduction of the Clan System to Ro'nikonhrowá:nen (He Who Has Great Ideas).

night. Some refer to it as *the long, long night*. And some interpret it as *the big, big sleep*. That's what death is. And so this big thing, this power that the Creator commissioned, it comes to get people when it's time to go. And this power they call Ahsontowanenkó:wa has no face, and it has no heart.

"It has no mercy. So that means when it comes there, you can't negotiate with it. When it comes there, you can't cry and beg for another day or another week because it has no compassion. It's got no mechanism in itself. It's only job, the way I made it, was to come directly and take, without question. And so therefore no army can alter it, no amount of money can stop it. When it comes, it's time. You gotta go. And that's the way it's gonna be," He said, "You tell the people that.

"So that's why they're to cherish whatever days they're allowed to live on the earth. And while they live on the earth, they're always supposed to carry a good mind day and night. And they're also to have compasssion and love in their hearts every day because nobody knows if tomorrow will be their last and the following they're gone. And if they don't have goodness in their hearts and in their minds, then it will be hard for them to find that path to the next world. If they have not done right to the people, then they may not find that path." That's what it says in there.

And he said, "So whenever somebody dies, they will send one or two messengers over there to the other side of the house. They will cry."

So when somebody dies on one side, you send a runner, a messenger of your people to cry on the other side. And there's a way you do that. Depending on if it's a Chief, it's a Clan Mother or a regular person, there are certain ways that you do that. You holler.

The messengers tell the leaders over there what happened, that somebody died, the name and everything about the person who passed away. And those leaders will embrace the messengers and have sympathetic words for them, and tell them to go back where they live and that, "Now that we have been notified of this, we will gather all our people on this side of the house."

So the side whose minds are strong has a meeting, because the other side are all crying now. And one woman will say, "I will stand in the front. All the food things, I'll organize them."

And the women, they'll say, "And we'll help you."

And then the men will say, "Who's gonna do the talking when the body comes back? Who's gonna do the dressing of the dead, wash them or dress them up in Indian clothes? Who's gonna welcome them back to their house when the body comes back? Who's gonna talk in the Longhouse? Who's gonna talk at the grave?"

And at Akwesasne where I'm from, since I'm a Bear, that means the south side of the Longhouse. That's where I stay. My mother and all her relations, we sit on the south side.

And with us on the south side for the Akwesasne people are the Snipe Clan people, our Eel Clan people, and our Beaver Clan people. They all sit with us over there. So all of those, the anthropologists refer to as my moiety. But we don't say moiety in our terms. We call it, skanonhsakará:ti, *one side of the house* or the other side of the house. That's what we call a two-party system.

So then they will gather all the grieving people over here, and they've got a name for when that happens. Their name is "their minds fell on the ground." We call those people that are on that side of the house, of the nation, Roti'nikonhrakwenhtará:'on. *Their minds have fallen flat to the ground.* Or sewa'nikonhrakwenhtará:'on. *Your minds are on the ground.* Because you lost somebody, because your loved one died, you've all got tears in your eyes. It means that you don't know how to think because you're so sorrowful about your loved one.

But our name for our people over here on this side is, Roti'nikonhrakáhte. Translated into English, it means *their minds are strong,* or *their minds are tough and upright* (because they didn't lose anybody). There are no tears in their eyes. There's no impaired hearing, because of death. There's no sadness in their head. They're still healthy, over here. They're all okay. So because we're healthy, it becomes our duty to go over there where the death happened to them, to those clans and help them.

That means we're gonna wash their dead; we're gonna dress their dead; we're gonna speak for their dead. That means our women are gonna cook for them. It means we're gonna clean their house; we're gonna carry the body; our men will dig the grave. And so nobody over there has to do anything for their dead. It's gotta be us on the other side, because they're crying. They're in tears. The dust of death is in their brains, which impairs them from thinking what to do next. And that's why there are condolences. That's why there are those ceremonies for the dead when that happens.

So all the women and the men whose minds are strong, we go over there, where the man or woman lived. We scrub the floor. We wash the walls. We put new curtains on or wash the curtains really well. And we make the house spanking clean, almost brand-new, so that when that body comes back, it comes back to everything fixed up.

We're obligated to them for nine days and we aren't released until the tenth day, which effectively means ten days.

When somebody is laid out in your house, the way we did it when I was growing up is we cover all the mirrors. What we call atátken in my language, I guess it's *mirror*, in English. You look at yourself in there. All the mirrors in every room, even on the dressers, we put sheets over them. Even a toaster that's made out of chrome. It's not a mirror, but it can catch your picture. We cover anything that can catch your picture.

And that's because when somebody passes away, for nine days, we're supposed to be in mourning. We're supposed to be in grief. For nine days, that's when we cry. Everything comes out. So, for nine days, we're not supposed to beautify our hair, not s'posed to wear lipstick, not s'posed to put mascara on our eyes. We're not s'posed to do any of these things. Because those nine days, they belong to that loved one, not to us. We're mourning. That's why no mirrors.

Long ago, the loved one's remaining relatives, they would even put ashes in their hair. O'kèn:ra, we call it, that's *dirt* or *ashes*. Some of them also used to cut their hair real short and leave wood ashes in there as a sign that they were in mourning until the tenth day. Then they would go back to normal. Not many people do that any more.

In the past, they commissioned certain ones from our side, to stay with that family for the whole ten days. So in case they relapsed or in case they really needed help, there would be somebody there. See?

For the last thirty years or so, they have stopped doing that. Once they bury them, everybody goes home, and they kinda take care of themselves. But for nine days, they gotta put food out and stuff like that.[2]

And while the body's still there, we stay overnight, or have some of our members stay overnight, twenty-four hours a day, so that it's never left, the dead body. At least they are doing that, yet today. And at Akwesasne, every day for the rest of the ten days, we send somebody over there, to go check on them. We don't stay overnight anymore.

And then on the tenth day, we go back over there. And this time it's *that* family and *that* clan, that are gonna do all the cooking. And that's what they call ahoti'nikonhrakétsko. It means they will raise their mind up again. We will do that to them. They're gonna cook and they're gonna feed all these other people, on behalf of their dead one, as a form of gratitude, because they were taken care of, in their need.

And so this family will honor these people. And they will have a giveaway. That's when they take the dead person's clothes and whatever they have and they assign it to whoever carried the body to the grave, whoever dug the grave, whoever cooked, whoever cleaned. Whoever did anything, they all are given something, as a remembrance from that dead person. They call it a giveaway and that's on the tenth day.

If the family wants to keep something that belonged to the dead person, it's gotta go through that speaker from the other side, through that ceremony. He has to say words over everything. He will say, "This is now gonna go to this person that's your son," for example. "Now it's *his*, not yours any more."

You can't bypass that. If that boy doesn't put it through that ceremony, then he will have trouble or he'll get sick. That dead person will bother him. Or else that act will not allow his father to go on to the spirit world. There are many things that could happen. Nobody knows what they're gonna do,

---

2. Tom is referring to other practices that still continue even though those who are grieving no longer have those whose minds are "tough and upright" with them during the nine days.

until they do it. That's why we have to put everything through there, so we try to make sure that we cover all bases, see?

It's an elaborate beautiful ceremony, *very* touching. I'm just telling you a little bit of it. There are beautiful words that go with it. And even the non-Native people who have ever seen it or been part of it, they're completely awed by it. They say, "We have nothing equivalent to that." In any of their stuff.

It is important. It's probably more important than almost everything 'cause everyone's gonna have death tomorrow or the next day or the next day. We're not immune to it.

While I'm on this subject, I might as well tell you that the Iroquois believe that the day that one is born is also the day when your death date is set. The six nations have a stick that they use to send runners out and for meetings. It's got marks on it and it's got wampum hanging down. That's sorta like what we have, when we're born. That's the way they used to say it. At our birth, the Creator marks down how many days each person's gonna be here.

But as I mentioned in the Opening, the Creator doesn't show us that stick, because he knows that we have a handicap: that for us people it's hard to tell the truth. Us humans, there was something messed up in our creation 'cause we were the last to be made.

And as I was saying earlier, that's why we have the Four Sacred Beings, because of that handicap. And that's why the Creator doesn't tell us. He doesn't show us that stick; he keeps it a secret because we will try to change it. So he doesn't trust us.

But even the Four Sacred Beings can't prolong anything. When it's marked on that stick at your birth, that's it. No one's gonna change that, *nobody*. The only one that can change that is the Creator, and he never does.

The Four Sacred Beings watch over everybody. They specially watch kids and people who do the Creator's work, the ones who are always doing ceremonies, always helping the people.

Some of the old people used to say that when your kids are growing up, you're s'posed to tell them, "You can be foolish and make a big mistake *once*. You can do it twice. You do it the third time, *maybe* you might get help. But after the third, you're on your own. They're not gonna bother with you anymore 'cause you're a fool. They're not gonna waste their time on you."

So my old people say "three times."

Anyway there's confusion here. Earlier I talked about the two boys, Shawískara and the other one, who made the people. But in the funeral, it talks about the Creator making the people. There is a contradiction. Maybe there isn't to some people, but there is to me. And I still haven't figured it out. But I'm called upon to bury people *a lot*. And that's the only way I know is what they said, so even though I think it's contrary, I repeat it and I bury the people, because I don't know what else to do! I don't know any other way.

People could ask the elders on their territories. Maybe they might know. Nobody has ever explained it to me—well, I guess I just never asked either. 'Cause there was never time and I didn't wanna *bother* them. But in my own self, I think about it, that there *is* a contradiction. And as for influence from the white brothers, I don't know, because our whole funeral stuff is so different from any of the Europeans'. The faceless one,[3] some compare to the newcomers' grim reaper. But it could just be one of those universal truths: for some power to come after us, that's its job. It can't be susceptible to tears, so it has to be faceless. Rather than being influenced, it could be the same truth.

You have to come to your own conclusion about it. But it seems to me that the Creator manifests himself in you and me. So we *become* the arm of the Creator or the actual body of the Creator. In certain instances, when a certain job needs to be done, he'll enter our body and make our body do these things that we thought could never be done. *We* are even sometimes amazed, at what we were able to do. It wasn't *us* that did it. It was that power, one of those Four Sacred Beings or it was directly from the Creator. But it was a power beyond our power.

---

3.   Ahsontowanenkó:wa, *the great, great night*, as mentioned a few pages earlier, is the faceless one.

And I tell you, that even a lot of the talks that I've given for our people throughout the years have been because that power took over. It wasn't really me, just my body was used. And that's why when you finish after that happens, you get real tired, like you're a rag, like you're just going to fall down. It uses all your energy. It's really hard, if the spirit uses you.

If you're just gonna do a lecture, an academic lecture, just from research, that's no problem, I don't think. But if you open yourself to let these things *use* your body, then you get zapped. Mmhmm.

Well anyway, the little tiny girl had died and they were all upset 'cause they didn't know what to do. They had never seen death before, so there were all these feelings, that there was no direction for. If they didn't deal with it the way they did, it might have turned into wars or anything, you know. Undirected energy like that, anger or hurt or whatever, can hurt *more* people. So this is why they asked that medicine guy to use whatever power he had, to ask the Creator what this was and what they were s'posed to do.

And the message was to go ahead and do these things. He assigned the clans to take care of each other, so if somebody dies over here in these clans, they have to go over there to the other clans and do the same. It's like an infrastructure of how cooperation occurs in our nations, see? So that's how I know where to get married and what kinda name my child's gonna get. I know if I get sick, which medicine society is gonna doctor me or perform, to get me well or to help make me healthy. I have to go to the other side to get doctored from their societies. When somebody dies, I know where my grief is gonna be handled. When I die, I know who's supposed to dress me, who's supposed to talk for me and who's the one that's supposed to put me under the ground. All that stuff. And so it's a hand-in-hand kinda thing. It's a system. And it's all dependent on what clan you belong to.

And that's the process of how we are. That's why it's important that you are born with a clan, knowing what clan you belong to. When somebody dies, you know what you've gotta do.

Chapter 13

A Language Dilemma

What they're talking about is renewal of all the things that give us life for all the people. Yet the people don't know what they're saying.

My grandmother and different elders told us that if you're born a Mohawk, then whenever you pick tobacco up or you're gonna offer a ceremony, you should talk Mohawk. If you're a Seneca then you should talk Seneca, when you talk to the Creator. If you're an Ojibway, then you talk Ojibway to the Creator. If you are a Lakota, you talk your language, or a Cheyenne, then you talk Cheyenne to the Creator.

Because that's the one that the Creator made you to be, when the world was new. And he gave you that special Seneca language or that special Ojibwa language. He gave it to you as a present, so that you would be proud to use it. And when you talk to him, he says, "I wanna hear the one I gave you." He doesn't want us to use another one. So that's the way our grandmother told us and our elders told us. And so I try to do that all the time.

I speak Mohawk and understand everything in my language. I was an interpreter for the Mohawk Nation Chiefs from the age of thirteen. When government officials used to come from Albany or some place, or the state police came, or somebody was in trouble at the reservation, I was the interpreter. I was just a kid, only thirteen. And I would translate from Mohawk into English, to these government people. So I've been doing that a long time.

Our Akwesasne Longhouse is about, I forget if it's fifty or sixty foot wide, and a hundred foot long. It's a log house Longhouse. And it can hold about six hundred or seven hundred people in one sitting, our Longhouse. So today at Midwinter, everybody comes to the New Year's dances. And you can't find a place to sit. They even bring extra chairs, but there's hardly any room to dance, it's so packed.

But now today, we're in a dilemma. We're in a *real* dilemma. It makes me feel *sad.* You know why? The majority of them, about three-quarters, if not more, of all the Mohawks that are jam-packed in there, they don't understand what the Faithkeepers and Chiefs are saying, when they're speaking at Midwinter. They don't really know.

So I think about it. What they're saying and what they're praying about in their Midwinter talk is renewal of all the things that give us life for all the people. Yet the people don't know what they're saying. For about four, five hours every day. Can you imagine?

I can. I'd be sitting in the Longhouse for five hours listening to the Russians talk. And I wouldn't even understand one word. It's my Midwinter, but I don't know what's going on.

And so I feel sorry for my people. They're sittin' so long and they don't understand. So what we try to do at our Longhouse is, ahead of time, before the Midwinter starts, we have a big meeting of all the people. And we translate everything that's gonna go on in the whole Midwinter. In generalities. So at least when they go there, they know what they're doing, more or less, even if they don't follow word-for-word. At least they know what that day is for. And that's the best we can do. That's why it's sad. We are supposed to know that. And that's how much we've lost our language, in Mohawk country.

I don't know about the Senecas or Cayugas, if they're better off than we are, or if it's the same thing. But it's sad.

So me, I'm always the interpreter.

When somebody dies, they talk.

When there's a death, usually people come there 'cause they're family or they're good friends of that person that died. And a lotta times that family is in tears and are devastated by their loss. They need support. They need condolences or sympathies, in order to go through it. And even really good friends, they cry too, some of them.

And so when there's a funeral in Mohawk country, when a Chief talks to the people, what he's doing is he's trying to wipe the tears from everybody's eyes, because their minds are falling on the ground in sadness. What he's trying to do is use words to get all the tears out of you. To make you cry more, so that nothing will bottle up in your body and get you sick from the pressure, the nonrelease of your sadness.

They're doing all these speeches, so that it'll help the people get over their grief and go on with life. And yet sometimes 90 percent don't even know what they're saying. So the funeral speeches are almost for no one, just a few people. And the hundreds of other people, it doesn't help them, because they don't understand what they're saying. So it puts us in a real funny position. How do we fix that? How do we help that?

So what the Mohawk Chiefs did is usually right in the Longhouse, they asked me. As soon as one finished talking, he'd say,
     Ahsathón:tate ken tahsewennaté:ni ahsén:nen tsi nihawennò:ten?

Okay. *Can you translate it into English language?* So I'd tell what he said, almost word-for-word. He'd be talking for pretty near an hour. And I'd try to remember what he said. Usually I'd come pretty close. And it helped the people. Now they'd understand about death. Now they could cry. Now they could get better.

And then the other side gets to talk now, to answer. And then again, we translate it. I really salute the Mohawk Chiefs there in Akwesasne for doing that. Because now people don't have to carry around this big black burden of grief all the time. At least they get relief from that, see.

Other Longhouses, they never translate. They say you're not s'posed to talk English. And I can see that and I can buy that. But it makes my heart cry and it makes me sad 'cause lookit all the people: they got no help. 'Cause they no longer talk Indian. So we're caught. And I don't know what to do about it either. 'Cause some Longhouses just will not allow English to be used. But that's their decision.

Chapter 14

The Fog

Grandma said, "You're not s'posed to complain about the fog."

Maybe I will just leave you with this image: one time I had to go somewhere, and it was really foggy outside.

And I said, "Oh geez, it's foggy. And I gotta travel." So I was complaining about it.

And my grandmother said, "Oh, oh, oh! Don't say that. Don't make a mistake."

And I said, "What do you mean?"

She said, "You're not s'posed to complain about the fog, because over there in Kariohià:ke is our Creator, Shonkwaia'tíson. And this earth where we live, Ionkhi'nisténha Ohónstia, this is the Mother Earth. So this is the Creator's wife, this Mother Earth. They're married together.

"And every little while, the Creator and the Mother Earth come together, just like a husband and wife. They're having a 'get-together.' And the steam comes from their affair.

"And after, from that, lots of things are gonna grow because they got together. They became fertile. And so now there will be life. If you complain about the fog, you are interfering with your father and your mother. And if you interfere with them, then there will be no more babies born of life. So don't ever bother the Creator and don't ever bother the Mother Earth. Don't ever complain when you see fog."

So I'm glad she told me that 'cause after, I never ever complained about that any more. In fact, I look at it differently. And I look at it as, "Oh, maybe she's gonna grow again now."

We see fog a lot here in the Mohawk Valley. And when we look out there in the early morning, we say, "Oh, gee, Mother and Father, they were visiting each other again last night!" And the grass is going to grow. And there's going to be lots of food. So this is always the affair of the Creator and our Mother the Earth. And the animals and everything else, we're their children.

Chapter 15

Where We've Settled

The Iroquois nations really all have the same father and mother. The only difference is where we've settled.

You know the only reason there are Oneidas, the only reason there are Onondagas, the only reason there are Senecas? It's a very simple reason.

When the Mohawks broke off from the main group, they settled here by the Mohawk River, and in this area, they noticed that they had seen flint rocks all over. And if you walk in the garden, you'll come up with dozens of them, right here at Kanatsioharè:ke. If you walk in the woods, you'll see stone that's made of solid flint over there, that they used to make arrowheads with. And so they called those of us that lived here, from that same group Ratinien'kehá:ka. That means *the people who live where the flint stones are*. Not Freddy Flintstone, so don't get mixed up with Wilma and Fred! But it's because that's how they identify us.

So when the Oneidas and the other Indian people named us, they called us *The People of the Flint*. Simply because there was flint all over, where we live.

And then the Oneidas were another group that splintered off. And they moved over, just about an hour from here. And over there where they went, there was a stone that was standing up. There were a few of them, I think, the way I have heard it, standing up. And so they called them Onenio'tehá: ka. That means *the stone that stands up*, see. And so that's how they became known.[1] But they're actually Mohawks; they're actually Seneca. They're all the same people, you see. The only difference now is that group lived where the stone stands up. And that's what they became. It's no big deal.

And then, of course, another group of the same people, they settled by Syracuse and around that lake over there. And they named them Ononta'kehá:ka. And all that means is they're *the People of the Hills*. They settled where it's hilly country. So they call them, I was gonna say "Beverly Hillbillies" just like the Flintstones, you know! They're not the Beverly Hillbillies; I'm just joking. But it does mean *People of the Hills*. And so that's who they are. And no big deal. They just live where the hills are. And that's what identifies them.

But today we've evolved to the point where we don't realize that all those Iroquois nations really all have the same father and mother. The only difference is where we've settled, you see. That's the only difference.

Now about two hundred years ago, the Senecas got attacked by George Washington's army, by General Sullivan. And they ran away, lotta Senecas. And they went to the Akwesasne reservation land to take refuge.

And a lotta Onondagas, when they got attacked by General Sullivan, during the Clinton campaign, they went north and ran to Akwesasne, too. And they took refuge. And Cayugas too. They ran away when they got attacked. And they came to Akwesasne, a lotta them.

But, us Mohawks, we have no Eel Clan. We have no Snipe Clan. We don't have Beaver Clan. We only have the Bear, the Turtle and the Wolf. We have no Deer Clan, either, but the Senecas do. And Onondagas have it. The Oneidas are almost exactly like Mohawks. They don't have the Snipe Clan

---

[1.] Literally *the People of the Standing Stone*.

either. Only Bear, Turtle and Wolf. But two hundred years ago or more, when they all came up north to live with us, most of them never went home. They stayed there, and they intermarried with all the Mohawks there.

Next thing you know, they were all talking Mohawk too, the Senecas and Cayugas and Onondagas. And so today in Akwesasne, the Mohawk Indians have almost two thousand people that are Snipe Clan. That's how we know those are Senecas and Onondagas and Cayugas. And we have Deer Clan up there, we never had before.

Now at our Longhouse . . . I guess different nations do it differently. But the way we do it at our Longhouse, the men come in the eastern door. And the western door, the women come in over there. So in one end of the Longhouse, everybody on both sides is a woman. And from the middle going to the east of the Longhouse, it's all men on both sides. That's the way our Longhouse is.

And the way they fixed it is on one side, all the Wolf and Turtle are together. So everybody on one side of the Longhouse is Wolf and Turtle, in a Mohawk Longhouse. And then on the other side is all Bear Clan.

So because of that, what they did is everybody who belongs to these other clans, they said, "Go with the Bears. Go sit with the Bears, because they're all alone. And us, there's the Turtle and Wolf, we are partners. And they're alone. So you can go help them."

So for over two hundred years, the Snipe, the Deer and the Beaver and if there are any Hawks, they go sit with the Bear Clan. And that's how we do it over there.

Chapter 16

The Four Sacred Rituals Part 1:
The Teacher

So he was restoring their first truth.

Sometimes this story gets confusing too. And I'll admit it to you right here.

Even when Roy Buck and Jake Thomas were telling this, they always mixed parts of each of these topics together: the Creation story, the Clan System, the Four Sacred Rituals, and the Great Law. They used to confuse me, but I never said anything. I never asked much. I said to myself, "Well, if I'm meant to know, it'll probably click after awhile." But it obviously didn't click! And they're gone. I don't know if they knew or didn't know. But that's probably how they heard it and so that's why they said it like that.

You would hear this story of the eleven kids when they did the Great Law. And it doesn't belong there: it belongs here with the Four Sacred Rituals. It's a whole different era, a whole different event. But then again, maybe it's that process that when it breaks down, you start all over again. So you hear it there because it's being reinserted. It's like on your computer: when you add a word, you've gotta push that insert key, then do it. If you don't, it'll mess up everything. You see what I mean? And that's probably what they were trying to do. I'm not sure, but that's what I think.

But it doesn't bother me that much, when I say to myself, "Well, something happened that was way before my time." I just go with the flow 'cause it's all right. Because between these events there was a lot of time. It took thousands of years to get from one event to the next.

First, Creation happened at the beginning of the world. Then the Clan System happened. Then, the Four Sacred Rituals came. Now this is all before Columbus came here. There could be maybe twenty thousand or forty thousand, maybe more than that, years between. But our people don't ever say this happened in 2000, this is 2003. They don't say dates when they tell history like that: they just say "Yesterday. It happened yesterday."

I think this probably took place before there were Onondagas, before there were Senecas, before there were Cayugas, before there was such a thing as the Oneida. It probably took place when all of the five nations or even six nations were only just one people. And that was quite some long time ago.

But remember our yesterday could be two thousand years ago or ten thousand years ago or twenty thousand years ago. It's still like it happened yesterday 'cause it was yesterday, but *many* yesterdays. See? So when we refer to the history of the Iroquois people, we don't talk about antiquity; we're not talking about ancient things. Even the beginning of the world is not considered ancient, because it's still here. Do you see what I mean? It's a different conception, a different way to look at it. It's dictated by our teachings, that our past *is* our present. And our past and our present are also our future, all in one, never changing.

Okay. So the third big event is this one.

Now each time there was a necessity for another event to happen, it was because the people of the society had neglected to follow and to teach their next generation what *they* were given. And as another generation was born, they neglected even more to tell them what they were supposed to know. And as they didn't do this, then chaos became normal in their communities. And then there were conflicts. And then there were wars, fighting. And so the society became decadent. There was no more direction; there was no more purpose; there was no more meaning.

And each time they had to redo everything. Whenever they forgot, the Creator made them restore them. They had to relearn the Thanksgiving Address before they were taught the Clan System. And then when they forgot those, which they did, that Teacher came, and he made them redo them both, before he taught them the Four Sacred Ceremonies.

So every time they fell down and lost it, he made them start all over from the beginning, just like AA tells you. To become a drug addict or an alcoholic, you have to give up your spirituality, your spiritual connection. And when you give up your spiritual stuff, then anything goes. Then there's a whole sequence: anger, madness, sorrow, and grief. You just go where the wind takes you. And if it's headed for disaster, that's where you go, because there's no spiritual anchor to hold you down to where you belong, you see.

Most of the time it's that way. So in order for you to get well in the AA program, what they usually tell you is you gotta get your spirituality back, reclaim it again. And then you can deal with your anger; you can deal with your addiction, if you've got that anchor, see.

Okay. Everything had gotten bad. And confusion had come. And it was because there were too many people. And as people spread out, the control of elders, like grandmothers and mothers, weakened. Their kids moved away, or moved to other villages through marriage or whatever. So there wasn't a tight rein on what was happening. Things became more relaxed, and families became less close. And when that became less, it was looked at with less respect.

So there was a need at this time for something to reestablish the closeness and the respect. And that's when this young boy was born whose story I'm gonna tell you. This is one of these events when an arrangement was made between the Creator and those Four Beings, that one of them would be born here, in order to be able to help the people become strong and to become good again.

Some people say this story is very much like the story of Jesus Christ. And they have cause to think that. When you first hear the story, you probably will also. 'Course I use to think that myself, that the missionaries musta taught us that. We musta mixed our knowledge with theirs and got it all confused like muddy water. See my problem is every Monday, we used to go to that Catholic religious instruction, so I heard stuff here and there, and I never listened very hard. But I can remember some of it and it's similar to this.

It throws me sometimes. I try not to let it bother me and so far I've been successful.

As I told you before, when I got older, I said "No. There will be similarities because the sun that's shining here today is the same sun that shines in Arab country or in China. So that's our commonality. The corn or the food that grows all comes from Mother Earth, whether it's in China, Africa or here. And so there *have* to be commonalities. We're eating from the same source, from the same mother. And the sun is the same brother. And so on. So of course there won't be coincidence: there will be commonalities."

It doesn't mean that because I'm an Indian, I can't have original truths It doesn't mean that until a missionary came and taught me something, I knew nothing. You know what I mean? That's what it sorta seems is the general opinion about it. And a lotta times we Indians believe that too, of ourselves. And of course when we do that, then we spin our wheels and we don't get anywhere. So we have to reclaim our independence and our freedom as well. That's the hardest thing for Indians to do, or anybody that's colonized to do, is to get back their freedom, the real freedom to think, be thinkers again.

So I'm gonna tell you just the way they told me, and then you can draw your own conclusions.

Okay now, it happened at this time that there were conflicts. There was confusion. And there were arguments going on.

And so the Creator summoned these guys, these Four Sacred Beings. And he said, "We need to use one of you as a messenger, to be born on the earth as one of the people, so that you can talk to them. And you can remind them of how they're supposed to behave and believe. And replant it again, the goodness."

And one of them did agree. And he was born. And the Creator chose one woman who was living amongst the Iroquois. And here's where it's similar to the Christian or to the Chinese, to the different prophets that were born in other cultures in the world. It's usually a woman who never had affairs with men. Usually it was a woman who didn't know men, who knew nothing about them. And so they called those "virgin births."

And so it was like the Peacemaker's[1] birth too, huh? That's the way his was. And this is what happened to the Sky Woman too, in her time. So it didn't happen just once, it's happened several times in our history.

But once a woman's gonna have a baby, she's not a virgin anymore. So regardless of how that happened, it's really none of our business! That's not the focal point, that part. So one of these women who was said to have been unmarried, without a boyfriend or anything, she became in a spiritual kinda way, chosen to give birth to this child.

And unknown to her or to each other, there were eleven other women that *had* husbands, that *were* married. And these other eleven women became pregnant, almost simultaneously. But it wasn't planned or anything. It was just a natural occurrence.

So that made twelve of them. And then again people say, "Well, that sounds like Western Christianity with their apostles." Well, I don't know if it is or it isn't, but this is the way our old people told us. And it may have been influenced and it may not have been influenced. I don't know. But I'm just gonna tell you what they told me.

These women didn't know each other either. They all came from different places. And they began in their pregnancies to get bigger and bigger. Towards the end of the nine months, then this woman gave birth, the one that didn't have a husband, didn't have a man.

When that baby was born, those other women had babies too, the *same day*. And somehow, they received word that this baby that's got no father, was

---

1.   See chapter 26, "The Great Law of Peace Part 1: the Birth of the Peacemaker."

born. And so they went over there. They all wanted to go see 'cause their babies were born at the same time. They thought something was strange or something was curious about it, so they all wrapped their babies up and they carried them.

There was something like a magnetic thing pulling them. You know how if you put a nail on top of a paper and if you put a magnet underneath and you pull it, how the nail follows that magnet? Well, this is what happened to these eleven women.

They felt this magnetic pull. And they needed to travel. They didn't know exactly where they were going. But they followed whatever it was that was kinda pulling them. And they all ended up at this one baby's house, the one that didn't have a father. And he was a special baby; he's the one that became known as Shakorihonnién:ni, the Teacher.

And so all these eleven women were carrying little bundles of baby, that they just gave birth to. When they went into this house, they put all their babies on a blanket, on the ground there in that lodge. And so there were twelve of them all together. And somewhere in the middle I guess, there was that baby with no father. And so even though they were fresh new babies, they thought they'd introduce them! Let them visit each other.

Having their births all at the same time, all at the same moment, sorta united them. So after that, they continued to be friends. And periodically, they would bring all their twelve babies together. And then pretty soon they were all crawling around and those kids knew each other, huh? And then as they began to learn how to walk, their mothers still brought them together. So that way they continued to be friends.

And so after some years passed, they kept in touch. And when they began to become running-around kids, they visited each other all the time. They were raised together. As they got a little bit bigger, this fatherless one used to be the ringleader, the gang leader or whatever, and he would make plans for them. Early in the morning they'd leave, just at sunrise.

He'd take them way up the hill and into the woods, somethin' like these woods here. But in those days it took three guys to put their arms around the average tree. These trees you see around here now are just little matchsticks, third or fourth growth or whatever. Not virgin trees like there were then.

And up on top of that hill, surrounded by forest, they say there was a natural clearing, that was almost a perfect circle. There was a big woods all around, but in that one area, not that big a place, only grass was growing, no bushes or trees.

And never fail, that's where he would take them, day after day.

The elders in the villages, they used to say, "That's strange that these kids take off every day, early in the morning. And they usually come back once the sun has passed across half the sky, towards afternoon. They're all done whatever they're doing. But they keep doing it day after day, and week after week, and month after month."

Pretty soon the whole village was talking about it, "Where do they go and what do they do?"

And so finally one elder lady, the grandmother of that fatherless boy, said, "Tomorrow, I'm gonna get up before they get up and get ready. And when they're ready to go to the woods, I'm gonna trail 'em. I'm gonna stay way back and I'm gonna find out where they go and what in the world do they do, all this morning time, every day."

So that next morning, she got up and she trailed them. Sure enough, they went off following each other, just like a bunch of ducks walking. And they went up there. And she was way at the back, so they wouldn't know that she was coming. But that one boy, he had more than two eyes. You know what I'm talking about? He was like a seer, huh? So he was an extra special guy. He didn't just have the two ears, he had an extra pair somewhere. So he could hear noises that you and I can't hear. It was like a built-in radar system, within his being. He was the Creator-sent boy, huh?

And so even though that grandmother was trying to sneak around, that leader-boy knew everything that was happening. She wasn't fooling him at all. But he just made pretend he didn't know. He just kept on walking. When they got up there, the grandmother hid herself behind a big ol' tree. And she peeked out and watched what they were doing, spying on them.

She listened to everything that they were saying. And she was gonna tell the village what she saw.

And they had a big log on the ground, that was like their bench. They used to use that to sit on.

And here's what she heard. That little boy, he was teaching them, even though he was just a young kid. The way I did the Opening earlier, that's what he was saying. He was teaching them that, thoroughly, all eleven of them. He taught them the Ohén:ton Karihwatéhkwen, the *Thanksgiving Address* 'cause they had lost that. So he was restoring their first truth. And he would say, Eh kati . . .

And they would answer with tho. Then he'd go on to another part. Tho. And another. Tho.

Each morning before they did anything, they repeated that. A different one would do it every time they'd meet. So he knew they all knew how to do it: eleven of them.

And she was watching, the old grandmother, what was going on from behind a tree.

And then, when he had finished that one, he started talking about Bear Clan, Turtle Clan, Wolf Clan, Snipe Clan, Heron Clan, Eel Clan. He was talking about that, and what that means. And where it came from, and why we have the clans. And then he separated them too. And he said, "Okay, half of you are on one side of the log and half are on the other side of the log."

And with his grandmother watching, that's how this little boy had divided the clans in two, just like the Longhouses are to this day. And that's why it carries on like that.

Now, as he finished the Thanksgiving Address, the grandmother shook her head and she said, "Holy, how can a little kid be so intellectual and so philosophical and so spiritual?" I mean it was beyond comprehension. Just a little boy, and he was talking as if he were ten old men in one, with his knowledge and his sophistication. She couldn't believe it.

So, she just kept sitting there watching that. And all the while, those kids knew she was watching, even though she thought they didn't, see?

So, then, he told them all about the clans again, that you are not supposed to marry someone from the same clan. If someone is from the same clan you are, that's your brother or your sister, so you mustn't commit acts of incest. And he also told them, "Nobody whose parents are from the same clan should ever be a Chief, should ever be a Clan Mother, should ever be a Faithkeeper or anyone that holds office. For those people will lead us to our ruin. The nation will be ruined if we allow them to take positions of leadership."

That's why you must make sure that the clans operate the right way. You start telling them when they're little kids. So when they grow up they have full respect for their clan. So if you make a Chief, that leader has to have two clans, one from his mother and one from his father. It's just like a Longhouse is: it's got two doors, a door in the east and a door in the west (a door for the woman and a door for the man). And a baby has to have two doors too, one from his mother and one from his father. And they have to be different. It can't be a Wolf and a Wolf. It can't be a Turtle and a Turtle. It can't be an Eel and an Eel. It can't be a Bear and a Bear. Otherwise they're gonna lead us the wrong way.

And the way the old people quote the Creator, if they quote it right, he said,
> Tóka she ne shahoti'tá:ra. Enhotíniake í:iah ní:'i thakheiakia'táhrhahse ó:ni oh nà:ken nienhén:ke í:iah ní:'i thakheiakia'táhrhahse.

In English, that means the Creator's talking to them:
> *If the same clan marries together, I will not be a party to that. I will step back and I will not be in there, what they're doing. They will be on their own.*

So the little boy finished that. He had thoroughly told them about Creation and Thanksgiving. Then he had thoroughly retaught them about the clans, the structure of the Clan System, and how it operates. The foundation had been totally rebuilt. When that was all done, *then* he was gonna start the Four Sacred Rituals.

Chapter 17

The Four Sacred Rituals Part 2:
Three of the Rituals

And they're all doing it for that little boy. So you know what that little boy must feel like? That his *whole nation loves him. That he has a place in his own nation.*

The Four Sacred Rituals are:

1. Ostowa kó:wa *Great Feather Dance*
2. Onehó:ron *Drum Dance*
3. Atón:wa *Fire or Thanksgiving Song*
4. Kaientowá:nen *Peach Stone Game*

That's when he gave them the turtle shell rattle. And to make it, there's a special ritual that goes with it. Not just any Onondaga, not just any Mohawk guy can make this. You have to know the prayer to go with it, how to burn the tobacco and what kinda words to use. And if you don't get it at the right time, the shell will crack or break. So you've gotta know when to harvest that snapping turtle.

And then there's a big process that's gotta be followed by which you make that snapping turtle into a turtle rattle. You've gotta be a pretty brave man to do it. It's not for the weak of heart. Now when you look at this turtle's back, that boy taught them, if you count, there are thirteen sections to it. So, in our Iroquois year we have thirteen moons, not twelve. From the New Year's right to the next New Year's, it's thirteen moons. And it's on the turtle.

So, that's what Shakorihonnién:ni was teaching them. And then, he brought out his big turtle rattles. And he got the boys to use them. And he sang, "Yo, yo, yohooooooooooooooooo," like that. And then he was teaching them that Feather Dance, those little kids. They all knew it too. They took turns.

The turtle rattle represents the turtle in our Creation story. The woman who came from another planet was put on the middle of the turtle. And that's what made life. That's why the turtle is important in these ceremonies. So when you shake the turtle rattle, Mother Earth is shaking and is becoming conscious of life. That's her responsibility. So when they play this, hitting it like this on a bench, the world is shaking, and life is starting to loosen up and be born. That's why this is important.

It takes certain people to be able to sing this kinda song they call Ostowa kó:wa, the *Great Feather Dance*. When you dance this, you're supposed to wear a kahstówa.

A kahstówa is an Iroquois hat. The bottom part can be the hat of any Iroquois nation. But the top part, with the three eagle feathers up there, means that whoever wears this is a Mohawk Indian. There are three spindles on there, so the eagle feathers are free to move.

If there is only one feather sticking up, that's a Seneca. And then, if you wear a different style it'd be Oneida. And Onondagas and Cayugas, depending on the position of the feathers. And that's how you know that. If it's the bottom only, no eagle feathers standing up, it's a Tuscarora. And we call this "kahstówa." *Feather hat.* That's all it means. And of course the beadwork has the everlasting tree on it and the different symbols that are relevant to our history and culture.

This is a traditional hat for the Iroquois. In other words, you never see us (unless we're lost Iroquois) with a great big Sioux bonnet on. If you see an Iroquois Indian like that, that means that he's believing Walt Disney's stories! Real Iroquois will wear this kind right here if they're true to their culture.

Back about forty or fifty years ago, there were lots of Mohawks, Onondagas and Senecas, who wore those great big-feathered headdresses. That's because every time the white brother in America wanted us to do something, he made us dress like that. Or he gave us that and he told us that's what he wanted us to wear. And in those days, you didn't dare answer back. With those people, you just sorta did what you were told, if you wanted to live. I mean live in a relatively good way. You didn't rock the boat.

But nowadays we're more free to do what we want to do. And so now you'd have to pay an Iroquois a lot to wear that big Sioux bonnet! Yeah. If we were in a real ceremony with the Lakota or those people who wear that and they were to present us with one, then we would wear it, you know, but not just for our regular stuff.

Okay. If you don't have a kahstówa, then you put a feather in your hair. That's why they call it Feather Dance, Ostowa kó:wa. That's the proper way to do it.

In the Creation story, remember those two brothers, with the power of the Creator, made the human beings? They made dolls out of the earth to resemble themselves. Then, they opened the mouths of the dolls and they blew in there three times. And so, when the rattle is hit, they holler, "Yo', yo', yoooo," in a very loud voice. That represents the twin boys blowing life, soul, spirit, into the bodies of our ancestors. And giving them the life that they lived.

That's extended all the way to us now. It's that same fire that was blown in there, that you and I are still breathing. Because those were our grandmothers. Those were our great ancestors, see? It's reminding the Creator that no matter over thousands and thousands of years what happened to us, we never forgot. And it's very powerful.

We do it the way the woman from the Sky World was doing it, as she went around the turtle, when the world started to grow, when the plants started to grow, when everything grew, and all life was nourished.

So now every time we dance this one, at a certain time in the year, they produce the rhythm by hitting the turtle rattle on the wooden bench and they holler, "Yo', yo', yoooooooo." And every theme, every song they sing, at the end of it they say that. That's saying, "My Creator, and my Mother Earth, the three breaths of life are what made us live. And we've never forgotten, since the beginning of time, where our ancestor always walks and 'til now we still know where we came from, yo', yo', yoooooo." Those three hollers are our way of saluting our Creator, our Mother Earth and all the things in nature that give us nourishment and everything, the ability to live. And that's what we call Ostowa kó:wa.

It's at almost all the ceremonies. You cannot join in that dance unless you first ask repentance or forgiveness, in case you have been mean to somebody, in case you have offended somebody, or in case you have argued with somebody.

When we are mean to each other as people, the first one we hurt is the Creator because he's the one that gave us that life. And so every life that's here in this room is all hooked to the Creator, you see. And to our Mother the Earth. So when we hurt each other and we are mean to each other, we are disobeying our Mother Earth, and we are disobeying our Creator. They are our father and our mother.

If you argue with somebody or offend somebody, then the *Creator* has been argued with, has been offended. Remember when I told you earlier that he's in everybody? So the minute we get mad at somebody, we are also mad at the Creator because he's in that person too.

And a lot of times that happens, as we walk in our jobs or just in company.

So that's why every Iroquois, the ones that are *really* Iroquois, never touch sacred tobacco, they never touch sacred things like that, they never join in dances of ceremony, unless first they say, "My Creator, in case I have offended you in any way or something causes you to be offended, I ask for forgiveness."

And that's only part of it. Not only do you ask the Creator for forgiveness. The other part is not to carry grudges with each other. The best thing is, always get rid of it every day. If somebody gets mad, you try to find ways as soon as you can to fix that. Don't carry it around 'cause after awhile it gets heavy, *heavy*. And it turns into high blood pressure. It turns into a heart attack. It turns into sugar diabetes, turns into cancer. Turns into all kinds of stuff.

If you've made bad friends with somebody, you have to try to start reaching out to that person that you're angry with. Find ways. Give him a cup of coffee or tea or something. You have to start putting your hand out, even if it's only a little bit. And then maybe the next time a little bit more, until you're able to go over there and say, "I'm sorry, my sister, how I hurt you." Eventually you have to do that. Otherwise what you said to the Creator is not complete, is not finished.

And then, maybe gradually, you become good friends after that, you know. Because mistakes are what we need to use to make our character strong. That's when we learn how to be a good person: when we make quite a few mistakes. We learn from those mistakes.

If you don't have lots of scars by the time you're over forty, then you haven't *lived* yet. Just follow me: I'll show you how!

So, you can't just use lip service. When you say, "I ask for forgiveness," you've gotta do the other part of it. You don't push the automatic button and then the conveyer does it. No, that's why you've got two legs and you've got two hands, and you've got a mouth and everything. That's why you've got to smile; that's why you've got to cry, see? That's our second half. So if we make no attempts to try to fix the friendships, wherever we have bad friendships, then we shouldn't be in that dance, the Great Feather Dance. We should not be touching the sacred things that go to the Creator's world, if we're not ready to do that. You see what I mean?

None of this is play stuff. None of this is just that, "Well, it says we're supposed to do this, so we've gotta do it." Just because it says we've gotta do it. No. There are preparations for all of this. It's a very spiritual journey.

Usually the Great Feather Dance is done in the morning. All these Longhouse things are s'posed to happen before the sun goes past the middle of the sky, from sunrise until the middle of the sky. And when you bury somebody too, you're s'posed to do your funeral before the sun goes past the middle of the sky. It's the Creator's will. Everything that's from the Creator is from the early sun: that belongs to Teharonhiawá:kon. And then after the sun goes down, you're going toward the negative side. Early in the morning, at dawn, is the most powerful time.

So there are two powerful times, at dawn and at dusk. But the more powerful one is at dawn because it's the beginning of life. That's why when they have a Tobacco Burning,[1] they try to do it before the sun comes up, just at dawn. At dusk, it's the negative powers that are coming in. So you don't want to do it so much then, unless it's for the dead. But, even if you're doing a dead feast, they say it's better to finish before the sun goes down. Except for Ohkí:we because they have their own power. Their stuff is powerful then, so they go all night, 'til the dawn.

When I'm asked about the dark being negative or "evil," in my mind, I don't think it's evil. I think it's the mischievous time, more than the evil time. Because, soon as the sun goes down, that's usually when trouble starts. It's easy for kids to get in trouble. Even I have an easy time to get in trouble, when the sun goes down! But if it's broad daylight, it's not so easy.

When we're talking about comparative things, when we do the Creation story, that twin named Shawískara belongs to the nighttime. He's mischievous. That's why it's so easy to get into mischievous stuff at night. But we have to be careful not to talk about him like he's evil and to hate him, or to teach our kids to hate or mistrust him. You've just gotta be always on guard. It's like somebody's always doing tricks on you. If you don't want to get tricked, you have to kind of be alert. Well, at night, that's what you've gotta do.

That's why they tell us, "Tell your kids not to run at night, outside or inside." As soon as the sun goes down, the dead spirits are *all* over, not only the spirits of the people, but even the spirits of animals and birds. If your kids run at night, or you run at night, you might hit those spirits accidentally, and then you anger them. The consequence of that might be something

---

1. For more about Tobacco Burning, see chapter 29, "Some Notes on Tobacco and Other Medicine."

beyond what you can handle, see? So, that's why they tell you, you're not s'posed to run around at night, or move fast. It comes from that.

But when I'm thinking about the Western world, I think they have almost the same teaching as we do, except they went a little bit overboard. Because the equivalent to Shawískara over there *sounds like*—but I could be mistaken—it's what they call "Satan." It sounds like that might be the comparison. But the only thing is *there*, they made him out to be a *monster*—monster, like a real evil one, not to be trusted. And to be hated, almost like an enemy.

It's not right to do that because the left-hand twin or the negative part, which was Shawískara, or if it is Satan in the Western world, was given half the world's power. And the other brother has the other half of the world's power. So, our job is to appease the right side and the left side, to *appease* them, *not* to make *enemies* out of them. Just little old you and little old me: we're gonna make him mad, and he has half the world's power? Are you insane? He'll make mincemeat out of us. So, it's better that we make friends with him.

So, it's not evil, it's just mischievous. You've just gotta be careful. It's like when your kids are teenagers: you have to be extra alert at that time. And it's not that they're *bad*. It's just the fact that if you aren't alert, the consequences are big.

Another thing about the Feather Dance I was gonna tell you is in the Creation story. (That's where this all stems from.) They say on the other planet where that first woman came from, where we the Iroquois people, the humans came from, that's the kind of language that they talk, the Mohawk language, Seneca, Onondaga. That's what we're told. That's why we're told never to forget how to speak that.

And, in fact, they say that the songs that they sing with the Great Feather Dance are in the language that comes from that other place. And the reason why we use that language and we use that turtle rattle is to continue to bring life and miracles. When all this is going on, this is what energizes life, stimulates all life, so that it can be healthy, nourished, and have a vitality. Yeah.

So Grandma used to tell me, when I went to the Longhouse for this kinda ceremony, "When you're dancing, make sure you repent and clear yourself." She said, "And if you're dancing and you're ready to holler Yo', yo', yo', like that, try to look out the window and find a tree. Maybe a big tree, little tree, doesn't matter. And when you start to holler Yo', yo', yoooooooo,' aim it to that tree. Hit the base of that tree with your song. 'Cause what you're doing is you're saying 'thank you for my life,' when you say those three hollers.

"And when you aim it at that tree, it goes up that tree. And the ends of the branches point north, east, south, and west. They point this way, that way, in all directions, everywhere. Your three breaths will touch that tree. And so your gratitude will go up the tree and get thrown throughout the universe, by the tree's branch ends. And that magnifies and carries your prayer and carries your thankfulness, to all of the things in this universe that give life. And they will hear how grateful you are."

That's why we dance. That's the way I was taught in my family, by my grandmother. So whenever I do this, I'm looking for a tree, whenever it's time for me to holler. 'Cause I *believe* her. I don't know scientifically if that's true or not, but who cares about Mr. Einstein! In this instance.

Whenever we do the Great Feather Dance, well of course, the rattle is representing the earth. It's representing that turtle in the big water. So when they play it, the rattle is . . . the earth is moving, shaking. It's giving birth. That's what it's doing.

And as I mentioned before, on that turtle's back, there are thirteen sections, which is the Iroquois year. There are thirteen moons in our year, on the turtle's back. And then when you're singing, Mother Earth hears it because you're dancing on her. The Longhouse is on her and it's going through to the whole Mother Earth. And so she feels good. And so the turtle gets bigger, when you dance that.

When you dance that, the trees hear it, and they get stronger. And they get more leaves, and they get bigger. When you dance that, your gardens will hear it and they feel great and they are thankful 'cause you are dancing for them. And then they grow. And then the medicines all over hear it. And then they say, "Hey, they didn't forget. So we're gonna grow for them. We're gonna be ready for them." And *they* get stronger.

So this Great Feather Dance is like a car battery that's dead, and you put a recharger on it, so that it can do its job again. And so that's what the Feather Dance is. It's our recharger of all living things, so they can grow and be strong again. It's our way of saying thank you, and shaking hands with the trees, with the grass, with the medicine, the water, the wind, the sun, the moon, everything that's in the Opening Address. And never forgetting.

And they say if you do this right, if you have done all the protocol, and you've done everything right, they say in every Longhouse that I've ever been to, that when you dance the Great Feather Dance, that actually your feet won't touch the ground, that you'll be dancing on air. About one foot off the ground. When people look at your feather dancing, they won't even see your feet touch the ground. And if you are doing the dancing, you will feel like you're not touching the ground either. If you do everything right.

And I can say honestly, that in my close to sixty years of living on this earth, that I can remember at least a couple of dozen times when I was not dancing on the ground. I *know* the sensation. I *felt* the sensation. And I feel *very* privileged to have done that.

And in the Feather Dance, there are certain songs that are Chief songs; there are certain ones that are directed for Faithkeepers. There are certain ones that are directed to Mother Earth. Some of those young guys when they sing it in the Oneida or Mohawk, ooooh, it's *pretty*. That's really something here, our young men.

One is Thomas Deer. He sings that one so I understand it. He translates it from Oneida into Mohawk. It's great. This other Oneida guy is Mr. Music. And he's only a young kid too, you know, a young man. He comes here every once in a while. He's from Wisconsin, but he lives over at Oneida on the Thames River in Canada. And they've been teaching him his traditions all these years, over there. They're nurturing him, and they're doing a good job too.

When he comes here, he'll sing for me and the community here. And, oh, he's a bubbly guy. Just a wonderful young guy. And he sings the Feather

Dance in the Oneida language, which as I've been saying, is almost the same as Mohawk. So I understand everything. When he's singing it, he starts just like the Thanksgiving Address, that I did earlier. But instead of me speaking it, it's being sung. It's very meaningful.

Once you listen to his singing, you feel as if you were a bird, and you're walking around on Mother Earth. And then as you take off, you start to fly where the corn is, the bushes are. And you fly higher to where the trees are, to the treetops and into the clouds. And then into the top of the universe. And you actually feel like you're a big eagle or something. That's the way he makes me feel when I listen to him because I understand everything that he's saying. Very, very powerful.

And so that's what I share with you, about that one, the Great Feather Dance.

And so this woman, this grandmother, was watching the young boy, Shakorihonnién:ni. He was giving them instruction about the ceremonies, how they were to be. And how they were to be transmitted to the communities, and so on.

And the next thing you know, he was doing the Drum Dance. He was teaching them how to do Drum Dance. And the way I'm talking to you now is like the way he was talking to those eleven guys.

Now this Drum Dance, we call Onehó:ron. That means *the skin covers this*. So this is the cover of a water drum.

A water drum has a little spigot where you can put in and take out water. And to tune it, you pull the skin down and push a thong down around it. When it's tuned up, it's like a bell. You can hear it a long way. We use a water drum in religious dancing. And we also use it for social, fun songs. So it does for both.

And then, we have a certain water drum that's not used for any socials. And that's a bigger water drum. It's used only for Ghost Dance ceremonies. And after those ceremonies are done, they take it apart, and they put it away until the next one. They never practice with it unless it's a special procedure. So that one is sophisticated. But this one is the common one.

It takes two men to sing this. And one man carries the Wampum of Our Nation.

Wampum is made from a shell, called the quahog shell, that's only found in the Atlantic Ocean. I don't think they have it in Florida, just in the north part of the Atlantic, around the coast. I don't think it grows anywhere else in the world. You don't even see it over in the ocean off California, just here. And we use it to make beads. It's a hard, long process to do it. But they used to make thousands and thousands of them in the old days, before they had modern drills and stuff. They had to use those old hand drills.

There are two kinds of wampum. There's this pale or white kind, and there's this other kind, mixed with the purple. And usually a combination of these two are woven in belts or in single strands, like when it's used for the Nation Fires, the Mohawk, Seneca and so on nations.[2] Usually the darker ones have to do with death, have to do with when somebody dies. But when they're mixed with the white ones on belts, then they form designs that record history, events of our history.

So the one man carries the Wampum of Our Nation. Those are five white strings of quahog beads. And because of amendments of other villages, there might be more of them. (There are different lengths for the different nations.) And they call that Onkwatsísta, *Our Fire, Our Nation's Fire*.

The only place you get this is from the Six Nations. When you go there, they're gonna examine you. They're gonna look at you, study you. And if you meet the criteria, then they will take a part of the big fire that they have and give it to you, and now you have fire with your village. See?

So, no Longhouse can just be built, without taking a part of the fire, from the big fire. It has to go through an approval. That's the way the protocol is. Here in Kanastioharè:ke, we don't have a fire, although we probably could run most of those ceremonies that I'm telling you about, a lot of it probably 'cause I've done it all my life. But, we have not been given permission by the big fire to do this.

---

2.   As will become evident shortly, Tom is referring to the wampum that represents a particular nation, as its "fire." The wampum is not burned.

But, where I come from, they have permission over there from the big fire. And that's where I learned. So, sometimes these days, Onondagas call or Senecas call me, to go help them with their stuff. And I use their fire. I come under *their* fire because they called in a proper way. But it's under their direction. I can't do it on my own, myself. It has to be approved. You can't just go into somebody's reservation, and just go do stuff, without the Clan Mothers, or the Chiefs, and all their protocol. You need the leadership's endorsement, you see?

So the one man carries the Wampum, the Fire of Our Nation, in the Drum Dance. It's a long song. It takes perhaps two hours, maybe three hours. Just the introduction of that song, before they start to dance is almost half an hour. And that song is the equivalent to the Feather Dance, the Ostowa kó:wa: it's *almost the same thing*. Except they don't use that turtle rattle; they use the water drum.

And that song is also related to the Sky Woman's chant, when she was making the world. It's like a spiritual history of who we are. It's like what I'm doing here, except in song form.

So, there are two singers for Drum Dance, who sit straddling the bench. Another is chosen as the speaker for us. And then all of a sudden, the guy that's chosen is walking, carrying the Nation's Fire (that's the wampum, huh?) He walks from the east to the west. When he gets to the west, he goes back to the east. Following the trail of the sun is what he's doing.

And he has been asked to talk on behalf of every man and woman, every elder, every child, every baby. He's even been asked to talk for the babies that are not yet born: the ones that *will* be born. And as he goes back and forth, as they're singing, the whole nation dances. There are hundreds of Mohawks going around in the circle with him, men, women and children, all in this dance. And if they're too old to dance, they put chairs next to the singers for them, so that way they're in it too.

And then, as he's singing that Drum Dance, every once in a while that guy who's carrying the Fire of Our Nation, he says, "Yoho" and he stops. The drum stops. The whole dance stops. "And now" he says, "We face our Mother the Earth. All the people of our nation are standing up and we dance on you. We dance for you. We dance in gratitude for you, Mother

Earth. Our singers sing for you, and with all the power of our people we are going around for *you*. And we are letting you know, today, that we thank you and we love you." And he says, "Yoho." He starts singing again and we dance for her, for Mother Earth.

So he's making prayers, like the Opening Prayer, almost like a spiritual history talking. Then he says "Yoho" and then they dance again. Then, all of a sudden, he goes "Yoho" like that, and they all stop and he prays again. He addresses the Water, the Mountains, the Trees, just like we did the Opening Prayer. And it goes like that for two, three hours sometimes.

He's walking back and forth from east to west because the sun goes that way. That's the spiritual road, from east to west. So, that's how *he* goes, as he walks in the middle with the singers. It's like the Thanksgiving Address; it's like a Great Feather Dance, but in a different form. And that's what they call Onehó:ron. Right there.

And then, the next one he taught them, was Atón:wa. And Atón:wa is, of course, the spirit song. And I'm not sure if this is correct what I'm gonna tell you. But, it's the closest that I can deduce from my studies, and from my years of trying to understand. I also had to depend on a dream, through prayer, to get the understanding and definition of this. So, that's why, when I tell you this, I don't want you to write it in cement, and say that Tom Porter said this. You know, "This is the way it *is*," because I'm not sure. All I know is that's what spirits told me at that time. And I don't know if they were trying to trick me! Or if it's really true. But it sounds like it's logical.

And I give you this information, on *that* understanding. Okay? And here's what I found. The way I understand our language, Atón:wa comes from the word o'tónhkwa. In my language, o'tónhkwa means *fire* or *flame*.

In the Creation story, when he made the humans, he put them in the fire, so fire would come into them. When you touch your body, your body is warm. So, within every person, there is a fire. So, everything that has life, has a fire. So, if I'm right, that the root word for Atón:wa is o'tónhkwa, that means it's the spirit that makes us live. It's the fire, the flame within all of us that lives, see?

And the head fire is our Older Brother, the Sun. He's the one that takes us from here to the next world 'cause he's our Older Brother, and the big fire of all fires. And they say when you die, the fire goes out and your body gets ice cold. But as long as we're living, we possess a fire that burns. And so that's why they call this men's personal Thanksgiving, Atón:wa, because it is acknowledging thankfulness for your life or your fire. That's where that word comes from.

Only the men have these songs. One time a woman asked me, "How come the women, we don't have a Song of Thanksgiving, Atón:wa?" I asked the old people why, too. And they'll also tell you, without you asking them: because a woman is already more powerful than a man.

When a woman is born, she's already complete with all her power. And that's why a woman has her monthly all the time, until a certain age, and the man doesn't. The woman is the only one that can give birth, not the man. She's the only one that can make another human being. The men can never do that. And I'll betcha if a man ever did, he'd scream his head off!

A woman is complete with her power. A man isn't. So a woman is stronger than a man. So that's why the Creator sent the Atón:wa songs to the men, so they could walk alongside the women. So they would be equal with the women.

All Iroquois Longhouses know this Atón:wa. And the Chiefs have certain songs that are called Atón:wa. Faithkeepers have got certain kinda Atón:wa songs. It is the personal Thanksgiving Song of every man. Every individual has his own song, so that he will have a purpose, and he will have a way to say thank you for his existence in the world.

And when do you give the song to the man? When he's a little boy, about four, five or six. Then you start to find the song for that young boy.

So, if I'm a good father, then I will pray every day for my son. Or if I'm a good uncle, I'll pray for all my sisters' kids which I'm responsible for 'cause we're matrilineal. We are the ones responsible that they have spiritual knowledge, and that they are protected as they walk the earth. That's what uncles do, any woman's brothers. It's their job more than the father's. Do you follow?

So for my kids? It's actually my wife's brothers who are really responsible for making sure that my sons and daughters know their spiritual things, and

that they know how to do the drums, and they know how to make the rattle
and all that stuff. And then my job is for my sisters' kids. So, what they do in
Longhouse, as I'm the uncle to my sisters' kids, I'm the one that's supposed
to be sure that they know how to do this. Or that they attend these things, and
that those things are known to them, so that they are connected to them.

That's what an *uncle* does, more than the father. But that doesn't exclude me
from my own son as well. So it's reinforced by the fathers too. That's what
good fathers and that's what good uncles do. So a good uncle should have
a whole mess of nephews, a whole mess of nieces, that they have tutored
and that they have been a father to. That's how the Iroquois world is.

Okay. So how do I do this for my son? I pray through my tobacco that we
use. And I say to the Creator, "My son or my nephew needs a song. Can
you send him a song? A Thanksgiving Song?"

And when you do this, if you've done it properly, and if the Creator's spirit
favors hearing you, then the song can come. The Creator can send that song
by the water, or by the wind. He can send it by the birds; he can send it by
the trees; he can send it by a dream; or he could even send it by a living
person who knows how to sing well. And that person may intercept it on
your behalf. He may have caught your prayer.

So, if I'm walking, perhaps by the creek, I hear this water going over
the rocks. And it makes a particular rhythm: now I've got my rhythm. In
different ways, as it hits the rocks coming down the mountain, that water's
talking. That's its voice. Because I prayed for it, it's not just water going
over rocks. It now becomes music, a song, see? It's the Creator sending
you the song, through the river.

Or maybe the wind is blowing through the trees a certain way and maybe the
branches are hitting each other, and the wind is whistling or something, and it'll
turn into a song to you. When you hear it, it will sound like somebody singing.
And that would be the Creator speaking through the tree and the wind, giving
you that song that your father or your grandpa asked to be sent to you.

Or when a bird sings, it'll turn into a song for you. Next thing you know, all
of a sudden that sound translates into words in your head. So now there's
a story that comes with it.

Or you could be dreaming at night, and you'll hear maybe an old Indian man singing over and over to you this song. And when you wake up in the morning, you start singing 'cause you heard it all night. And that's the Atón:wa song.

Whoever prayed for the little boy—his father or his uncle—may hear it for him. Or the little boy may get it directly. And if he does, he's very privileged, huh?

So there are all kinds of ways to get your Atón:wa song, when you're a little kid. That's why you have to be sensitive. 'Cause you don't know what the spirit world is gonna do, or how they're gonna present what you're asking for. It can come in many ways. A lot of people, they don't know that. And so they ask and it's been given, but they don't know enough to take it 'cause they kinda have blinkers on.

And let's say, I'm just completely deaf to music (which isn't really true: I'm not a musician, but I can *dance!*). Then what I can do, if I'm deaf to music—you know what I mean, as far as singing—is, I can go to somebody who was meant to be a musician. All he has to do is hear a song one time, and he can repeat it. That's how good those people are with music.

So, if you can't find it through other means, and you've tried everything— and it happens once in a while—go to one of those singers. And those are the Roy Bucks, the Jake Thomases, the Hubert Bucks, George Buck and all those kinda guys, and old Harrison Ground from Tonawanda. That's the way they were: Mr. Music. And we've got modern ones like Nick and Mike McDonald. They hear it once and they've got it 'cause that comes naturally to them. They're gifted in that.

So I'll go to one of those and I'll say to him, "This is my son's name. We've been trying to get an Atón:wa song for him. And we haven't been able to understand the song. We know you are always singing and it's easy for you to find songs. So can you help my son (or my nephew)?" And I'll offer him tobacco, sacred tobacco.

And so he'll say, "Okay. I'll try." He'll say, "Give me a little bit of time." And he'll burn tobacco for the boy and he'll ask for a song for him. So he'll take a week or a month. And then finally, he'll find it. And then, he'll come and see me. He'll say, "I've got your son's song now." And he'll tell how it came, if he dreamt about it or if he found it in the woods or whatever. And then he'll take my son over there and he'll start singing for him, until he learns it. He'll say, "This is your song now; it's supposed to be for *you*."

So then, my son and I, we'll get a beautiful pair of moccasins, maybe a beautiful Pendleton blanket, or maybe the most exquisite ribbon shirt[3] that you've ever seen in your life. And we'll give it to that singer. Because, "Thank you, you found the Thanksgiving Song for my son." You can even give him money, give him whatever 'cause he did that.

Now my son can walk this earth in thanksgiving for the rest of his life.

I'm very proud of my son 'cause my son has tried to be a good uncle. And I've tried to be a good father. I *try*. And so I told my son one time, "You know," I said, "don't forget—now you're an uncle—all your sisters' kids." And they're the ones that were running around here a while ago. I said, "Those boys, those are your nephews, my daughters' kids. So," I said, "you should get 'em all together." They're all little ones. "And start teaching them what you know about this."

So he did. One time, he got all those boys, my grandsons 'cause he's their direct uncle.[4] And he brought 'em from Akwesasne reservation all the way down here. And all the way from there to here, he was singing them songs, singing for them. By the time they got here, the *kids* were singing those songs. And the next time we went to Longhouse, they were singing there before four, five, six hundred Mohawks in the big ceremony. And when they did this, here's what all those people did.

They did like Grandma. My grandmother was a seer. And whenever my grandmother would look in a cup, read for somebody, if she saw something that was really *something*, she would say Waaaaah, like that. If it wasn't really fantastic, you wouldn't hear her say that. So, at the Longhouse,

---

3.   A ribbon shirt is a traditional shirt, which has colorful ribbons decorating it.
4.   Elsewhere, Tom has talked about the use of the word "uncle" for any man of
      your father's generation.

when we have an Atón:wa song, that's the word they say. Ah wa waaa wa wa waaaaaaaah, like that. That's how they'll say it.

And then all the men, hundreds of Mohawk men in that Longhouse, go like this, He he he haweeee, as backup for him, while tapping out a beat with their feet. Hundreds of them will be doing that on the floor, while they're sitting. And the women in their half of the Longhouse, they're clapping a slow rhythmic beat, keeping the rhythm for him. Two, three hundred women. For that one boy.

That boy stands up and he puts his kahstówa on. He's just a little, tiny guy. It takes a lot of courage for a little boy to do that. He's all dressed in Indian clothes. And he says Ekaeia waaaah. And the people say Wa wa waaaaaaaa. They all do that for him. And that little tiny boy, he starts singing. He goes I:ke i:ke i:ke i:ke i:ke wentsia kiiii. He's even got his rhythm. He sings all the way to the middle of the room. And then he stops. And he says, "Creator, I thank you. I send you my love and my greetings. And I sing for you, my Song of Thanksgiving that I'm on the earth." And he yells again I:ke. And the people say Wa waa waaaa. Two, three hundred people saying that. For him.

He turns around and he goes back. I:ke, i:ke, i:ke, i:ke, wentsia kiiii. Or songs similar to that. And when he gets back, he'll say I:kewe. And everybody'll say Wa wa waaaaaaah. And he sits down.

That's a whole nation of grown women and men, who are acknowledging a little six-year-old boy, when he sings his Thanksgiving to the universe. So you know what that little boy must feel like? That his *whole nation loves him. That he has a place in his own nation.* And they're all doing this for him. So there's a lot of *power* there. And that's what they're teaching him.

And that's what our job is, as uncles. It's to make sure our nephews know how to pray; they know how to sing; they know how to be grateful and they know their place on Mother Earth. That's what Longhouse is for. What a wonderful thing the Creator gave us. And I am so grateful for my grandma and my grandfathers, and the ones who were so stubborn. When people in the world told them to quit the "pagan" way, they said, "*No way.*" That's how come I know what to talk about today. 'Cause I was born from the most stubborn grandmother on the face of the earth!

When it's Atón:wa, when the men sing, that's also the time when boys are named. They let the girls get named then too. But the girls usually get named at the Strawberry time—just the girls, not the boys.

This Atón:wa song is sung twice a year, at every Harvest and every Midwinter. But you can sing your Atón:wa song every single morning if you want to. In fact if you do, the Creator *loves* it. If there's something that happens to me in my life that makes me really grateful and really pleased, and I'm so happy that it happened to me—like a grandchild being born—as a grandpa, I can go out there in the sunshine on the Mother Earth. And I can say, "My Creator, I'm going to sing you my Thanksgiving because my grandson, my granddaughter, was born." And I can go He:ie, he:ie. That's saying to the Creator, *Thank you.*

For any occasion that brings you happiness, where you need to feel gratitude, you can sing that song. 'Cause this is your individual Thanksgiving Song, for what you are living, the miracle of your life.

So then finally, this is the song that the anthropologists who have studied us, have called the "death song." And they can't be more wrong at all. Because you know what? I've used that song two thousand times since I was born. And I'm only gonna use it once, when I'm ready to leave this world. So it's a death song only once. But all the other years I've been living, I've been singing it, all the time. So it's not a death song; it's a song of *life.*

And I've seen real Iroquois men of ninety, a hundred years old, at the end of their lives with no more power to live, sing their songs with their last breath. A man will barely be able to get out of bed, sit on its edge and he'll say,

> Takia'tíson niá:wen. Niá:wen tsi nikarì:wes wa'tkatawén:rie tsi iohontsiá:te wahskenaktotháhse takatawén:rie. Ne ká:ti ne Takia'tíson ó:nen ká:ti tkaié:ri ó:nen ká:ti enwá:ton enskahtén:ti. Ó:nen enkoniaterennotháhse.

And what he's saying is,

> *My Creator, thank you for the wonderful life that I lived, since I was born. My Creator, thank you for the children that were born to me and my wife. My Creator, thank you for all the grandchildren that were born, that I've seen get born. Thank you for how I was*

able to take care of them, all these years. And now my Creator, I know that my journey and my visit here is close to being over. And so I'm ready to come to you now. I'm ready to go home. And so I sing to you for all the wonderful gifts, all these years since I was born, my song of thankfulness.

Then he'll start to sing his song. And he lies down, still singing while he's lying down too. And when he finishes singing his song, his breathing stops. He's gone. Died. I've seen that happen. I've seen the people do that.

And that's why they say,
Kwah ratirennotákie Karonhià:ke wahón:ne. *They're singing as they go to the next world, the world of our Creator.*

And that's where our grandmas and grandpas are. They're over there, waiting for us. Got a great big corn soup cooking ready for us, a big feast. Got strawberries growing, big fat juicy ones all over that land. Water drums going, all kinda dancing over there. That's where grandma and grandpa went. And that's where I'm gonna go too, one day. And how many more times I'm gonna sing this song, I don't know. But I'm gonna sing it.

Okay, now that's Atón:wa.

Now there are more teachings to these things of preparing yourself, and what it means. But we'll leave it at that for now.

So that woman was standing behind the tree, watching what I just told you. That little boy was telling those eleven boys, almost word-for-word, what I've just been telling you now. And that old grandmother was trying to hide and see what they were doing.

And then when she was satisfied, she turned around, thinking they didn't know. She went back down to the village and she broadcast it all, down there to the people. She said,
Ne ne ionerákwat tsi nihonkiehrha thí:ken ratiksa'okon'a iethiiatere'okón:'a ne ne ionerákwat. Í:iah nonwén:ton tesathonté:'on tsi na'teiotenonhianíhton tsi niióianere nahò:ten rotitharáhkwen.

That means,

> *You will never believe the scope and the magnitude and the*
> *sophistication of what those kids are talking about up there. The*
> *way that they see the world, the way that the world was put together,*
> *they're putting all together. That's what he's teaching them, that*
> *boy, my grandson. Unbelievable.*

And so they finished all these first three on the list: Great Feather Dance,
Drum Dance, and Thanksgiving Song. Only these first three. That's what
he taught them. With the Opening and all the clan stuff. He reinforced
that. But the fourth one, the Peach Stone Game, he didn't teach them that
right then.

So then, as he taught those kids, he said, "The reason there are eleven of
you is because humans tend to forget. No matter how well you've rehearsed
something, or studied something, you always forget some little piece of it.
And if that happens to you, that's why the others, the tenth one or the ninth
one or the seventh one, they will patch up your stuff, wherever you left a
hole in it. So that way, among all eleven of you, you won't forget anything
because you're gonna help each other. Whatever one lacks, another one
can get right in there, and add. It's like a canoe with a hole in it. Patch up
any hole right away and keep that boat going. And that's why there are
eleven of you, to do that. No one can do all of everything." And that's the
psychology behind that.

So finally, all of the eleven kids were dispatched back to their villages,
after they had thoroughly gone through the university of the forest, the
clearing in the forest that was a perfect circle. So they went back home.
And so all the people of the villages were to do Feather Dance. "Eio hio
hiooooooooooooooo." Drum Dance. Atón:wa songs. And all villages started
to do exactly this, all this stuff that he had taught the eleven. Everybody
started to be grateful for their life. And everything was hunky dory for
quite awhile. Yeah.

Chapter 18

The Four Sacred Rituals Part 3:
Peach Stone Game

So the winds stopped. And the birds all rested on the nearest tree and kept still. Even the deer all came there, from the woods. Still. Only their ears turning forward; big black eyes, looking at them.

So then when the time came, the Teacher said, "Now I have to go. I must leave you." So he gathered them together, and he said, "Now, I've finished my job, what the Creator sent me to do. And I'm proud of you guys and all you Onkwehón:we people. You embraced all the Creator's teachings. Oh, you are such a nice people." He said, "We've done everything we're supposed to do. So now I'm ready to journey. Come with me to the edge of this turtle."

"Oh yes, we will go."

So all the young guys walked together with him. And all twelve of them got to the shore of the big turtle, where the waves of the ocean come in. And he said to them, "Across this big water, there's another people: they're different than us. And those people are worse than us, meaner than the people here, more violent: the killing and the things going on over there, not following the Creator's way at *all*. They're more wa'onthahará:ko. They have gone away from their spirituality more than here."

He said, "And those people over there, they've got mustaches and light skin, and blue eyes. That's where I'm gonna go. They need the teaching of the Creator. They're even in more need than here. The Creator said that I have to go there. So I've finished here, and now I'm going over there."

And my uncle and some of the elders say that all the winds stopped, and the sun even dimmed at that time. You know when your car has a surge of power and it dims? Or sometimes it even happens to your electricity: everything looks like it's gonna go out, but it doesn't quite.

Whenever that kinda spiritual thing happens, life's forces get dim. In order for a great thing to happen, it puts a strain on them. So the winds stopped. And the birds all rested on the nearest tree, and kept still. Even the deer all came there, from the woods. Still. Only their ears turning forward; big black eyes looking at them.

And Shakorihonnién:ni said, "I'm going now to where the rising sun comes from. That's where these people are, that I gotta go to next, to give them the teachings. I don't know what's gonna happen to me 'cause where I'm going is rough. I don't know if I'll make it. But, if someday you get lonesome for me, and you wonder about what happened to me," he told them, "there's a tree over there on that hill," just like in the Great Law[5] time. "You go scratch the bark of that tree, and if blood comes out, you'll know I was not successful. But if just sap comes out, you'll know I'm all right. That's how you will measure it, if you ever wonder."

So then, when he finished that, he said, "So you will still continue this." He had told them when and how to do everything. They all knew it thoroughly. They were well instructed. "Now," he said, "don't ever stop doing this, as long as the sun shines in the sky. As long as the waters are moving in the rivers, don't stop that. As long as the grasses and the vegetation grow, don't stop." He used the same language that's embedded in all the treaties that

---

[5.]   See chapter 26 "The Great Law of Peace Part 1: the Birth of the Peacemaker."

were made with England, Holland, and then the United States, the same kinda words because they're significant of a universal truth.

He said, "Now, my brothers, I have to leave." So he went down the hill and then he started walking, almost like in the air, over the water. Just walking on the water, like the white people say. 'Cause he did that to go there. And they watched him, as he went across that big water towards the east, into the sunrise. And his body got smaller as he went further, and smaller, and smaller, until he became nothing but a little dot. And then even the dot disappeared. He was gone.

And the birds started flying again. And the deer started jumping around again. And all the eleven guys turned around and they went home, back to their respective villages. And they continued to do all these things they'd been taught to do. And those rituals are the ones that most of the Iroquois nation Longhouses have never stopped doing.

We, the Mohawks of Akwesasne, *did* stop it for almost one hundred years, or close to it. We stopped, and then we tried the other way. But it didn't work for us, so we built our Longhouse again one hundred years ago, to bring it back. A hundred years ago, and that Longhouse stands yet today. And that was my grandmother and great-grandparents, who did that. And I'm happy they did.

So now, for many years, these young guys were teaching all the while in their villages. And all the villages were doing well. The people were caring for each other. There was brotherhood, joy and love, and everything was good.

The years went by, and, after awhile, the eleven guys began to get older, and older and older. And they all could hardly walk: they were so old now, ancient. A lot of them were walking around with sticks and canes, some even with two canes. Some people used to say that in those days, people could get up to 150 years old. However old they were, they were *old*. But by this time, there are hundreds of them, that can do these things that those eleven were doing.

And, all of a sudden, this one old man got this urge. It was nothing you could see, but somethin' was kinda pulling him, you know, just like when they were born.

Then the next old man—and this was unplanned, unorchestrated, unintended—that same sensation came to him. There was this thing that drew him, almost like magic, without touching him, or without sending him an invitation or anything. So he took his old walking sticks, two of them. And he started walking, barely walking. But he started following that.

And then another man, same thing happened to him. And they were all living in different villages. Nobody said, "And today we're gonna do this." No. There was nothing physical. They just kinda wanted to go. And of course they were spiritual men, so they were never reluctant, they never hesitated about anything spiritual. They'd go with it, see? And that's the way we are. I know 'cause I've studied this. And I'm like that too.

So these eleven old men from the different villages start walking aimlessly, without direction. But something was taking them somewhere, so they just followed the instinct, the feeling, and it took them, barely walking. But then all of a sudden one of them got to the edge of the water. And after another half a day, another one got there. And they hung out there, where they were taken by that Teacher they had years ago, 'til all eleven showed up.

And so when they finally got there, they saw each other and they knew each other. And they said, "Gee that's strange, we all came here. How come we came *here*?" And they were so surprised that they had all come at the same time.

"Well," one said, "I just got this urge to go where the earth took me. And this is where it took me."

Another said, "Me too, that's what happened to me."

They said that to each other. And they embraced each other 'cause they were old friends. They sat there in a circle by the edge of the water over there, at the big ocean, and they started to reminisce.

One said, "Remember when we were little kids, and our Teacher was here with us? And he used to take us way in the woods in that clearing? 'Member that?"

"*Yeah,*" they said.

"You 'member he taught us the Opening, the Ohén:ton Karihwatéhkwen? 'Member that?"

"Remember that log up there? We sang Feather Dance and everything and we learned that and Drum Dance and all that stuff?"

And this and that. They were remembering how much fun they had, as little kids.

"Remember his grandmother came to see and sneak up on us and we all seen her," one laughed. And they all started laughing. They were talking about old times, the way it was and they said, "Geez it's wonderful we all sit together, reminiscing."

"And then," one said, "our Teacher left us and that's where he went, years ago. We haven't seen him since."

All those old men were gathered there by the ocean, at the edge of the ground, the turtle. And all of a sudden as they were pointing out to each other where he went, they saw something like a dot. Just like that one that was gone. And as it came closer, it got bigger and bigger and bigger.

And it came not *right* on top of the water, but *above* the water, flowing like a cloud, below the other clouds. And it was this form of a man. He had all white clothes on, white garments. But they didn't know who it was. And they'd never seen anything like that before. And so finally they were all really straining their eyes looking to see, "What's that? Who is that? What is it? What does it mean?"

All of a sudden, when it got really close to them, they noticed it was their *Teacher*. But he looked different. Dressed different too. So when they recognized that it was him, the Teacher, they all jumped up. They even left their canes on the ground. They forgot to use them, they got so excited. They jumped up with all their strength, and they ran over there. They were so happy, immensely happy, they wanted to hug him 'cause it was so many years since they'd seen him.

He said,
Í:iah thaón:ton. *It's not possible.*

He stopped them. Can't do that.

They said, "What happened? Why? We're so happy to see you."

He said, "When I left here, when I left all of you to go to another part of the world, remember I told you, I didn't know what was gonna happen to me? Well, what happened when I got over there: those people didn't want anything to do with the Creator's teachings, at all. Not only that, *they hurt me*," he said. "Wa'onkkaré:wahte." And he opened up his white garments. He was wounded. There were scratches all over his body. And there was fresh blood coming out of the wounds, out of his chest.

And he showed them his hands. "Iokahrón:ton, *holes in there.* Blood coming out . . . taiotiiakenhákie ne onekwénhsa, *my feet are bleeding.* Ionekhwá:'on kahsi'tà:ke, *blood all over.* Hé: eh akwahsi'ta'kéhshon, *there, all over my feet.*" He said, "They don't want peace. That's why I'm going back to Karonhià:ke now. And there, I shall make a report about everything that happened."

He said, "When I get over there, I'm gonna go close that door because of what they did to me. And so from here on in, until the sun doesn't shine any more, and the rivers don't run any more, it is going to be: they will never stop fighting over there where they did this to me. They will fight each other and blood will be always over there because they refused the teachings."

And so that's why right now in the Middle East there's lots of fighting. No matter what anybody has said, they don't want peace. They say they do, but they bomb each other just the same. And of course we've been hearing this since I was a little kid, that it's gonna be like that. I've been hearing that for over fifty years. And I don't know if it's true or not true, but that's what they told us.

And he said, "I'm gonna tell him everything about you, too, you Onkwehón:we." (That means *Indian people in North America.*) "He'll be proud." He said, "Thank you. You didn't hurt me when I was here. Thank you, you opened yourselves, and you embraced the Creator's teachings. And you gave me great honor. You Indian people, you don't know how lucky you are, what you did. Such a multitude of honor. So when you finish this earth, that road you're gonna go take is so easy."

So I always say to our people, our little kids, just the way they said it, "You're lucky. Your grandpa didn't say 'no.' Yeah."

And then he said, "I'm not real *real*, like you are now. I'm only in the spirit. So that's why you can't hug me. That's why you can't touch me. The reason the Creator sent me back here was to show you, to give you the evidence of what happened across the ocean. 'But,' he told me, 'while you're there, I want you to deliver one more sacred thing.'

"When I was here, when you were little boys, and I was little and I grew with you, when I was teaching you the Creator's three sacred things, there was one thing he forgot to send with me. Until now. And I shall give it to you."

So he opened up his white garments, and from under his arm, he took a wooden bowl. And in that wooden bowl, there were peach pits, that were burnt black on one side and white, their natural color, on the other side. Six of them. And he had beans in this bowl.

And he said, "This bowl was sent to you by the Creator, as a special gift to celebrate your *life*. This Peach Stone Game is the Creator's favorite, most enjoyable game, the one he loves to indulge in more than anything else in the whole universe.[6] Whenever the Creator likes to relax, he plays this game. And anybody who plays this game will get the attention of the Creator immediately because he loves it so much."

My people call it Kaientowá:nen, which means the *big wood*, because it's a big wooden bowl that they use. And they throw that bowl with the dice[7] in there, black or white in combination. That's how you know if you win or not.

---

6. Another version Tom has mentioned elsewhere is that the Peach Stone Game came from the Creation story. In that version, they used the heads of the chickadee. And they rolled them like dice.

7. Tom is referring to the peach pits as the dice.

"And so when things are going nice, everything's going good, whenever you have a big celebration, make sure you play this game." And so he told us that at Midwinter (the beginning of our new year) and at Harvest ceremony, you're gonna play. And then, again you're gonna play at planting time, men against women. But in the Midwinter and also Harvest, it's gonna be the clans against clans.

We are to play the big Peach Stone Game, to entertain the Creator and give him enjoyment because we are enjoying our life. "And so together, there will be enjoyment. Let it be a part of your life, and you will tickle our Creator's heart, when you play it."

And so every time we do play that. And that's why this Peach Stone Game wasn't given to us until his return trip many, many years after these three other ones. And it became the fourth ritual.

So that's what we call now, Kaié:ri Niiorì:wake, *The Four Sacred Rituals*. And these are done in almost all the Longhouses yet today.

And so that's the way The Four Sacred Rituals is told, as far as I know.

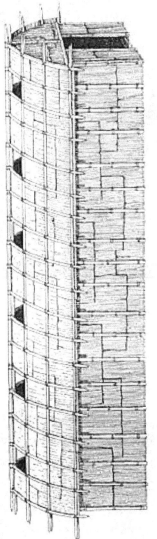

Longhouse

Above: drawing of a Longhouse made of elm bark

Below: Akwesasne Longhouse, photographed in 2008

Grandma
Above left: "Grandma" in her apron
Agatha Harriet David Chubb,
March 22, 1889-May 29, 1978
Mohawk name: Konwanataha   Nickname: Hattie

Top right: Grandma's rocker (in 2008)
Middle right: a modern corncob pipe

Bottom: Grandma's
house at Akwesasne
(2008 now inhabited by
one of her grandsons)

Grandma and Grandpa
Right: Louis Chubb in later years
Bottom: Hattie and Louis Chubb as a young couple

Ahkwesáhsne Freedom School
Top: Students/staff, many in traditional clothing
Middle: Tom's grandkids currently attending:
   Left: Konwahonkarawi
   Middle: Rowennaskats
   Right: Iakokwenienstha Porter
Bottom right: Photo of school, March 2008

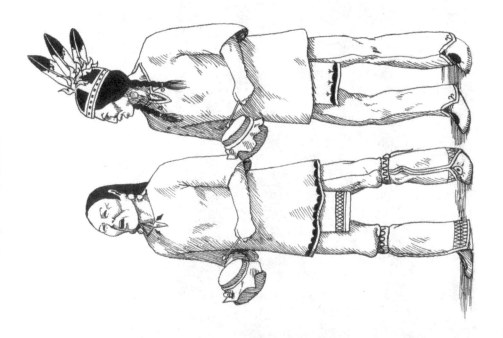

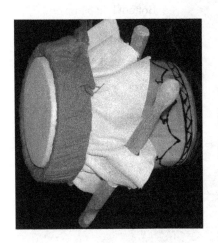

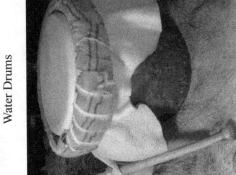

Water Drums

Wampum

Left: replicas of the Wampum Strings for each of the five original Haudenosaunee (Iroquois) nations: Mohawk, Oneida, Onondaga, Cayuga, Seneca (right to left)

Bottom right: quahog shell, from which wampum beads are made

Bottom left: pump drill, used to drill holes in the wampum beads

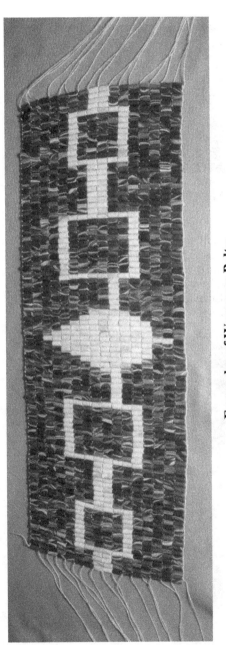

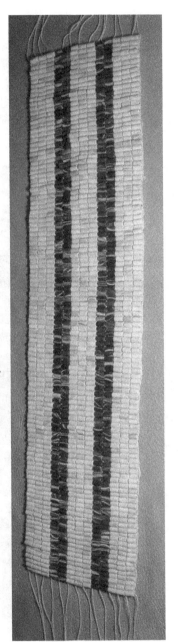

Examples of Wampum Belts:

Above, a replica of the "Hiawatha Belt," symbolizing the union of the Mohawk, Oneida, Onondaga, Cayuga and Seneca in the Haudenosaunee (Iroquois) Confederacy. Below, a replica of the "Two Row Wampum" agreement between the Haudenosaunee and the white settlers, not to interfere in each other's affairs

White Corn

Left: braided white corn
Right: field of white corn
Bottom: Atenaha (The Seed Game)
with dried white corn for scoring,
hickory dice, half of which are
blackened on one side,
and hide carrying bag

Tom and Alice's Wedding
November 7, 1970

Middle right:
another example of a
wedding basket

Bottom right:
Tom (Sakokweniónkwas)
and Alice in 2008

Tom's Six Children

Left: Aronienens Porter and Yvette Ashinawey

Right: Katsitsiahawi Perkins, Kanastatsi Porter, Tewasontahawitha Porter, Katsitsiakwas Lazore

Wedding of Aronienens and Watenonsiiostha Porter
August 18, 2001

Left: Aronienens (Tom's son) and Watenonsiiostha (Sherri)

Right: Aronienens and Tom

Bottom: (left to right) Kanastatsi Porter, Yvette Ashinawey and Katsitsiakwas Lazore, (Tom's daughters), Alice (Tom's wife), Watenonsiiostha, Aronienens, Tom, Tewasontahawitha Porter (in front of Tom) and Katsitsiahawi Perkins (Tom's daughters)

Tobacco

Right: old-style Chief's
tobacco bag

Left: oien'kwa'ón:we
(Indian Tobacco)

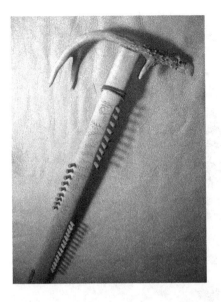

Haudenosaunee (Iroquois) Chiefs

Top left: a condolence cane, showing the marks of each of the 50 Chiefs in the Confederacy

Top right: drawing of a Mohawk Chief's kahstowa

Bottom left: drawing of the Circle Wampum, with a wampum string for each Chief in the Confederacy

Bottom right: a deer antler such as those used on a Chief's kahstowa

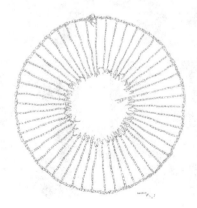

Tekáhstia'ks

Tom bought the parrot
Tekahstia'ks, to show
his grandchildren that even
a parrot could learn Mohawk.
Shown here are grandchildren:
Top right: Rahnienhawi Burns
Opposite: Rahente Perkins
Center left: Tsioweriio Lazore;
Center right: Roweren Lazore
Bottom left: Konwanontiio Lazore
Bottom next: Karhatiron Perkins
Bottom next: Ronatiio Perkins
Bottom right: Karonhiate Lazore

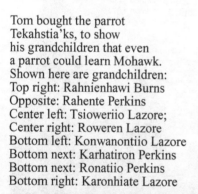

Carlisle Indian Industrial School, 1879-1918
Top left: main entrance
Bottom left: Chiricahua Apaches on arrival at Carlisle, 1886

Top right: student body assembled on the grounds, circa 1900
Bottom right: Chiricahua Apaches four months later

Kanatsioharé:ke

Top: the West Wing, and the Bed and Breakfast

Center left: horses grazing

Center right: the "clean pot" for which Kanastioharë:ke is named

Bottom: recent restoration of the barn

Chapter 19

Atenaha, the Seed Game

They played it only in the wintertime. And usually it was at night, when the kerosene lamps were going

Another thing that Grandma always did is the seed game, "Atenaha." A lot of Mohawks in my reservation don't even know that game. Certain families do, but the majority of families don't play it any more. But it was normal in our house.

It is different from the Peach Stone Game, the fourth sacred one. This one is not made out of peach stone; it's made out of hickory, from the hickory tree. There are eight pieces; you use eight of them. Atenaha has got its own rules too.[1]

They played it only in the wintertime. And usually it was at night, when the kerosene lamps were going. They put a white sheet on the table and that's what they played on, the whole family. Even the grandkids would play, against the old people.

[1.] See Appendix B for detailed rules.

Chapter 20

The Four Sacred Beings

During times of need, they're the hired messengers of our Creator . . . They have nothing to do with angels.

At the beginning of the world, when the Creator made human beings, as I've mentioned, we were not made complete, like other animals. We're the most pitiful of all life forms, us humans. We're the ones that make the most problems, for ourselves and for everybody. Because of that fallibility that we have inherent in us, as I've said, the Creator was too busy all by himself, to keep track of our mischievous stuff. So he appointed or commissioned Four Sacred Beings. We call those Four Sacred Beings, Kaié:ri Niionkwè:take.

In every Longhouse, you'll hear them say all the time: Kaié:ri Niionkwè: take. Then they'll say, Ratironhiakehró:non, the Sky Dweller Beings. Ratironhiakehró:non means those *men of the sky, the universe.* Usually the Iroquois that are Christianized, they'll call them "angels." But they're not angels to us that grew up in Longhouse 'cause we don't have that concept. They have nothing to do with angels. To us, they're just some kind of powerful beings, four of them in the universe, the sky between the next planet and this planet. And their job is to keep a connection between those two lands 'cause of our life.

And like I said, they really love children. And they love old people too because old people are *like* children. They'll help us older people too, but not as much as children. Their priority is kids. During times of need, they're the hired messengers of our Creator to help, to keep order. Whenever there isn't order on this earth, he will send one of them, two of them, or all of them, to come and see if they can fix it, or get it back in order. You see what I mean?

And so when there was a need for the Peacemaker to be born, he summoned them. And one of them used his power to be born as a person *here*, in order to bring order back. If some kind of a strange thing we've never seen before, or stranger from another place, came and we didn't know him, we might not listen to him at all. We might hurt him. See? So he sends one of them to be born like we are, so he's one of us and so we listen to him. And so one of them volunteered, and was born the Peacemaker. See?

And then earlier, at another time, they came to visit this man, Ro'nikonhrowá: nen, the Big Idea Man, the Big Head Man when the clan time came, that we talked about earlier. They influenced him with messages and ideas of how to bring order. And he brought the Clan System, via their influence. They weren't born into him this time. He was already born and they entered his world and his mind and they brought the Clan System.

And then later on, when the Four Sacred Rituals came, it is one of these powers, that was commissioned to be this little boy that was born. And so I say in the world, wherever there was a need for a messiah to be born, it's one of these powers that were born, whether he's Chinese, whether it's a black person, or whether it's whatever. So each of the messiahs of peace is one of the Four Sacred Beings. And so that's why there'll be similarities about lots of things. So that similarity doesn't bother me any more. But if you try to be purist it will! And when you're young you try to be purist. When you're young.

Chapter 21

Three Souls or Spirits and Ohkí:we

Our life is like a braid, like a sweetgrass braid.

I've heard elders say that our life is like a braid, like a sweetgrass braid. And when you braid something you have three parts. So in the Great Law, this three is always carried over. In almost all of these sequences, you'll hear the number three being quoted at various times in these events, so there's always a consistency to it. It doesn't really change all that much.

But in this reference to life, one of my uncles used to say to me, that when we were created in the beginning, the power of Karionhià:ke, the place where our grandmother came from is the first one, the first power, the first source of who we are.

Then when she arrived here, she used the earth's power as well, and that became another one, a second source of spirit.

And then they used the actual dirt from the earth and the elements of this earth which came alive. And that's what we are, what our flesh and blood is. That's the third source. And then we will return, when we're done.

And those are all referred to, when we have funerals. They recite that part. So there's the three.

So the Creator and Mother Earth and all that, they took those three and they intertwined them together so that we have three sources that made who we are. So in other words, my uncle said we have three souls and three spirits. Soul and spirit are almost like the same thing. In fact it sounds like it's the same thing. (But I never questioned him further on that.) So there are these three.

When we finish our stay on earth, these come apart, and go back to where they belong.

So the spirit or the soul that came from Karonhià:ke goes directly back there. It doesn't matter what you did. If you were a thief or you were a killer or you were a rapist or whatever, that doesn't even enter the question. That's got nothing to do with it. When you die, the part of your spirit that came originally from Karonhià:ke, goes there no matter what.

And the second one of our souls or spirits that came together as one to make who we are, goes back to the Mother Earth. It goes back here and it roams the earth. That spirit stays when we pass on.[1]

And the third one, which came from the earth itself, who is our mother, becomes that again. It goes back to the dirt itself, which then makes life go on. Because it's the physical dirt that makes corn grow, that makes watermelon grow. So that part returns back there. It's the ongoing life-giving force. That's the one we call Mother Earth.[2] That's where our body came from, in order for these other two souls or spirits to find a place to live.

So when you're decomposing, there's a spirit in that too. That third spirit comes back to the Mother which is again, the giver of life. I guess you

[1.] These are the individual souls or spirits that are honored in Okhí:we, as Tom explains further on.
[2.] This is part of the spirit of Mother Earth, the spirit that is acknowledged in the Opening Address.

could call it recycled, if you wanted to. It is recycled because you return back to your Mother. When we pass on, our spirit continues in the life of many things. So it's wonderful: it's a beautiful thing.

What happens is like when you take sweetgrass, you get three parts of the sweetgrass. Then you crisscross them and make them one. And that's what our life is. See? When we're born, it's braided together. And then, when we die, it comes apart. It undoes itself. So that's why we're temporary. That's why they say we are only visiting.

And that's why they say when somebody dies, you tell the people, "Don't be afraid." Don't be afraid of death. Because all death is, it's just like a baby being born. It's another stage. It's another graduation. That's all it is. So.

While we're on the subject, when somebody dies, that's why we have Ohkí:we: what you call a Ghost Dance. We have two Ohkí:wes, one in the spring, one in the fall. All the Iroquois have this. Ohkí:we is an all-night Ghost Dance to feed the dead people. It's for the spirits that are all over, roaming the earth. They say once the sun goes past the middle of the sky, and it starts to lessen in its heat intensity, that's when the spirits of the dead start to roam around the earth. See?

When the sun goes down, it's really cool out, and so when you touch the dead people they're cold. And the night is like that. And so that's why they say, whenever you do a dead feast of some kind, a memorial feast, you usually wait 'til after three o'clock to do it. That way you're assured that they're up and about on the earth.

And 'member when we were talking about Shawískara, I said that at nighttime, you're not supposed to run outside? Because the spirit of a lot of living things is all over. And you could hit them accidentally, you could offend them. And they could retaliate. You know what I mean? So that's why you don't want to.

Most of our old people, the grandmothers and grandfathers, they used to say that to us, when we were kids. They would tell us right away. But we don't do that anymore. Now there's a lot of grandmothers and grandfathers who don't say anything to their kids. They don't warn them.

So everything is going wildlike. There are no more guideposts. All those things made you move respectfully. It was almost predictable, the movements. And right now everything is erratic; anything goes. The kids don't have anything to go by. And we have lost that sort of thing.

So that's why we have memorial feasts all the time, and that's why we have them individually in the house as well. We have two of them that are national—the whole nation does it—two a year, for sure. And that's so that the whole nation is protected, see?

And then we also have individual ones in our own homes, for our own families. We usually have two of those, too, per year. So we have at least four times in the year that a normal traditional family will have a memorial feast. Twice nationally and usually twice just for your family, to make sure you cover all the bases. That's a normal traditional family.

This goes way back to the beginning of time. And that's one thing you'll find amongst every Iroquois reservation. No matter how modern or progressive we are, most of the reservations have a segment of their population that are traditional. And some almost, we could say, "ultratraditional" in their thinking. Most have that.

Some reservations don't, one of those being Tuscarora. They have traditional people, but not near as much as the other ones because when the Tuscarora came here, from North Carolina, they were already all Baptists. They were already converted, and part of their training was that it was evil, and that it was Satanism to do that kind of behavior. So they've never had a Longhouse over there—ever since they have been here, I think—for over two hundred years. However, they have kept other aspects of the tradition. But in this part, I think, not so much.

But in the Onondagas, Senecas, Mohawks, Oneidas, and Cayugas, you usually see this still existing. Very strongly by the way.

It's the same thing with you, the same thing with me. If my wife doesn't cook for me, and my aunt doesn't cook for me, or my daughter or whoever doesn't cook for me, then pretty soon I'm gonna get skinny. And as I get skinnier, I might get a little bit upset! And then I have to cook for myself.

And then if I don't cook right myself, I get upset again too! And then the next thing you know, I get angry.

Well it's the same thing. If you don't feed these ancestors, and you don't pay attention to them, they're gonna get upset. They're gonna get angry. And what they're gonna do, if they're angry or upset, depends. You might die. They might make you or your children get sick. Or they might make your whole clan, or your whole nation, get sick. So that's why we don't take a chance on that.

That's why we're always doing these memorial feasts. We want to show the highest respect to our grandmothers and grandfathers. We don't want to take a chance. They're the ones that gave us birth and life. See? So that's not even a question; it's an obligation.

And that's why, when the Iroquois do feasts for the dead, we always serve the food clockwise. It's very different. That's the only time you do that: when it's for the dead.

Any other ceremony we're doing in all the Longhouses is done counterclockwise, for the living.[3] And that's still understood by all of them, even the ones that are Christian. It's so ingrained from our ancestors, that even the most Oral-Roberts-Christian guy, couldn't change their minds. It's still that strong.

We just had Ohkí:we here at KanatsiOharè:ke in early October. Whenever our people come to fast here, they do it. And then in the spring, they do Ohkí:we again. Plus we do it ourselves, for our own families. When they do it for the nation, when the speaker burns tobacco, he's talking to all of the spirits, on behalf of everybody in the nation. See?

Where we grew up, even though they do that in the Longhouse, we always do it at home, as well. And Grandma did it that way, and her mother did it that way, and way before that. So us, we're always doing those memorial feasts: we've never quit.

---

3.   See chapter 28, "The Great Law of Peace Part 3: Keeping and Preserving It" for more information on the concept of direction.

Also that's why we have seers. So if you notice at your house that something just doesn't go right, no matter what you do to try to fix it, that's usually when you go to see a woman or a man who has the ability to *see*.

And they will look into what your life is, and then they will see right away what's causing this irregular pattern. And so they'll tell you. Your people in your family who have died, like your grandmother or somebody—they even sometimes specifically say who it is—and they'll say, "They're so hungry for *you* to feed them." They already went to the big feast, but they're lonesome for *you*. They want to sit down with *you,* their grandson.

So that's what seers are for. Whenever there's something irregular in your life, that you notice, that's the time you go seek them. The dead people are gonna do things, if they have been somewhat neglected. Whether it's by intent or not, or just forgetfulness, or not knowing, it doesn't matter to them. The dead people don't know what "postpone" means, in their world. So they're sort of always following around living people.

When you commit to doing that feast and you get together your family, or when the seer tells you to do a feast especially at *that* time, now you can't ignore that. 'Cause once that seer has told you that, now you have no excuse of any kind. Now the dead people are gonna get stronger, if you don't do something about it. They say, "Now you were *told*." And if you say, well, I'll wait for six months or the summertime or when the weather gets better, I'll do it then, if you do that, they intensify their desire to be visiting with you and the food, whatever it is.

And that's when you're gonna get trouble, start to get sick. You may get physically sick, heart trouble, migraine headaches or pain or whatever. They're gonna make you that way. It's like a sliver. You can't rest until that sliver gets out of there, see? And the longer you wait, the worse it gets, huh? And you can die from it. And that's the same thing here. You ignore that: you can die from it. So that's why when you set a date that ceremonies will take place, you better *do* it when you said you would 'cause that's when they're gonna be there.

And if you're not doing it at that time, you're gonna get in trouble. 'Cause they don't know why you weren't there. They say, "He lied to me." And sometimes they bring friends with them from their world, so you're in even more trouble!

There's a society of people that's in charge of the Ghost Dance—the nation-scale one. Only the initiated members belong to that. You have to belong to it because you got healed by them, or the dead people have invited *you* to become part of that. You and I can't say, "Well, I think Ohkí:we society is a neat society. I'd like to be a member of it." You don't do that. That's the way it is with all the medicine societies that the Iroquois have. And we have a lot of them.

We never say we'd like to join them, or we think it's nice the way they do things. No. It's because we got sick, caused by that power of that society because our ancestors who belonged to that long ago, miss us. So once we become that, we've become initiated into that kind of society. For the Ohkí:we it's a very strong society, a very strong initiation.

They're the ones that are in charge of the food, of the singers, of everything that goes on. It's a women's society. One or two men dance with the women for just a little while, not all of it. Otherwise, only the women dance.

You should go whenever you are asked, invited to go. But if you are not a member, you don't *have* to go. You see? Because that's *their* job. They're gonna feed the dead, on behalf of everybody. That's often when the Longhouses get really full. Sometimes there's not even enough room for all of them to go in there 'cause everybody has lost somebody that died.

But then a lot of the time, if people don't go, they'll send food. They don't go because they don't belong, and they know the society is gonna do it "on my behalf" anyway. And they say to themselves, "I'm gonna do the one that's in my house." But a lot of the people do wanna go because they dance all night until dawn. That's when they quit. And the kids like going because they give out ribbons and candies and stuff, on behalf of the dead.

So that's enough on this subject because I only started out to talk a little bit about the braid, huh? That's what my uncle said. I don't know if that's the way all the Iroquois believe, but that's the way my uncle explained it to me, when I was younger. And I have always maintained that because he told me that. But I don't have any other way to know. So that's what I share with other people about it 'cause people wonder about death a lot of times.

But he says that our thinking, our conception of it is different than the European way. He says, "It doesn't matter what you did in life, that one spirit's gonna go back to Karonhià:ke, that other one's gonna go back to roam the earth, and the third one's gonna go back to the Mother. And that's that. No matter what you say or what you do," so he says.

So you know that. We are in charge of these three powers, when we're born. That's why we should always take care of ourselves and our spirit, the spirits we have within us that make our existence. We should always try to walk this earth in a respectful manner, so we do justice to these. You make them happy, not make them cry.

We are the example, the exhibit of the oneness of those three spirits or souls. When we die, they come apart. It finishes. But while we're living, it's one, through our body. It's like the braid. It's three different strands, but once you've braided it, it becomes one. And so that's Creation.

I've been asked if the three can be compared to the biblical trinity. I don't know because I don't know anything about the Bible. So I'm a poor one to make comparisons with that.

It's the same thing when we talk about our Constitution. Some people ask me, "Can you do a comparison?" Well, I don't know the Constitution of the United States. I don't know what the articles are. All I know is our Great Law. So I can say what I remember of our Great Law, and then *you* know the law of the United States. Well then, *you* compare it, once you've heard what we have to tell about ours. Now you can do a comparison, but *I* can't 'cause I don't know how America works.

Someone said the Bible trinity is "the Father, Son and Holy Ghost, but no women." So now we are talking about the women. Course this story I'm gonna tell you is more like a joke or something. Or maybe it isn't, I don't know!

They said three women became good friends: the Jewish woman and the Polish woman and the Mohawk woman. And they became friends through

AA. That's where they met each other. And so they were going to travel around now 'cause they got a new lease on life, I guess.

So they were going somewhere towards New York City, on the thruway here. They were riding together. And a great big, ol' eighteen-wheeler hit 'em head on. They died right away. And 'cause they were on the right road now, AA, their spirit went right away to heaven, I guess. And they said Peter was there waiting for them. And he took them around, showed them where they're supposed to go, the pearly gates and all that. They went right through there.

And then they came to the middle of the land, the next world, and there was a big ol' throne. That's where God sits, and it's got diamond studs, and pearls and rubies, and all that. So God is sitting there, you know, and so Peter brings them before him. And he says, "These are new arrivals, right here."

And he looked at those three ladies. And he looked at that Jewish lady, and he says, "My little sister, come on, sit here in this chair next to my throne." And that throne is completely solid gold. So the Jewish lady sits there. And he looks at the Polish lady and he says, "My Polish sister, come and sit on the left-hand side of my throne." And he looks at that Mohawk woman. And he didn't know what to do with her, I guess.

And she looked at him and she says, "What are you doing sitting in my chair?"

I love that story. It's real descriptive. I mean that would probably be true!

So anyway, we simply started to talk about the Thanksgiving Address and it led to all this other stuff. Wonderful. And I guess that's what my uncle meant when he said, "It's never the same." Whatever spirit comes, whatever power comes, it wants to be exposed; it wants to be known; it wants to be aired. And that's where this took us. It's an example of it, huh? See, we're s'posed to be doing this, but the other ones wanted to come in. They wanted attention, so that's what we talked about. And a real Iroquois teacher, that's the way they are. You never know what it's gonna be, you know. But it's gonna be something!

Chapter 22

Weddings

My grandmother told me that we follow the way of the eagles.

Say a young man of the Bear Clan and a young woman of the Wolf Clan plan to get married. This is proper, and their children will become good candidates to become Faithkeepers, Clan Mothers, or Rotiianéhshon.[1]

A couple cannot marry unless they have the consent of both their mothers. In traditional marriages, you can be forty years old, but you would still need the consent of your mother.

A couple desiring to get married must make a request to the Council of Chiefs, and together set a date for the wedding. When the Council of Chiefs and the couple agree to the date, the Rotiianéhshon will publicly announce the date, and the whole community is welcomed to participate. There are usually no individual invitations sent unless the couple has relatives and friends living far away.

[1.] For more about this term, and how it differs from the English word "chief," see chapter 30, "The Leadership."

For a wedding, the man and woman and their families dress up, from head to foot, in the most beautiful and elaborate Mohawk clothes. In the middle of the Longhouse, a wooden bench is placed, for the couple to sit.

At the side of the groom-to-be sits his mother. At the side of the bride-to-be sits her mother. The Rotiianéhshon will choose one of their own, or a Faithkeeper, to conduct the actual wedding on behalf of the entire council.

The person chosen to perform the wedding will begin by doing the Opening Address, holding the Nation's Wampum (Katsísta). Now the woman must promise to her husband, that she will fulfill and honor all the commitments of marriage.

The man chosen to conduct the marriage speaks at great length to the couple. He explains the duties and formula for a healthy, stable marriage. Now all the Rotiianéhshon address the newly married couple, with their encouragement and advice.

The couple now takes our nation's Katsísta, and agrees to pledge to one another, and to our Creator, that they will honor and embrace, for the duration of their lives, the sacredness of all the pledges of marriage.

Now they are almost solidly married. The Chiefs, Clan Mothers, Faithkeepers, the elders and all people, form a single-file line in a counterclockwise direction and shake hands with the newly married couple.

Now the first duty of the married couple will be to feed all their people. And they will, in a counterclockwise direction, give every person a small piece of the kanàtarakhón:we, *corn bread.*

The next step calls for the bride and groom to lead the people in the Great Feather Dance, which finally sanctions and seals the marriage. In all traditional marriages, there is absolutely no alcohol or drugs of any kind permitted. The entire marriage ceremony takes about two hours and sometimes longer.

Now there will be a big feast for the wedding. Generally, gifts for the married couple are now opened and viewed. The couple thank the people for each gift. In the evening, there will be a social wedding dance. Traditionally, there is no such thing as a honeymoon.

Another thing that our elders said was, "When a man and a woman are married, they have committed themselves, promised to take care of each other for the rest of their lives." I suppose that that's probably the biggest teaching. The elders told us that we are just like the eagle. The eagle flies the highest; it is the most valuable of all the birds. The eagle is considered the leader of all the birds. And once a female and a male eagle get together—we will call it marriage—if one of them should die, the other one never looks for another partner for the rest of its life. That's the way the eagles do it. That's their way. And so my grandmother told me that we follow the way of the eagles. We always try to stay with one mate, as much as we can.

Growing up,[2] I never used to go to the hospital, and I never went to a doctor because my grandmother was a medicine woman. Most old people were medicine people. They knew what herbs to pick for all different kinda sicknesses. That's one thing that's very seldom true anymore in our communities. But when I was a young boy, even the old people that were Christianized followed the same law of medicine.

My grandmother, she was a seer. That means that she had an extra eye, not just two eyes. She didn't just have two ears. She had extra ears. Her antenna in her body received many more things than regular people. Most old people were like that.

A seer is almost like having a dog next to your house 'cause a dog can hear more than a human. A dog can see better than a human. A dog can feel more than a human. So if somebody's coming to your house, that dog, he will tell you ahead of time. He will bark.

That's the way seers—human seers—are. They're like the protectors of the community. That's why the Creator sent them to be born—if they're real. But there are many seers that are not real. They only use it to make money.

[2.] This next section, recorded in July 2007, is Tom's description of his own wedding and how it came to be.

My grandmother was a seer. And my mother was one of those. Lotta people in my family were seers. I have one granddaughter that's like that too. We took a picture of her. Her whole body was lit up, glowing. Not the furniture, not the room, just her. That's my son Henes's daughter. She will be growing up, and she will probably have a gift like that.

But anyway, my grandmother didn't know how to talk English, just Mohawk. I didn't really have a father when I was young. My father had left us, five kids. They had problems, my mother and my father. So I never knew him, growing up. My mother raised us. And the one who helped raise us was my grandmother. She took the place of my father. I had a grandpa too, and uncles. So even though I didn't have a father, all my aunts and my uncles and my grandma and grandfather, they took the place of my father.

When I was about eighteen or seventeen years old, most of my cousins were not traditional. They didn't believe in our traditional ceremonies. They liked to party, go to taverns and dances. They used to invite me to go with them. I only went once or twice, just to go see what it was like.

They invited me many times, but I belonged to the Longhouse. In our Longhouse ceremony, it says us real Longhouse Indians, we are not to touch alcohol. We are forbidden to drink or touch anything that changes or alters the natural state of mind. So that's why I didn't want to go with the other young people. But it was a struggle because I also wanted friends, and I didn't wanna be lonesome. Our elders were telling us not to do it. Yet the young ones were doing it. And I was in the middle.

But I listened more to my grandmother. When I was around seventeen or eighteen, my grandmother looked at me and she says, "What's wrong? Somethin' wrong." She just had to look at me.

I said, "Oh nothing."

"Oh no," she says. "Somethin' wrong." She says, "Come on over here. We'll make some tea." She uses the green tea. And she has a little pipe. She puts prayer tobacco in there. When she prays, she burns the tobacco, and the smoke goes up. It carries her words into the universe. That's how the Mohawk prays.

She says, "I'm gonna find out what's botherin' my grandson. His name is Sakokweniónkwas." (That's my name—Sakokweniónkwas—when I was born.) She asked the Creator to find out why my mind is *heavy*.

After she finished praying, she took the cup. And she says, "Drink it."

I drank it. 'Course all the time I'm growing up, from when I was a real little boy, I'd watched her do that. So it's not new to me. When people are sick, they come to her, and she gets them to do that. She's gonna find out why they're sick and what kinda medicine can fix them. Sometimes she makes the medicine that'll fix them too.

I drink the tea. And I'm done. And what's left, I pour it out, slow, and don't look at it. I wait. She turns the cup around three times. Then she looks at it. She says, "Oh, waaaahh aahh."

That means she's seeing something, really *something*. If she does not see anything good, she will not say that. Even in our Longhouse, when they have a Spirit Song for the men, that's what they say, "Oh waaaahh aahh." That's how we do it in the ceremony. And how my grandmother does it.

She says, "Oh, it's an amazing thing. I know what's wrong with you. I know what's wrong now. You're a young man. You're thinking about woman. You're thinking about the woman now."

She looks, "Oh yeah, I seen one woman in there. That woman in there, she's looking at you. That woman in there, she's gonna come see you. When she comes next to you, she'll hold you like this, and she's gonna rub her breast on your shoulders. When that happens, you're gonna go crazy. You won't know what you're doing, and you won't even be able to find your way home. She make you wild. Because a young woman has lots of power."

She says, "But don't marry her because that woman just likes to make party. She don't know how to cook the good food. She don't know how to clean clothes. She don't know how to keep a house clean. She don't know how to make moccasins. Just only party woman. So do *not* pay attention to her. It's all right to say hello, that's all."

Then she said, "Lemme look again. Oh, waaaahh ahh. There's another one. That woman's got short dress on, above her knees. Got nice long hair. Got just like this[3]—just looks like doll. Pretty, pretty woman. That woman's gonna sit next to you at a dance. When she sits next to you, she's gonna make her legs touch your legs. When her legs touch your legs, you will go crazy again. And you don't know where you live anymore. If you wanna follow her, you're gonna get lost because that woman's got power. And she'll use it on you.

"But that woman, she likes all the men. She put her legs on all the men, not just one. So don't marry her. Just say 'hello.' That's all. If you marry her, you will always be sad and crying. Don't bother with her."

She looked again, "Aaaahh." She found another one. "This woman here, she's got a nice hair, little bit heavy, but lots of fun. She likes to laugh. She likes to dance and party. She's gonna come next to you. She's gonna touch you too. She's gonna hold you. And when she does, you will get lost again, you don't know where your home is. Do not go to her because she just wants to be happy all the time. No work, no housecleaning, no cooking, just party and laugh." She turned the cup. And she seen it.

Then she looked again and she said, "Oh waaaahh aahh. I found one away over there. This one is little one, not too tall. *Real* Indian woman. Black hair away down, almost to the knees. When she sits down, almost she sits on her hair, such a beautiful long hair. She looks nice shape too. But this woman can cook. Corn soup, corn bread, all the old food that we eat, the Indian people. She can make her moccasins and sew a shirt. She can make a quilt. She work in the garden. She knows how to plant. She knows how to make the garden harvest lots. This woman is a real Indian woman. And this woman won't bother you. She do not rub her body on you. She don't come after you. This is the woman that's a good woman for you. But you have to wait for her."

She said, "Maybe five years, maybe ten years more. Not tomorrow. You wait for that woman, the last one. When you see her, you will know. When you see her, you will know her."

[3.]   Tom moves his hands to show a woman's curves.

I asked my grandmother, "Where does this lady live? That last lady? Does she live in Cornwall Island or Snye or St. Regis or Frogtown?" (On our reservation, see?)

"No, she comes from where the sun goes down. In the south."

"Oh, must be from Syracuse. Must be Onondaga."

"No," she said, "farther, farther than that. She talks different than us, a real Indian woman."

That's what Grandma told me. And so one year went by. I met that girl that put her legs on my legs. She almost drove me crazy. I didn't know if it was day or night. She could snap her fingers, and I'd jump. She made me blind, and I couldn't find my way home. I met her.

Then later on I met the other woman, the one who rubs her breast on my shoulders. Again, I didn't know if it was day or nighttime. I lost my way home. I went with her.

Sometime later, I met the other woman that likes to dance and laugh, short dress on. I met her too. And I didn't know where's my house.

Three different times, I almost got married. I just narrowly escaped every one of those. Yeah. But none of those were really committed to belief in our Longhouse, in our spiritual way. Every time we were gonna get married, we cancelled it. Just in the nick of time too.

Many years went by, and I didn't get married to any of them. And then finally, I thought, well, maybe I will be a bachelor all my life. I'm never, ever, gonna get married.

Then in 1969, we were traveling with the religious leaders from our Longhouse. I was one of their speakers. I was just a young guy. And we were traveling all over: South Dakota, Montana, Arizona, British Columbia, Florida—everywhere. We were trying to make a revival of the Indian way, just like the American people revive their history. We were gonna do it too, but our way.

We had met in Choctaw country, in Mississippi, with the Choctaw Indians. We had a dance over there. Bobby Joe, he was a young Choctaw boy. He never went to school, so he mostly talked Choctaw, and only very simple English. He says, "Can I go with you guys?" He was only about seventeen or sixteen years old, maybe. He said, "Can I go with yous and travel with you, when you go to Arizona and Louisiana and Texas and California?"

I says, "Well, if you wanna. If your mother and father let you go, you can go with us."

He said, "Okay. Can you drive me back to my house, and I'm gonna go and ask my mother and father? If they say, 'Yes,' then wait 'til I pack some clothes, and I'll jump on your bus. I'll go with you." So he got in our mobile home and we went down off the main paved road onto a side road, a clay road. It had been raining, and the ditches were deep, maybe five, six foot deep. You didn't dare go off: you couldn't get out. That was a kind of reddish brown dirt, that clay, not like here.

We were going kinda slow. That Bobby's with us, to show us where he lives. There were two girls walking on the road, two Indian girls. And we passed them. I looked out the back window of that mobile home, and I seen them. It was that Bobby Joe's sisters, but I didn't know that. And I seen Alice. I said, "Oh, that's my wife, right there." I knew right away, just like Grandma said. I recognized her *right away*. I'd never seen her before. Only, I know it's my wife now.

I shouldn't have said nothin' because all the guys heard me. Now they were gonna tease me 'cause I said, "That's my wife." So they stopped the van to give them a ride, and I'm in the back, *way* in the back, kinda hidin' 'cause these guys are saying "Hey, go meet your husband," to her. 'Cause you know . . .

And so they wouldn't look back there. And I wouldn't look in the front either. That's how I first seen them. That was Ida Mae, with her, the one who lives with us now, yet. Alice's sister.

While I was traveling, I was making a beautiful necklace with nice stitches. I was really working a long time on it, every day. I had finished it. I knew that that was gonna be my wife because of what my grandmother had told me.

But they can't talk English. And I can't talk Choctaw. So I gave it to her, that necklace. I remember, there was a little tear come down. But we can't talk because we don't talk the same language.

Bobby went with us through Louisiana. Then he says, "Tommy, I don't know how to read, and I don't know how to write. Can you make a note and write it for me, to my mother? Let my mother and father know that I'm okay. I'm with yous yet."

So I wrote it for him. I got a little piece of paper, and I wrote on there another little note. I said, "Hello, Alice. I hope you're fine. From Tom Porter." And I put it in there, for the sister, the one that I know is gonna be my wife.

About a week and a half later, at another place on the road, a letter comes over there. We picked it up. The mother and father wrote back to Bobby Joe. (They can't write either, so the next-door neighbor has to write for them.) And there was a little note in there for me. It says, "Hello, Tommy, I hope you all right. From Alice." And that's it.

Next time I sent a letter, I said, "Hello, Alice. This is Tommy. I'm okay. I got your letter, and I wanna know if you're gonna marry me now." (That's all.) "Tom." I sent it back.

Now we're going down farther into Texas and going towards Arizona, I guess, and wherever. Next place we stop, we got a letter over there waiting for us. Another letter comes. This time we open it up, and it was a letter from her parents. Inside, there was a little letter from her.

It said, "Hello, Tom. I don't know if I can marry you. I like to. But I don't know if my mother and father will agree. Gotta ask first. And if they agree, here's $10." (It was an American ten-dollar bill.)

"If you see nice material . . . if we get married, we gonna get married Mohawk way. Because you said the Mohawk people, traditional people don't touch alcohol. They don't drink in their Longhouse, their ceremony.

So that's how come I wanna marry over there, *if* we get married. Because Choctaw, they like to drink. And I don't like that," she said.

"If you see a fancy store that's got nice material, use this $10 and buy it. And that's what I'm gonna use for a Mohawk wedding dress."

So we stopped at a place—I think it was somewheres in Texas, or maybe Arizona—where they sell material. I went and I bought navy blue velveteen, I think you call it—like a velvet—for her dress. I start cutting it, and I make her wedding dress. I start beading it, day after day, in between our stops. The guys even helped me to do some of it.

When I got back home to Akwesasne, after our tour, my sister helped me make the top part. 'Cause I didn't know how to make that, for girls; I only knew how to make it for guys. She helped me make it for her, to match the dress on the bottom.

When I got back home to my reservation, I said to my mother, "Ma, I think I found that woman I'm s'posed to get married to, the one Grandma found. Is it all right?"

I asked my mother 'cause in our tradition, you can't get married unless your mother agrees. Not father, *mother*. 'Cause we are matrilineal. She said I'm old enough, I should know. That was her answer. It was up to me.

Then I asked my grandma, my mother's mother. She said to me, "Well, many years has passed, and you found that woman, the one I was telling you was there. Okay, good, then get married to her."

My mother and my grandmother sent my aunt (my mother's sister), over to Mississippi. We went there to go meet with Alice's mother and father to arrange it. So we did. And we brought Alice back. They agreed.

We were scheduled to get married at the Longhouse, and one of my relatives died, an older lady. So we had to cancel our wedding because somebody died, a relative.

We rescheduled it another day. But this time *another* relative died. So we couldn't get married again.

We rescheduled for November 7. On the last night, my friends were helping me. We were making three wedding shirts. Then I was gonna try all of them, to see which one I liked the best. One was blue, one was red, and I forget what color the other one was.

One of my friends who traveled with us, he was seventeen. He was our head singer for Stomp Dance and all across the country. They were helping me hand-sew these shirts. That night, a group of young guys came and knocked on the door. They said to this young man helping me, "They're having a Dawn Dance down Snye area of the reservation." They call it "Dawn Dance" because it's an all-night dance—until sun comes up. And they invited him.

He asked me, he says, "Tommy, my friends are outside waiting for me. They're inviting me to go to the Dawn Dance with them. But I'm not done helping you to make the shirts."

I says, "Well, we just gotta put the buttons and the cuffs on. I can finish the rest myself. And the other guys'll help me. Go ahead if you wanna go." So he went to the dance.

About four o'clock, four thirty in the morning, a man come. Bang, bang, bang (knocking real hard on the door). He woke us up. We opened the door. He's crying, that man. He said, "Bank Leaf, he just died." The one that was helping me make the shirt.

Before he had gone to that dance, you know what he said to me? "When we finish it, if you don't choose to wear this red shirt for your wedding, why don't you give it to me? I *like* this shirt." See?

So that man came with the news, at four thirty in the morning, and told us, my best friend just got his neck broken. He died in a car accident. Now this was gonna be the third cancellation. And they had food fixed for hundreds of people.

I started crying 'cause that young boy—he was only seventeen. What happened to him: he was at that dance. Somebody was driving, and they were drinking. They were going real fast, and the car was swerving. And he's in the back seat. He knew that car was gonna get in an accident. 'Cause somebody's driving drunk-like.

When it went in the ditch, he opened the door. And he was gonna get out of that car. But when he dove out of the back seat, there was a tree and the door hit the tree. It hit his head and broke his neck. Died right away. That's how he died.

So it was very upsetting to me.

That morning, we were gonna cancel the wedding again. Third time. But my grandmother, who was the seer, she said, "If you cancel this wedding, that means you and Alice can never ever get married. You must separate. 'Cause after three times, you can't do it again. Bad luck more. If you're gonna get married, you should get married."

My aunt, my oldest aunt, she went into the Chiefs' houses. She gathered all of them together. They had a meeting with my mother, and my aunt and my grandma. They talked about it. The Chiefs said, "It's better you get married today. But first, go check with that boy's mother, the one who just died. If she says it's okay to get married, then you go ahead and get married."

And so we went to see her, the mother of the boy that died. The mother says, "He was helping you to paint the floor at the Longhouse. He was helping you to sew your wedding shirt. He was so happy you were gonna get married. He was trying to help you. So don't stop because he died. Go ahead. It's okay with me."

Then she says, "Well, my son doesn't have no burial clothes. He's got no clothes to wear, to get buried. Can you help him to get dressed for his burial?"

I said, "I think so." I was s'posed to get married at eleven o'clock that morning. And here it's seven o'clock now, in the morning. Four hours, s'posed to get married.

But I said, "Okay." I took that red wedding shirt that he liked, the one he wanted. And I said, "I'm gonna give it to him. I'm gonna dress him in his burial clothes, with my red wedding shirt. I will use the blue one." I took it to the town of Massena, to the undertaker. We dressed him up in the red wedding shirt.

By eleven o'clock, our Longhouse was packed with Mi'kmaqs, Indians from Montana, British Columbia, Oklahoma—everywhere. I knew Indians from all over. And they came to my wedding. So eleven o'clock, I'm not there. Twelve o'clock, I'm not there. The people were waiting in the Longhouse. One o'clock, I'm not there because we're trying to dress that boy. We're trying to help the family.

Finally, at two o'clock, we went to the Longhouse. They waited three hours for me and Alice. And everybody's crying. *Everybody* was crying in the Longhouse. Even me. It was the saddest wedding. And it was also a happy wedding too. But *both*, at the same time.

The Chiefs had said we could get married, but no fun dancing at the wedding like we usually have. We were just to get married, have the ceremony, and that was it. No dance. So we got married, and right after the wedding, we ate. Everybody ate. But there was a lot of food left. So we took all the food and we went to my friend's house where his body was laid out in a coffin. We gave all our wedding food to everyone that came to see him, at his wake. We sat there all night with him, *all* night. The second night, we sat at his coffin all night. And right 'til they buried him. We didn't have no honeymoon. We just sat, with the dead.

That's how I got married. That's what my grandmother arranged through the medicine.

And the Choctaw, they had a Chief Wesley. I think he was 117 when he died. He was also a seer. He told Alice when she was young, that she was gonna marry me, from the north, northeast. So she knew it too, see?

We got married November 7, 1970. We're still married. Just getting old, that's all! Our wedding picture shows everything we're wearing, that I made. My clothes too. Except the top part of hers—my sister helped me. We still have her dress. It's in the closet upstairs.

When we get married, we don't use rings. We exchange baskets. That's what the basket's about, in that picture. In my basket, I've got corn bread, mixed with strawberries. And her basket, she's got moccasins and cloth.

That's what I wanted to share with you.

We have six kids. One boy and five girls. And eleven grandkids. And only half of my kids are married. My youngest one is working in the craft store. She just graduated from high school. She's been accepted at Syracuse University, one of the top universities in the state of New York. So she'll begin her classes in the middle of August.

And of my six kids, I have one daughter that's not with Alice. There was one of those ladies that my grandmother was talking about. 'Member she told me to be careful? We weren't too careful, and we had one baby! So! But she comes to visit me sometimes. Her mother's an Ojibway.

During our marriage, me and my wife's marriage, I was part of the Council of the Mohawk Nation Longhouse for many, many years. And one of the principal Chiefs, I took his place for almost thirty years. So I used to have to be at the council all the time. Because of that, I was never able to work like a regular person. 'Cause any time trouble comes, we have to attend to it, as leaders in the nation.

That also means, when we get sent to some meeting, in Onondaga or somewheres we have to go, too. And so even though we're married, your first wife is the nation. Then your physical wife is second. And even your kids are . . . But first comes the nation. And your wife and kids comes next.

As a result, my wife and kids never had me much, to be with them every day and do the things that fathers usually do. And a lotta the time, women don't like that. But my wife never really complained.

Once in a great while, she'd say something. But not often. Mostly, she was totally supportive. When I was gone, sometimes I'd get home at two or three o'clock in the morning, from Onondaga or Seneca country. She'd never get mad at me or yell at me 'cause how come I'm so late. Used to be she'd warm up food for me, and she'd just think I was tired. And I was. But she never argued with me or said, "How come you're so damn late?" or something. She has always just been supportive. Always been like that. Yeah.

That's why now, she wants to go back up north to Akwesasne, when I retire in two more years. She wanna build a house up there where we'll have a private life now, for the remainder of our lives. Before, I was always giving to the nation. My kids never even had a father. They had to share me with the nation and stuff. And my grandkids. So she wants us to devote it to our immediate family now. I think that I owe it to her.

If we were a normal people, we would have divorced a long time ago. But because she is the way she is, she was always patient.

So I hope you enjoy. That's a true story. That's the real story.

The old people that used to know how to talk and how to do those kinda things, most of them are gone. And just me and people like me are left. Compared to them old people, we don't know how to do much anymore. That's what's sad.

We can't really afford to fool around too much. There's decisions we've got to make because once the hourglass is turned over, the sand is going down. Once it's gone, it's gone. I mean we're just little fragments of the greatness of what they were. That's why we have to be careful what we're doing. That's what's scary to me, at my age.

All the things that my grandmother and all those old Chiefs did—they acted. Even though they were poor, they moved. They did things. The only thing I wonder is if we're doing enough for our young. Compared to what our old people gave to us.

That's why, I think, each time another generation comes, there are more people, more Indians that want to be Indian, but there's less substance of Indianness for them to have and to hold, and to embrace. That's where there's a question.

But maybe that was true with me too, and my elders. They were probably thinking the same as I'm thinking. I don't really know 'cause I never have nothin' to measure it with.

Chapter 23

Pregnancies, According to Mohawk Tradition

In the eyes of the Creator, there is no more valuable life form in all of the world or the universe, than a brand new baby . . . whether it's an animal, a bird or a human.

Okay, now the subject that we're gonna talk about is pregnancy, according to the tradition of the Mohawk people or the Iroquois people.

And I say Iroquois because all the nations of the Iroquois have the very same tradition, the same value system and everything. So when we talk about the Mohawk, we're also talking about the Seneca, the Onondaga, the Oneida, the Cayuga, and so on.

Our elders told us many things about how a man and a woman should prepare for a baby to be born. There are different rules, dos and don'ts about having a child. They need to be prepared, so that they know the exact details and the amount of work that's needed. So that when the baby arrives, the baby is taken care of, in the most sophisticated and the strongest, most secure way.

One of the main teachings that has been given by our elders is that in the eyes of the Creator, there is no more valuable life form in all of the world or the universe, than a brand new baby. The Creator values any new life the most, whether it's a human baby, whether it's a tadpole from a frog, or a baby deer. Any infant, it doesn't matter whether it's an animal, a bird or a human.

One of the teachings is that you're never supposed to touch the nests of the birds. Or any animal's nest. You never bother them, when they're having babies. That's the worst thing that one can do. Our elders often told us about that.

Now, within the marriage, the commitment of a lifetime, that's where the children will be born. A nice family will come from there, with security. In the Iroquois tradition, when a father and mother are gonna have a child, the mother is pregnant, but the husband is also pregnant. There is no such thing as just the mother, the woman being pregnant. The father is also pregnant because it took two to make that baby. And it takes two to take on the responsibility of that child. There's no such thing as only one.

There are many things that the man and the woman are told: certain things they should not do and certain things they should do, for the duration of nine months. In that way, the baby will be healthy and the baby will be strong, when it is born. And that's what I'd like to talk to all of you about, some of those dos and some of those don'ts, so that you may spread the word to your relatives, to cousins you have or whoever. So that they may know this as well. And then our tradition will be strong. Because if our tradition is strong, our children are also strong.

Number one, the way my grandmother said it is that when a man and woman are pregnant, the husband is going to be just like a pillow for nine months. A pillow is soft. And when you touch it, it just bends and conforms to your hand or whatever goes onto it. And that's the way the man is gonna be.

The woman's body is changing, in order for a little baby to be developed and made. These changes affect the chemicals in her body very radically. And they cause her personality to have mood swings here and there. And when that's the case, sometimes she becomes angry fast. And she's sharp with her words. And she might try to hit you with her words, or even actually physically hit you with something. And that's how come Grandma said the husband has to be like the pillow.

Now what does she mean by that? She means this: he has to be man enough to take those sharp words. He has to be man enough to take it even if she punches him, or pushes him or something. The husband has to absorb it like a cushion. He must not argue back to his wife during this time of nine months.

And that's nature, the way it naturally is.

Now if you aren't able to do that, this is what's gonna happen: if the father and mother are arguing or fighting, the little tiny baby who's within is going to feel that. It is understood, in our traditions, that the little baby is going to feel everything, the moment there's a conception. Even though the baby is just a little tiny dot, it is already in the process of learning how to be a human being. And he learns that from his mother and his father, while he's inside getting developed.

And so all the things that happen in the nine months, the spiritual things, the physical things, the emotional things, everything, is going into that little baby, to that fetus. Is that what they call it in English, the fetus? Yeah. It's transferring. So therefore, our elders told us, and among all the Iroquois it's understood, that if a father and mother argue, this little baby is gonna feel that as well.

And then this little baby inside the mother is going to be thinking, "How come my father and my mother are arguing? I'll bet you that I'm the cause of this dispute that's going on. I don't wanna come to this earth to cause trouble between my father and mother. So I'm just gonna go back to the Creator's land." And the baby will abort its own self and be lost. That's what might happen. And it's likely that that could happen.

That's why my grandmother and different elders told us, "Don't be arguing" during the pregnancy. Sometimes the mother will initiate an argument, but the father is not to argue back. He is just supposed to take it. And if you, as the father, can't take it, well then hold your breath, turn around and go outside. Just go away and then come back later. 'Cause it'll cool off, and then everything will be all right. And that's what one of the teachings is, so that the baby won't abort, see?

And all the dos and the don'ts that the wife has to do: they apply to the husband. That's pretty good, huh? Shared responsibility, all the way. And I want to expand a little bit on that. Whenever the husband and wife are pregnant, the man is not allowed to go hunting deer. He's not allowed to kill a chicken. He's not allowed to butcher a cow or a pig. He's not supposed to touch it 'cause he's pregnant, the man.

So one time I asked my grandmother, "Well, what if I was hungry, my family's hungry? And I have to go hunt for a deer or go fishing?"

You're not even supposed to go fishing because you see blood. You have to gut the fish. When we shoot the deer, we see tragedy. And so it says, in the old teachings, that whatever your eye sees is transmitted to the fetus, to the baby inside, that's being developed. So whatever the mother and the father see, it's all being gathered in that baby that's getting created.

Now another thing that the elders have told us about is that because in the eyes of the Creator a newborn baby is so highly prized, the Creator, Shonkwaia'tíson, has bestowed upon each expectant mother and father seven times the power that they had before pregnancy. So whatever our power is now, when my wife becomes pregnant, she and I will have seven times more power than we normally have. The Creator gives the father and mother that much power so this baby can have a chance to survive and to be born on this earth. So in effect, this man and woman who are gonna have a baby, are just like a nuclear power. You know how nuclear power is? You can't see it. You can't feel it, but it can kill you. It can knock you down. And that's how an expectant father and mother are.

To illustrate this, the older people used to take medicine all the time. When they got to be seventy or eighty years old, they always had tonics, which they made by the gallon. And they would drink that to fix their blood, to fix their bones 'cause they needed lubrication. And these tonics that they used to make from herbs, did that. Sometimes they used to live to be a hundred years old, a hundred and ten years old, long ago, when they did this.

And so one of the teachings is that when you are pregnant, the man and the woman, you are not to go visiting house-to-house, unannounced. You can go visit some place, but you've gotta tell them ahead of time, that you're coming there. Don't go there and just surprise them. Because if you do, you may ruin their medicine.

I always used to go to see my grandmother, every day. 'Cause I loved my grandmother. So one time, when my wife and I were expecting our first child, I walked in there thinking nothing of it. She was old. And here she was, pouring her medicine from the jug she always had it in. And she says, "Ooooooooh." She says,

Wahshétkenhte kí:ken akenónhkwa.

That means, *You ruined my medicine.* Just simply because of my presence, because my wife was pregnant, see? That's the seven power.

It took them a long time to gather these herbs, to dry them and to prepare it and everything. And here I come and ruin it.

But my grandmother said,

Ahhh í:iah ki' thé:nen teiokié:ren. *It's all right.*

She says, "Come here." So she pours me a little glass of that medicine.

And she says I am just to take one swallow. So I drank one swallow. "Oh," she says, "you just made my medicine seven times more powerful than it was before." She says, "Now put your finger in the jug."

So I put my finger in and touched the medicine inside the jug. She says, "Now you restored the power, even seven times more than it was before. You help me out now." So what she did was, she turned a negative into seven times the positive. What a wonderful way our tradition is, you know what I mean? To turn something like that right around and really make it much better.

"But," she says, "that's why you mustn't go house-to-house unannounced because you may ruin somebody's medicine, and it won't be intentionally. And it'll hurt your baby, and it could hurt the medicine too." That's one of the teachings.

And then Grandma and elders used to say, "Now, during this nine months of pregnancy, don't ever put anything around your neck that's tight or snug. Don't button the top of your shirt. Don't put a necktie on. Don't put a choker on. Don't put anything tight on your neck, the husband or the wife. Because, the little baby that's inside the mother has what they call a cord, a birth cord. And it hooks the mother to the baby. That's how the baby eats and gets oxygen.

"Now if the father or the mother is to button the top of their shirt or wear a choker, you know how it feels when you wear a tie, very uncomfortable. Well, if you do that, the baby also feels that inside. And so that baby will try to move around, maneuver around inside the mother, until he feels or she feels the same sensation as the father or the mother, who has the choker around the neck. But many times the birth cord goes around the neck and causes the baby to be strangled. And it will die."

And so that's why we are told not to wear anything close to our neck. We are always to keep things loose, when we are pregnant.

Another teaching that we have is this: Grandma used to say, "When you're going in your house, don't stand in the doorways and rest your elbow against the doorway. Go all the way through. Don't ever pause or stay at the door. When you go up the stairs of your house, don't go half way, and all of a sudden you remember, 'Oh, I left something on the kitchen table.' And then turn around and go get it. Go *all* the way up the stairs, then go get it, what you left. But don't stop and go back down from halfway. Because if you stay in the doorway or you go halfway upstairs, when the baby is ready to be born, he's gonna start going down the birth canal and when he gets at the doorway, he'll stay there and he'll put his arm up there. He'll take his time. Or else he'll say, 'Oh, I forgot something.' And he'll go back.

"And the mother is gonna have a hard labor, and the baby's also gonna have a hard time. Stubbornness like that's gonna take place. Also that baby will inherit that thing, always forgetting something, see. So don't do that when you're pregnant. Go through all the way, even if you forget something. Or then go all the way and turn around. And complete your thing. And so the baby's delivery will also be complete, when it's ready to be born."

Another thing that I remember our elders telling us is that the mother or the father must never just flop across the bed. You lie in your bed with your head at the pillow end, and your feet at the other end. If you flop across the bed, when the baby's ready to be born and travel the birth canal, he's gonna lie across there the same way you did, and block the pathway down to get born. And you're gonna have a hard time, and the baby will have a hard time. So you always begin to do everything in the natural way, so that the baby understands and can flow through, so the birth can be easy, see. And it takes the whole nine months of preparation for that.

Now, another teaching that the elders told us about was this. You never go into a crowd or into a meeting somewhere, where there are a lot of people. And the reason why you don't do that is because many times you don't know who's going to be in the crowd. And if you go into the crowd, you might see somebody with a birthmark on their face, or maybe you'll see somebody with a leg cut off or limping or you know, something wrong with them.

And it's just a natural thing to find yourself staring at them, even though you don't mean to be disrespectful. Because anything that doesn't look normal, catches your eye right away. You don't do it intentionally and you don't mean any harm, but a lot of times because it's not natural, you stare.

And if you're pregnant, if you're either the father or mother, that may transfer and mark the baby. The chances of it marking the baby are great. So that's why you don't wanna go into crowds where there are lots of people 'cause you don't wanna get that mark on that baby, you see.

These are only some of the teachings, the dos and the don'ts about the baby.

Now, another thing that's *very* important is this. My grandmother said, "When you are pregnant, get up early in the morning, father and mother both. Get up early. Don't sleep late, 'til nine o'clock, ten o'clock, like that because if you do that, that baby is gonna learn how to do that too. And the next thing you know, that baby will be up all night, sleep all day. And you'll have to work hard, see."

So that's why she said, "Always, go to bed early, when you're supposed to. And you know if you get tired during the day, it's all right to go take a nap, as long as you make sure you get up when the sun gets up, you see. Then that baby will follow the same pattern as a human being. And you won't have no trouble. You won't have to stay up all night long with the baby."

And there are all these little teachings about such things.

And now, I'm gonna give you the biggest teaching about a father and a mother. In the teachings that we call the Karihwí:io, it says, in Mohawk,

Tóhsha nonwén:ton ensewatsté:riste oh nahò:ten teka'nikonhraténies.

That means the Creator said to the Indian people,

Don't ever touch anything that alters or changes your natural state of thinking, your mind.

He sent this message almost two hundred years ago. And what that means, in plain English is, the Mohawk people by our tradition are forbidden to touch alcohol, whisky, wine or anything with any alcohol content. It also means marijuana, cocaine, or drugs of any kind. We're forbidden to touch that, if it changes the natural state of our being. The Creator doesn't want us to do that. And if we do that, that will hurt the kids. It will hurt our partner. It will hurt all our family. And it will cause a big blemish upon our family, and there will be misery.

And so that's why I always include that in the teaching. That's the most important one, no alcohol or drugs when the baby is coming, or even when the baby is here. Stay away from it because it's gonna contaminate that baby.

And another thing that Karihwí:io says is if you see somebody that's drinking coming to your house, *hide your children.* Send them upstairs. Don't let them be there in the same room with a drinking man or woman. Because if they grab that child . . . You know how sometimes they like to play with kids? They'll grab them and throw them up in the air? They might drop him and break his neck, when they don't realize 'cause they're drinking, you see.

And also if they breathe the fire breath of alcohol on that baby or little child, then it will go in and it'll act like a seed in that little one. And as soon as that baby is a young teenager, he'll start to follow his uncle, or whoever it was that was drinking because it contaminated him. That's part of the teachings of the Karihwí:io in the Mohawk tradition.

Another teaching that goes along with this is that the father should be close by when the mother is ready to have the baby. It's even better if he can be right there, at the delivery. If the mother doesn't want him to be, then he should stay in the next room, so in case his wife calls him, he can be there in just a split second. That's what our elders told us is the proper way. My grandmother said that you're not a real man, if you're not there when your child is born. That's the most important thing, for a woman and man to be together when their child is coming into the world.

And something I'm gonna add on to the teachings of the elders is that when your baby is first born, make sure that the first words that your baby hears, once it comes out of the birth canal, are in your own language. And whatever is the first one is going to be kept in that baby's body.

And when that baby hears Mohawk after that, that's the one that's gonna stick. But if you take the baby to the hospital or somewhere and he hears French or English, then that's gonna be the first language. And she's gonna always lean towards that more. She won't even want to hear Mohawk later, see. So I don't know if that's true, but some of the elders told us to make sure of that.

Now, I wanna tell you something. I've told these things to different people in my travels. And sometimes people say, "Oh, I heard a little bit about that before." And it's not just Indians that say that either, specially that marking of the baby. Even descendants of the European people say that. But they say, "Oh, we thought those were old wives' tales."

If someone has the opinion that these are old wives' tales, I think they're missing the whole point of being a human being, really. Because the point is, if a man and a woman adhere to all these so-called old wives' tales for the whole nine months, you can pretty much be guaranteed that by the time that baby is born, they will really love that baby. And that baby is gonna be wanted, in the most complete and the most dignified way. That baby will never be subject to any danger, and will have a very good life. And the point of it is that we prepare for our children. And our families are kept strong and sacred.

And I will also add that cigarette smoking is not supposed to be done by our people either, even though I used to do that myself. The smoke of tobacco is to be used in a sacred spiritual manner, not to be put in our mouth and smoked. We are committing sacrilegious acts when we do that.

When you're pregnant, you're also not s'posed to smoke 'cause it can hurt the baby. Now even the doctors are saying that too.

When you have a baby you're supposed to have a name all ready, a female name and a male's name. A baby needs a name from almost the moment he is born because you don't know how long that baby is gonna be here. And as long as he breathed the breath of life of earth, then he should have a name, like everybody on the earth. Then even if he should pass away quickly, he's already got the name. He came here to this sacred place and he's going to another sacred place, you see. And that's understood.

Okay now, I wanted also to mention that once the baby is born, in the old Mohawk tradition, there is a ritual or an observance that is done by the mother, the father, or the uncle (the mother's brother), specially the father or the uncle. And it's called "welcoming the baby."

In this ceremony of welcome, you know how they do the Opening Prayers at the meetings and stuff like that? That's what you use when you welcome the baby. So the father, most likely the father, and the uncle, maybe both, together, will take the baby. As soon as the baby's passageways are cleared, you know the nose and the mouth and everything, and before they even give him a bath, they take that little girl or little baby boy. And they sit somewhere and hold that little baby.

And the man says to the little baby, "I'm your father. And this is my name. And this is the name we give to you. The women chose this name for you." And you'll tell him the name.

And then you'll say, "Takia'tíson, my Creator, I wanna give you my love, my greetings and my thankfulness, that you send this, my little baby, here to be born, safely. First, I thank you, my Creator."

And then you say, "Creator, this is the name the women chose for the baby. And Creator, I wanna introduce you to the earthly name now."

Then you start with the Opening Prayer. You know how they start with Mother Earth. You hold your little baby. And you say to the baby, "I wanna introduce you, my daughter or my son. This earth is your mother, our mother. And she's gonna give you all the things you need to live, all your life. And so as you grow up to walk, to become a man and to have children yourself, you will develop this good relationship with your mother. And you will respect her."

And you say, "Mother Earth, this is my baby's name." And you tell the Mother Earth what your baby's name is.

You finish that and then you talk to the Water, the rivers that quench the thirst of life. And you say to the Waters of the World, "This is my baby's name. I want you to have a good relationship. You will be interdependent with each other, for the rest of his life" (or her life).

And you do that to the Trees, to the Medicine, to the Wind, to the Sun, to everything that contributes to that little baby's relationships. You introduce him. It's called introduction or welcoming the baby.

And, I did that with all my children, so that they would have reverence for our ways of belief and our Mother Earth and everything. Even when my kids were born in the hospital, I did it there too.

Sometimes, nurses watched me and even asked me if they could stay there and listen. Everything was in Mohawk, so they couldn't understand. But later they asked me to translate what it was I was saying. And I did. And those nurses, they thought that that was the most beautiful thing that they ever witnessed, the way the Mohawk people welcome their new babies.

And I think that's so wonderful, that children have such a nice place in the old tradition. I think that's what we need more for all families is to get back those traditions. Because then we will have strong, loving families.

Most of our grandparents are gone now, the ones that used to know these things. And many times we didn't take the time to listen to them, or to gather their knowledge in one place, to make practical use of it. So here's another chance, so that people may do that.

Chapter 24

A Spiritual Ladder

I thought I would have to go to university for about six years just to learn that.

The most important thing to unity, to becoming united, is to communicate. That's what our Peacemaker did. And that's what Aionwahta did. And that's what the old leaders did. In order for there to be unity, people have to talk. They have to understand each other.

And when they understand each other, then they say,
Ó:nen ska'nikòn:ra ón:ton. *Now there's one mind.*

That's the trick of it. That's the formula. Gotta talk. If they don't talk, they can't be of one mind. And so what I wanna talk about today is Tobacco Burning because that Tobacco Burning is hooked to the way we do the Opening, the Ohén:ton Karihwatéhkwen. It's almost the same thing.

I'm gonna explain the Tobacco Burning. But while I'm explaining about the Tobacco Burning, I wanna make it a lesson at the same time. The Tobacco Burning follows the same sequence as the Thanksgiving Address. It is so close that we can feed two birds with one corn. Did you hear that? Until now, everybody says, "*Kill* the birds." But this time we are saying, "We *feed* the birds with one corn."

When I was a young kid, I used to listen to them at the Longhouse. And they used to talk for about an hour, maybe more, when they did the Opening. Just that. I can name all those old men and all those old Faithkeepers who did that. They were orators. They were such good orators, that one hour seemed like only five minutes. We never got impatient because they spoke so nicely and so well.

I used to say, "When I grow up, I hope I can do the Opening just like them. But," I said, "how would I ever remember one hour's worth?"

So I used to go see the old Chief in my clan. And I gave him tobacco. Because that's the way you learn. If you wanna do it the real Indian way, you have to give someone oien'kwa'ón:we, *Indian tobacco.* And you ask them for what you want. And they'll tell you because you've got Indian tobacco.

He ignored me the first two times I gave him tobacco, until the third time. And it probably took a little over a year between my requests. Because I'm kind of funny. If somebody gives me the brush-off, I get real brushed-off! And I won't come back for a year. I don't know if it's just me, or if I learned it from my mother. She was worse than me! Never forget either. Anyway, I've been trying to get better! So that's why I didn't go back there, to ask him again. It took me a long time.

When I went there the last time and gave him tobacco, he finally answered me. He said, "I can teach you. Gimme five minutes, maybe not even that. And I'll teach you the whole thing. And you'll learn too."

And I looked at him, "Five minutes?" Here I thought I would have to go to university for about six years just to learn that. 'Cause I thought you would have to put the same words, in the same sequence, all the way through, each time from memory. But that's only what I thought. It isn't like that at all.

And so he said, "Five minutes."

I wanna share that formula with you, if you will, how he showed me. It was true, it took five minutes. Anybody can learn it. And so people can use that in schools, or when they do workshops, to help them to learn this.

And here's what he said, "When you do the Opening, it's almost the same as you do Tobacco Burning, just a little different."

"First of all, who's gonna do this? Us, the people. But where do we get our power from, as a people? It comes from Shonkwaia'tíson. So the first thing is that we have to say thank you for our life from the Creator, the source of our life, before we do anything. So we acknowledge the Creator. That's number one.

"Then, who's gonna do this Opening, that says thank you? It's coming from the people, from our mouths. So the next thing is, we have to acknowledge the people, say hello to the People because we're gonna do this together.

"Then for the third thing, we sort of take two steps back and then start at number one. Even though it's actually number three. This earth is our foundation. This earth is a woman. This earth is not just a woman, but it's the Mother. And different than a regular mother because it's the mother of all the humans and all the trees and all the animals, all of life, in its totality. She is where we plant our feet. And we do everything upon her body. That's why we call her the foundation.

"Then, we're gonna take a ladder. And this is a symbolic ladder, an imaginary ladder. And we're gonna sit that spiritual ladder on our foundation, on our Mother the Earth."

And then the ladder is tall. In order for you to climb a ladder, you have to put it on a foundation.

But the top has to be secured too, right? You can't just put it in the air. If you climb it that way, it might fall right down.

So the old Chief said, "Hook the top of that ladder on Karonhià:ke, the Creator's land, up in the universe. What we call the Thanksgiving Address or Opening Prayer or Tobacco Burning is our spiritual ladder that hooks our Mother Earth to our father's land, the Creator's land. So now our ladder is secure. It's not gonna move. 'Cause it's anchored at the top and it's anchored at the bottom."

Because of that, they say they put a ladder on our women's dresses. When you see a traditional Iroquois woman, who has a dress for Longhouse events, it has, on the bottom of the dress, what they call the Earth Dome, representing the earth that we live on, Mother Earth. And then there's the Sky Dome, and that's of course coming from the sky. And so a lot of times you'll see these two domes, beaded, on the old dresses of the women. And even sometimes on the men's leggings or breech clouts, you'll see that kind of design. And that's where it comes from: the Earth Dome and the Sky Dome.

So we derive our life from this planet and the other planets in the solar system. And with all those together, that's how we came to be. And so our job in the Thanksgiving Address or in a Tobacco Burning is to connect these two facts. The earth dome is called Ohóntsia, *the Earth*. Or in Iroquois they'll say, Ionkhi'nisténha Ohóntsia, *the Mother the Earth*. And the other one is called Karonhià:ke. And what that means is *the Place in the Sky*. And when we refer to our spirit, that's going to leave us when we die, we say it's going back to Karonhià:ke.

So the rungs of the ladder between these two domes are all the different parts of Creation that need to be mentioned when we say the Ohén:ton Karihwatéhkwen.

All the ceremonies that the Iroquois do in our Longhouses are actually this ladder. And ceremonies are used to connect our present earth with our origin in Karonhià:ke, the Sky World. One end of the ladder is the Creator, and the other end of the ladder is Mother Earth.

The first two steps were to get the ladder in position, to be secure in what we're gonna do. So now we take some steps back and we begin. Now that it's secure, we say, "Mother Earth, we thank you." And then you use any words that you think are befitting and are proper, nice and good, to praise Mother Earth and express your thankfulness.

And then as you are on the Mother Earth, you take your first step on the ladder. What's the first thing that comes to mind, the first life form that you see that's the closest to the Mother Earth? And there's not just one answer. There are many answers. Which life form on Mother Earth is gonna come to visit you when you're talking about it? That's the one you choose.

So what life do I think is the closest to the Mother Earth? Well, I could say "water" 'cause it goes right in the Mother Earth. Or, I could say "grass" 'cause it comes out of Mother Earth. Or I could say, "medicine." So there are many answers, to which is the first rung. It depends which one of those comes into your head, when you do it. That means the power of that life is coming to see you 'cause it wants to be mentioned.

Then we're gonna speak to the Water that quenches our thirst. And that's what we did out there this morning. We said to the Water that's in the ponds, in the lakes, and to the Water that moves in the rivers and the streams all over the earth, "Your job is to quench the thirst of the humans and the animals and the birds. And since the beginning of time, that powerful Water that you are has been quenching our thirst. We know that. So that's why we use this tobacco that the Creator gave to us to communicate with you today because our mind is one."

And our thankfulness and love, we put it in the tobacco. And when that tobacco touches the fire, the fire's power raises the smoke up into the universe, carrying our love and carrying our thankfulness to all the lakes and rivers and streams in the whole world. "Because you quench our thirst. And we're still able to find clean water to live some more today." And we throw the tobacco in there as a gift, to carry our thankfulness to the Water's Spirit.

So then on the ladder that's hooked to the Sky World, I take my second step. So in my mind, what's the next thing that's close to the Mother? And this morning I said, "the corn and beans and squash, all the things that are in the gardens." So I took the tobacco and I said, "The good group of people here today, they all give tobacco. They touch this tobacco. And that means that their minds are agreed in unity to do that. And so with oneness of mind to all the Gardens, your people, your children, wanna say thank you.

"Right now, some of them are already eating corn from the garden. We are eating beans already too. And some of it, we didn't harvest yet. It's still growing. Those gardens are in good health and they're doing exactly what they're supposed to do, so that we may live. And so on behalf of all our families, our elders, and our young, we take this tobacco that you gave us, Creator, and we put our thankfulness in it, and our love, and we throw it on the fire."

And the power of the fire is gonna carry it to the universe, so that every Garden that's been planted, not just by Indians, but by the people all over the whole world, will be thanked. And then the Gardens will feel honored. And because they were paid attention to, they will become healthy. And they will grow lots of food to feed the people.

So now what's the third step on that imaginary ladder? What's the next one I see? Oh, I see berries. And not only that, I see the strawberry. I know that after the big snow of winter, the very first to come is a blossom of the strawberry. And then that strawberry blossom turns into a green kind of a berry. And in a little while it turns into a great big, juicy, sweet, red strawberry. Before any other berry. And that's why we call the strawberry the chief or the leader of all the berries.

And when the strawberries are finished, then come the raspberries and the blueberries and the blackberries and the gooseberries. Right until snow comes again, there's another berry ready to take its place. So they help us and the deer and the bears and the birds, to live. We all depend on the berries. And so we take that tobacco and we throw it in the fire, with our love and our thankfulness. And the smoke goes up into the sky so that every Berry that's growing will see our words, and feel our words, that we appreciate their life. And now they will grow even better.

So then you take your fourth step on the ladder. What's the next one I see? Oh, I see the Bushes, and I thank them.

And I take another step. I see the Trees, big and little, the Maple Tree. And I send the tobacco and say, "Thank you for the things you give us. Even the fire itself is burning because it came from your life, for our prayer." We make the fire from the trees. They are what make it burn.

Then you take the fifth step, the sixth step. And then you go to the Deer, the Animals. You even include the ones that are domesticated, like your dog or cat, and the ones that live next to your house. You include them there too. And you offer them your thankfulness and your tobacco.

And then you go to the next step, to the Birds. So as you climb towards the Creator's world on this ladder, everything that you see, that's the order by which you recite. And when I do it tomorrow or the next day or the next day, it will not be the same as yesterday. Because the spirit of that life is free and it comes to me when it wants to, you see? That's why it's never the same.

So we Indian people never use a stagnant prayer. Our prayer is always different, every time we do it. It's always in a different order. It's almost the same, but different. That means it's spiritually alive. It isn't a prayer we recited or learned word-for-word. It's not a prayer that somebody else made five hundred years ago that we're still saying. No, we find the words for today's prayer, at the instant we are speaking about the Creator's life, and us. It's *living*, just like the river. The river water moves all the time; it's never the same water as yesterday. It's always new. And that's the way our ceremony is, when we do it. It looks the same: it's the same river, but it's always fresh.

When I do a Feather Dance, you're not gonna see me doing the same hoochy-koochy moves twice! No, the next time I may do fancier ones. That's what our ceremony is about, taking life as it is right now.

And then you offer your greetings and thankfulness all the way up to the Wind, to the Rain, to the Thunder Grandfathers, to the Old Brother Sun, and to the Grandmother Moon who regulates the women's cycles, so little babies will be born. And if our Grandmother should stop, and not shine any more, the women of every nation would not give birth to any more children. And humans would stop living. So we send the tobacco, thanking her for the births of the children, thanking her for the fact that they're with us. And also that some more will be coming. Look how small they are, and Grandma's the one that made them come. She had a little help, but she's the one who initiated it, our Grandma. Little beautiful babies. And we say thank you for all of them.

And then we go all the way to the Stars. And then to the Four Sacred Beings that help us to live. And then finally we go to our Creator.

And when we got to our Creator,[1] I said, on behalf of the people, that right here at this Centre, there were problems. The Centre is meant for the people, Ojibwa and Haudenosaunee nations, Crees, Mi'kmaq, whatever Indians set foot in the door. And they can drink a coffee or find something helpful. That's what it's for. To help them out.

And so we ask that whatever problem there was, whatever it is that caused a problem, that it be slowly taken away, moved, cleaned up. Make the Centre what it's supposed to be meant for. Help the people to have a good mind, so they can do that. That's why, a while ago, I talked about how we have to communicate. If we don't talk, and speak the truth, then we won't fix it. It will never get fixed. So we need help from the power to be able to do that.

Because the little ones, the young people, they need a place to shelter. They need a place to get knowledge. And they need a place where they can feel secure, where they can find elders to talk to, if they need to. And a place where they can find each other, to support each other. Even language program, the young ones could do it here too.

So what is here is very valuable. That's why it's important that the Creator help. And we help along with the Creator to make it a place of peace here, for tomorrow and the future. That's what we ask for. Whatever's in here, that may have interfered with that, we ask that the Creator move it out, take it out, if it's gonna hurt us. And leave it a nice place. That's what we asked for over there this morning.

Then as I looked around, it was overwhelming because when the message went out that we were gonna have a Tobacco Burning, a lotta women came to that fire, that circle. And men, elders, middle-aged and young, even babies came. You saw how many ribbon shirts, kahstówas there were. Wow!

And I said, "Gee, these people. There are really good-looking women and handsome men, standing at the fire for the Creator." I said, "That is really something."

---

1. This next section is an example of how Tom ended a Tobacco Burning for a specific purpose, to help with the problems at the Fort Erie Friendship Centre in 2003.

So I said, "Creator, here are your children. They all come from different places, almost at the same time, to the sacred fire. They send praise, thankfulness and their love. I'm talking for them: they asked me to. And it is a great pleasure to be proud of them. And so the people send you our love today, as this smoke carries it to the universe. Good, good people."

Right at that moment, my hair wanted to stand up! I knew that the spirits were coming there. I don't know if you felt it, but I did. And did you see that fire, when that smoke twisted like that? You know what that was? That was our Indian brothers who live where the sun goes down. They've sent their wishes for us here in the east, from out in the southwest. 'Cause they told me before, whenever you burn tobacco, we want you to watch now. And this was a few years ago.

They said, "Whenever you burn tobacco, especially when you send the young men and young women into the mountains to fast for four days and four nights . . ." 'cause we do that where we live. "When you burn tobacco for them, before they go to the mountain, we will send all our prayers from our nation, from the southwest. And we will come there in the form of like a twister in your tobacco fire. And when you see that, you will know that the nation to the southwest of you, your Indian brother, will be standing there holding your hand and holding onto your shoulder, to support you in what you're doing."

This morning I saw that again. So our brother nations from the West, they have joined us too. And the smoke goes up.

And so finally, we said to the Creator, "Our elders, some of them are at home. And they've gotten to an age where they can't move fast any more. And some of them don't feel good enough to go far. They know, though, that we're doing this. But they couldn't come because they don't have strong enough bodies 'cause they got old." So what we said was: "Those are our elders. Those are our grandfathers and grandmothers, that are home. They couldn't come to be with us. But we include them in what we're doing. And so with this tobacco, Creator and Four Sacred Beings, we ask you to go touch them. We ask you to go protect our elders, the ones that couldn't make it.

"And if they're not feeling well, do what you can to make them feel good. Help them, so that the remaining days they have to live will be comfortable.

And they won't hurry to leave us. And so that last tobacco, we send it to them, for their health." Because if it wasn't for them, you and I, we wouldn't be here. So they gave us life. And we must never, never forget them for that.

And then when we finished that, we said to the Creator, "For these three days that we have been having a meeting here at this Centre, we were called to try to remember whatever our grandfather and grandmother told us, whatever our leaders told us, about our ways, about the way we're to believe, the different symbols and traditions that the Creator gave to us. We were called to talk about it, so that the people will hear it, the young will hear it, and maybe they'll even learn it. And then they'll practice it. And then our ways won't die. That's what we're trying to do here. And," I said, "it's not just the young either 'cause I've seen elders here every day. They too are learning and getting support from what we're doing. And so it is we put the tobacco in the fire."

And we said, "Creator, help the people, young and old and middle-aged. Help us so that we become like a sponge. And all the good things that we're supposed to know about our ways, that they will be absorbed by us, and they will become real and alive, especially to our young. We ask you that favor. We don't want our ways to die. And we ask your assistance." And it went up.

Again the little whirlwind spun the tobacco smoke. I almost had to ask somebody to get me some Kleenex.

And then finally, the last one we said was, "I'm only a human, and I might have forgotten something very important. So with the last tobacco that's going up, I ask that if I forgot something that's supposed to be said, that you, our Creator, will sew up any hole that wasn't patched by me in this prayer. So that it will go up to you whole and full of goodness, and be good for our people." And then it went up.

And there's another thing I said this morning: "I suppose there's a bowling alley somewhere. People coulda gone there. There's a shopping center and a Wal-Mart over there. People coulda gone there. And there are a whole bunch of things that are going on, that people could have gone to. But look, they all came here instead, where the fire is. See that, Creator? Your people came to you. Look at them, how nice they look. Help us Creator. We send you our love, our thankfulness, for all these good people." And the fire, the smoke went up.

So that's how you do an Opening or a Tobacco Burning. That's also a translation of what we did outside this morning. We do it by using the ladder. We put it on Mother Earth and we hook the top to the Creator's world. And then we take one step at a time. And express our gratefulness to our Creator. And so that's that part now.

Oh, and I forgot to tell you at the beginning, before I started, I asked my younger brother to holler to get the attention of our Creator and the spiritual world. That's why he hollered three times. So that the Creator would know that we were ready to salute him. Because do you remember the first day we talked about Creation, that he took the dolls he made to be humans, who are our grandpas? And he opened their mouths, and he blew in their mouths three times. And after the third time, the eyes were blinking, and the arms started to move on those dolls. And he put them upright on their feet. And they had life.

And so whenever we have a big ceremony of some kind, we always holler three times, three breaths of life, because we have never forgotten how we started. All the years we've been walking this earth, we still know that we came from that power's three breaths of life.

And then when he finished hollering, I just said to the Creator, "I ask for forgiveness. And while I've been walking the earth, if I did anything wrong to hurt you or the people, I ask you to clean me and forgive me. Because I've been honored that the people asked me if I would speak on their behalf, to burn their tobacco. And I don't wanna hurt them. And I don't want any blemishes, from my yesterday, to interfere with their walk today, and into tomorrow. And so I ask forgiveness." Then I started.

And so it is that's what happened. Niá:wen.

Chapter 25

Child Rearing Methods, According to Mohawk Tradition

And it is said that water possesses the power to cleanse and to purify.

Now I wish to talk about something else that's very important. And that is some of the teachings of the Mohawk people that refer to the discipline of children, and how one is to raise them.

First of all there is a tendency, sometimes a strong tendency, to favor one child over another. And when one raises children, it is important not to get trapped into that, but to look at all your children in a way that's equal. You must treat them in an equal fashion.

The second thing I think is important is that the father and mother, according to the teachings, should never argue in front of their children. If there is a disagreement, you should do that when your children aren't around. Never argue in front of your children because it will lead to problems later on, behavior problems, and problems with discipline.

The other thing is, when the children are around, or even when the children aren't around, it's a good practice, the elder people say, for fathers and mothers not to gossip, or say anything bad or negative about other people. Especially in front of the children.

Those are some of the teachings that a father and mother should know.

The elders tell us that babies are not born with a knowledge of what is right or what is wrong. They have to be taught everything about right and wrong, moral issues, and so on. And so when your children are growing up, one of the elders' teachings is that you must never scold them or raise your voice to them. You must never holler at them.

The other thing is, that it is forbidden, amongst the Mohawk people, or the Iroquois nations, to ever hit, push, shove or kick your children. You aren't to hit your children, in any way.

What will we do then, if we are going to raise our children and discipline them? Well, first of all, you never yell at your kids. That's for a simple reason. As adults, if somebody yells at us, out of the clear blue, our first reaction is to put up a wall and just ignore them. We certainly won't listen or pay any attention to what they're yelling at us about. And so if we would feel that way, then for sure a small child will have the same reaction, and won't listen either.

That is why the elders tell us that the Creator does not want us to yell at our kids. If we have something to say to our children, then we must speak to them in a good fashion, with kind words, nice words. We must speak to them calmly, and then they will respond. They will listen to what we have to say.

If a father or mother scolds or yells at their children, then they will put up a wall. And that means that thereafter, they will then have to yell and scold their children all the time. And nothing will sorta ever get done. So you don't want to start a cycle that's going to be fruitless.

So the first lesson, I suppose we could say, is to talk calmly, to tell your children exactly what you expect, and what is right and what is wrong. That's how they're going to learn.

Now if for some reason, when you speak calmly in a nice proper way, and the child doesn't seem to absorb what you're trying to teach him or her, and behaves in a negative way, then after two warnings, the third time is the time for action.

After asking the child twice, to behave in a proper manner, a parent or a grandparent will take a glass of cold water. Or they may use a cup or a dipper of cold water. And they will throw this water into the face of the child.

The water will startle the child. It won't injure the child. It won't cause a cut or bruise. And it won't break a bone. But it will startle him. And it is said that water possesses the power to cleanse and to purify. So our elders in Mohawk country will use this water, hoping that it will wash away the negative behavior patterns of that child. And startle him back into reality and to positive ways of behaving.

That is what is done. But you never use that water unless first you have tried twice in a real nice way, in a calm, quiet-spoken way, to tell your child what you want her to do and why she's doing wrong.

Most of the time, the water is sufficient. But if it doesn't work, then it is possible to take the child down to the river or to the creek. And there, again, you don't just do this out of the blue or abruptly. You explain to the child why you're doing this.

So after two times that you have spoken to the child with no response, then you'll take the child to the river or to the creek and you will submerse him under the water a couple of times, real quickly. And then, it is said that the negative things that are on this child will be taken down the river with the current. The power of the water will cleanse him and leave only the positive again.

And so usually that is sufficient. And the child will learn from that experience.

But let us continue. Let us say that the water methods didn't work. The first method of splashing her in the face didn't work. And the second method of taking her to the river and dunking her was tried, and that didn't work. There is a third course of action that is told in our teachings, in the Mohawk nation.

That third one is, of course, a very difficult one to do. But it is done in this way. After two warnings, after several attempts with the water, then, if there is no positive result in the disciplining of your child, then what you will do is you will take your child by the hand and you walk with him. And then you will take him into the field or to the woods.

You do this when you are not angry. You do this when you are not mad. You do it when you are calm. And you explain to him in a calm way again what it is that you don't approve of, what it is that he is doing wrong.

When you get into the woods or to the field, there is a bush that grows there. We call that the red willow bush. It has really bright red bark, and it usually grows in a clump. A whole bunch of red willows grow together. When you get there, then you will take your sacred tobacco, and you will make an offering to the Creator. And you will tell the Creator the name of your child. And you will tell the Creator that you seek help from the medicine plants of the red willow, to help your child so that he will be disciplined, and he will act in a proper manner.

Once you have left tobacco for the Creator, then you find out which plant grows there that is the leader of the red willow bush. Every town or village of people has a leader in their community. And it is viewed by the Mohawk people that the medicine bushes and medicine plants also have leaders, and subleaders, and so on. And so according to our tradition, you will then take a pinch of tobacco, sacred tobacco, and you will talk to the leader of the red willow plant.

And you will say, "This is my child's name. And he has not been behaving in a proper way. He doesn't listen the right way. And so therefore I need some help. I need medicine to doctor him, so that he may behave in a proper way, and he may grow the right way."

So then, once you have identified your child to the leader of the red willow, you will go beyond the leader. You don't pick that first one. And you don't pick the second, nor do you pick the third one. Because it is understood that the two that are next to the leader are their subleaders. And you don't want to disrupt the community of the medicine, just like you wouldn't want somebody to come here and to remove or to take away our leadership. It would cause the people of that village to become angry with you. And it is the same way when you pick medicine. You don't pick their leaders away.

So you go beyond the three. And you ask your child to cut from the middle, a slender stick of red willow, which is like a whip. You make sure that you tell him to pick a slender one, not a big fat one because the big one will break easily and it will be of no use. He needs to pick one that's thin. Then it will be pliable and flexible, and it won't break.

When he has picked it, he will give it to you as he is told. And you will walk back to your house. And when you get back to your house, you will fix a place high on the wall, with nails or a shelf, where you can put that red willow stick. And that red willow stick is gonna belong to that child for whom the ceremony or the prayers were done. And you never use that stick on that child unless you follow the procedures. You never use it when you are angry, or your temper has flared up.

Now, if things are going on again, you warn your child the first time, and then the second. And if he or she doesn't heed your warning and behave in a proper manner, then on the third time, you can take that stick off the wall. You use that stick on the child's leg or on his arm on the bare flesh. And you hit it only one time. You don't just touch it, you make it sting, so that it feels like little needles on there. And that's all you do, only once.

That little stick, that little whip will only sting and tingle the skin. It won't cut it. It won't break the bone and it won't injure the child. But it will cause that child to take notice that something is wrong, and that he needs to pay attention. And he needs to behave in a proper manner. Then you put the stick away.

But again, before you use that stick, you have to give that child an understanding of what it was that he or she was doing wrong. And you have to give them two chances to ask for forgiveness, and to show that they are not gonna do what they were doing wrong again. The third time, again, is always the action time. If they don't follow through with behaving the way they said that they were gonna behave, then you use that stick.

And that's generally the way, the traditional manner, that every Iroquois nation, from Mohawk to Seneca, uses to discipline their kids.

But as I said, if you carry on right from the very beginning, by talking gently and calmly to your children, chances are you probably won't have to use that stick. Of all the children that I have, I had to use the red willow stick on only two of them. And I only had to use it on them twice: I mean once each, on each child. And my kids are all grown up now.

And I will tell you also that if you have to use this stick on your children, it's gonna hurt you, more than it's gonna hurt the child. I know when I used it, it kinda broke my heart. And I wanted to cry. In fact, I did cry some tears because I felt sorry for my children. 'Cause I love my children very much. But I did it because if I'm gonna be a proper father, then I have to make sure that my children are disciplined, so that they will have a chance to be good human beings when they grow up.

And so this is what the elders told us is the proper procedure to bring respect and discipline to our children.

I also wanted to relate one story that is said to be true. Way up in I believe it was Manitoba or Saskatchewan, I was visiting one time, maybe fifteen or more years ago.[1] And up there, there's nobody that has a road. You have to get in there by airplane because they live in the extreme north. And this one Cree people that I visited, they told me this story. They said it was true. I don't know if it is or not. But this is what happened.

Because the location is so far north, there's no electricity there. They live on trap lines. And there was this one Cree man, who had three or four kids. And his wife died. And he had to raise his kids. And while he was raising his kids, he never ever struck them. He never punished them in any physical way. Nor did he ever scold them because he loved his kids so much.

Well, all his kids grew up. And as they grew up, he became older. And the day finally came when he passed away. Because there were no funeral parlors or undertakers, his kids and the neighbor that lived a little distance away, prepared the body and put him on a high table or something, on some kind of a platform in the house. And they waked the man.

And while they were sitting there all night waking him, sittin' with the dead body of the man who loved his children so much, they had a kerosene lamp

---

[1.] Tom made this speech in about 1989.

going. And they noticed his eye began to twitch. And then they noticed he began to move his arm. And the next thing you know this man sat up. And needless to say everybody in the whole room was frightened, almost to death, that they had seen this dead man sit up.

And in the Cree language, the man said, "Don't be afraid. Don't be afraid of me. I was traveling to the Creator's land. But the Creator won't accept me because I didn't finish my job on the earth."

And so he got off the platform and he said, "Wait one minute." And he went outside. In about two minutes he came back. And he had this red willow stick. And he came to each one of his children that was in the log house. And he told them to roll up their sleeves. And they did.

And he said, "This is what I didn't do. I didn't finish my job as a father on this earth." So he took that red stick and he hit each one of his kids once on their arm. And he cried tears because he hard a hard time doing it. He said, "That's what the Creator said you must do. You must discipline your children and not be afraid to, if you love them. For if you don't do that, then you won't be a proper parent."

And so I thought I would share this with people. I know it's hard to do that, but you have to think. You have to use your mind. It's better to follow the Mohawk way. The results are going to be gratifying and positive. But if you neglect to be a parent and to tell your children what's right and wrong, and you don't discipline them, then you'll have wild horses as the end product. And they will hurt themselves, as well as they will hurt you, their father and mother. And there won't be peace in the family.

So these are the few words I thought I would share about discipline, according to Mohawk traditions. And I thank you for listening and I hope that you may apply some of those, if you think that they're not too outdated. If they can be used today to bring health and peace to families, to make healthy families, then by all means use them.

Chapter 26

The Great Law of Peace Part 1:
The Birth of the Peacemaker

The elders tell us this was another one of those dark times in our history, when the culture, ceremonies and the peaceful ways of life were almost lost.

Now I'm going to attempt to recall the epic of the Great Law of Peace. And again, the Peacemaker was one of those Four Sacred Beings.

I really want to emphasize that this is the reader's digest form. I've heard it myself recited for ten days, on three different occasions in my life. In fact for two of those, I was asked to be the interpreter, in the afternoons, for it. At the time it was scary because there were no notes. It was almost like a simultaneous recitation, in the afternoon.

So it meant that I had to listen to all the Mohawk language of the recital, from eight or nine o'clock in the morning until one o'clock, with no breaks, no stops, from eight to one. That's the Great Law in the Mohawk language. Then after we had eaten, in the afternoon, I had to repeat what he said, recite it, with no tape recorder, and no writing either. So it was frightening for me. I was familiar somewhat with it, but I had never actually done it. But on two occasions, or maybe it was three times, I did it. So I have a pretty good familiarity with it. All I would need to do is dust off things, I think, and I could make it come alive again, if I attempted it—maybe.

But just to give you a time, it took the reciter ten days, just for the Constitution. So if that took ten days, with four or five hours per day, that's fifty-five hours with no coffee breaks—just the straight teachings, to recite that. And that's only the reciting of that. Then, once that's done, you have to see what you heard, what that means. How does that unfold? And how is it put into reality? How does it become real in one's life?

Usually before one recites the Great Law of Peace, the reciter will go to the birthplace of the Peacemaker. And just as dawn is coming, they will have a Tobacco Burning over there, requesting the spirit of the great Peacemaker to guide the speaker in the reciting of the law that he gave to us. They will usually do that one to two weeks in advance, or sometimes even earlier than that because the speaker needs to have that spiritual help, in order to remember ten days worth of speeches.

Whenever someone recites the Great Law, the people that are present there will make a big circle. They will lock their arms together or clasp their arms together in a big circle. And they will burn tobacco there as well, at the beginning. That's what they usually do, when they do the real Great Law readings.

The Great Law, I guess, came to be probably—and this is just guess work—about a thousand years ago, maybe more. I don't know if it was less, but probably it was more than that. Some people have even suggested—even that Jan Swart who used to come here—suggested that he thought it was more than two thousand years ago, that the Peacemaker was around. That's what his opinion was. And he was an archaeologist. That's what he did; he liked to do that. And his dad was; and his grandpa too.

Some people ask me whether the date was 1141 AD, during an eclipse of the sun. An eclipse would dim the sun and so it might be, but that always happens on all of those events. Like when the Teacher left to cross the big water. Remember? It always does that. Everything goes dim for awhile.

The only problem is that I haven't heard that myself. As far as the people that have recited the Great Law that I've heard, I've never heard them say that. But that's not to say that it isn't so. So we'd have to see where that source came from.

There was a time in this world when there was peace and tranquility, and spiritual things occurred day-to-day amongst the people of the Iroquois nations. But the elders tell us this was another one of those dark times in our history when the culture, ceremonies and the peaceful ways of life were almost lost.

All over the world, what happened is that people began to lose their spiritual knowledge and the things that gave them tradition and their ceremonial life. And this is what happened to the Iroquois people again. When people neglected their spiritual things, ceremonies and so forth, then turmoil and chaos became the rule of the day. And so this is exactly what happened again.

Almost all the people had strayed away from the Creator's ways. This period of time was perhaps the darkest, most violent, and hopeless, of our entire history. This was a time when blood stained Mother Earth. This situation was caused by the bloody wars taking place in every village.

So much so that there were killings almost every day. The war leaders, who were called the War Chiefs, began to recruit the nephews and sons, who were the children of women who were crying all the time. When the war leaders would come back, many times, they did not return with the nephews or the sons of these women. And they were killed. And so that is why there was grief all over the place.

There was no peace. Families argued and fought one another, and people didn't follow their clans. Some families even lost any memory of the clans. Things had simply been allowed to fall apart.

Things became so bad, at that time, that cannibalism evolved, and the society became very sadistic. In fact, it became the norm, that people relished causing pain to one another and took joy in seeing gruesome things occur. Thus it was that way in the world, when there was chaos. In amongst all the nations, this occurred.

The Creator was very sad to see the deplorable situation the people were in. It is for this very reason that the Creator sent one of the Four Sacred

Beings to be born among the people. The mission of the Peacemaker was to restore kindness, love, joy, and peace to the villages of all our people.

The Huron Indian nation is a sister nation of the Mohawk. They have a similar language, similar customs; they're almost a duplicate of the Mohawks. For some reason, something occurred in the history between the Mohawk and the Huron, many years ago. So many years ago that I don't even know what the reason was, for their conflict. But the fact of it is that a Huron and a Mohawk could not be put in one room or one area for very long, before they would attempt to fight each other and even kill each other. There was no love between them.

The Huron Indians were located along the north of Lake Ontario at the Bay of Quinte, in that general area. They were also very ferocious and they were very mean to one another. And there was this one woman amongst them. And this woman had a little girl. Just a little, tiny girl.

And for some reason the people of that Huron village had forgotten what spirituality was about. They had even forgotten the word "Creator" or "God." They didn't even know what that was. They had ceased to use those kinda words or practices for so long, that they had just become a vague, vague memory.

And so you can see the bad situation that they were in. But because this one Huron woman had this little girl, whom she loved very much, she began, independently, to become concerned about the little girl, about all the backstabbing that was going on in the society of their village.

She also became concerned about the physical violence that was occurring in the village. And it was just a sad thing to be in, that kind of environment. And so this woman wanted to safeguard her daughter, wanted her future to be more hopeful and more consistent, more stable and more peaceful.

And so on her own, she decided that she would leave her relatives and the village where she was born and raised. And that she would take her daughter. They would remove themselves from this terrible, violent society. And so that is what happened. She took her daughter and their belongings, and she began to walk in a certain direction.

And after she got many, many miles away from the main village where she was born, she started to build, along what they call the Bay of Quinte, west of where Lake Ontario joins the St. Lawrence River. In that area, near present-day Kingston, Ontario, and close to Deseronto. And when she arrived at what she felt was a far enough and safe enough distance from her village, she began to construct a little lodge, made out of bark and the saplings of trees, along the Bay of Quinte, on top of a hill.

She and her daughter then resided there, by themselves, day after day, month after month, and that's where the little girl grew. And because they isolated themselves, the little girl did not have any company. She didn't have any friends. She didn't have any relatives. She didn't have any cousins to play with. Just her and her mother. But life was peaceful there.

And so the mother had to hunt like a man. She had to fish like the men did. She had to cut wood. She had to make fires. She had to carry the water from the Bay of Quinte to her lodge, and to do all the things that are necessary, that usually a whole village does in order to survive together. She was doing it by herself.

But her daughter was helpful. As years passed on by, the little girl grew into a young woman. This young woman would fetch water, using clay pots that were made by her mother and herself, at the bay.

And by this time, something strange occurred, very strange both to the daughter and to the mother. It was some kind of a supernatural occurrence that happened. This young girl, for some reason unknown to her or her mother, became impregnated. And as time went on by, her physical appearance began to show her pregnancy.

One day, as she was standing in the doorway of the lodge, her clothes settled in such a way that they showed her pregnant body. And when the mother saw this, she pulled the garment of her daughter and it hugged her pregnant body. This was a great surprise to the mother. There was no man within miles and miles of where they lived. There was no hunter that ever stopped there. There was no one else except the mother and her daughter. So how was it possible that this young woman could become pregnant?

And so the mother demanded to know who was the father of this child. And when she was asked, the daughter said, "My mother, I don't know."

And the mother said, "Don't tell me you don't know. It is not possible that a girl or a woman can get pregnant without a man. I want to know who's the man involved in your life."

And again the daughter said, "Mother, I don't know. I've never seen anybody. I've only seen you. I only know you. I don't know any man."

Of course, the mother could not understand and did not accept this answer. She thought that her daughter was lying to her. And from that moment on, the mother turned her feelings off, the great love that she had for her daughter. And it had been almost indescribable because that's why she moved from the wicked village: to protect her daughter because she loved her so.

The daughter couldn't answer her, as to who was the father of this child. The mother thought she was being deceived and lied to, and there was no more trust. And how could this be? And so the only way she could deal with this situation was to shut herself off, from any emotion for her daughter. She had no words of encouragement for her. She had no sympathy for her. She just had no feelings.

In fact, what would happen is when the sun would go down, the mother would order her daughter to carry the clay vessels to the Bay of Quinte in the darkness, to fetch water for the following day. If somebody were to, by chance, pass there or by their lodge, they would not see her pregnant body. So she tried to hide it. And for weeks and weeks and then months, the mother treated her daughter very coldly, and without feeling. And this was rough on the mother, as well as the daughter.

Finally, after the elapse of nine months, the daughter became very big. And she began her labor and she gave birth to a little boy. Even when she was in labor and not knowing what to do or how to give birth, the mother didn't help her daughter, just ignored her. But nevertheless, the daughter, in her own way was able to give birth. She and the little baby boy were all right.

Only a few minutes had passed, when the mother went over there to where the baby was and looked at them. And she took a hatchet and went outside. She went down the hill to the bay and there she began to dig a hole in the ice. And the ice might have been somewhere between six and ten inches thick. And when she had made a hole there, she went back up the hill to the lodge where her daughter and grandson were lying on the bearskin rugs and blankets.

She grabbed the little baby away from her daughter, with no explanation of any kind. And she wrapped that baby tightly in a soft deerskin blanket and carried him down the hill to the place where she had dug the hole in the ice. And then she placed this little bundle, this little grandson of hers in the hole under the water. Not only that but she had a long pole that she used. And she pushed her tiny grandson way under the water to make sure that no one, animal, bird or human would ever know that this baby had been born to her and her daughter, to this family.

Then, she turned around and went back up the hill, where the lodge was. When she entered, she heard the gurgling of a little baby. She was very shocked that she would hear this. She thought her mind was playing games on her because of what she had just done.

And then she walked in there. She saw her daughter lying on those bearskin blankets. And in her daughter's arms was her little grandson, that she had just got through drowning, with the long pole pushing him under. When she saw this, she couldn't believe her eyes and she jumped back. She was bewildered because she had just killed this baby. Yet here it was. It was living yet, nursing from his mother.

And so the old lady, the grandmother, was now convinced that this little baby that was born, was evil. That's what she thought all along. There was some sort of witchcraft going on, or something bad. And she must do something to get rid of it.

And so the next thing that the grandmother tried is she went over there to the woods and she began to chop away at the frozen ground. And when she got below the frost line, she dug a grave. And when she finished the shallow grave, she went back up the hill, into the lodge. She pulled her little grandson away from the arms of her daughter. She grabbed that baby and took it to the woods.

She put it at the bottom of the grave, and she buried it alive. So that way no one would see or know that this baby was born.

And each time this was done, the baby's mother went through agony because there was nothing she could do.

When the old lady who was the grandmother finished burying the baby, she went back up the hill and went into the lodge. There lay her daughter on the furry blanket, and there again in her arms was this baby nursing from his mother. And there again, she jumped back with fear. She said, "Now I know this is an evil baby. This is the second time I have attempted to kill it. There is nothing I, as a human, can do to destroy this evil baby."

And so the grandmother, in her knowledge of the universe and its truth, thought that even if it was witchcraft and evil, it would really be no match for fire. And that fire would be able to destroy this baby. So what she did was she gathered dried grasses and branches. And she gathered the fallen limbs from the trees, until they made about a five- or six-foot pile. Then, she began to kindle that and make a fire. And she waited until those branches and wood that she had piled started dancing with flames, and it was apparent that they wouldn't go out, that it would be a real fire.

Then, she went in the house and she grabbed her grandson away from her daughter. And she took this little baby, this little bundle that he was, and she placed his whole body upon the dancing flames of the big fire in the woods. And she stood there and she watched until that baby turned into black charcoal to make sure that he died. When there was nothing but a little charcoal left, she turned around and she went back into the house where she and her daughter lived.

And when she went in there, again she heard the gurgling sounds of a little child. And then when she went right into the house, there her daughter was on that fur mattress. And there in her arms was this little baby nursing from his mother, gurgling, making baby sounds. And so the grandmother was even more furious, was even more bewildered as to how this baby could survive even the fire, and not die. She was completely astounded. She didn't know what to make of it.

And so she went to where she herself slept. She sat on her bed and she was trying to figure out what was the nature of this child. What protects it? Why can nobody harm this child? She sat there thinking and contemplating, meditating about what happened. Her eyes were closed and she wasn't sleeping: she was thinking.

All of a sudden, she could hear in the distance in front of her, the noise of branches moving, hitting each other as if there was a big moose with big antlers, going through the underbrush. But it was in her lodge. And when she opened her eyes and she looked, there was a strange man standing before her.

This man was very handsome, someone that she had never seen in her life before. She looked at him and she said, "Who are you and what do you want?"

And he said to her, "I have been sent by the Creator to come and see you, and to tell you that you are an evil, old, wicked woman. What are you trying to do, to kill a little baby? In the eyes of the Creator, any little baby is the most precious creature, whether it is a deer or a human. And here it's your own flesh and blood and you tried to take his life away. That's evil."

And he said, "I came to tell you that you must cease those attempts. And if you don't, then I will do to you what you were trying to do to that baby, and see if you like it."

And then the old lady looked at him and she said, "Who is, what is Creator?" Because remember, the people from the village that she came from had ceased to practice ceremonies. And they had forgotten even what the word meant, Creator. That's how far gone they were.

And so he said, "The Creator is the great power of all the universe and lives within everything that lives."

And so, "Oh, I think that when I was a little girl, I remember real old elders talking about Creator in that context. I vaguely remember it. I think I know what you mean."

He said, "Yes, that's the one I'm talking about. He's the one that sent this little baby, to teach people how there can be peace, and that there can be a good life and a good mind used amongst people. No more war. No more violence. No more bloodshed. He is the messiah from the Creator, to bring peace. And you, old lady, were lucky that the Creator chose you and your daughter from where such a great man will be born."

And then he said, "Do you know what you did to your daughter? When you noticed that she was pregnant, how mean you were to your daughter? And that's the time of life when a daughter needs the love of her mother the most. And yet you went the opposite way."

And he said, "Now, I want you to reassess everything and I want you right now, to make amends for what you did wrong. Your daughter is lying over there. Go see her. Your grandson is lying over there. Go hold him like a grandma is supposed to do. If not, you will see what I'm going to do."

She opened her eyes and realized he had disappeared. But the message was profound. And she got scared. Not only was she scared, but her heart really began to break. It had been broken all along, but she was in denial of that. And now she came to the realization of the feelings that had been almost destroyed, between her and her daughter.

And so she said, "My Creator, I ask for forgiveness that I was so mean to my daughter. I ask you, my Creator, for forgiveness, for the attempts to take the life of my grandson. I thought I was right. But now I've found out I'm not right to do that."

And so she sat up straight on the bed where she was sitting. And she tried to muster all the power and the strength she could, to stand up on her feet and walk over there where her daughter was lying, and her grandson. And she did find that strength and that power. And she stood up. That was the hardest thing in the whole world that she ever did.

And she walked over to her daughter. By this time, the daughter had pulled her baby close so the old woman couldn't take it because she thought she was trying to kill it again. And the grandmother said, "No, my daughter, I don't want to take him."

And she stood before her daughter and she kneeled down by the blankets and she said, "My daughter . . ." And she had big tears in her eyes, barely able to talk. And she said, "My daughter, if you never ever talk to me, for the rest of the days that you and I live, I will not blame you. If you don't accept my words when I speak to you ever again, I will not blame you. For I have done great evil. I have done great wrong. I treated you so mean and so cruel, when you needed me the most in your life."

And with big tears in her eyes, the grandmother said, "So I just want you to know that if you don't ever accept it, I deserve that."

And so she touched her daughter on the head, as she was lying in the bed. And of course the daughter was starving for affection all these months. So the daughter sat up and she was holding the baby. "Mother," she said, and she cried. They both cried. And she said, "I'm so sorry too. But I'm glad you told me that. I've got my mother back again."

And the grandma held her daughter and in between was the baby. And she held the baby for the first time. To *really* hold her grandson. And she said. "To you, my grandson, I ask for forgiveness. I am so sorry what I tried to do to you. I thought you were evil. But now I understand that the Creator has sent you here. I know now that you were born to bring peace to the world. And so now I will nourish you. I will protect you and I will let nobody hurt you. I will feed you. I will care for you. We will be a family.

"My daughter and my grandson, I vow, I pledge to you today, no matter what comes tomorrow, I will stand with you. I will love you and I will support you right to the very end, whatever we gotta do."

And that's what happened when he was born. So then everything was fine from day to day, normal. Just how a small family should be. And there were no bad feelings anymore. They truly had forgiven each other.

And I think this is the most important part. For I think all families in the world have problems with their children, their offspring. Sometimes words are said, and actions are done, that under normal circumstances wouldn't be done. And at some point all families need to reconcile that, need to find forgiveness and compassion. And mend those things that are sacred.

And in my opinion of the Great Law, that is one of the biggest stones or markers of the journey of the Peacemaker: his birth.

And it's the part that touches my heart, because even though it took place one thousand years or more ago, those feelings and the hurt that people do to one another is still going on today. Young girls still need their mothers. Young boys need their fathers. So we're doing that to the young. That's why it hurts me. Also that's what my father did to me. He left us all. So when I talk about it, I can't help but touch my heart. So we all got lots of work to do from the Great Law.

So then, as they became a close family again, the little boy began to grow, and he grew fast. He was almost like a magic little boy. He was always doing things that were astounding, unbelievable. He had the power to do miracles even as a kid. And so he used to leave his mother and his grandma early in the morning. And he'd go up into the woods, not too far from the bay.

And there, there was a big boulder, a white granite boulder. He'd go there by himself. And what he would do was, he'd use other stones like a chisel. And he'd hit that big boulder and he'd chip away at it as if he was making something. Well, the fact was, he was making something. He was making a canoe. He hoped, at some point whenever he finished it, he could travel in it, and do the job that the Creator sent him to do.

But months and months went by, and finally his grandmother wondered, "Where does my grandson go every day? Every morning he's gone for hours by himself, and then he comes back in the afternoon." So one day she said, "I'm gonna get up real early in the morning, and I'm gonna follow him. I'm gonna go see, because I'm nosy. I'm curious to know what does he do, and where does he go."

So she did. But of course he was kind of like a magic boy, so he knew that his grandma was following him. So as he went into the woods up there where his project was, where the big stone was, his grandmother was hiding behind the tree and kind of looking around as he was chiseling away.

Finally he saw her. And she went over there, and she said, "Grandson, I was so nosy. That's why I followed you. I thought you didn't see me, but you did. But I want to know what you're doing. Why do you keep hitting that big stone? Why are you chipping it away like that, a little bit at a time?"

He said, "I'm making a canoe out of this white granite stone. And I'm gonna use that one day, some day when I'm ready to travel. That's what's gonna carry me."

And the grandma said to him, "Well aren't you kind of foolish to make a canoe out of a stone? Don't you know that stone goes always to the bottom of the water? It don't float. So you're wasting all your time to do this boat. You should make it out of birch bark or elm tree or something, better chance."

"No," he said. "Grandma, the one who made the universe instructed me to use this white granite stone. I have to use that."

"Oh," she said. "Well, when the day comes you will finish that project and you're ready to put it in the river, I'm gonna stand there and I'm gonna laugh at you, as your canoe goes right to the bottom."

He said, "Okay, Grandma, you can watch me when I'm ready, when I'm done."

So she went home satisfied that he was doing this project. And while he was doing that and traveling up there by himself in his solitude, he began to find small wampum beads here and there where he was working. He would put those wampum beads inside his pouch, and then, once in awhile, he would string them in a certain sequence. And as he did this, he began to foresee things in the future. And that these would be instrumental in those events that had not occurred yet. And he even began to compose speeches of condolence and things. He knew that's what he would use these things for, in the future. Because as I said, he was like a magic boy. And so he put those away.

So a couple of years went by and he was still doing that chipping away and it was starting to take shape.

One day, the little boy was having breakfast with his mother and his grandma. He said, "Grandma, do we have any relatives? Do we have any cousins? Do we have any uncles or aunts? Or is there just you and me and my mother in this world? 'Cause we never see anybody."

And his grandma said, "Oh yes, you got relatives. We come from a village down the way from here. I left that village because there was too much turmoil, too much violence and too many problems. I wanted your mother to grow up in a safer environment. That's why you don't see them."

"Grandma," he said, "do you think that maybe someday we can go visit them so I can get to know them, who my relatives are?"

"Well, I think that's a good idea, Grandson," she said. "How about we get up real early tomorrow and we'll fix breakfast, have a good eat, pack a good lunch, then we'll walk over there to that village that I haven't been back to in years? And I will introduce you to whoever is left of my relatives."

And he said, "Okay."

And the boy's mother, her daughter said. "Okay."

So that's what happened. The next day they got up early in the morning, and they began to walk. And after they had gone quite a number of miles, they came to this little bit swampy area, tall-grass area, but there was kind of a vague path that they were following. And all of a sudden, the one they call the Peacemaker boy, the grandson, he looked down where he was walking.

And I don't know how his grandma missed it and his mother missed it because they were in the front; he was behind. He looked down and he saw a shiny, white thing. He picked it up and he brushed off the soil that was on it. And do you know what it was? It was a flint knife. With maybe an elk handle on it. Really well carved. Really well fitted and everything.

And it appeared that whoever made it, must have worked on it for months, in order to get it just the way it was, so finely carved. But when this Peacemaker boy saw that, he began to worry. He was admiring the craftsmanship in it. And he said, "You know Grandma, Ma, somebody was walking here, must be years ago, and dropped his knife. And he worked so hard to make that knife, and he doesn't even know where he lost it. And I'll bet you that person got sick because he lost something that he had valued so much, that was so good. That guy must have a broken heart." That's what the little boy said.

He said, "So Grandma, can I ask you a favor? You know, that man that lost that knife must be looking all over for it, all the time. When we get to where you used to live, I know in the middle of that village there's a post, in the ground. So can you take this knife and ask the leader there to put a string or a rawhide on there, and hang it to the top of the post? Let that knife hang there, because people go by there all the time. And the one who lost this may see it and find it, and there will be great peace in his mind again, for something that he had lost so long ago. There will be great peace for him."

And that's the second part I like in the story of the Peacemaker. Because it means honesty. You don't take things that are not yours. If somebody has lost something, you try to make sure it gets back to them. It even goes beyond honesty. It's right-to-the-core-of-your-bone honesty. And that's what the world needs. Is honesty and trust.

And so it is, that when they got over to that village, they were introduced to the relatives. And they were surprised to see them. But the relatives had an inkling that something was really different. And they could tell because there were two or three boys, kids fighting over there. And that little boy got in the middle of it, and he said, "You're not supposed to fight and hurt each other. You're supposed to play together, help each other."

The old people were watching what he did, how he interceded in that and stopped the fight. And he started talking to them as though he was an old man, and he was just a kid. And so already word had got around that place, that that little kid was amazing. The way he thought, his philosophy, his sense of justice, was something else. Better than an elder.

And so they would ask their leader questions, to find out what he's about. And finally the leader of the village said. "What is it about this boy?" Especially because he wanted to hang the knife from that pole, and return it to whomever lost it. And they were always amazed at the little things he was doing.

So finally the leader said, "Who are you? What is it, you got some kind of message or something?"

And so the little boy said, "Yeah, yeah. I got three things. Peace, the power (strength) to live, and righteousness. That's what I have. And that's what the Creator wants the people to have. And love, compassion."

"How about we gather all the people up and can you tell us, can you explain it to us?"

He said, "Well, yeah, but not just like that. We have to have deer meat that we cook, and corn bread, corn soup, stuff like that. It has to be present; then I can talk. It goes with that."

And he told them the three things, well actually the four: the peace, compassion, the strength (the power) to live, and righteousness. And he said, "I have to teach that to the people who make war."

So they left that village and they went back home to their little hut, along the Bay of Quinte. And so what he wanted, happened. So then he went back to chipping that big stone, and gathering more wampum, and making his plan.

He was just a kid. But he grew fast. By the time he was thirteen, he was already like a man, just like a real man. And finally he finished that canoe. And he told his mother and his grandma, "I'm done making the canoe now. And so I have to begin my journey." He said, "So tomorrow can you help me? I'm gonna move that canoe into the Bay of Quinte. And then you can laugh at me Grandma, tomorrow. Or I'll show you, one of the two. We're gonna see tomorrow.

"And so" he said, "tomorrow we're gonna burn tobacco too, early in the morning. And I don't want you two to cry for me, because I don't know what's gonna happen to me. I don't know what my fate will be. Maybe I will never return and I will not be successful in the mission that I am to do.

"But" he said, "if some day you wonder what happened to me, you don't see me in the future, just go over to that hill, to that big tree that's over there. Just make a small scratch or cut on the bark. And if I haven't been successful on my mission, blood will come out of that tree. But if there is only sap coming out of there, like a regular tree, then you'll know I'm successful. But don't cry too much, if I don't come back. 'Cause I don't know what's gonna happen."

So they started. After they had burned tobacco and made prayers, they put rollers, in holes, in front of the canoe. They pushed the canoe on top of the rollers, so it was not so hard to push. Plus it was going downhill a little bit, so it helped them. And they got to the Bay of Quinte and they put it in the water.

And the canoe didn't sink.

And that grandma was looking at that 'cause she thought it was gonna sink. So already now, they were surprised. It was like a miracle, I guess you might call it. And so when he got in his boat, he had his pouch of tobacco and he had his pouch of wampum beads that he had strung and everything. And he said, "Now, I'm gonna go."

Chapter 27

The Great Law of Peace Part 2:
The Birth of the Confederacy

And together they traveled all over, to the nations that were warring, to bring them peace.

He said, "I'm gonna cross the river and the lake over there and start my journey. And where I'm going is to the place where the meanest, the most cannibalistic people, the fiercest people on the face of the earth live. That's the Mohawk people. That's where I'm gonna start. Because if I can't convince them, there's no use going any place else."

And that was his rationale. Start with the toughest, roughest one; then the rest will be easier. So they say that he got in his canoe, and he had a paddle. Then he sang this song and he just pushed the paddle once. And that canoe went almost like a bullet, like an arrow goes, that much faster than normal. Sometimes he would sing that canoe song, and that canoe would go out of the water, almost like an airplane goes through the sky. It traveled fast. He was a miraculous kind of person who could do those things.

So he went from the Bay of Quinte and he came across our Lake Ontario. "Kaniatarí:io" they call it. And when he got over there, there was a road that used to go from the east to the west. A small path that our warrior, fighter people always frequented 'cause it was the main throughway. In fact, the present Thruway follows that yet to this day, that ancient trail. Can you imagine that?

There was a woman living over there, and her name was Tsikónhsase. And there are different stories about her. She was a manipulative woman. A very controlling woman. She knew medicine, and she had the power to do things. Even to take people's life through medicine, if she wanted to. She had medicine that was like love medicine too. If she saw a man and she wanted that man, she could fix medicine on him and she'd get him.

There are all kinds of stories about her. She had many personalities and many moods and whatever. For some reason she had a unique power. All the men when they fought, back and forth from east to west, traversed that path that went past her house. Anybody, any men who went there, even though they would kill each other away from her place, when they got on her grounds, they didn't fight. She had that kind of power.

It was like a neutral place. And she used to feed the people, feed the men. Didn't matter what happened, she didn't take sides either. She was neutral. But she liked a good time. And she was friendly to all the men, in many ways.

So when the Peacemaker went over there, she didn't know who he was. And it was apparent that he was sort of strange or had a power. At first she became afraid of that. So she began to brew up some food for him, but it was made out of bugs and different kinds of stuff that could kill him.

But he was also powerful and could read minds a little bit too and foresee tomorrow as well. And he knew. So on his way there, he took those weeds that grow near the water, they're like a straw: reeds. And he put one in his clothing and under his leggings to the floor. So when she made these beans with bugs and stuff, so you could hardly tell the difference, he started to eat it.

But instead of eating it he put it in that hollow reed and it went down. So she thought he was eating it. And of course he wasn't losing consciousness. He wasn't under her control, and he wasn't dying like she wanted. So she knew he was smarter and stronger in medicine than she was. So finally she gave that up.

And so she said to him, "Gee" she said, "who are you? Where did you come from, and where are you going? And where did you get your power?" And all that kind of stuff.

So he began to talk to her. And he said, "The Creator sent me to bring peace and to do away with war and bloodshed and killing. The Creator sent me, instead of fighting, to bring peace and a good mind and love. And to teach people to help each other. That's why I'm going to where the sun comes up, to where those mean people live, the Mohawks."

And she said, "You better watch out if you go there 'cause they're really mean. It won't take much for them to kill you either. You're going to a dangerous place."

He said, "I know, that's why I'm going there, because it is the meanest, roughest place."

"Well, your plan, it is a wonderful plan. You have my endorsement and my support. Anytime you need my help, I'm there for you. And I think you're right."

And that's when he proclaimed her to be the Mother of all the Nations. And she became that. And then he went on.

The Peacemaker also had much more to confront 'cause the danger wasn't by any means over, as he continued on his journey. But he was able to withstand any test that they gave to him, to provide any proof that people needed.

So they subjected him to different things. And probably one of the most famous, at least for the Mohawks is that at Cohoes Falls they tested him, *really* tested him. Cohoes Falls is only about an hour from here, from Kanatsioharè:ke. And that falls is kinda high. It's not like Niagara Falls, but it's similar. They tested him by putting him on a tall, tall tree. He climbed the tree and when he was on top of that tree, they cut it down and let it fall into the gorge there, into solid rock. The tree itself was at least a hundred and fifty feet tall, at the edge of the cliff, plus the falls are probably another eighty to one hundred feet. So that's a two hundred—almost a three hundred-foot drop.

The next morning, all the Mohawk people thought that he had died, that he was killed because of the fall. When the people awoke, they saw white smoke, off in the distance from their village at Cohoes. They sent men, the warrior people, over there to find out who it was. They thought it was Penobscot or Mi'kmaqs or Mohicans or somebody coming to visit. They didn't think it would be the Peacemaker at all.

But when the young men got there, they found that it *was* the Peacemaker. He had survived that fall. And, of course, they were in awe, because they had witnessed a miracle take place before their very eyes. And so they welcomed him into the village.

That village at Cohoes was predominantly Turtle Clan. But there was also a mixture of others, some of the fiercest Mohawk people there are in this world. The Peacemaker had claimed that he was being sent there by the Creator. And when the war leader saw him, with no bruises, no scratch, not even a broken hair on his head, then he was convinced that he indeed had the power of a great messiah, and was sent by the Creator, the Maker of the universe.

So this test convinced the Mohawks that he had a supernatural element or nature to his existence. Up to that time, they weren't going to listen to a word he said. And of course the Mohawks, I guess, carried lots of weight, because they were a fierce people.

The contenders for being the most fierce amongst the Iroquois were probably the Senecas and the Mohawks. They were two of the bloodiest and most savage, the cruelest and the meanest people there were. I'm not sure which one was meaner, the Seneca or the Mohawk. But it appears that it might have been the Mohawks, because when you hear people talking, they always say they're afraid of them. People like the Ojibway or Penobscot, in their stories even today, always mention that the Mohawks are like the boogeyman, more than anybody else. So I suspect from that,

that probably the Mohawks were the meanest ones. And so if the Mohawk people were to support something, because of that, it would carry a lot of weight. It would mean a lot, in terms of getting the message across, or whatever you're trying to do.

And so the war leader said that the Mohawk people had seen enough. They said that was all that was needed: he had passed their test. They were now ready to listen, and to embrace whatever the message was that he carried. And so the Peacemaker began to instruct the people of Cohoes about the Great Law of Peace. And the word spread quickly among the Mohawks, about this great thing that happened.

While the Peacemaker was in Mohawk country, he had visions of a man who was going to be his helper or his assistant, in bringing the law to the people. This man, that he dreamt about or envisioned, was a man who lived in Onondaga. And some say that he was a Mohawk guy married to an Onondaga woman. And some say he had seven kids. Seven girls. They call this man Hiawatha in English.[1] In my language we call him Aionwahta. But later, people called him Hiawatha. That's the same character that they're talking about.

And also in Onondaga, there was this man who was evil, or like a witchcraft-man. He had the ability to turn his body into a deer or into an owl or into a wolf. Some people call that a shape-changer or something like that. Well, that's what we have in Iroquois country. (And the Ojibwa had the ability to do that before as well. Some might still have it.) So there was one of those kinds of guys over there in Onondaga. He had great medicine, but he used it in an evil kind of way.

This witchcraft-man, this evil man, used to look at Aionwahta's wife. And he fell in love with her. He wanted to take her away from Aionwahta. So he would make advances to her, but she would always turn the other way. He would talk to her, to try to lure her to be his girlfriend. But she was married to another man, so she wouldn't look at him. She wouldn't answer him or even acknowledge him. No matter what he did, she didn't like him.

---

[1]   This Hiawatha is unrelated to Longfellow's fictional character called Hiawatha.

So that man started to get mad, the one who knew bad medicine. And he began to make medicine to try and control that lady, so that he could take her as his girlfriend or his wife—take her away from that other man. But she was so strong in her love for her husband that the medicine didn't even sway her, couldn't pull her where it normally would have.

After a while, because that witch-guy could not take her with his medicine, he began to make a medicine to do away with her, that man's wife—the one he loved. "Because if I can't have her, nobody's gonna have her." That's what he thought. So he began to poison her life until she got sick.

Aionwahta, the husband, tried to find medicine to help her, but nothing he made could fix her. She got sicker and sicker. The medicine didn't have enough power. It wouldn't work. And so this evil man eventually won and he took the life of Aionwahta's wife.

She died.

Aionwahta was very, very sad because he had lost his wife whom he loved very much. When they buried his wife, he was lonesome. But even though he was sad, he had seven daughters yet to take care of, see. So he was able to have some hope.

But it didn't stop there.

The evil man began to also make advances to his older daughter. Because he could not have the wife, he wanted the daughter. She also ignored him and rejected him, and so he began to make medicine on this second person, the oldest daughter. And she started to get sick. And the father tried to help her by fixing medicine. But no matter what he did, he couldn't help her. Every day she got sicker and sicker, until she died too.

Now Aionwahta was not just sad from his wife dying; he was three, four times sadder because now his older daughter had died too, just a short time later. And then the next one: he tried to chase the next daughter. And he kept doing that until all the daughters were killed.

He killed all the daughters 'cause none of them wanted him.

And so Aionwahta became so sad that he was wanting to end his life. He became hopeless because his whole sacred family had all been killed, taken away from him. He had nothing more to live for in the world. And so he didn't take care of himself anymore.

He said, "I'm just gonna walk to the end of the world. And I don't care what happens to me. I've got nothing to live for. Nothing, no hope." And so Aionwahta walked, aimlessly, in no particular direction. He just walked. And he didn't care if he died during the night or the day.

He came to a small lake. It was a shallow lake, not too deep. Maybe it was a big pond or something, but they call it a big body of water. And as he came there, it was covered from shore to shore with a blanket of geese and ducks, water birds. There was so little room between them, you couldn't even see the water. It was all ducks and geese.

When he came to that he just went straight into the water. He didn't care if he drowned. He was gonna walk right through. But when he started to walk, all the ducks and geese, they jumped and flew up. And as they flew up, all the water stuck in their feathers. They almost drained that lake, the birds did. That's how many were in there. And so it was muddy and just pools of water here and there, after the ducks and geese had taken off.

As he walked through there, he didn't care if he went into quicksand and he drowned. He was just walking 'cause he was so sad. But as he was walking in that mud, he noticed something on the ground. It was a white, bright thing. And he picked it up. It was a quahog shell. In the craft shop here at Kanatsioharè:ke, we have wampum beads made out of the quahog shell. The shells are cylindrical. They're white, and they're purple. And he found those in that lake.

He didn't know what they were for. But he took some sinew that he had and he began to string them together as he found them. And so they formed different variations of white and purple. And when he would finish one, here's what he'd say. "With this string I made from this wampum that I found, if there is somebody in the world that is as sad and tearful, as full of grief as I am, with nothing to live for—the sun has fallen from the sky in my world, there's no sun in the sky anymore for me—if somebody was as sad as I am, I would go see them. And I would take from the very beautiful blue sky a pure eagle feather. And I would wipe the dust of death from the sad one's ears, so that he could hear the children talk and sing and laugh again. So that he could hear his children and nephews when they speak to him. That's what I would do with this wampum if I knew somebody who was as sad as I am. I would console them by taking the death from their ears."

And then he picked some more up and he strung them. And he said, "If there was somebody as sad as I am, walking this earth, I would take, from the very beautiful clear blue sky, a soft little deer skin that's like white cotton. And I would wipe the tears from his eyes. I would use that cloth to wipe the tears, the pain of lonesomeness away from him. So he can see again the beauty of our Mother Earth and the beauty of his children and nephews and nieces. So he can see life again. That's what I would do, if there was somebody as sad as I am, to lose their whole family that they love."

Then as he continued to walk, he found some more of those same beads on the ground. And he strung them up. "With this wampum," he said, "if there was somebody in this world who was as sad as I am, with heaviness upon them, what I would do is I would take from the very beautiful blue sky, a medicine water and I would offer it to him. So when he drank it, it would dislodge the grief and the sadness, about the loved ones who died in his family. That way he could eat again and the food would taste good. And that way he could speak without a stutter to his loved ones, the ones that remain on earth. And so I would say to him, 'From the very beautiful blue sky, I give you a glass of water so that you will be refreshed. And you can live again and you can speak, and you can eat again and be nourished.' And that's what I would do, if there was somebody who was in as much grief as I am."

And he went on like that. When he kept finding wampum, he'd put it in his pouch. And he said, "I'm putting it away, in case I do find somebody like that. That's what I will do for them."

And so he kept walking towards the east. He came to the Mohawk country where the Peacemaker was with the Mohawks. And the Peacemaker had already known this. He had known for years that that man would be his partner. So when that Aionwahta got over to the Mohawk country, the Peacemaker was waiting for him. The Peacemaker hung up a stick right there next to the fire. And the Peacemaker already had those wampum that he had from years earlier that he had strung and kept in a leather pouch, just like Aionwahta did.

And so when Aionwahta got over there, so sad, the Peacemaker stood up. He took that wampum and he said, "My brother, my cousin, I see you are so sad and your mind is so heavy. Your eyes are filled with tears. Your ears are filled with the dust of death. You can't hear." And so he went through the strings of wampum, which were the same as the other ones that Aionwahta made, before they met.

And the Peacemaker began to condole him and do everything that Aionwahta said he would do for somebody. And after that, Aionwahta began to be the interpreter or the spokesperson for the Peacemaker. And together they traveled all over to the nations that were warring, to bring them peace, the peace plan.

And so in Mohawk country, they started the first part of their work, by putting up three Chiefs, three Turtle Clan Chiefs. And those are the Chiefs that they try to keep installed right to this very day.

And after lots of things going on over there, and instructions, he began to teach them different things about the social/political structure.

Then the Mohawk delegation went with the Peacemaker to the Oneidas, for they're the next people that live to the west of us. And there the Oneidas were more receptive, because the Mohawk leaders, who used to be war leaders, had been converted into men of peace. The Oneidas were somewhat subservient you might say, to the Mohawks, because the Mohawks were noted for being the fiercest people.

The fierce war leaders no longer had the hatchet of war: they radiated peace. And so the Oneidas didn't resist. They said if the Mohawks were accepting that law, then they too would also accept it. And so they asked about the law, and asked to be taught it. And so it was that the Oneidas also put three leaders up, three Chiefs or "three men of the good." Only three.

And then they bypassed Onondaga. They skipped over it, because in Onondaga country there lived a man who was the fiercest man, I guess, on the face of the earth. Probably even more fierce than the Mohawks were before they accepted the Great Law. And this man was so mean and so fierce that he couldn't live with people. He had to live by himself in the swamp, in Cicero Swamp. They called him Atotáhrho.

And Atotáhrho was something like the plant over there on that bench, that aloe vera. His head looked like that. His hair was almost like those Caribbean guys with their dreadlocks. Something like those two, mixed together. And this man was a mean man; he was a witchcraft-man, a sorcerer. He used that evil medicine.

And his problem was that he wanted to be the controller of the world. He wanted to control everything, even the animals. They say he was so tied up with that kind of notion that there were rattlesnakes that nested in his hair. And they were his protectors. So if anybody came there, to try to talk to him, they would hiss. And if you came too close they would lunge at you and they would bite you. And even today Cicero Swamp is full of rattlesnakes, something like maybe those Massasaugas over in Canada. They're not too big.

His skin was just like fish scales. And they said he had seven crooked places on his body and that added to his misery, I guess, 'cause he was so mean. His hands were so bent they almost looked like a turtle's feet. His hands were—I don't know if it was arthritis or what, but—they were all deformed.

And this man was so powerful, in a supernatural way, they say that he could even make a tornado come. He could make the clouds move and a big wind or hurricane come, and knock everything down. Or he could make twisters come at his will. He could command that. That's how powerful he was.

And if somebody tried to go where he lived, tried coming onto the lake close to Cicero Swamp there, he could cause the wind to blow, making the waves go ten feet high and capsizing canoes. He was noted for that. People had seen that before, so they knew he could do that. Also if you got too close, he could even make an earthquake happen. And of course all that would stop people from going where he lived.

So this is the kind of power he possessed, this man they call Atotáhrho. And Atotáhrho was a manipulative man. He had to be the boss of everything; he had to control everything.

The Onondaga people themselves, they didn't live with that Atotáhrho man, even though he was an Onondaga. He lived by himself, because he was too fierce and too mean. But the Onondaga people themselves had heard about the Great Law in Mohawk and Oneida country, because news traveled kinda fast, even in those days. Now I'm talking one—to two-thousand years ago, when this took place.

The Onondagas didn't like him either, but he was controlling them. And so even though the Onondaga people desired to embrace that law, they were deathly afraid of their leader. Nobody dared to say anything against him 'cause there would be reprisals. They didn't dare to do anything without his approval, or without his knowledge. So they wouldn't try to embrace the Great Law right away: they were afraid.

The Mohawks and the Oneidas knew this and they said their strength was too weak yet, because they were just newly united in this law of peace. They knew they might not have enough power or smarts to outtrick him, or to outpower him either. They decided they shouldn't try to tackle such a big power right away, not until they had a chance to become strong in it.

So they went around the Onondagas. The Onondagas lived next to Syracuse, New York. (And they're still there.) And so they went around Syracuse and on farther west to between Syracuse and Rochester, which is the traditional territory of the Cayugas.

And the Cayugas, just like the Oneidas, didn't offer any resistance, because they had seen that the Mohawks and the Oneidas had agreed already, to do this with that Peacemaker. So in Cayuga country, the Peacemaker began to instruct them about what the Great Peace meant, and what it was about. And also at that point, they installed or stood up three leaders of the Cayugas.

And so now you had Mohawk, Oneida, and Cayuga: three leaders from the Mohawk, three from the Oneida and three from the Cayuga people. And they said they were still not strong enough to confront Atotáhrho. They possibly wouldn't make it, because they were not strong enough yet.

So they said, "We will continue on west to the land of the Seneca." That's next to Buffalo and west of there and south of there. Between Rochester and the other side of Buffalo is where the Seneca people lived in their villages.

And in one of the lakes over there, close to where the Seneca lived, there was a young war leader. And this war leader was a very capable man and a very powerful man, physically as well as intellectually. He was a tactician. He knew how to fight. He knew how to defend. He knew how to lead a whole lot of people in war. He knew how to do that.

And even though he was way younger than all of the other War Chiefs in all of the nations, he had gained quite a reputation and was revered by the people all over, because of his fierceness. He had like a dominance, or whatever, and he relished that too. He was quite proud of it. So he had become quite well known and feared by all the different Indians that went from east to the west along the old trail.

When they propositioned him about the law and everything, he didn't feel like he wanted to share his power or his successes. He thought that the Seneca people who were under his leadership, were undefeatable. They didn't need anybody else to help them.

So the Seneca man said, "We see the Mohawks, Oneidas, and Cayugas have agreed. But we don't know if we need to unite with you because we're *strong*, strong enough, just alone. We can handle our own battles. We can handle our own affairs. We don't really need anybody to help us. We're powerful people, Seneca people. We're not afraid of nobody, to fight them." And he said, "So therefore, we don't think that we are interested in joining what you call this Great Law of Peace plan."

And so after he told this to the delegation of Mohawks, Oneidas, and Cayugas, they all got into their canoes and they left him.

So there was a problem. But I don't know if you could say it was more of a problem than the Mohawks. With the Mohawks, if the Peacemaker hadn't survived that fall, he'd have been dead. And with the Seneca, well, he had these other nations with him. But the Seneca didn't put him through a test like the Mohawks did. Maybe they didn't have to, because they were told what happened with the Mohawks. And it was verified, so they had a tendency to believe him without really testing him.

But anyway, one of my uncles talked about it, saying that the young Seneca guy, the war leader, was really thinking that he didn't need anybody. He thought he was so powerful that he could control the world, I guess, at his will. But this Seneca guy had a daughter. I don't know if he had more than one daughter, but he had one little girl that he especially was fond of, and he had a real good relationship with her.

When the delegation left, there was a big storm that came—clouds, thunder, and lightning. The lightning hit that Chief's daughter, the one that he really liked. And that little kid died right there, by that lake. He had just got through saying he was infallible, he was invincible, he didn't need *anybody*. And look at what happened.

So it made him realize that things were not quite the way he thought they were. It triggered his mind to kind of flip and kinda humble himself. It humbled him so much that it changed his view, his thinking. The Seneca leader realized that he had no power. Not compared to the kind of power of the supernatural and of the Creator. When that big storm came and it hit his girl, he picked her up and he realized that there was a bigger power than he was.

And so when that happened he sent a little boy. He said, "Go run over there to the lake and beckon them back, that delegation. Tell them to come back, that I want to listen to what they have to say." He wanted to know further what this peace was about.

And so they did come back and they had council. And when they counciled, that Seneca war leader said, "It sounds like it's doable. It sounds like we might be able to be a part of that plan of peace. But," he said, "the only thing we don't understand is what happens if a war party comes from somewhere, and they begin to use their hatchets and whatever weapons they've got, to kill our women and our children, and the people of our village? Because we live by the trail that goes from the rising sun to the setting sun. And this east-west road, everybody travels it, enemies and everybody. And so we always have to be vigilant."

"And in your proposal," he said to the Peacemaker and to the Mohawks and the Oneidas and Cayugas, "you want us to bury all our weapons of war, which will leave us defenseless." And so he took a stand on that part.

And then the Peacemaker said, "In place of the weapons of war, I will give you this sacred tobacco. And this is what you will use in times of need. When anything like that comes to threaten you, you will build a fire and you will offer this tobacco that I have given to you. When you burn the tobacco, that will summon the spiritual world. And you will call to the Creator and you will call to me. And we are the ones who will stop whatever threat comes to you."

But the Seneca Chief still wasn't convinced. He was still doubting what the Peacemaker said. "That sounds good, but I don't know if it's gonna work. I don't know if I can put the trust of my people in that," the Seneca war leader said, "because if somebody comes, then we have to be able to defend ourselves. If that don't work, then we'll all be killed."

And so the Peacemaker listened to him some more, and finally they came up with something. The young Seneca War Chief, he said, "Well, in the chieftainships that are gonna be set up, how 'bout if two of them retain some of the qualities, some of the authority that the War Chief had. And in case there's a need for it, then it will be easily accessible for defense as they know it."

And so they contemplated. They thought about it quite a bit. Finally the Peacemaker and the other delegations did say, "All right, we'll compromise on that, then. You will let go of all your weapons of war. There will be two Peace Chiefs, two sachems or two chieftainship titles in the Seneca that will have a part-time war capability, a calling of men, to make an army or defense. If something like that happens, those two Seneca leaders will be the only ones that will be able to call a war. They're the only ones."

And they made it difficult to do. If any of the nations need soldiers, they have to go through there: the process is there. And this was mostly done for the sake of compromising, see.

"But at the same time," the Peacemaker said, "what we will do is we will take precautions so that it doesn't happen, that there is the least chance for it to happen. We will take slippery elm bark and put it at the Seneca door, at the western door of the Longhouse. And also where the Mohawks live, we will put slippery elm bark over there at the eastern door. If somebody came here with the wrong intentions, came here to the territory of the Iroquois, from the western door, then when they stepped on that slippery elm bark, they would slip and fall and they would be incapable of going into the house and doing damage."

That means that the Seneca people will act as the most vigilant ones, the forewarners. That's the symbol of that slippery elm, I believe. There may be other things too, that I don't know about, but that's what I think. And if the time comes where they see that there is a need for warriors to fight, they will be the ones who will make the call, the summons.

If in Mohawk country or in other parts of the country, they see the need for warriors, the only way that they can do it is to go through those two Seneca Chiefs, who then will be in charge of opening up the thing for the whole Iroquois to raise an army. But the process is such that it's hard to get that to happen. Technically, the protocol or the channel that is made is not the easiest thing to use.

So you can't just go like that . . . Or maybe you could, depending on the severity of it, providing those two leaders okayed it. Do you see what I mean? But it's sort of a big responsibility, of that Seneca people. There are two names of them,[2] that are just for that, and I've forgotten them 'cause it's been years since I heard or talked about them.

So the Seneca did agree, and they too put three leaders up. So now there were four nations that had agreed. And then after that, they began to put the other leaders up. The Mohawks put up six more. So that made nine altogether for the Mohawks. And the Oneidas, they put up another six and they already had three. So that was nine. And the Cayugas, they put up seven more leaders and they had three already. So that's ten they had. And

---

2.   Two inherited chieftainship or sachem titles.

the Seneca, they had put up three and then they put up another five. And that made eight for the Senecas: that's how many leaders they had.

And once they had been instructed about the law, about how the government would work, each nation came together into a confederacy of nations. So now they felt that they were pretty much of sufficient power and strength. Now, the Mohawks, the Oneidas, the Cayugas and the Seneca, they would all go together to Onondaga, to Cicero Swamp. And they would now confront the Atotáhrho, the one who could make tornados and hurricanes. The one who could make the earth shake.

And they would begin to confront him and change him. They would have to heal his body from the wretchedness and evil that he stood for. And so when they went there, they were instructed by the Peacemaker on how to go. That's who they were taking their direction from.

And from there, the Oneidas, Cayugas, Mohawks, and Senecas began by the hundreds to go to approach Atotáhrho. And the Peacemaker said, "When we go there, Atotáhrho is gonna do all kinds of destructive things, to stop us from getting to his place in Cicero Swamp. So you be watching out."

So they did. When they started to walk over there, there were eagles flying in the sky. And in between their feathers, those eagles had lots of wampum. And when they got over the people, they dropped it. And even their feathers fell down. That's what that Atotáhrho made those eagles do, so that everybody would fight over those feathers and that wampum, and they wouldn't go to see him.

That didn't work. They got through that part all right. So they got in their canoes, dozens and dozens of them, and they started to cross the lake to go to Cicero Swamp. But the blackbirds were all his protectors. They told the Atotáhrho that all those people were coming to see him in canoes.

And so he began to make medicine. Next thing you know a big hurricane came, and the waves capsized the canoes of those delegations from the Mohawks, the Oneidas, the Cayugas and the Senecas. Some of them drowned. But most of them survived. And so finally they got across.

The Peacemaker had said, "When we get over there, there will be wolves or rattlesnakes on the road. And they're gonna try to bite you, try to poison you, see. But as long as you sing this peace song I'm gonna sing, Aionwahta, and as long as you sing it without hesitation, Atotáhrho's power cannot find a way to get in there. But you cannot hesitate."

And when they got across there, Aionwahta began to sing. And as they started to walk in there, rattlesnakes even came close from the bush, hissing and ready to bite. But as long as he sang that, the rattlesnakes couldn't bite them. They couldn't get through that.

And so finally when they came close, all kinds of things happened. At that time too, Aionwahta kind of got nervous 'cause they were getting too close and he hesitated. And so then the Peacemaker said, "Whoa, you can't do that. I'll take over, I'll sing. You back me up." And so he took over.

There was turbulence all over 'cause they were having to fight this evil of Atotáhrho now. But all the delegations came and they didn't hesitate. And eventually they got there.

And when they got to him, what they did is they doctored him, and they took the snakes out of his hair. They combed his hair to straighten his mind. And then there were the seven crooked places on his body they had to straighten. They doctored his body and they took the crookedness out of it. And they turned his skin back into a normal skin. They were doing this together. So they got him in pretty good shape, but it took quite some doing.

And that Atotáhrho saw all that. And in a way he was relieved 'cause he was possessed or something. He was relieved somewhat, and yet he was somewhat ornery. *Still.* But finally they talked to him enough that he would reason. And so they told him about the peace plan and he began to listen. But the big thing with him was he wanted to control everything. So he wasn't willing to accept the Great Peace.

So they said, "Okay, you can be like that. You can. You'll be the head Chief of the whole Iroquois. You'll be the head. But you won't have any more power than anybody." It's something like the Queen of England. She's the head of state, but she has no power. A figurehead.

You can see their markings on our condolence cane. Each represents one of those chieftainship titles of Onondaga. And the Atotáhrho one is the one with the snakes coming out.

He has power, but it's the same power as all the other Chiefs. Yet his name will always be above them, in a sense. So he was tricked or I don't know if you'd call it tricked, but he liked that idea. He could live with it. He thought that was acceptable, so he went along with that part. And they said that Onondaga would be the capital or the main fire of the whole Confederacy. That would be the headquarters, the place where the Grand Councils would be held 'cause it's central.

And the Onondagas would have fourteen leaders. That's almost twice as many as any of the other nations. But the Onondaga people, they have the smallest population, by far, of all the five nations. They're not even an eighth the size of the Mohawks, yet they were going to have almost twice the leaders, the most Chiefs, as a compromise. That was appealing to the Atotáhrho too. So they used all these kinds of things that would butter him up and soothe his ego.

But the reality of it is, in all their negotiations, he had no more power than any other one. 'Cause all the leaders are equal. It doesn't matter if the Onondagas have a hundred and the Mohawks only have one, because that one Mohawk can stop anything in the big Council. It has to be unanimous. The numbers don't mean anything because it's a consensus of all.

He may have had a little more influence, but not more power. And so as a result of this deal, he was the only one, Atotáhrho, who would not have a Clan Mother or be nominated by Clan Mothers. All the other forty-nine leaders, they would all come from clans and they would all have a Clan Mother. But not Atotáhrho.

Atotáhrho is created from the decision of all of these leaders of all the nations. They're the ones that nominate or they're the ones that select him or confirm his chieftainship. And he's the only one that's like that.

And he was satisfied: he accepted that. And so to this day, he's considered like the head, leader of all the Chiefs.

And now the Onondagas agreed to all of that. And so they had fourteen leaders. Now the peace was planted. They put up all their fourteen leaders over there with Atotáhrho as the head one of them, of all the Iroquois, Mohawk included. And when they finished that, they made sure that there were fifty Chiefs in all, for the five nations.

And then the Peacemaker told them to hold hands together in a symbolic way: lock their arms together. "And in a big circle the fifty Chiefs will be and," he said, "in the middle of that circle where the Chiefs are holding hands, I will plant the Great Tree of Peace. And it will be so tall that it will pierce the sky. And it will be the symbol of sharing, the symbol of brotherhood and the symbol of peace in the world. And the roots will be so big and they will be white, one to the north, the east, the south, and the west. And they will carry peace to the world. And those roots are white, so they can be noticed by all. And when people see the white roots, if they want peace, they can follow them. And they can make their minds known where the Tree of Peace was planted, in Onondaga country. And there they will seek to sit in peace, in the shade of the tree, with all of us Iroquois nations."

He said, "But you must hold tightly in there. For inside of that circle are your people, your territory, your clans, your language. Everything that you have is in there and is protected by the fifty leaders."

And he said, "But I want you to know that in the coming years, there will be a people coming here that you've never seen before. And they will carry an axe with them. And they will sneak under the arms of the leaders that are in the circle surrounding the tree, when they are not looking or paying attention. And they will come in there, trying not to be seen, and they will try to destroy the Tree of Peace. And they will take the axe and they will hack the roots, the four roots, because they want the tree and what it stands for to fall. They want to kill it."

And he said, "When that has been done, the tree will begin to die, because it'll be getting no more nourishment from its roots in Mother Earth. When it dies, it will begin to fall, and all that it stands for will begin to fall. But because those fifty leaders are holding hands together around it, it will fall on their clasped arms. And therefore it won't hit the ground. But it will hit a blow to them, because it's so big and heavy. And now they must hold it on their arms, whereas before it was upright."

So they're gonna go through *trying* times, because of the heaviness and the drastic impact of that tree falling on their arms. Do you see? So that has a symbol too, by itself.

"And for many generations, those leaders will struggle to hold the tree from hitting the ground. And the time will come when there's almost nobody left, except those leaders holding hands. And now, after so many years, they're just trembling from the weight of it, because they're losing the power to hold such a heavy thing by themselves," he continued.

And in our prophesies it says, "But when those people, like culprits, run away from chopping the tree's roots, when they run away from their evil deed, they'll know it's evil, what they did. They will run to escape any consequences that the people might do to them, but they will never be able to escape, because" my uncle said, "They will run, but it won't be too long."

(When the old ones used to say, "too long" or when they said, "one day" it could mean ten years. So they don't mean it literally. They mean it can be a long time.)

"But one day, the supernatural will come. And those people will hemorrhage from their eyes. They'll hemorrhage from their noses, their mouths, their ears and their bottom parts will hemorrhage. And they won't go far, and they will drop. And they will die, for what they have done." The Peacemaker said that's what was gonna happen.

And that leaves the leaders, having to hold up this very heavy thing, all by themselves. No help. So that means that the people are in disarray. The Chiefs have got no more people. So if you look at the Longhouses in the last hundred years, most of them were run mostly by those leaders. The rest of us weren't there by their side. We weren't with them through thick and thin. And they did this, all this time.

And so we blame a lot of stuff on them. And sometimes we even get mad at them, because we think they're not right. But they didn't have much time to do anything else except strain all these years, under tremendous ridicule, under tremendous suppression, oppression not just by the society but even from *our* people. They had to try with all their might not to let go. More than any human should have to do.

And it says in our prophesies, "And so there will come a time when they will tremble and they will come to the last fiber of their strength to keep this tree from falling. And it's already fallen, it's just that they're holding it from falling on the *ground*. And just as they're ready to let go, and as the tree begins to fall the rest of the way to the ground, you will notice from the north and the east and the south and the west, our great-grandchildren will come running, the girls and the boys. All of our children will come running when they've seen the last Chief let go. And by the hundreds of them, they will grab the tree for the last time. And they will push it back up upright *one more time*."

So right now the grandchildren are trying to push it up. They didn't get it up yet. But they've got it going from all over.

And in the prophesies, it says—I used to hear it quite a bit:
Né:'e ne katkekshón:'a tá:we awenhnísera. Ne iethiiatere'okón:'a né:'e ohontsiakwé:kon enhonwatihtháhrhahse ne ahonwanatahónhsatate.

That's what they used to say. That means:
There is a day coming in the future when our grandchildren, our great-grandchildren, they will speak to the whole world, and the whole world will listen.

When I was a little boy, nobody spoke anywhere. No Seneca, no Mohawk, no Lakota, no Navajo, nobody could talk anywhere 'cause we were *nothin'*. When I was a kid, "you don't even talk to no white man 'cause you're not good enough." Even in Massena, the closest town to us, they were never gonna listen to us over there 'cause they didn't have any regard for us. It didn't matter what we thought. And we were even nothing to each other. So it was beyond comprehension. When we heard that as kids, it was almost unbelievable, it seemed to us that it could never be.

But in my life, just since I was growing up, we have sent our leaders, our delegations, many times to Geneva and they have spoken there on the floor of the General Assembly of the United Nations. We've done it in

New York City too. I was even part of that delegation a couple of times. And we've spoken to the nations of the world. And now, our people are recorded in documentaries. You see Oren Lyons's name everywhere internationally. And that's only a recent development. So now it has come to be, just in my lifetime. It has fulfilled those parts of the prophecy and will continue to.

And you go to the Mohawk's Longhouse, where we have our ceremonies, and our Longhouse can hold six hundred to seven hundred people. You go there at Midwinter, and there are people standing up 'cause there aren't enough chairs to sit down on: it's so packed. Onondaga's the same way. And I hear almost all the Longhouses are all like that. That wasn't like that twenty years ago; twenty-five to thirty years ago it wasn't like that. There were only a few sitting there. And in the last thirty years, many of our nations have built Longhouses two or three times bigger than they had. And it's still standing room only.

So all of those things *are now true*. Our young stood up. But the thing of it is: will they know what to talk about to the world? That's the question. So if they don't do it in the right way, their action, even though it's massive, may just miss the boat yet. They may all jump in the ocean. 'Cause the last of the teachers are already at the doorway that goes to no more. The last of the real teachers are almost gone. And so it's the trick in time: is that generation gonna be able to learn enough, absorb enough, to be the talkers to the world?

Because even though you're standing in front of the United Nations now, if you keep saying "Ah, ah ahh." See?[3]

So as I said earlier, and just as they let go and the tree is ready to fall, our great-grandchildren will come from all the directions. They will rush to push the tree back up, so it won't hit the ground one more time. *One more time.* But even when they put it back up, it won't last forever either. It'll fall again, but this time when it falls that means the world is gonna turn on

---

3. In other words, if you don't have the words, if you are stumbling in your speech, you will not be effective.

its axis. In my language, Tenwatkarén:ron tsi iohontsiá:te. *The earth will rock.* That's like a rocking chair, how it goes back and forth.

And that tree will stand there a little while and it will fall again. But when it falls this last time, that is the purification of the world. That's when the Creator is really gonna order the universe. That's when the earth will *rock.* And the sun will come up where it didn't come up before. And the cold will be where the cold wasn't before. And the heat will be where it wasn't before. 'Cause the whole thing will rock. They used to say that, see?

The world will do this and then there will be big changes in climate, all over the place. And also the different poles, the North and South Pole will change. And there will be lots of people who are gonna die all over the place, when that happens. And that begins the process of purification. And the Creator will come back one more time and redo the order of the universe, one more time.

And also I heard some uncles say this. Now I'm not sure what source they're pulling from: if it's from Creation or what, I forget now. But I *heard* it someplace, there will come a time in the future that the different races of the world that were from here, will come back.

We don't go there. We don't go to Africa. We don't go to England or France. We don't go anywhere. But those people will come here from those races. And they will have a meeting with our Indian people, our religious leaders or whatever we have as the leaders.

And when that happens, even the sun will dim. You know like I've talked about before when there's a power surge? The sun will even do that, when. That's how you're gonna know, eh? And some Indian people say, even the wind will almost stand still. And the birds will even stop flying. They'll all sit in the tree and be watching, for just that moment. Then they'll fly again. 'Cause they all recognize and acknowledge that, see?

So they're gonna request a meeting to come here in North America. And when that happens, that's when the process of the cleansing of the world will come very fast. And that's where everybody has to be scared, because when the water starts to clean, it cleans everything. When the wind starts to clean, it can take down big buildings. And it'll clean. When Mother Earth starts to talk and act, she can shake her body like you won't believe. And everything will fall down that was mighty and big.

And so that's prophesied to come sometime.

Chapter 28

The Great Law of Peace Part 3:
Keeping and Preserving It

Put your whole heart in what you learned, so that the spirit of our ancestors, our Creator and our Peacemaker can talk right through your body and use you, so that you can communicate peace. And then our people, we will get better. Our people will be united again.

Our young men and our young women, when you study the law and the way of Longhouse, keep your heart clean and pure. And when you interpret the laws, interpret it with love and compassion and kindness. Don't learn the law to use as a club, to hurt your family; don't use the law to clobber somebody, because they make a mistake. That's not what the law is for. That law, it's like that daughter who forgave her mother, that's what it's about. Forgiveness and love. And that's why when I talked about it awhile ago, that's why it touched my heart. It always does, because I know that's what the nations of the Iroquois, the Ojibwa, and all the nations need today is that tolerance for one another, in order to forgive and go on. That's what I know.

So when you younger people learn these things, put your whole heart in what you learned. Dedicate your whole life to it, so that the spirit of our ancestors, our Creator and our Peacemaker can talk right through your body and use you, so that you can communicate peace. And then our people, we will get better. Our people will be united again.

Sometimes I have heard that the Chippewa or Ojibway, they don't like us Mohawks or Iroquois. Some of them still talk about it, because of the days when we used to fight, long ago. Sometimes I even hear in Cree country up north on James Bay that they're still afraid of us, because their grandparents told 'em that the Iroquois are too mean and gonna kill 'em, even eat them. Some of them tell it yet.

But we made a treaty with the Ojibwa and Chippewa people in 1763. There's a wampum belt about it. Yeah, we used to fight at one time. But in 1763, there was a great treaty made between the Iroquois nations and the Ojibway that dedicated us to peace. So now, whenever I see Ojibwa or Chippewa people, I *love* it 'cause they're my sisters and my brothers. My great-grandfather promised peace, and I will never raise a hand to hurt the Chippewa or Ojibway or the Cree.

And so how I look at it today is that all our Indians, never shall we make fun of each other. I don't even really like to make jokes like we do sometimes with each other, because sometimes that one Ojibway or that one Cree isn't quite in the mood for a joke. They might misinterpret my joke, and I don't want there to be a chance that we have to fight or get mad at each other.

For example, when we smudge with sage the direction we go around in, that's the Iroquois way. What we do is, in our spiritual things, we always go this way. I guess they call that counterclockwise. (I always get mixed up when they use the clock 'cause I don't look at the clock much!)

And when we go that way it's for birth, and for life, and for the daytime, and for positive things. And then the only time we go the way the clock goes is if somebody passes away on us, then we'll go that way when we serve the food. Or even if it's a ceremony, we'll go this way for one circle. And then we'll go back to the regular way of *life*. That's the way we do it.

But the Ojibway and out west the Lakota and different Indian nations out there, they go clockwise. And when they go clockwise and we're over there, we go with them, the way they go. Always. We follow what they do. And then when they come over here, when we're going this way, counterclockwise, they go this way.

But sometimes the younger people, they'll say, "Oh you Iroquois, you're backward people, you don't go the right way." That's the younger ones who will say this. But if there's an elder with them, he'll cut 'em off right away. And he'll tell them, "You're not supposed to say that. You don't say that."

And the same thing: sometimes when our young go over there, they might say, "Ah, you are going the wrong way over there." But if there's an older Iroquois with them, they won't say that either. 'Cause they're gonna get checked, right away.

Because the older Indians, they respect each other all the time. They always honor and respect each other's way.

If I'm there, I tell them, "Both of you stop it *right now*. Because the Creator told us Iroquois to go this way. And we listen to the Creator. The Creator told you, Chippewa, and you, Lakota, to go this other way. So go that way. And it's right too.

There's a reason why they go that way. And there's a reason why he told us to go this way. So it's not up to us to change the foundations of these great peoples. We're not supposed to put each other down for the way we go. We're supposed to honor each other that we're *still* going the way he told us. So we must promote love and understanding."

If the Ojibwa people or Mi'kmaq people or Cree people invite me to their place, I follow the way they go. I'll eat the way they eat. I'll do what they do. It makes peace.

So anyway, if ever you get a chance to really hear the Great Law, it takes about ten whole days. In fact, the honest truth, I don't know, since Chief Jake Thomas died, if there is anybody left that can come close to doing it from its *a* to the *z*, from one end to the other. Maybe there is, but nobody told me yet who it is. So maybe we will never hear it again.

But I do know this one thing for sure: that in Mohawk country, in Seneca country, in Cayuga country, Onondaga country, Oneida country, there are various individuals that know by heart, half of it or a quarter of it. And I know in the other nations, there's another guy knows another part of it. And I know that in the Cayugas there's another man over there that knows the other parts. And I know that in Seneca they know these other parts.

So if there isn't a Jake Thomas now, the Chiefs of our Confederacy better hurry up and have that meeting amongst those that know. And put it together before they die. Because then we will be in trouble for ever. So my advice here is whatever Chiefs are still living in the Longhouses, go see them. Go tell 'em to put that on the front burner, to see if that Great Law can be recited again. You see that little one we just did, how powerful that is? Ten days of power, I don't know if we can handle it.

I don't write all this to say, "Do this, do this, do this." It's only a suggestion, what I've been saying. If it helps, use it. But don't ever feel that Tom Porter twisted our ears and twisted our arms: this is what we have to believe. No, because the Great Law threatens nobody. The Great Law is a law of peace and love. And that's how I talk to you, under those circumstances. And if I used the wrong words that mighta hurt you or offended you, then I want to let you know that I apologize to you, ten feet tall apologies, because my mission here was not to make you grieve or be sad, but to be positive and loving, as our law said we should be. And so for the honor that I had to talk and share with you, I say "Niá:wen 'kó:wa, tekahna'netarion" *layers and layers*. And that's all I have to say. *Thank you.*

Chapter 29

Some Notes on Tobacco and Other Medicine

And the Creator said, "Any time you are walking the earth, that you need some kind of special attention, that you need a hand, or you simply want to say thank you, you will have this tobacco."

When we talked about Creation, 'member I told you that Sky Woman mounded up the earth over her daughter, after she died? And plants grew out of there? And directly above where her heart was in this mound, grew that plant we call oien'kwa'ón:we. That's *sacred tobacco*. And the Creator said, "I give that to you, as a special gift through your mother." That's why it came from her heart. And that's where prayer has to come from—is the heart.

If you were to take our Indian tobacco, you could look at one seed from that seed ball. It's just like when a fly goes to the bathroom on a wall. You can hardly see it. That's how tiny those seeds are. And yet that seed can grow into a beautiful lush plant, from that one little thing. That's the miracle of birth. It started there.

So that's where the tobacco came from. We plant it all the time. And us Iroquois, we're a little different than the Western Indians. We never use the tobacco that comes from the store: Buglers, Smokey Joe's, or any of these tobacco outlet places that are on the reservation. We don't use that kind. The Western Indians, they use anybody's tobacco. They use Bugler's and all kindsa stuff. They don't care what kind it is.

But we Iroquois, when we burn tobacco or make little bundles of tobacco for somebody, we don't use just any tobacco: we use the kind that Grandma gave us, the kind Grandpa gave us. And they got it from their mother and father. And they got it from their mother and father, way since the time when the world began, when the world was new. And that seed continues.

We are the only ones that touch that seed. A woman who has her monthly never comes near it. And it's never disrespected. It's completely pure.

Whereas commercial tobacco, probably hundreds of people have touched that. And they're not supposed to be: if they do it'll touch our prayer, as well. So that's why I really salute a lot of the Iroquois people. They're still really strict about that. Even the ones that are not really strict about other things are strict about it, which is really good. So when I'm with my brothers out West and I see them using that tobacco, a lot of things go through my head about it. But they accept it completely, the use of whatever.

In contrast, the traditional people out West are very careful about women's moon time in other ways. Both them and us understand that this is a time each month when the woman's body is going through a very powerful cleanse. 'Member I told you how a pregnant couple have seven times the power they usually have, in order for that baby to cross over into the world?

Well, each month, the woman's body prepares a very special place for that baby to grow in. We could maybe call it a special medicine for that baby. If she doesn't become pregnant that month, then the body needs to shed that special lining and prepare a fresh new one. Well, if you can imagine that she has seven times her normal power when she's pregnant, imagine how much power she must have for her body to move that special medicine out of her body.

So during that time of cleansing, her spiritual energy is very, very strong, so strong that it can interfere with other medicine, with ceremony, with food that is being prepared by her, and with the spiritual messages that anyone else is putting into their tobacco.

So when I say that her energy can affect things around her, and that there are lots of precautions that Grandma said she needs to take during this time, our people think of that in a very respectful way. Just as we celebrate it when a girl has her first moon time. Now she becomes a woman and her body is capable of this miracle of growing a baby.

So I want to be clear that this is different from the kinds of attitudes I have heard about among non-Indian woman towards this time of the month. It's not a negative attitude we have. It's simply an understanding and respect for the power a woman has at this time. And a desire to make sure that her power doesn't kind of unwittingly interfere with things.

Well, how it seems these days is that the Indians out West are more careful about a lot of this than we have become. Yet with respect to tobacco it's kind of the opposite.

When I was a kid, some of the older people used to tell us not to eat in American or Canadian people's restaurants, because some people are using medicine. And if the waitress or the woman cooking that food has her monthly, and she touches what we're eating, it's gonna mess us up, make us weak.

So in the older days, that's why some of the older people used to tell me, "Try not to eat in any restaurants, unless you know who they are, who is cooking and they know what they're doing." Even that's almost like water over the damn now. There are not many people that even think about that, or consider that. But I wanted to share that with you, so that you might give it some thought 'cause we're all guilty of it now, I think.

Remember in the Creation story, it talked about how in this universe that we're in, there are thousands and millions of things going on, it's so busy. And so 'member, the Creator said to us when the world was new, "No matter how busy I am, in running this universe, as vast and big as it is, I have given you this tobacco. Any time you are walking the earth, that you need some kind of special attention, that you need a hand, or you simply want to say thank you, you will have this tobacco. And then I give you fire with it, and the power of this fire. And you will put this tobacco on the fire, and when the smoke goes up, I will *stop* what I'm doing, running the universe, the business of the world. No matter how busy it is, when you make that smoke go up, I will stop and I will listen, and I will pay attention to *you*, to what it is that you have to say to me. And that's why I give you this tobacco."

And so that's why the real Iroquois people don't like to see it when people are smoking a cigarette or a cigar. To them, as soon as any kind of tobacco smoke goes up, they know that the Creator stops everything in the world, just to listen to them. People are out there smoking away for their own pleasure, and not being at all spiritual. But the Creator is holding up the world, while they're fooling around. He's waiting to hear what it is they want. A lot of people are doing that to him. And it's not fair to life. And that's what some of my uncles used to tell me, when I was doing that.

Okay, I'm gonna try to see if I can remember more now.

One of the things that my grandmother and different elders told us—even the Chiefs, Faithkeepers, and my uncle—is that number one, you talk your language. When you pray or you burn tobacco—or you go talk to the dead people, because somebody died in your family, you go to a funeral or a wake—there are certain things you're supposed to say, when you go see them.

Whenever you do a Sunrise Ceremony, or say thunder comes, there are ceremonies for the thunder. And there's a way you talk. I guess you could call it prayer for the Thunderers. If we're gonna use that word, prayer, huh?

And as I've said earlier, what they told us is that if you're born a Mohawk, then whenever you pick tobacco up or you're gonna offer your ceremony, you should talk Mohawk.

But right now, I wanna show you this tobacco bag. Made out of a deer—deer skin. And this is the kind of bag that our old Chiefs used to carry when I was a little boy. And they were old men, they were almost ninety years old when I was a little boy. That's fifty-five or more years ago. This kinda bag has four sides to it. Sometimes we put fringes on it, hanging down. I had one of their bags, so I got the pattern, how they used to make it. So I'm only one of a few people in Mohawk country now that make bags the way the old Chiefs made them.

And it is usually Faithkeepers or Chiefs that carry this size of a tobacco bag, prayer bag. And medicine leaders in societies who doctor people, the ones who are always doing ceremonies for people, they carry this size, because it holds a lotta tobacco, because a lotta people depend on them. Usually I call it the old Chief's tobacco bag.

But regular people, just regular men or women, they carry tobacco bags that are about half this size, or even sometimes smaller than that.

Now the real Iroquois people, every man and every woman that is Iroquois, like Mohawk, Seneca, Cayuga, Onondaga, never go *anywhere* outta their house, without carrying their little prayer bags. The traditional people. It's probably the same with the Ojibway, and the Cree too. Maybe, I'm not sure.

Today, the majority of the Iroquois Indian people, even the ones that have joined Western religions, will carry tobacco with them. The really traditional ones *always* carry that. But I would say about three-quarters of the nontraditional ones also do, because it's so inherent in our society that it still goes on. It's hard for an Iroquois to forget his tradition, all of it. It doesn't wanna die.

The women usually carry them in their purse, and lots of them even carry an extra one in the glove compartment of their car. So I almost guarantee you if we see a Seneca's car out there in the parking lot, if you open that door and they let you look in that glove compartment, you're gonna see one a those in there. I think I can almost guarantee it, that if we see an Onondaga's car parked out here in the parking lot, and you look in their glove compartment, you're gonna see one of those extra bags in there too. Because us Iroquois, we kinda know what each other are doing. So it's predictable, which is pretty good. Yeah.

So we never go anywhere without it. That's what our uncle told us, because you never know when you're traveling what might happen to you. You might get an emergency and then you have to pray: you have to use that tobacco. That's why we carry it.

One of my sisters, this morning, gave me this prayer tobacco. Some of you've never seen it, I suppose. And some of you did. And probably most of you grow it.

And that particular plant, we plant it every year, all the traditional families of the Senecas and Mohawks and Cayugas. So we're never caught without our pants on. That's what I say. We've always got our tobacco. We've *always* got it. And we have to grow it and we have to take care of it all summer.

'Member how I said when you walk in the garden, how you have to talk and pray? Well, we do that for our tobacco all summer. So our sacred tobacco, when we're ready to make it into tobacco for smoking or offerings, is full of prayer from all through the summer.

I want to show you what one of the leaves looks like. This is the one we call oien'kwa'ón:we. And that's the one we Iroquois use.

In a pinch, if we didn't have any for some reason, and the likelihood of that is just about nil, we will use maybe a cigarette, and break it up as a substitute. Most of us probably would prefer not to do that, but just to use pure words. I've seen some use that, break up a cigarette or use pipe tobacco from the store. But mostly we use this oien'kwa'ón:we.

This kinda tobacco, you can't smoke it really, like you know when people inhale cigarette or pipe tobacco. You dare not do that to this kind 'cause this one is so strong, it will knock you down.

I was gonna tell you a story, but I better not 'cause there's little kids here! One time when—I'm not gonna tell all of it, just part of it—and this was one time when the Six Nations' Chiefs back in the '60s, they sent us out all over the United States and Canada, to send messages to all the big reservations, the Cheyenne and Navajos and Lakota. And so I was the head one for the Mohawks, carrying wampum and messages to them out West.

They used to call it the Unity Caravan. Yeah, and so they assigned one young guy from my reservation. But he didn't grow up in the Longhouse.

He was never taught the real Longhouse way to do things. He wanted to come with me because he was a mechanic. And if our car or any of the caravan of cars broke down, he could tune them up and fix them.

In return, myself and others would teach him all about tobacco and the pipe, how to make Sunrise Ceremonies and how to talk from nation to nation the way the Chiefs do it. And he would learn that in exchange.

And so we went all across the country. After meeting with the Winnebago and the Sioux Indians, Lakota and Blackfoot in Montana, we went through the Rocky Mountains and we were on the West Coast. And I think that highway name was 101. Is that right? Did anybody ever go there? Anyway, it's a small kinda road. It's not like the thruway. Only two cars can go on there.

And along the coastline, as you go towards San Francisco from up north, like Washington, those roads curve all around like this. And there are no guard rails. When you look from your car, you are up so high you can see for three hundred miles, and the big waves are coming onto the rocks like this: shhhhh. And no guard rails. I'm s'posed to be a Mohawk: I'm s'posed to be tough, so I was tough. I didn't show I was scared, but I almost fainted when I saw it!

So my car, it would squeal: drrrrrrrr, zrrrrrrr, like that. And my friend, the one that's the mechanic, he's sittin' in the backseat. It was just him and me. He's sweating. And he's a toughie, a rough and tough guy. He grew up rough. He's used to fighting anybody, you know, that guy. And all of a sudden I feel a hand touching my shoulder as I'm driving . . .

I wasn't going fast: it's just the roads are like that. So you squeal just going slow. And if you miss that road, you're dead.

So a hand touched my shoulder. And he says, "Tom. Tom. You know that tobacco bag you got in the glove compartment?" He's talking about this. And I've always got a pipe in there too. I've got two pipes in mine. We use them to pray with. He says, "Well, while you're drivin, I'm gonna open the window a little bit. Can I borrow your pipe? Because this road is dangerous." He says, "If we fall down there, then nobody will ever find us. Those waves will take us in the big ocean, car and all."

So I was kinda proud of him because when he saw danger, he associated it with our Creator; and the power that the Creator gave us, the tool he gave us to meet danger. That was the tobacco. But he'd seen how I always do it, coming across the country. And I was proud of him 'cause it was him who asked. It wasn't my idea. And my knuckles were turning white, holding that wheel.

And I said, "Help yourself in the glove compartment." So he reached over and he took the tobacco bag and a pipe out of the glove compartment. He's sitting back there and I'm drivin' away. And he started putting tobacco in the bowl of my pipe. And he lit it. And he smoked it. And he pretty near died! He didn't know that we never inhale it. He puffed that thing, and he took it all down. He started chokin'. He *was* chokin'. And I thought he was gonna die.

And all of a sudden when he caught his breath a little bit, you shoulda heard what he said! He used English. He really swore. Yeah.

And at first I got scared. I said, "You're not s'posed to do that when you're talking to the Creator." But then it was so doggone funny, who could get mad? So I said, "I'll betcha the Creator's laughing his head off at my Mohawk guy!"

He said, "Son of a . . . Why the hell didn't you tell me how to smoke this thing?"

But he didn't mean it, like to be mean. He meant to be honest! And so I suppose the Creator forgave him.

Anyway we got off that road all right, almost. After going like that, over those cliffs and drop-offs, we'd just got out of those mountains. And we were just coming in—I've forgotten the name of the town in California. And we'd just got into the town off the big dangerous road. Guess what happened? The front wheel on my car came right off. But I was only going five miles an hour, around the corner. It coulda happened over there on the cliff road.

So maybe the Creator did hear his prayer, even with his swearing. And I just wanted to share that with you. Because sometimes when you're learning, it's funny too. Like that was funny. Uh-huh.

Whenever you're gonna make a prayer, or in the Longhouse, if you're gonna have a Feather Dance, or some kind of a Longhouse dance, my grandmother always said, "Before you join in that Feather Dance or any kinda tobacco burning, don't touch the tobacco when they're collecting it, unless first, here's what you say:

Ne Takia'tíson tahskwatahontsi:iohst ne ne sakoniatathré:wahte tókat nahò:tenk wa'konrihwákhsa'se tsi wa'tkatawén:rie tsi iohontsiá:te. Ne tewakatahontsión:ni aóhskon ka'nikonhrí:io enwatstónhake ó:nen enkaien'kwarakétsko.

That means in English,

You who are my Creator, I ask you to listen to me. I want to ask your forgiveness, my Creator, if I did something as I'm walking this earth to offend you or hurt your feelings or anybody. My Creator, I ask you to forgive me, so that when I touch my hand on my prayer tobacco or I become part of your Great Feather Dance, I carry no blemish, I carry no sin, I carry no bad things. But I come, my words come to you with complete pureness of love and compassion.

That's the words you use before you touch the tobacco.

So when there's a Thunder Dance gonna happen, or if there's somebody collecting tobacco, don't put your tobacco in there 'til you have addressed that as an individual. So that when the man who's chosen to burn that on behalf of all the people, burns it, it holds the pure power and love of the people. Let that go to the universe.

And so that's the way I wanted to share with you. Before you ever do anything sacred like Sunrise Ceremony, always clean yourself. Some people use their sweetgrass. That's just as good. Some people use sage. Some people use cedar, they burn cedar. But a lotta people will just say what I told you. And that's the same as that cedar, the same as that sage. You're cleaning yourself, to make yourself presentable to the power of our Maker. And that's what we use, see?

So we call this oien'kwa'ón:we.

The other thing I wanna show you, any pipe will do, the Iroquois say. Long as it can make us fire. Long as the smoke can go up, anything will do. And so a lotta Iroquois, like Grandma and them, they had pipes made out of corn cobs. And those were their prayer pipes. A lotta times for thunder, they use a corncob pipe 'cause it's easy to make it. And it's even easier to buy at the drugstore! When I was a kid, they made them. But now it's the drugstore.

Anyway, this is one of my prayer pipes. It's just a regular pipe. I bought it somewhere. And it's even got a filter in there. 'Cause sometimes the old clay ones that my nephew made, you wanna smoke to pray, and half the tobacco goes in your mouth 'cause it doesn't have a filter. You know what I mean? And then you have to chew that tobacco.

And then here's how we do it. We take a piece and you hold it like this.
Ne Takia'tíson ne watkonnonhwará:ton ne ó:nen ne wa'konien'-kwahshonnia'te.[1]

Then you put it in the bowl of the pipe, after you've done your purifying. Then you take another one and you say,
Ne Takia'tíson ne sé:ron onkwaia'tákta enkaién:take otsísta ne ne sé:ron eniohsatstenhseraién:take ne ne tsi iotékha ne thí:ken otsísta enkakwé:ni enkahará:tate ne enkaronhiáwe'ehste ne enien'kwa'ón: we ne enkawennahá:wihte onkwawén:na.

So the second one that you put in the pipe, that's to acknowledge the power of the fire. And the Creator said he put that fire next to the humans where we walk the earth, to help us to live. And we use that to cook. We use that to make medicine, that fire. We use that to pray with, so that it burns the smoke. And the smoke goes up, whether it's in a pipe or whether it's in a regular fire. So now this second one, it goes to the power of the fire. You acknowledge your fire, the special gift that the Creator gave to us, to help us live. And you put it in there.

And then the next one, the third one. This time you say,
Ne Takia'tíson ne shiwá:se tsi iohontsiá:te tehseiá:wi ionkwah-satstensera'kénha ne shiwá:se tsi iohontsiá:te ne oien'kwa'ón:we ne sé:ron ne ó:nen aionkwatonhwéntsionhse kaia'takenhnháhtshera

---

[1] Loosely translated, this means, *My Creator, I send you my greetings, my thankfulness and my love, as I make this tobacco smoke for you.*

ne ká:ti eniakwawennakén:seren oien'kwa'ón:we. Ne enkakwé:ni enkahará:tate onkwawenna'shón:'a tsi nón:we tisatahonhsiióhstha.

That means,

> *Now my Creator, you gave this tobacco to our grandfathers long ago, when the world was new. And you told us that whenever a time comes in the future that we the humans ever need help or assistance, or we wanna talk to you, that we could use this tobacco and make a fire. And the smoke of the fire will carry the tobacco up. And that smoke will catch our thinking and our prayer. And it will carry it to the top of the sky, of the universe, to where you listen to all. And so now, to the power of the tobacco that's been working since the beginning of time in this world, that we are still using for all this time, now we offer the tobacco to the tobacco, for carrying our message.*

And you put it in there.

And then you can say,

> Ne shiwá:se tsi iohontsiá:te ne wahsherihontónnion ne Kaié:ri Niionkwè:take Ratironhiakehró:non.

The next one you say,

> *In the beginning when the world was new you commissioned Four Sacred Beings.*

We call them the Sky Dweller Beings, or sometimes we call them the Mysteries of the Universe, the four of them. They watch over us and help us, and are messengers between us and the Creator. "And so to your helpers, the Four Sacred Beings, I take this tobacco and I acknowledge them. And I offer to their power and their existence this tobacco."

Then you can start with the Mother Earth. And you can be detailed about the different things on Mother Earth, like the Opening Prayer, or you can talk to everything that grows on Mother Earth, and make it all one. There are ways to make it longer, medium, or short. That's up to you. And you put the tobacco in there, until you get, again, to the Creator.

And then you say, "Creator, I began with you. And Creator, now I ask you, our people need help right now. Our people . . ." Then you tell what it is that's needed, some assistance or some strengthening up. And then what you say is, "Creator, this is what I need help for." And now the smoke will carry your plea.

Then when you've finished packing your pipe, now you light it. All the prayer is in there already. And then you smoke it. And you always try to, at first, put three breaths in there, when you're using a pipe. Three, that's how Grandma does it. Because 'member yesterday we were talking about when they made the human beings out of the dirt and all that? Then what did they do? They opened the mouth and they blew the breath of life into it three times. So when we do this, we always blow three times to remember the miracle of our beginning. We never forgot, since the beginning, all this time.

And then you keep smoking. And if there are people there, you can share it, go around to everybody. Even if there are little kids, they can do it too. My kids were only two years old. Even if there is a little one-year-old, they do it. But when they're one year old, all you do is just touch their lips. They don't have to put it in their mouth.

Two years old, my son started. He didn't know how to smoke. He didn't pull: he just touched it with his lips. That smoke went up too. 'Course he's twenty-eight years old now. Now he has his own pipe.

And that's how you make these prayers with a pipe. So the first offering is to the Creator, the Maker. The second one is the fire, that he gave us the gift of fire. And the third one is the one that carries our message, the tobacco you offer to the tobacco. Then to the Four Sacred Beings. And then you start with Mother Earth, however you think is right.

And then when you finish, you finish with the Creator. You put everything in the Creator's hand. And that's how you make prayer with the pipe and tobacco.

And me, I'm different than most Indian people. I'm not afraida anybody. I mean I'm not Superman either, don't get me wrong, what I'm saying. But some people, they hide their medicine. They hide their tobacco, prayer tobacco. They say, "Don't let anybody see it and don't let anybody touch it." But not me. I say, "My tobacco, it comes from my Mother Earth, and it's going to the Creator. Who do you think's got more power than Mother Earth and the Creator, to mess up my tobacco? There is no man, no woman that can stop my prayer."

So that's the way I think about it, see. If I have to discriminate against somebody, I'm not gonna do it. Let the Creator do it. Leave it in his hands. So I'm inclusive when I pray. I pray with anybody, you see.

I didn't used to, though. 'Cause I used to be brainwashed too. But I learn because I listen to my ceremony. I try to follow it. And it tells me not to be afraid of anybody.

Now when we make a fire for prayer, usually we use a maple tree, the tree that makes sugar. It's a hard wood. We use that to make the fire. My grandfather said, "If you can find a hard maple tree, sugar maple, that was struck by lightning, if you find that one, it's the most powerful one to use. It's almost like a direct line when it's like that. That's what I heard."

In older days, there were different ways to make a fire, for different things. When you're gonna do just a regular Tobacco Burning to the Creator, you make your fire like a Lakota person's house, like a teepee. You make it like that.

When you're done, about one hour or two hours after you've done this, you go back there. And what you will see are little white wood stubs in a complete circle around that fire, ashes. When you see that in a complete circle, it is the same thing as the Chiefs' Wampum of Our Confederacy. They call it Kenkiohkwahnhákstha. They're holding hands together, and the Tree of Peace is in the middle. Well, when you finish your sacred fire, that's what the remains of that wood look like, just like that sacred wampum. Then, you've done it right. That's what some of those old guys said.

Whenever you go pick medicine, somewhere in the woods or in the swamp, you have to talk to the leader of the medicine that's growing. You have to get permission from the leader of the medicine to take the other ones with you, to doctor somebody. And usually when you go to pick medicine, you're supposed to tell that medicine the name of the patient that's sick, the one that needs the help.

But if you're picking for a whole village or a whole community, then you just say it's for the people. "We don't know yet whose coming to get the medicine." That's how you say it, when you make your prayer for picking medicine, if it's not particularly for one person.

When that person who needs it, comes to that lady or man's house who has lots of medicine, then they're gonna burn tobacco again. 'Cause now you know what their name is. Now the medicine that you pick knows who they're gonna doctor, specifically.

Used to be some of the Mohawks where I lived, they weren't real traditional. But they still used medicine. And sometimes what they would do is, instead of leaving Indian tobacco when they picked medicine, they would put pennies in there. Or sometimes, quarters in there.

My grandmother and different elders, they saw that. And they said, "We understand what you're trying to do. And it's sorta almost right, what you're doing. But it's not right. Because you're supposed to use Indian tobacco, not money, not pennies." But in the mind of those people, they were thinking that you can never take medicine from Mother Earth without giving back something.

And so the elders told them, "You're supposed to use Indian tobacco. That's what those medicines are waiting for. They don't know what to do with that dime."

They don't know. I've never seen the medicine go to Wal-Mart yet! So you always use Indian tobacco, oien'kwa'ón:we.

And another thing I always tell is that when the old, old people make medicine, they say that when your body's in balance, that means you're healthy, you're all right. But when something is broken, it's because you're unbalanced. So now you're not walking right. Your mind isn't straight or balanced. Nothing is right about your being 'cause there's an imbalance. Sickness is making the imbalance.

So when they make medicine, you hear them say that they use only one root, or three roots, or they use five roots, or seven roots, or nine roots. When you're gonna doctor somebody, with medicine, you have to take the imbalance of the medicine to the imbalance. And that's what makes it straight. You can't take match balance with imbalance, and get health. It's not gonna work. 'Cause that isn't balanced. So you have to add something to make it straight.

So they never use two or four. They always take an odd number because they're gonna doctor something that's unbalanced. So they have to use the unbalanced number to prop it up where it's balanced. Now you have health. See?

And that's still practiced amongst the medicine people, the ones that do medicines.

Now, I wanna share with you what happens when somebody passes away. All of us have to go see people who have passed away 'cause we have relatives that die. Or friends that die. When you go to see dead people, you're not supposed to go over there if you're using Indian medicine. Because the power of the dead will neutralize your medicine.

Whenever you're taking herbal medicine, don't go where the dead are. You gotta wait 'til you're done your medicine. Or, if you go see the dead, then you gotta stop your medicine. You can't touch it right away. The dead are more powerful than that medicine. That's what is told to us.

That's why when we go see the dead, they make that medicine, the one they made yesterday for me, here. We call it otsionehskwén:rie. And whenever we go see a dead person, we take that. In English we call it *ginger root, wild ginger*. You make a tea out of it.

Before you go see the dead, you put the tea in a saucer or a cup. And you put it up high on a shelf, or on top of the refrigerator, where you can't see it. Then, once you've finished making that tea, you go see the dead people. And you come back . . .

They say that the dead people are *so strong* . . . It's the same thing when a new baby is born. It's almost the same as the dead in terms of power because they had to have a lot of power to get born here, and to enter this world.

When you die, you have to have a lot of power, to exit this world. It's like those rockets at Cape Canaveral. Can you imagine all the fuel, the energy it takes that rocket, to get out of this world? Well, the same thing when you die: your spirit has to have lots of power to get out of here, to go to the next world. And so it is the teaching of our old people that when a baby is born, the Creator gives the mother and father seven times the power that you normally had before pregnancy. To the mother *and* the father. So that that baby can be assured to make it into this world.

So this is the same door as death. When we're ready to leave, after we're finished on this earth, he gives us seven times more power, in order to get out of this world into the next. And that's why they tell us, "Don't touch dead people." You're not s'posed to go there and touch them, when they're laid out. You're not s'posed to hug them or anything because they have seven times more power than normal.

That's why you have to fix your medicine *before* you go there. When you get done looking at the dead at a wake, and you come home to your house, you're carrying the seven powers of contamination, from exiting this world to the next, with you. It's like a stagnation power. It's touching you, and it's going all over your body. So when you look someplace, the hand of death is between you and what you're looking at. You don't really see it properly. Even when you're doing something, you're carrying death with you, see?

So when you get home, what you do is you put your hand up on that medicine, way up, so you won't see it. Because if you see it, it could ruin *that* medicine too. That's why it's up. You put that on your hand, and you take the juice, and you sprinkle it on your face. You take some more and you go over the top of your eyes. And then you sprinkle it all over, washing your body—but not every inch. And then that otsionehskwén:rie takes it. It removes the hand of death from your body. And now you're free to go back to normal life. And even today, all the Iroquois, the ones that are real Iroquois, still do that.

Chapter 30

The Leadership

You have to have skin seven spans thick.

We talked about the Clan System earlier. Now I'm gonna talk about how it was revitalized and incorporated into the Great Law by the Peacemaker.

When the Peacemaker put up the new leaders, the Rotiianéhshon, he instructed them to remember what animal they would see. The next day each Chief, each Roiá:nehr did see an animal and that animal became his clan from that time on. The women received their clans in the same way. And as we discussed before, it is said that was how some of our ancestors received their clans. The Peacemaker also, at the time, instructed the women that they would be the holders of the clan, and that they would pass the clan down to their children. This too was a reaffirmation by the Peacemaker of the ancient Clan System.

We can think of a big circle, a pie, representing a nation. And think of this particular pie as the Mohawk nation. And then we can divide that pie into nine pieces. And then we can just take one piece of that pie and magnify it. In the middle we can put the Clan Mother, the Chief, the male

Faithkeeper, the female Faithkeeper, and the Sub-Chief. And we can put deer horns on the Chief's head. That's the symbol when they are leaders. They put those horns on their hats. And that's how people know that they are the leaders.

Now according to our Constitution, this circle represents the Mohawk people. And the Mohawk people have nine clans. Three of those clans are Turtles, three of them are Wolves, and three of them are Bears.

The Turtle Clan people have three principle Rotiianéhshon titles and they are listed as follows:

1. Tekarihó:ken, *split ideas*
2 Aionwahta, *he who wakes them up*
3. Sa'tekarí:wate, *equally important issues.*

In the Mohawk nation the Bear Clan people have three principal titles and they are as follows:

1. Tehana'karí:ne, *the horn leader*
2. Ahstawenserenhtha, *he drops or strikes down the rattle*
3. Shoskoharó:wane, *the big tree.*

The Wolf Clan people have three principal titles and they are as follows:

1. Sharenho:wane, *a type of big tree*
2. Teionhehkwen, *food plants or sustenance of life*
3. Orenhre'ko:wa, *a type of big bird.*

In the Wolf Clans, there are the Gray Wolf, the Timber Wolf, and the Little Wolf—like a coyote. And they're all wolves, but they're separate.

The same with the Turtle: there's the Snapping Turtle, there's the Mud Turtle, and there's the Box Turtle. Those are different clans, but they're all turtles, so they're closely related, but they're different. They're all different families.

And then the Bear Clan: there's the Brown Bear, and there's a Black Bear, and some call it that "Big White Bear" from way to the north.

Tuscaroras have that. Probably it's the polar bear. I'm not sure. But the Akwesasne Mohawk people, all the clans over there, except for one that I know of, don't know which of the three types of bear they are, anymore.

So there is one Roiá:nehr title per extended family. In times past, the people of Akwesasne knew which family they came from. Within the Bear Clan, for example, there are three distinct extended families and three principal Roiá:nehr titles.

So now I'm a Bear Clan, but I can't tell you if I'm a Black Bear or a Brown Bear or a White Bear. And the same with the Wolf in Akwesasne. They can't tell you if they're the Coyote Wolf or they're the Timber Wolf or they're the Gray Wolf. They don't know. They lost that somehow, along the line.

But the Snipes that came there in Akwesasne, some of them can tell you they're the Big Snipe Clan. And then some of them say, "We're the little one." And there are a few of them that say that. So some of them know which one they are. And I think I used to hear Jake Thomas say that too. I forget which one he used to say he belongs to: the big one or the little one.

The Snipe Clan have a number of principal clan Rotiianéhshon titles. These titles are held by the Onondaga nation, the Seneca nation, and the Cayuga nation. The Akwesasne people who belong to the Snipe Clan are originally either Onondagas, Cayugas, or Senecas. Most likely they are from the Onondagas.

So maybe in Grand River, some people can tell you what kind of a Turtle they are, what kind of a Bear they are, but in Akwesasne, we don't know. We've forgotten. I don't know when was the last time that somebody was able to do that. It's back before I was born 'cause I never heard it. They tell us it was like that, but they've lost track themselves.

And Onondagas, I don't know if they know the ones that are Eels there, if there are different kinds of Eels. Or the ones that are Deer 'cause there are different kinds of Deer too.

Amongst the Onondagas, the Rotiianéhshon titles for the Deer Clan are:

1. Arirhonh
2. Dowayonhnyeanih
3. Se a wi

Amongst the Cayugas, the Roiá:nehr title for the Deer Clan is Kadagwarsonh. I do not have the translation, the English meaning of these titles.

So let's magnify one piece of that pie. And I'm gonna describe to you the formula for the political/social function of that. We can divide that piece of pie in half, so one is the man's and one is the woman's side. That is one political party. So let's say that it's the Bear Clan, one kind of a Bear. I don't know what kind.

So all the people that are in that Bear Clan are Wakskaré:wake. That's one kind of the Bear Clans. Let's say it's a Brown Bear. I don't know if that's true or not. I don't know what kind it is. But I know I'm that kind, whatever it is.

So in the Mohawks, there may be two thousand people that belong to that clan. Or something like that. (If everybody were Longhouse there would be maybe two thousand in my clan/family. But they're not. A lot of them don't even want to be a part of it.) And so that clan consists of children, men and women, and elders.

So when they have meetings, they can have meetings of just the women or just the men, or they can have meetings with men and women together. It's up to that Clan Mother if she wants to do that. And it's up to the men too. But the woman usually initiates things.

Now we're gonna try to list some of the criteria that the Constitution says that you must possess, in order to be a candidate or nominee to be a Clan Mother or to be a Chief:

1. You have to have a clan from your mother. You also have to have a clan from your father. And it has to be different.
2. You have to be married.

3. You have to have a minimum of three children. (I'm not just sure if that's really true as a criteria for chieftainship, but I *think* it is.)
4. You have to be knowledgeable both politically and spiritually.
5. You can't have any human bloodstain on your hand, which means you can never have killed anybody.
6. You have to have skin seven spans thick.
7. You have to be what do you call it when you take care of your wife, you take care of your kids; they've always got food? A good provider.
8. You can't have any disabilities, physical disabilities or mental disabilities to be leader.
9. You have to be a good-minded person.
10. You have to be a community-minded person.
11. You have to be fair.
12. You have to speak the language.

I think there's more to it than that, but those are a good foundation. That's the criteria that the Clan Mother and the people use when they're gonna look for the next leader. It's what you have to have.

By the way, it's part of our mentality amongst the Iroquois that you are forbidden to *seek* leadership. The elders used to say that any man or woman who said, "I wanna be a Clan Mother when I grow up" or "I wanna be a Chief when I grow up," those are the ones you make sure never become leaders. Because they're sick. Somethin isn't balanced. There's a mental sickness going on in their head.

When I see some of the actions going on elsewhere[1] I wonder about that a lot. I think about that.

You're never s'posed to blow your own horn. So if you have accomplished something, then your cousin, your aunt, your mother, your grandma, will talk about it. Your village will talk about it. Your community will talk about it. It's all right if your teacher says that. It's all right if your uncle says, "My nephew has got a doctorate degree."

[1.] This comment came in response to a TV interviewer's comment about mainstream politics.

But you, yourself, aren't s'posed to say that. In the Indian world, you do not tell them, "I'm great" or "I accomplished . . ." or "I did this." You never really say, "I graduated from . . ." even if you did.

You're considered to be sick, mentally sick, or something wrong with you if you blow your own horn.

Now, the way this magnified section works, every one of those other ones works exactly in the same manner. And the way this Mohawk circle nation works is the way the Onondagas, Oneidas, Cayugas, and all do it 'cause they're all constitutionalized.

And I call this clan a political party. So if you were to compare with America: America has Democrat and Republican, two political parties, essentially. In the Mohawks, we have nine political parties. And these political parties are not just political parties, but they're also our religious parties as well. They're one and the same.

Unlike America, we don't have a separation of spirituality and politics. Ours: if you do that, you're committing a crime. The minute you take spirit out of anything, you have already defeated yourself. That's the way we think. You've probably already caught on since we started, how important it is. Because we don't have religion. Maybe you can take religion out of it, but not spirituality.

And there's a difference, I believe. There's a *big* difference. 'Cause religions are just like a shoebox, really empty. And spirit doesn't stay in there anyway.

So for each political party, they will have five people that are the leadership. They have the positions of responsibility that I mentioned at the beginning of this chapter: the Clan Mother, the Chief, the male Faithkeeper, the female Faithkeeper, and the Sub-Chief. Since the Mohawks have nine of those political parties, if you multiply that by five, it would give you the total Mohawk nation's leadership: forty-five.

There can be more Faithkeepers, but for the chieftainship, there's only one man and one woman. A clan can have as many as four, five or six Faithkeepers if they want to. But they're not the political ones, they're not the Chief ones. They're the Faithkeepers for the ceremonies.

In our language we call it Kaié:ri Niiorì:wake Roteríhonton. That's how we say it. That means they're in a position that takes care of the Four Sacred Rituals. They're the *Caretakers of the Four Sacred Rituals*. That's what it means when we say it. So I don't know who said *"Faithkeeper"* or how that came, but that's commonly used now. It's quite acceptable to most all Iroquois.

Often they will be able to recite lots of things too.

In our language, the Chief is Roiá:nehr and it means *he's good*. And the woman is Iakoiá:nehr, *she's good*. And the law is called Kaianere'kó:wa, *the great good*. That's the Constitution. So compared to that, the word "Chief" sounds degrading, it doesn't do it justice.

Getting back to this section which has these five people who are the head of it . . . Next to the Chief is a woman. She is the Clan Mother of that political party. It is her job to initiate the selection of people who will be nominated to these positions. She only initiates. She is not the one to say it ends there, as if she selects and that's that. That's not the way. Some people *say* that nowadays, but that's not the way it goes. All she does is she's the voice of the people of that clan or that family.

And we call that clan *a family*. And that's why people sometimes get confused 'cause they consider their father, their mother, their brothers and sisters the family. But when they say "family" in this context, they're talking about everybody that's in that clan. *That's* the family. So that family may include two thousand people. So the next male leader has to come from those two thousand people. The next Clan Mother has to come from those two thousand people, not from the immediate family of the mother and father. You see?

And that's why the people on a lot of the Iroquois reservations are getting mixed up, when someone says, "I'm the next in line." Their family is two thousand people. It's up to all the people in that family. And you belong to that clan family through your mother. It's only from the mother's side.

But the father's clan also factors into it: that's what makes them eligible to be considered. Now if their father is a Bear as well, then they're *not* gonna be considered because they're the product of incest.

The Clan Mother, she will initiate the nomination for that man next to her, that's a Faithkeeper. During all the national ceremonies, like New Year's, Maple Dances, Strawberry Dances, Bean Dances, Harvest Dances: all those where the Four Sacred Rituals happen, his job is to prepare songs and prepare whatever paraphernalia is needed for that ceremony. And speeches: he's got to make sure that there are people there that are gonna be able to do them for that Chief, or with that Chief, however, so that it gets done. That's his principal job.

That Clan Mother, she also nominates a woman who's a Faithkeeper. And the woman Faithkeeper's job is the same thing as the man's, except it's for the feminine part of the spiritual stuff. So that Clan Mother and that Chief have assistants. They're gonna do any running around and gathering of the stuff. And making sure it's ready.

She also initiates the nomination of the fifth person. He is what we call the Raterontanónhnha. And literally translated into English that means *he's the caretaker of the big tree.* In general English, they refer to him as the Sub-Chief. The Chief is the tree, the big timber tree. So if that tree gets dry, this man's job is to bring water to it. If somebody tries to cut the tree, he stands in front and doesn't let you. So he's the one who helps that Chief in anything. He's just like him, except he makes sure that the Chief stands and he functions. That's what a Sub-Chief does.

So if the Chief were to get sick, he can go to a meeting in his place, as long as it's a small issue. If it's a big issue, he can't make a decision: he has to bring it back over there to see if the main leader is gonna agree or not, and then take it back.

And so to summarize, for each principal Roiá:nehr title, there are five people, the titleholder and four assistants:

1. Iakoiá:nehr, *Clan Mother*
2. Roiá:nehr, *principal male leader*
3. Raterontanónhnha, *male subleader.* "He Takes Care of the Tree" is the literal translation.
4. Kaié:ri Niiorì:wake Iakoteríhonton, *Faithkeeper (female).* She is in charge of the Four Sacred Rituals.
5. Kaié:ri Niiorì:wake Roteríhonton, *Faithkeeper (male).* He is in charge of the Four Sacred Rituals.

Now the job of the Clan Mother is a critical job, an almost overwhelming job because like all of those, none of these things are from nine to five. None of these things are forty hours a week either, from Monday to Friday. This is a full-time job, around the clock. And these aren't two-year terms or four-year terms, these are *life* terms. So once they become that, it's for their whole life. Except for the subleader, the nourisher of the tree. If that Chief dies, he's automatically free, upon his death, because there's no more tree to take care of.

He would not automatically step into the Chief's position, unless his clan chooses him to be that. When the Chief dies, he's done. If they're choosing the Sub-Chief to take over, he would not be Chief until they go through a whole process. Between his death and the process concluding, he wouldn't be the one who takes over.

But the same Faithkeepers stay in. They don't change, 'til they die. When they put the new leader in, that's who they're working for, and the Clan Mother. So that means that this woman, this Clan Mother, on behalf of the people of that family is always vigilant because life is unpredictable. We don't know if that Chief's gonna be here next week, even if he's young. Because we don't know how long we're gonna live.

She always has to be ready to have nominees, to initiate at the drop of a hat. It's s'posed to be like that. Not just her, but all of the leadership have been thinking like that. And not just them, but even the rest of the people of that clan, or that political party, have been thinking about that as well. Thinking about who has the qualities of a Chief.

And when you raise your children, you're raising them in case they're needed. Maybe they can help. So mothers and fathers, uncles and aunts and grandmothers are raising the kids, so they can grow and be able to do that. It's not necessarily that they're doing that *in order for* them to become leaders, but so that there will be a lot to choose from. Just like when you plant corn, you don't just plant one corn. You plant the whole field, so that you have lots of corn from which to pick. And so when you raise kids, you do this too.

Even though all my older kids know most of this stuff 'cause they were raised up in the Longhouse, *my kids* can never be that because their mother's a Choctaw. And since she's not of the Mohawk nation, my kids are not Mohawks.

Some of my grandkids can. My son's wife is a Mohawk. So all his kids are Mohawks. It's not my goal for them to be Chief. But I want all my kids to be of the caliber where they *could* be that, even though they're not Mohawk. Because if they can be like that, they will be wonderful people.

Everybody wants their children to be of that caliber, but they don't always know that this offers that. It's a matter of reeducation and rediscovering your own identities. And then this is a windfall.

And you know what? Let me just add something here that I have noticed. A lot of times when I talk about the Great Law and the qualifications of our leaders for the future, I include all these things. And you'd be surprised how many people have said, "You're defeating any hopes of a nation for tomorrow. You're too rigid. You're putting too many rules in there; the standards are too high. 'Cause if you look at that, who among all the Iroquois is gonna be eligible?" That's where they're coming from.

In my mind, it's important though. But it means that we have to invest time and energy and education in the young so they can become eligible like that again, and so they'll be plentiful. Don't do it the other way around and take us further down the road to destruction, to the demise of our people.

Now let's go through the criteria for our leaders, in more detail.

1. A Different Clan from Each Parent

There have to be two clans: one from the father and one from the mother. They've gotta be different to qualify you. If your parents are Wolf and Wolf, you can never become a Chief. If your father and mother are both Bears, you cannot become a Chief, or a leader. Remember the teacher telling the little boys in the forest clearing: it's forbidden to marry within your clan. That's called incest.

But there are a lotta people nowadays that have done it. Lots. There's hundreds of them. And that's what's gonna hold us back, drag us 'cause when you bring it up, they get real mad. You talk about getting *mad*.

Now I'm not sure if this is part of the Constitution, but I've heard it spoken by a number of our elder people. It sounded like they were quoting the Constitution, but I don't know if it *is* a direct quote from it. Here's what they've said:

In my language, it says,
>Tóhsa nowén:ton ne shahoti'tá:'a enhonterihón:ten tókat tho neniá: wen'ne katkekshon'a ne ká:ti enionkhihetkénhte.

That means do not ever make a leader or a Chief (or positions of whatever) from somebody who's from the same clan on both sides, their mother and father. For if you do this, the Creator said, "I will not be party to anything that they do. And if you do this, those people will lead our nation into ruin." That's what they say. It's always part of the discussion when it comes to that.

People don't like to say what I just said in any of the Longhouses because so many marriages between same clans have occurred. Even some of our leaders are like that, or have married somebody. Maybe their parents aren't, but they married somebody whose parents are, so their children are. And so they get very angry. More the women get really angry than the men. The men, they kinda just say, "Yeah we did wrong." But the women, they'll say, "How come you're always picking on me?" They get real mad right away.

When parents do that, all the offspring usually end up doing the same. And when the parent tries to say something, they say to their mother and father, "That's what you did to us and it was all right. Now I'm in love with this woman that's the same clan I am. And if it's good enough for you, I can do it too." And so the parents don't say anything after that. They're afraid to.

2. You have to be married.

Before the Europeans came here, marriage wasn't quite as elaborate as it is now. Our people used corn bread. And we still use corn bread and baskets yet, in our marriage ceremony. Basically it's almost the same: it's a commitment that the two of you are gonna take care of each other.

The Longhouse marriage takes about two hours, maybe more than that actually 'cause there's a lot to it, uh? Whereas a civil marriage or a Christian marriage is very fast. And in the Constitution it says, skanáhkwa. It says, *only one partner*. If the husband dies, she can remarry. But you can't be married to one person who's still living and then marry someone else. That disqualifies you.

3. Children

I'm not sure if there are three in there, but it says you have to have children. And if you don't have three children, 'cause biologically you can't, then your sisters or somebody in your big family will give you their children so that you'll *have* children. And that's a common practice even yet today, amongst the Iroquois. Sometimes a woman can't have any children and then her sister's got nine kids.

So a lot of the time, one of the sisters will give one and another sister will give one; another sister will give one. So now she'll have three kids. She can raise them. That's her flesh and blood too. It's as if she gave birth to them 'cause it's her sisters' kids.

The way my grandmother used to say it was: "one to replace the woman, one to replace the man and one is extra for the Creator, make sure it goes." It's the same thing when we plant corn or beans: we always plant three or four, so if some don't grow, the others will grow. And we'll have something. I'm not sure if it says that in the Karihwí:io, that we, as humans, don't finish our job, unless we produce three kids. So that's why I got six of them. I made sure!

So that's the way the Iroquois, the way we think. If somebody can't have kids, they can adopt these other kids, and that's the same as if they've got their own kids. So don't make a mistake about that one.

4. You have to be knowledgeable both politically and spiritually.

In other words, you gotta know the spiritual ceremonies and how they go, and you have to be familiar with the Constitution. To be spiritual and political, that means you have to be knowledgeable about how this all works and functions. And you have to have not just knowledge about it, but you have to have a love for it, or a compassion for it.

5. You can't have any human bloodstain on your hand.

No bloodshed, otherwise you cannot be considered. That means that you can't have killed anyone, regardless if it's a war, or by self-defense, or anything. And it doesn't matter what the circumstances are: there's no such thing as a justified war. If you kill somebody in a war, you can never hold office as a Chief. Once you take the life of somebody, accident or no accident, that blood is on you. The only one that can take life is the Creator. Nobody else. So that's why the Iroquois are s'posed to have foremost interest only for peace.

But some people make a discussion about this too. It almost is like the discussion of the Great Law, when they approached the Senecas. Say I'm a Chief or a good Iroquois (and I will try to be like a Chief even if I'm not: that's what all our young are s'posed to do anyway) and somebody says to me, "What if somebody came and hit you? Maybe you won't hit back 'cause of the way you're talking. But what about if somebody came and they beat up your wife, and they used a knife on her, or an axe, a big stick, or something. And then they started on your kids and did that right in front of you. Are you just going to stand there and say 'I want peace'? What are you going to do?"

And I will say, "Well, I guess that's why they call us 'the Rattlesnake People,' us Iroquois people."

And what would I do? For myself: I don't even know what I would do until it happened. But I suspect that I would tell you to stop immediately, and if you didn't stop immediately, I'd probably take that thing and hit you with it!

And if you hit my kids, maybe I wouldn't stop hitting you until you didn't breathe any more. And I'd break my law. But I don't know if that's what I would do in fact, until it happens.

I would *try* to avoid that, but if you get me mad enough, I'm like a rattlesnake. Most all the other Indians call us "the Rattlesnake People." If you approach a rattlesnake, the ones we have here, they don't do anything. They just go the other way. But if you pursue them, they'll shake their tail and that says "Don't bother me." And then they still won't bother you, they'll just shake their tail. And then if you keep on going after them, and you're gonna step on them or something, that's the third time: they'll nail you. Now. But you're the one that asked for that.

So I'm gonna be like a rattlesnake too. I can be peaceful, but don't make a fool outta me. You want to step on me, then you're gonna get it. And if you get me to that point, this is why everybody used to be afraid of Mohawks, of Iroquois before. 'Cause if you get them to that point they go insane. Like, "All right, if it's gonna be a fight, well then let's get it over with." And it's almost like an insanity at that point. And how do you reason with an insane person? It's very difficult.

You know the young Indians who wear the so-called Iroquois haircut, shaved, with a stripe of hair down the middle? Well, a lot of the older Indians, they don't like that haircut because when the peace came, they stopped that. The men mostly all have long hair. But when you go to war, that's when you shave all this off and leave it down the middle because this long hair represents your affiliation and relationship with the Creator. And the Creator doesn't kill people. So if you have to fight or kill somebody, then you gotta cut your affiliation off with the Creator, and you don't drag the Creator in that war with you.

You go on your own. But at the time you go there, you also declare a world of insanity that you're stepping into. And once you step in it, it's almost like quicksand, so you have to be prepared for the consequences of your insanity.

But you don't take God with you.

Among the Iroquois we say, "One, two, three." So if you are like Atotáhrho and you say you want to change, okay then we try to be like the ones who helped him. And so we help you. But don't you make a fool outta us. Don't you lie to us.

You get one chance. You muff that chance, we're not so willing to give you a second chance, but we *will*. But it will be with more skepticism than the first. Because you're the one who set it up to be that way. Then the third time, now there's real reluctance, but *still*, we'll give you that chance. But if you mess up on that one, now you're *done*. That's when the snake bites you. If you go on beyond that, then you're Superman, or else you're the biggest fool in the world.

You see, once Atotáhrho said that, he followed through. He didn't backtrack on them. And the Peacemaker had a supernatural power to begin with. He was sent specially, divinely like, you see, so . . .

But there are people, specially some Onondagas, who spend *many* many years being drunk and stuff. They'll say to me, "Well, when the Peacemaker put up all the Chiefs, they were murderers. And they changed their lives. They were allowed to be that." They think that's an excuse for all of their foolishness. And so they say that's the way the old law was.

I say, "Well, if that's the way you think, then you've got a lot of studying to do! And you're gonna ruin your life." I say, "That's not what it means. I don't think so."

The first Chiefs were cannibals and murderers and they were all forgiven, by the Peacemaker and the delegations of the time. And they became the Chiefs. That's a *fact*, they did. But that was by divine intervention, as far as I am concerned. And they became the examples that people *can* change. But that doesn't give you the license for ten years, to say, "Well, I can be drunk, and I can be womanizing, and I can do all this stuff. And I can make babies and not take care of them, for ten years. And then after ten years of foolishness, then I want to be good now." They're trying to use that as an excuse to be forgiven, to be allowed to be foolish.

And so they want me to say, "Oh yeah, that's right."

So anyway, if a leader commits one or all of the three major crimes, he is automatically removed. The three crimes are murder, rape, and stealing.

6: You have to have skin seven spans thick.

When you skin a deer and you take the hair off and you don't tan it, it's just rawhide. When you let it dry, it gets thick, just like a board, very rigid, very tough.

Well, what they're talking about is that the skin of a Chief has to be seven of those dried skins of the deer. So that if you try to push through and puncture the heart of that person, you *can't*. And even if you holler bad words, sharp words meant to hurt somebody, it's gotta go through those seven skins.

So that means that those leaders are protected. They have to have those seven skins, so that if somebody criticizes them or calls them down, whether privately or in public, it never pierces their heart, to cause them to speak in an unjust or a mean way to that person. So instead, the Chief, the leader, if he's been criticized by someone, he'll just say, "My nephew, I'm sorry you feel that way. That's your opinion and I'm not angry with you. But maybe that can be fixed tomorrow or next month. Or maybe the next decision will be more pleasing to you. There was no choice, the way we fixed it. But it wasn't done to hurt you or to attack you. And if you feel that bad about it, I'm sorry that it has that effect on you."

That's the way they're supposed to respond. They're not supposed to say, "You no-good scum. Don't you talk to me like that." If you answer that way, that's grounds enough for you to be impeached. If a Chief does that twice to a person, the third time he can be removed. That's how high that standard is.

It means lots of patience, compassion, and when the people holler at you, or are dissatisfied with you, or are angry at you, you can never be angry back at them. No Chief can do that. You have to be compassionate and kind, even to the most severely critical person.

So that's the seven spans, what it means.

7. A Good Provider

A good provider means your wife and your kids have always got food, and they're always warm. They've got a nice little place to be dry and comfortable. And you take care of your relatives, and you take care of your Longhouse. You take care of your community. You're always ready to benefit somebody who's sick. Or if somebody's house burned, you're right there, trying to help make another one for them. So you're not just a family provider: you're an all-around provider. And the leaders have to be like that.

8: In Good Health

In good health means you can't be hard of hearing or deaf, and you can't be shortsighted or blind. You have to have full physical mobility, hearing and sight. You have to have all your full health faculties because you have to lead that nation.

You've gotta be hearing well, everything that the nation says. So when you're in Council, you can't be saying, "Huh? What'd you say?" You can't hold up the nation like that! They get that way sometimes. That's why Sub-Chiefs sit with them. That's what the Sub-Chiefs are for, if that happens to them along the way.

When you become a Chief, it's really demanding. You have to be on call twenty-four hours a day. And a lotta times the meetings are far away, that you've gotta go to. And you've gotta be able to do all that.

9. Good mind

Good mind means that you're never gossiping; you're never making rumors; you're never assassinating people's character. The Clan Mothers and Chiefs and Faithkeepers all are not to do that. They're supposed to be the examples for their whole clan or their whole family, not to do that. They carry a good mind and they always talk about positive things. That's what their job is. That's what "good mind" means.

10. Community-minded

Of course that's where somebody's in need of help, somebody dies, you're right there, right away, ready to go, and ready to help them. You are always helping the community.

11. Fair, objective

You have to be fair and objective because you have a dual responsibility. It means that not only do you have your family, but by the time you become a Clan Mother or Chief, if you are that, now your family grows from six kids to two thousand. Not only two thousand kids, but to forty thousand because everybody in that Mohawk Nation now becomes your children. You become like a father to all of them.

If there's some problem that comes up, that maybe involves your nephew or your son or your sister's son, you're not supposed to show favoritism, even though that's your son or nephew. You have to be able to divorce yourself from your blood when it comes to that, which is hard for a lot of people to do. But you have to.

I was on the Council for twenty-five or thirty years, however long it was. And I was meaner, way more strict to my own kids, to my own relatives and I had more sympathy for people who I wasn't related to, when it came to fixing their problems. I didn't show favoritism to any of my own 'cause I expected them to toe the line more than anybody, and be the example.

So when you have to make decisions about your immediate family, you can't use the fact that you're their father, or their uncle, and give them a break. You can't exempt them. You have to be objective and fair. And your close blood relatives don't count for more. You have to do it like it's just, right, fair, not your child. And that's a very hard thing to do.

And if you can't, then you have to speak up, right away, to remove yourself from that discussion, or that decision. And I've seen Chiefs do that, excuse themselves. They'll say, "That's my nephew and I don't think I can really fairly do it, and I would like to ask to be removed from . . . The rest of you take care of it. And whatever all of you decide, that's what we'll do."

12. You have to speak the language.

And then of course the language, that's just common sense. You need that. It wasn't an issue before 'cause you can't do the ceremonies without knowing the language. And you can't counsel without the language. When I was still a teenager, they forbid any foreign language, of any kind, in our Longhouse. You could only speak in Mohawk. Otherwise, they would stop you right away.

They don't any more. But in those days, I've seen how they would enforce that. Mostly it was the Clan Mothers that stopped people. Everybody knew the language. In those days, you never heard an English word in there from anybody, kids, old people, anybody. I don't remember when I heard the first English word in there, but it would have been really strange if you did.

But you go in Longhouse today, any Longhouse, and you hear mostly English. It's the other way now. It's kinda sad.

So now, those are the criteria which you use to look for the new leaders, including the Clan Mothers. In many cases, in older times, that Clan Mother was a midwife. So a lot of the people who were born amongst those two thousand, she was there to help deliver them at their birth. Not only was she their grandmother or their great-aunt or whatever, she was also the one that pulled them into the earth, as a midwife. She's known them since the minute they breathed their first breath. Literally, she has. So in some cases it's like that.

Now say that Chief becomes old, and the Chief dies. He's a hundred years old and he passes away. She has to be especially ready to initiate the process of getting a new leader, for the one that just passed. When the Clan Mother's Roiá:nehr passes away, she will be ready to put another man up within three days after the funeral; if that's not possible, then no later than ten days. And so what she will do is she will call a meeting, maybe before he dies, to be ready. And she can call a meeting of just the females of that family or that clan, or she may choose to include the men together with the women, instead of two separate meetings. They can have it either way. It's up to her how she wants to proceed with that.

A lot of times, they'll include the men because of the time; it takes time. So they figure if they can include the men, it'll get to a conclusion quicker. And a lot of times that's true. And it's not unusual that they would sometimes—not always but a lot of times—send these men that they're thinking of nominating, on missions away, either to Onondaga or to Seneca country. They'll make up an excuse to get them out of town. The reason they're doing that is because they want to talk about them. And they don't want them to know, I guess. While they're gone, then they'll do this discussion without them knowing that. 'Cause if they suspect that, I suppose, if they say, "Watch out because we're gonna talk about you . . ."

Sometimes they are in there, but it makes the person they are talking about uncomfortable. So they usually try not to have them there. So they have a meeting together, the men and the women. They open it up with a prayer like we do. And then the Clan Mother will say, "The Chief is *real*, real sick. And we don't know if he's gonna last through the night or he'll be here two more days: we don't know. But he's on the verge: we know that he's gonna leave. So we have to be ready for it. That's why I'm calling this meeting."

And so she'll say to them, "I have, over the years, given strong thoughts and lots of consideration, and I have a list of men who I think fill the criteria and they measure up to the . . . And they would make good nominees for a new leader (a new Chief, a new Sub-Chief, whatever). And so that's why I called this meeting, to see if what I have thought or have come to the conclusion, if it's close to right, or is it the opinion of you as well, that it's true and that it's right.

"And if not, I'd like to know if there are other people that maybe I have overlooked, that I haven't even considered. Maybe you can bring forth their names, and then we'll see if they're qualified and if I overlooked them."

And she approaches it in that way. And she says, "Okay." So she'll ask them, "Anybody has somebody that they think could be a good leader?" And if not, they'll say, "No, we want to hear what you think first. And maybe that's enough."

So then she'll get up and she'll name them. Then she'll tell what she knows about them, how long she's known them. And that's where sometimes she'll say, "I was the one that was the midwife when he was born. So I've known him since he was first born to the world. And I've known him ever since. He's a man now with a wife and children. And I know that when they cut wood for the Longhouse for all ceremonies, he's always in those cutting bees. And I know that when somebody has an unfortunate incident, and we raise funds to help them, he's always in there. He's always trying to be helpful to the people.

"And I notice also" she might say, "that when elder people's wood runs low in their house, he'd be leading a bunch of guys to go to the woods and go cut them wood. For the elders. And nobody tells him to do that, and he's always just doing it 'cause it's common sense, to him. And that's the kinda people is a real good people. So therefore . . ." and she'll go on with other things. "And he's always good to his kids. Good not just to his kids but to his *sisters'* kids. He's always a good uncle. He teaches them and he takes care of them. And he's always at the ceremonies, cleaning up, washing the floor, piling the wood, going hunting for deer. He's got lots of deer meat ready to feed the people. So all of those things. And he's been faithful to his wife and his kids, his community. He doesn't get mad easily at anybody. And so that's why I put him up."

And so in other words, they're going through that list. And then she says, "Then I have another one that's almost like him, but I favor this one first. As a second one, if there's something wrong with him, then this other one is like that too. And then maybe I got another one after that too. So in case those two don't make it, if there's some reason that any of you know that I don't know, well you need to tell me. So we can review it. And if you disqualify them through the process, then I have these other ones that are ready to go, huh?"

So that's the process they go through. Once she finishes telling who the nominee or nominees are—usually it would be singly—she says, "Now it's gonna go around. I wanna hear from everyone so that we can become one mind." So now it's gonna start and that woman's gonna say, "It's your turn. Next woman, your turn. Next one." All the way around. If there are a thousand people, then it's gonna go all around 'til they hear them. That's just the *women*.

And if the men have been invited, if the women finish, then they're gonna ask the men. And if they all agree to that, now she can say, "That's the one now. It's been confirmed: we are all of one mind now." The whole clan.

And if there's a reason why somebody is not going to agree, then they will have to state the reasons why. And you can't just make up a reason why not. It has to be true, valid. So if you bring up something that's foolish and nonsense—that's rumor or gossip—that's gonna reflect on *you*. All of those two thousand people know you're foolish. So they don't dare to do that, in that kinda group.

So then, what steps have we followed so far? I would say two.

Now, that's only the beginning. When that's done, she has to call a meeting of the eight other Mohawk Chiefs. She has to appear before them. And she has to tell who her nominee is, to fill that. If that Chief dies, this is who she's gonna put in there. Because that family that's nominating has to sit with him for the duration of their life and his life. So they best be compatible. Or at least be able to work together. If not, it will also hamper the nation, see?

So the third step is she has to present it to the eight Chiefs there. And they also have to approve because they have to sit with him after, once he's a leader. So there's the third step. She must receive approval of the entire Council.

So once he dies, say he dies now, these steps have been followed. Now they've gotta send a runner with a wampum. 'Cause he's a Mohawk, they gotta send it to the Younger Brothers: that's the Oneida and Cayuga and Tuscarora. It will be their duty to gather the whole Confederacy, to set a date when they will conduct the Condolence, and the raising of the new Roiá:nehr. They're the ones that conduct the raising of a new Chief for us. So now those three have to agree. And not only that, but the Older Brothers have to agree: those are the Mohawk, the Seneca, and the Onondaga. We're the Older Brothers. So they've gotta agree too.

Those are steps four, and five. Then, finally, they set the date for the Condolence. And they all come here. They come hundreds of miles, hundreds of people do. Maybe even thousands of people, to Mohawk country. And then they condole them: they give them sympathy 'cause they lost their leader. And there are hundreds of these Cayugas and Oneidas coming, to conduct the raising of the new leader.

So then they ask the Clan Mother, "Show us the face that your family has chosen. What does he look like?" And a lot of times, whoever it is that's gonna be put in there, doesn't even know it. And a lot of times they do. So that Clan Mother's walking amongst the hundreds of people. And then she sees him and she goes over there and grabs him.

"You're the one we're gonna put up."

And they put him over there. And they show what he looks like. So they look him over, from head to foot. And if they agree, they say they agree. Then the last part of that is they'll say to the hundreds of people assembled (and there will be all nations coming to see it, to be a part of it): "Does anybody know any reason why this man that's standing before us cannot be a leader, and have the horns put on his head? Anybody? If you do know of a reason why he can't or shouldn't be, you tell right now. And if you don't, he's gonna be the leader."

So that means any child, any woman or any person who has a gripe about him that's real, can stop that. But if not, then they put him up. So can you see how many checks and balances there were before he became that? And that's how it happens. That's how they're selected. That's the process.

That's why we call it a *true* democracy.

Because that leader doesn't campaign. He doesn't say, "I'm the good guy; I'm a good candidate," like you see all over the place. He's really chosen by the people, for the rest of his life. And if he doesn't do things properly, the Constitution also says the process by which you remove him. If he doesn't uphold the law. That was later adopted by the United States and called the impeachment laws.

This is not the way it's being done now. Similar. The last Chief we had was Brian Skidders.[2] This process was pretty near followed to the *t*. But he *died*. He was only a Chief for two years, or something like that, not even two years maybe. He was a wonderful Chief 'cause they followed this. But he had a massive heart attack and died. In that two years he was a Chief, he did more than most of the other Chiefs, combined, did in fifty years. In *two* years. Because he had the right everything.

If a Clan Mother just picks her son because he's her son, then that's not a basis ... It's not right. It's wrong, *very* wrong if he doesn't fulfill those

---

2.   Tom made this comment in 2003.

things . . . It's not wrong because it's her son. It's wrong because he doesn't have those qualifications.

If he fulfills those criteria, it's quite normal for a Clan Mother to choose a son. And usually that guy is knowledgeable because he is in there and exposed to it. So he would be the most *likely* candidate. But sometimes it works the other way. A lot of times those Clan Mothers and Chiefs' sons are the worst ones you'd want to become a leader. And in other cases they are the prime candidates too. So just because it's her son doesn't elevate him and it doesn't stop him either.

With a Clan Mother, usually what will happen is when she realizes that she's too old or she's sickly too much, then she can nominate women in her family. Now when we say her family, we're talking about the *whole* clan.

So they will have a meeting again, the people of that family, and they'll all approve it: they'll all become of one mind. That's the process, but a *lot* of them don't do that any more. They just get a few people together and that's it. They don't include the whole family any more. They don't think like that any more.

And I don't know if we can blame them too harshly because in the past, they were always being attacked. The colonizers wanted to get rid of them. So it diminished their mobility, and they tried to keep things going secretly. And the more secret they could get, the less attack they would get, see? So after four, seven, eight, ten generations of doing that, I can see where a woman in a family would say, "This is in my family." You know?

So we have to love them. Even though it's not right, we still have compassion for them because at least that family kept that going all this time, on our behalf. So that's why when we fix these things, an extremely good mind is necessary. So we have to learn . . . Some of these things are going to cause anger, like I said awhile ago. So we have to be prepared. The people who are gonna facilitate this should have been the Chiefs. But many times it's them that act angrily 'cause they're hurt.

So you almost need professional interveners 'cause a lot of times those Chiefs can't do it. In this Constitution, they're the ones that are supposed to do that. That's their job. But they're the *victims* of it. So it's hard. 'Cause they're the ones we're supposed to look up to, but they're the ones that are perpetuating these inequities. They're the ones that are doing these foolish kinds of things. And some of it has to do with power. They feel that they have prestige and power because they are called a Chief or a Clan Mother.

In the process, the women and the men have their roles. For example, the men don't have the right to tell the women they can't be at the Council meeting. In fact, they're supposed to be at the meeting, to make sure that the men behave properly.

And if they don't, that's when the Clan Mother intervenes. But in the discussions when Council's going, neither the people nor the Clan Mothers are supposed to interrupt that. The Clan Mothers and the people are supposed to know that. If the people want to have a meeting and be a part of the discussion, they can say that or send a message to their leader, their Clan Mother, whoever, and then what they can do is have a meeting for that, where it can be discussed.

But during the regular Council discussion, they're not supposed to stop that, or interfere with that. Because that's the *process*, how it goes. But when I was on Council, I used to get flack from the other clan leaders because I was a people person. I always wanted to have meetings that involved all the people in my clan, so that whatever decision we were making had the *full* support of the people. So if there was a snag, and then it had to be supported or backed up, those people would do it.

But if not, if you don't have the people discuss something, and you just assume that you're the representative of the people, well then you don't know if they liked it or not. Or if you're doing right, really. And so then if you have a snag or some trouble, the people say—and they have said it to them too, before—"Well, *you* made the decision and *you* back it up. Don't involve us. You didn't involve us *before*."

Now you need an army!

But I know that the other clan leaders, they didn't used to like to hear me when I was there 'cause I was always taking too long, always involving the people. "And when they get involved, we're never gonna finish." That's what they used to say to me!

So there's a lot of reeducation to do, within and outside, for this to be resurrected and to be reinserted into our life.

I used to call Bear Clan meetings on our *own*, about almost all the issues. And none of the other clans did that. 'Cause they said that I was being foolish and wasting time. But most of the Bear Clan used to feel included, huh?

Akwesasne Mohawk Nation Council and the Clans

There is a special seating arrangement of the Chiefs, the Rotiianéhshon. This seating arrangement enables laws to be made in a structured way. Years ago some of the leaders at Akwesasne changed the seating of the clans and their functions. They kept the format and the same procedural structure.

The following explains the way the Council functions today:

The Council is separated in three parts. The first part of the Council is the well. The three Rotiianéhshon of the Turtle Clan sit on the northeast side of the Longhouse. This particular set of leaders are the well. The well is a symbol which means that issues or problems are deposited here, and remedies by the entire Council are initiated or begin with the Turtle Clan leaders. These Turtle Clan leaders have the duty to arrange and prioritize the issues for presentation, review and resolution.

The second set of Rotiianéhshon are from the Wolf Clan and sit across the Council fire on the southeast end of the Longhouse. When a resolution is formed and agreed to by the well or Turtle Clan leaders, it must be sent across the Council fire (Tenkatsienhì:ia'ke) to the Wolf Clan leaders. The Wolf Clan leaders must reject or approve the pending resolution.

The third set of Rotiianéhshon are from the Bear Clan. The Bear Clan leaders watch and listen as the issues and/or resolutions are being heard and formulated. When the first party, Turtle Clan, and the second party, Wolf Clan, have all agreed, the pending resolution is then passed to the Bear Clan leaders, for acceptance and ratification. Through this process, the law is made. If the Bear Clan rejects the pending resolution, then the whole process must start all over again.

All Council meetings of the Rotiianéhshon are opened with the Ohén:ton Karihwatéhkwen (Opening Prayer, Thanksgiving Address). At the conclusion of the Council meeting, the Ohén:ton Karihwatéhkwen must be recited, to officially close the Council meeting. Another very important part of the Council meetings is that the nation's Katsísta (Wampum Fire) must be present, for the meeting to be official. There can be no official meetings after the sun has gone down. The Katsísta must be put away before sundown. Informal discussions can take place after sundown, but they are not in any way considered proper or official in terms of the law.

The present Akwesasne Chief Council's seating arrangement was changed in the 1950s. Originally before the '50s, the Wolves were the well keepers, the Turtles were the firekeepers, and the Bears were across the fire from the Wolves.

So anyway, those are the highlights of the Great Law. But like I said before, it takes them ten days to talk about it. And we just took this little while, so . . .

There are reasons why we don't say the Peacemaker's name, except at very specific times. And one thing may be of relevance here. Did you know that the Mohawks, the Senecas, the Onondagas, the Cheyenne, the Lakota, the Navajo, the Hopi, the Seminole, the Choctaw, and every single Indian in this Native North America don't know how to swear?

Did you know that there's no such phrases in our language or dialects that can call the Creator down? That if we want to swear, we have to speak French or English. But we cannot do it in Indian. There is no way. There's just no proper way for it to happen.

And it's sorta relevant to this. We can say the Peacemaker's name, when they are putting new Chiefs up, or new leaders up, installing a new leader. We can say it 'cause it relates to that. Or, if I'm telling my grandkids who are around six, seven years old, about the Peacemaker, about the law, so they can remember. I may say it once to them, what his name is. And I'll tell them not to say it any more. And I'll tell them that they're not gonna hear me say it any more. Just that one time.

We were forbidden to say his name because, as I told you earlier, in the prophecies of the Constitution, it says the day is gonna come, in the future, when there will be discord. There will be confusion. There will be turmoil. The Great Tree of Peace will be chopped down, but the leaders will hold it up. There will come a time when Clan Mothers will become indifferent to each other, and they won't have compassion and love. There'll come a time when even the male leaders, who were put in their positions with well-defined duties, will neglect them, even though they are still the leaders.

And it will be the same as if the head was cut off the body, severed. And the body is in one corner. And the head is rolling in blood, hitting the other heads in the other corner over there. That's how confused, and how disoriented from the reality of peace, that they will become. It will get so bad that people won't respect each other any more. They won't even follow the Clan System any more. All this confusion's gonna come.

Whatever confusion you see now isn't even close to what's coming. And when that happens, the prophecy says, "There will be three left." And when I asked different elders, "What does it mean 'three left'?" They said, "We don't know 'cause it was never told to us."

It could mean three nations of the original five nations, that still follow these things. Or it could mean three clans, that are still true. It could mean three Chiefs that still follow this, or three Clan Mothers. At the very minimum, it could mean three people, that still follow these things.

If it comes down to the three left, whatever that three means, when this turmoil and this chaos comes, they will go into the woods, where there are really big trees, like a real forest. And there they will kindle a sacred fire. And they will throw sacred tobacco onto that fire. And they will cry the name of the Peacemaker, three times. They're not gonna call him; they're gonna *cry* his name three times. You know what it means to cry a name? It means in your sincerest belief, from the very bottom of your entire being.

And then he said, "And if that happens, I will come back."

That's part of the reason.

Now, to explain it further to you, my grandmother used to use this example. There were three boys playing by the river. And you know whenever you get people together, there's always one who's the clown, who, you know, makes people laugh.

And so these three boys were playing around the river. And this one boy said, "I'll betcha I can fool my buddies." So he jumped in the river, and he started swimming to the middle. And he made pretend that he had cramps. He started screaming his bloody head off. And he was jumping, moving his arms, "Help me, help me, I'm drowning." And he wasn't drowning. He just wanted to fool them, be the clown. You know, silly guy.

They didn't know if he was drowning. So they jumped in there and they went over to save him. And as they swam to the middle of the river, and they were ready to grab him, he jumped up and he said, "Aha, I fooled you guys. I made you get wet." He made a big joke out of it. But the other two boys didn't think it was so funny.

So then a couple of weeks later, this same kid said, "Well I fooled them once. I betcha I can fool them again." And so they were swimming there again. And that boy started swimming. And they told him, "Don't go that far out in the middle. It's rough over there."

"Ahhh," he says, "come on. Swim." They wouldn't go. He went. And then again, he pretended he was drowning. He went under the water and came up yelling and screaming his head off, like he was really drowning. And so one of them said, "I don't know if he's just fooling us or he's really drowning. Ahhh, let's go get him, maybe he is." So they did. And again, when those two boys were about to grab him, he jumped up and he laughed his head off at them. "Once the fool, always the fool," he says to them. "I gotcha again."

They didn't like it. But after about a month or so went by, that same kid said, "I made them jump in that river twice. I tricked them, I fooled them twice. And I'll betcha I can do it again." So he went out again. And he didn't even get half way this time, and he really did get cramps in his body. And he couldn't move. He was frozen up and in a lot of pain. He started to go down and scream. That's all he could do was scream.

Those two boys were at the shore and they said, "He made us jump in there one time. And he made us jump in there twice. Let him *swim*." And they turned around and they left. And he drowned. He died.

And that's the reason why we are not allowed to say our Peacemaker's name, over coffee, or tea, or over just a conversation. We're not allowed. Because when the time comes when we need to cry his name, it has to be for real. And so that's why we only say that name in the context of truth and honor and peace.

Chapter 31

Casinos

Sugar is laid down and sweet things are laid down to the big trap.

I want you to understand one real important thing that's gonna affect Indian country, that already has affected Indian country. You maybe are aware that most of the Indian nations have casinos: bingo and casino gambling establishments.

Those casinos and gambling things, I think President Reagan's the one that opened the door to this kind of a world, of this kinda thinking. I don't know that for a fact. But he was the president when it started to come.

And there was always a plan, called a one-hundred-year plan, by America, Canada, and Great Britain for us Indians. They wanted to make us forget who we are, to forget the notion of nationhood. They projected a one-hundred-year plan, by which they would slowly remove the Indianness from our thinking. And turn us into mainstream Canadian or United States citizens.

There are documents that say that, from Ottawa. There are actual documents that state that that's the intent. And that was also the intent of the residential schools. It's a process.

In our Iroquois teachings, we are forbidden to have casinos or gambling. We do have a little bit of gambling in the Longhouse, but it's religious. It's not like these casinos. You can't lose your house, can't lose your fortune. You can only lose a pair of moccasins or something. And so the Iroquois don't want that because our spiritual teachings say we're not supposed to do it.

But many of our people, Mohawk, Senecas, and so on, have forsaken their spiritual ceremony life. And they have turned to European or Western religion. So they don't have the same soul or spirit anymore like we do.

Over there in Connecticut, there's a people. They are married to black people and European people, and maybe their Indian blood is only a little bit. And they don't have land anymore. They don't even have a tribe anymore. And they haven't known how to talk their language for more than one hundred years, maybe. So they've got no more ceremony, only just a little bit of blood in their body.

When they tried to make casinos where we Iroquois, we Mohawks live, our language is still spoken. Our ceremony is still going. So there was opposition. We have too much tradition left, that protects us and tells us not to do this. So it was a great controversy. Even amongst the Iroquois themselves, there were people who died, who got shot over that issue.

But among those Pequot over there, in Connecticut, where there are no spiritual Indians anymore, there was no opposition.

So the government recognized them as Indian, even though they're not *really*. They recognized them, and allowed them to put up a casino.

And now it's a multi, multi, multimillion, probably billion dollar affair, okay? Beautiful, massive, hotels that touch the sky. Gold faucets, rug, marble, like coliseums. Millions and millions of dollars comin' in. And the Pequots' casino over there, they gave ten million dollars to the Smithsonian Institution Museum in Washington, D.C. And the newspaper headlines read, "Pequots donate ten million dollars to the Smithsonian Institution." "Pequots donate some more million dollars to the Red Cross." Money all over.

So now, the government says to the Lakota, who are poor Indians, "Go see what the Pequot are doing because they've got a casino. And see how nice it is."

"Seneca, Mohawk, Ojibway, Menominee, Shoshone, Navajo, go over there. Go see."

And so they go. And their eyes get big. Then they become envious. Now they want one too. And now, the trouble starts on all the Indian reservations. Now almost all the reservations have a casino. Not every one, but many.

Before, whenever the United States government or the Canadian government wanted to abrogate treaties or terminate the Indian lands and Indian reservations through legislation, they were never successful. You know why? Because many American citizens—not Native, but *American* citizens—have a mysterious feeling of support for us. They think of us as the "underdog." They like to support the underdog. And so they have been our allies.

They are the ones who would protest, and organize, and help us to defeat these termination bills, that would strip the Indian of *everything* that we have from the treaties. Always, because we were poor, no voice, we were called "underdog." And we had a lotta allies to help us, okay?

So America couldn't do that. Canada either. Now, in times past, Canada and America came, and they gave the Indian leaders whisky and rum to make them drunk. And then when they were drunk, and they didn't know what they were doing, they made them sign treaties. That's was the past.

Civilized people are not supposed to do this, but this is what America did. And Canada and Great Britain, too. They used coercion. And that has been outlawed by the United Nations, to do that to somebody, see?

So because American people know this, they were helping us too because it is not right.

Okay, so they tricked the Indians before, to sign these documents. They used tricks and coercion.

But now, guess what?

When the Seneca and the Lakota and the Cheyenne saw the Pequot's big multimillion casino at Foxwoods, giving away money here, giving away money there—they have so much money—now the Cheyenne, they say, "Get outta my way, Mohawks, Seneca. Let me sign first. I want casino now. Let me sign the compact."

In order to get a casino, you have to sign a document called a "compact." And this compact is an agreement with the county, the state and the federal government, saying that you will give a certain percentage of your profit to them. That's called *taxation*. Now taxation comes.

Then you have to allow the state police and the federal police to have jurisdiction to oversee the casino. And they use their jurisdiction also against the Mafia. "To protect the Indian."

So the Cheyenne and the Lakota and Seneca push each other aside, "Let me sign. I want a casino right away." So now they sign. They're pushing and asking to sign the compact, which says they're gonna give their police sovereignty to America and to the states. And also taxation, they gotta give so much million to the state too.

And now the Indians have lost . . . They can't say anymore, when they sign this, "They coerced me. They got me drunk." They can't say that because they're the ones pushing. They said "Let *me* sign" for the first time. Do you follow?

So the Indian is now trapped, after all. Sugar is laid down and sweet things are laid down to the big trap. Now all Indians, all the rats are going there, and now you close the door. Snap.

And when the door is closed, United States will now allow casinos to be run in Niagara Falls and all the big tourist places. Then nobody will go to the Indian casinos anymore. They will go to American casinos. Now all the Indian casinos will become ghost towns. And we've got no more land. Now we pay tax. No more nation. And we signed.

And all the people in America that used to support us because we were the underdog, they'll say, "Lakota is not poor. Mohawk, Seneca is not poor. They gave ten million dollars to the Smithsonian Institution Museum in

Washington. They gave twenty million dollars to the science project over here. All the headlines in the papers, they say Indians donate millions to this and to that." So now to those American allies, they're not underdog anymore. "They're richer than we are."

So now our natural ally is gone. There is nobody to help us anymore. Those are the last nails in the coffin. And that's the way I read it. That's the way I see it. That's the last now of the sovereignty of our nations. And once that's gone, then the money's gone. The land is gone too. Now everything is gone. That's the end. The plan was for a hundred years. It took two hundred years—but it finished.

So that's our dilemma. How are we gonna get through that one? How do you erase that fresh ink that my leaders, whoever they are, signed? They were tricked, big time.

Although it seems bleak, and maybe it seems almost hopeless at times, we still won't give up, though. Because the Indian people . . . I know sometimes when we were kids, we would fight, my brother and me. And he would put his hands around my neck and try to choke me. We were just kids. And he would ask me, "Do you give up?"

And I would say, "No."

And he'd squeeze harder. I couldn't breathe, and he'd say, "Give up?"

"No."

Pretty soon, I'd be almost dying. And he'd say, "Give up?"

"No!" Until I'm pretty near fainting. Then he'd let go.

Same thing when I grabbed him. I'd hold his neck and I'd say to my brother, "Give up?"

He'd say, "No." And I'd squeeze harder. "No," he'd say. He'd pretty near turn purple. And he'd pretty near fall down. But, he wouldn't give up.

That's the way the Mohawk and the Lakota are. We never give up!

So what we're going through is going to be another era, another era, another era. But I feel good about everything we did, all the struggles, all of the fighting. Even the internal fighting, though it was hard. Well, it was specially hard for me because people I grew up with in my Longhouse, when it came to money, some of them took the money. And I couldn't understand that. And it really . . . it hit me hard. 'Cause I didn't think that my own brother, my own family, my own, can do this, for money. I couldn't conceive of that. I thought we were stronger.

But that only showed me how strong America and the Western thing is. And how tricky they are. No matter how much confidence you thought you had, they'd get one step or two ahead of you. So you couldn't sleep. You've gotta keep one eye open, all the time, if you don't wanna get completely tricked. So what we're gonna do nowadays is, we have to be very careful. Very aware, and very conscious. That's the message I guess I wanna leave. Not one to give up, but to become extra aware.

And myself in my older age, I will mostly need to be advising the younger people, when they ask for advice. And also to give them advice when they don't want it, I guess is what we gotta do!

But I think that we'll probably do all right though. We'll swim to the last one anyway, no matter what. But I said all this just to give you a full, rounded picture, you know.

Chapter 32

Prayer?

Holy! All these years, I've been saying the wrong word.

I want to tell you the prayer, one of the prayers I learned when I was a young guy, a kid. It's one I've never forgotten, all through the years. It's s'posed to be a prayer for little kids, but I'm almost sixty years old now[1] and I still use the same prayer. I've never changed it because it's so easy and simple and to the point. And I wanna share that with you 'cause my grandmother and my uncle told me how to do it.

Whenever I see the younger women and younger men—doesn't matter if you're Ojibway or Cree, Seneca or Choctaw or Hopi—I always look at you as if you were my own nephew, and you were my own niece. That's the way I look at you. Sometimes I even take it a step farther. Sometimes I look at all of you as if you're my own daughters and my own sons. Yeah.

---

[1]. This section came from an address Tom made to youth, at the Fort Erie Friendship Centre, in 2003.

So what we're gonna talk about today is in the old traditional way of how we are supposed to talk about certain things. And I don't know if I say "to teach how to pray," 'cause I sorta mean that. But I don't know if praying is the right word for *me* to use.

Because what happened to me is I didn't go really far in school, in American or Canadian school. (I went to both.) I didn't go very far, mostly because I didn't believe either one of them! So I kinda blocked my ears 'cause I didn't like what I heard. And also for many other reasons . . .

And so I think I am at a bit of a disadvantage.

So how I learn is I watch different people that I know, and sometimes I listen to the English people or French people talking. And I listen to how they talk. What kind of words do they use? And then I try to use them too. That's where I learn most everything that I know. It didn't really come from school.

My grandma, unlike many grandmas, I *think*, didn't really want me to go to school. Because she said if I go to the school, pretty soon, I'm just gonna talk English only and I won't know how to talk my Mohawk language any more. That's what happened to a lot of people that went to school, who are Indians. They went there talking our language. And when they finished, they couldn't talk it any more.

And my grandmother said,
     Né:'e se's ken thí:ken iotéha tsi nihotirihòten.[2]

She was talking about our own Indians. Because they go a little bit to the white people's school and they come back, and they make pretend they don't know how to talk Indian any more, as if our language isn't good enough or something. They start to feel ashamed and kinda hide their language, or hide their Indianness. You know what I mean? And she didn't want me to do that.

So that's why I didn't go to school right away, when I was a little kid. And there are other reasons too, but we won't go into them right now.

[2.] *Isn't that shameful, the way that they are./ Their ways are shameful.*

Anyway, here's what she said to me. She said, "It begins this away. When you're laying down in your bed, in the early morning, you notice that the light starts to come in the window of the room where you're sleeping. Yet you're laying on the bed, only your eyes open. You didn't even get out of the bed yet. That's where you begin your talk." She said, "As soon as that light comes through the window, what's happening . . ."

Remember the story about the Creation? See we have to remember all those stories and how the sequence of the story goes. Because it's gonna help us to put our puzzle together of who you are and who I am, tomorrow. So when I get a problem, I can reference my story in my memory, that something happened before, like that problem I got, and what did they do? So I'll use that as an example. See, that's what it does. That's why you need to remember things.

'Member I said that the Teharonhiawá:kon power, he's a big giant man. The two twins were big giant guys. 'Member I said that the biggest tree just comes to their knees? So you can imagine how tall they both are. And 'member at the end of the whole thing Teharonhiawá:kon became the sun and the oldest brother of you and me.

And always an older brother or an older sister, they are like mothers to us 'cause we're younger. So anything we do, our older brother right away comes running. We're in some kind of trouble, he's gonna come, try to help us. 'Cause he's older than us. He's gonna try to take care of us. So that's the job of the sun, is to take care of you and me because we are the younger brother and the younger sister to the sun.

But also we must remember that Shonkwaia'tíson, the Creator, is very powerful. And is the source of life all over the whole universe. And Shonkwaia'tíson, our Creator also has qualities of a magician. He can do things that most people can't do. So he's multitalented, multipowerful, multisensitive, multiknowing. He has to be, in order to keep a hand, you know, on everything that's going on in this world. And sometimes it even gets away on him too.

So Teharonhiawá:kon in a sense is the power of the Creator. (And so is his brother. He's got the power of the Creator too, the one that likes to make trouble. He was given half the world's power.)

Anyway, so when you're sleeping in that bed, Grandma said, "The sunlight is coming in your window. And you're laying on that bed. And you're just a little kid. Or a man or a woman, whoever it is. And so when that sunlight comes in that room, it goes where you're sleeping. And that sunlight is the hands and is the arm of our Teharonhiawá:kon, of our Shonkwaia'tíson, our Maker.

"And so when that light comes in that room, that light surrounds you, as you're laying in that bed. So it's the arms of our Creator, that light."

And it came to you and you and you this morning, every one of you, when the dawning of the new day came in that window, where you were sleeping. And that Creator comes and he holds you, as you just begin to open your eyes. And he holds your whole body, every inch of you. And he caresses you with the brand new light of the new day.

That's the Shonkwaia'tíson, that light that did that to you. So nobody can run away from our Creator's touch. Because we're walking in the miraculous light of his day. Philosophically, isn't that something? I mean even poets would get jealous! Yeah, yeah for Indian!

Anyway, so each one of you, I guess you could say it, was visited individually, young, old, this morning by the power of our Creator. That light of that sun, that's the Creator surrounding us.

So Grandma said, "What do you do when that happens every day? You can't just do nothing. If somebody comes and he shakes your hand, or somebody wants to hug you, you don't just do nothing. You better hug them back. You better put your hand out *or something*. Acknowledge."

A while ago, 'member I said we maybe call it a prayer? I forgot, though, to tell you, that because of my lack of formal education, I just pick up what people say. And if it sounds good, I put it into my head and then I use it. And I get in trouble for that too. 'Cause sometimes I make a mistake, I use the wrong word. 'Cause in English, there are words that sound the same, but mean something different. But they didn't tell me that part!

Son of a gun, I got in trouble a couple of times! I thought I was real smart, talking English so well, and I made a fool outta myself. I could tell you that, and I mean it's funny too. But we'll save that for another day.

Anyway, in my learning as I'm growing, I just put one and one together the way I think it should make two. You know what I mean? A teacher didn't have to tell me. I just did it myself. And so I *thought* when people all over were talking about prayer, I thought what does that mean? So I put together myself what prayer means. And here's what I thought it meant. And this is what I made it mean, for many years:

Prayer to me was when you as an individual remove yourself from everything, the busyness of the world, and you find a real quiet place, a place of solitude, and you ask the Creator, the Maker of the Universe, "Let's have moments to talk together. Listen to me, Creator, I'm your son."

And when you talk to the Creator, whatever it is you're gonna talk about, to me, that's what I thought a prayer was: when you had quality time in solitude and sacredness, with the Creator. Man or woman or child. That's what *I* thought it was.

And all the years I was using it as such, until the AA Partridge House over there at Akwesasne asked me to come teach different Indians there. Different tribes from all over come there for alcohol and drug rehabilitation. And so I said, "Before I go teach them there, I'd better double-check my English." So I grabbed Webster's dictionary, the big fat one, the one that knows the most. And the bigger it is, the more it knows!

So I looked in there. And I looked for where it says "prayer." I wanted to just double-check if this Tom Porter added one and one to make two right, when I say "prayer," huh? By golly, I had it *wrong*. All these years, I was saying the wrong thing. 'Cause you know what it says in that Webster's dictionary?

The number one priority meaning was "to request something." That's what "prayer" means. Holy! All these years, I've been saying the wrong word. 'Cause whenever *we* talk to the Creator, we're not saying "Gimme, gimme something."

We don't say that. All we do is say, "thank you, thank you, thank you." We hardly ever ask for anything. 'Cause everything we need's already here. So it's opposite, like.

But I still like the word prayer anyway, even if it's not my word. Because I like my original definition better than Webster's. I think of it as a time to be with the Creator, and talk to the Creator. That's a prayer, see?

So I'm somewhat at a loss when I try, yet today, to incorporate what I learned. 'Cause I don't want to mislead somebody.

Okay, so anyway, this talk, "spiritual talk" we'll call it. So what you say when that sunlight comes, the light of day surrounds you, when you open your eyes . . . Here's what Grandma told me to say. And this is what I want to share with you. If you wanna use it, you can use it. And here's what she says, before you even get out of bed,
Niá:wen Takia'tíson ne watkonnonhwará:ton.

And that's it.

That's not hard to say, huh? Can you all say it?
Niá:wen Takia'tíson ne watkonnonhwará:ton.

Come on, say it,
Niá:wen Takia'tíson ne watkonnonhwará:ton.

And here's what it says. I'm gonna translate it word-for-word, literally tell you what it really means. Niá:wen means *thank you*. Takia'tíson means *you who made me*. In other words, *Creator*. But you're personalizing it 'cause you're saying, *you*, directly, *Creator, who made me*.

"Ne." Lotta Iroquois, they like to say "ne." Everything is ne, ne ne. Well, ne is just, in English, what they call a connector word. It's like *and, the, but, also*. It adds one phrase and another phrase. It hooks it together. Like a big train, if you've got another train, where it hooks together, that's ne. Makes it one long train. So ne is a connector word.

Watkonnonhwará:ton means many things, not just one word. Like yesterday, I was sick. I've got a cold, I guess. And they made medicine for me, yesterday. All day I was drinking that. So I said to them, "Thank you, you made medicine for me." That means watkonnonhwará:ton.

If I come here and I see you and I say, "How are you doing? You're doing good? I'm glad. Good to see you today, you're here with us." That means watkonnonhwará:ton as well. It's the same thing. So now there are two things it means. You greet people, you thank people.

Then when you listen to the word watkon*nonhwar*á:ton it comes from the root word sa*nón:wara* which is *your brains*. What it means is that my brain intentionally did this "thank you" or this greeting. It wasn't just an accident. I used my o*nón:wara*, which is in the word, watkon*nonhwar*á: ton. So it isn't just by chance. It's not accidental: it's with direct intent.

Then, if you look at the word watkonnonhwará:ton, you will notice the other root word in there is konnorónhkhwa. The word konnorónhkhwa should not be taken lightly. Don't just say konnorónhkhwa, if you don't know what it means. Because if you do that, you cheapen the word. It becomes cheap.

So let me see if I can translate it to you. In English, there's a phrase that you could use. I don't know if it justifies it, though. And the phrase is *I love you*. But I don't know if *I love you* means the same as when we say konnorónhkhwa. Because, when we say konnorónhkhwa, this is what it means: not just now, and not just today, the whole day, but tomorrow, the next day, the next day, the next year, all the way until I'm not gonna breathe any more breath of life, and maybe I have two canes walking around, I'm so old. That time. From now 'til then.

When I say konnorónhkhwa to you, or to my mother or my father or my wife or my kids or my nephews, my nieces, it means from now until the end of my life. If something comes that's gonna hurt you or injure you, I'm gonna stand right in front because konnorónhkhwa. And I will stand there today and tomorrow and the next day, until there's no more danger. That's because konnorónhkhwa to my wife or my daughters, my sons, my people. Forever konnorónhkhwa.

So that's why you don't hear Indians say that too much. Because when they say it, they *mean* it. And so that's in that word, watkonnonhwará:ton. It's not just for now, it's forever, my Creator. I will stand with you, Creator, forever. Until I get old, and I don't live any more. So you're saying that the commitment is forever, as long as you live.

So you see when you add up all those things that say watkonnonhwará: ton, you're dealing with a mighty powerful word. In fact, it takes three paragraphs, four paragraphs in English, just to describe that one word watkonnonhwará:ton. It's in there: konnorónhkhwa.

And so you're saying, *Thank you, you who made me. I send you my greetings; I send you my love and kindness; I send you my thankfulness. And I will be with you forever, my Creator.* And that's what that's saying, that prayer. Isn't that beautiful? So simple. And we just say to the little kids who are growing,
Niá:wen Takia'tíson ne watkonnonhwará:ton.

And I was just telling my younger brother Dan, here, I said, "You know what? I have at my house this African gray parrot. He's about four or five years old, right now. And he can live to be about seventy-five years old. So I'll be gone a long time, and he'll still be here."

And this African parrot talks. He can *talk*. I don't know if it's a he or a she 'cause he never showed me anything to prove which! But anyway, he talks Mohawk. Mostly Mohawk. Very few English words. And he says that every morning . . .

You know why I got him to begin with? Not because I love African birds, but I heard that the African gray parrot has the biggest vocabulary of any bird in the whole world.

And I have a strategy. I have a plan why I bought that bird. It isn't because he's a bird. I have—what do you call it in English?—an ulterior motive. I was gonna say an alternative moment. It sounded better! But anyway, my reason is because I noticed a lot of times when we tell our young people, our kids and grandkids that they should learn our language . . .

A lotta time we just say it because it's s'posed to be popular to say that to your kids, whether you mean it or not. It's just a dress-up like stuff. Some are serious though. Some *really* do it. But a lot of us aren't. We just say it, just because that's what we're supposed to say, I guess, and hope they do it. But a lotta times we don't do anything to make sure it happens.

And so I said, well, when I tell my grandkid to talk Mohawk, sometimes he says, "But everybody talks English. They won't understand."

He's only a little guy and he's arguing just like a lawyer, the reasons why he shouldn't talk Mohawk. 'Cause the whole other world won't understand. He's so sorry for them!

And so I said, "When this bird is gonna talk and if he talks Mohawk . . ." But I didn't know he was gonna start praying right away! I didn't know that. That's a *bonus*. That was a windfall. Yeah.

And so now, early in the morning, my bird, every morning *without fail*, he says,
    Niá:wen Takia'tíson ne watkonnonhwará:ton.

Every morning without fail. Sun goes down in the evening, again,
    Niá:wen Takia'tíson ne watkonnonhwará:ton.

He says it. He copies the way I talk.

And then, when my grandkids are there, I say, "Did you hear that? Was that me talking?"

And my grandson says, "No, it was that bird. But Tóta Tom,[3] it sounds just like you."

I tell him, "You see that little bird? He knows how to pray and he knows how to talk Mohawk. My grandson, how come you don't? Try harder. If the bird can do it, you're supposed to be a human being, you do it better."

And so they try harder because of the bird. They don't wanna be outdone by a bird. And that's my ulterior motive. Yeah! And he helps me out, that bird.

I was telling Dan, I said, "I should have brought my bird over here. And he could've helped us." But the only thing is he won't do it when I tell

---

3. Tóta is an affectionate term for *grandfather* or *grandmother*.

him. He only does it when the sun comes up and when the sun is going down. He just knows how to do it then. But I can't tell him to tell you that 'cause you'll be here all day. He won't say nothin'! He does it when he's supposed to do it, see. So it would be no use to bring him.

Oh, let me introduce you to my bird's name. His name is Tekáhstia'ks. That's the name that we gave him. And he knows his name, or her name or whatever, I don't know. Can you say that? Tekáhstia'ks. Tekáhstia'ks is our word and it literally means *the mouth that's going all the time*! And it's all flying-out words. Talk, talk, talk, talk, talk, talk: tekáhstia'ks. So anybody who's always talking frivolously, we call Tekáhstia'ks.

Don't call *me* that, though!

His name (or her name) is Tekáhstia'ks Porter. I didn't even give him that name Porter, but s/he took it. So sometimes . . . and I'm always on the road, you know what I mean? I'm always going somewhere. I'm never home. So when people call me, my wife or my kids answer.

And they say, "Is Tom Porter there?" And they'll answer, "No. He's somewhere, gone away."

So when I answer my own phone, I'm saying hello to them, and they'll say, "Could we speak to Tom Porter?"

Because I'm never home, they'll always ask for me, even if I answer. And so I have to say to them, "This *is* Tom Porter."

You know that doggone Tekáhstia'ks was listening to that. So every time that phone rings and somebody answers, that Tekáhstia'ks says, "Hello, this *is* Tom Porter!" I kid you not. He does.

Anyway, back to the spiritual talk, the prayer. So every morning that's what we say, the human people, soon as we open our eyes,
   Niá:wen Takia'tíson ne watkonnonhwará:ton.

That means *thank you, you who made me. I send you my greetings, my thankfulness and my love and my commitment to stand with you forever.*

And then the Creator is happy. And then, you're gonna have a good journey all day, see.

Now, you get up from the bed, you come downstairs, and if you've got a mother, you're lucky to have a mother left. And you see her cooking. The thing you gotta do next is you say, Istén:'a[4] watkonnonhwará:ton. Or else, Istén:'a kwé kwé. And that's considered a prayer, to acknowledge your mother every morning when you see her.

Or if you got up and you saw your father, in Mohawk we say, Ráke'ni[5] watkonnonhwará:ton or Ráke'ni kwé kwé, if it's early in the morning. Kwé kwé is an old word that just says *good morning*. I think we adopted that word from the Algonquins, hundreds and hundreds of years ago. But a lot of Iroquois use it 'cause it's an old word for the morning acknowledgements.

Then, if you see your kids . . . I'm a father and I see my kids. Or I wake them up and they get up. And I try to touch them. You don't have to really hug them, but just touch them with your hand. That's your son. That's your daughter. That's your flesh and your blood. And you say hello to them, watkonnonhwará: ton, kwé. And they say that back to you. That's a prayer too.

So all the members of your family, you never start your day, without acknowledging them. Fathers to their kids, and kids to their mother and to their father. You see your grandma somewhere, you go to her house. First thing, Akhsótha,[6] watkonnonhwará:ton. Or Shé:kon skennen'ko:wa ken?[7] That's the way you're s'posed to do. That's prayer.

Then every time that you drink water. Doesn't matter if you drink water twenty times a day; in that water that you drink, is the power of life that the Creator put in there. So water is a sacred thing. So whenever you drink

---

4. Istén:'a is the Mohawk word for *mother*.
5. Ráke'ni is the Mohawk word for *father*.
6. Akhsótha is the Mohawk word for *grandmother*.
7. Shé:kon skennen'ko:wa ken? is another greeting, which literally asks, *Is it still the Great Peace?* or *Does the Great Peace continue?*

water from the well or anywhere, when you finish drinking that water, you say Niá:wen. Some people will say,

Ohné:kanos watkonnonhwará:ton, niá:wen.

Again, *commitment forever, your love, to the water.* Because that water is gonna quench your thirst. And if you try to go for four or five days without water, most likely we'll have to bury you. You have to have water.

So our elders told us, "Whenever you drink water, don't take it for granted. Always acknowledge the Water, the spirit of the water, because it's living. It makes you live." That's another prayer.

Then when you eat your breakfast, your dinner, your supper or whatever . . . Whenever you eat anything and you put it in your mouth to eat it, all the real Indian people, all the real Senecas, all the real Mohawks, all the real Oneidas, all the real Cayuga people, the ones that follow the old teachings, whenever anything goes in their mouth, after they've eaten, you'll always hear them say,

Niá:wen.

That's a prayer to the Creator, for that food. Where you hear this the most is if you go to Longhouses when they have their ceremonies. If you go in the cookhouses of the six nations, you see the Chiefs in there. And when they get up from the table after eating, you'll hear the old Chiefs. They'll say, Niá:wen. They'll talk loud when they say it, they'll holler, NIÁ:WEN.

They're saying to the Creator, *thank you.* And everybody in there, they'll say, yo. On behalf of the Creator, they acknowledge.

But you say this *after* you eat. When you say niá:wen when you finish eating, number one is the Creator hears that. Number two, the second ones that are gonna hear it, are the ones who cooked the food for you. Now you touched their hearts because you said niá:wen. And then the third one that's gonna hear you, when you say that, is the spirit that made that corn grow and those potatoes grow. And that food that you're eating, it's got seeds that are gonna be put in the ground for a next generation of it. And when you say niá:wen, it goes there.

So whenever you finish eating, you say niá:wen once. And it touches the Creator, the preparers, and the spirit of the food 'cause it's living. That's what's gonna make you live. Every time you eat. Grandma said even if you are dunking a little piece of donut, you're supposed to say that, too, 'cause it's a food.

Now, it's still morning. And I go out the door of my house. And I'll tell you what, I'm gonna share this one with you, if you wanna be a real orthodox, traditional person. You know what I mean? To *really* follow the old ways. You know what they do? Before they go outside of their house, this is the real old time people now, they will take a broom. And they start right at the door, before they touch the threshold. And they push the dirt over. They sweep the entire porch and the entire steps at the entrance to your house, even the little pathway that goes to your porch.

And they'll say,
> Takia'tíson ne watkonnonhwará:ton tóka senh ónhka nahò:tenk wahéthken rokion tho tsi niwahsón:tes wá:s ísi tho wa'koniaté: kwahte.

That means if anybody throws something there that's not good, that will hurt my family, like a medicine of some kind, when they sweep their porches and their stairways, they say,
> *Go, anything bad. Go, anything that's gonna hurt my family. Get outta here. We chase it away.*

And that's why the real traditional Iroquois or Ojibway or Cree, they sweep every morning. That's part of their life. They sweep evil away, so nothing will come to hurt their family.

I used to see that. And I still do that. It's in my blood now. I can't help it.

And that's what you say when you do that sweeping. You give your greetings to the Creator. And with the power of the Creator, you sweep it away, any evil that may be thrown there, see? For the protection of your family. Okay, so when you do this, and also when the wind from stepping out there touches your face, that's when you can say,
> Kaié:ri Nikawerá:ke ne watkonnonhwará:ton, *The Four Winds that touched me, I acknowledge with love, you.*

Then you step on the ground from your house,
    Istén:'a tsi Iohontsiá:te ne watkonnonhwará:ton.

You say,
    Mother Earth, I acknowledge you, with love and commitment.

A lotta times when I have time to do my walk—'cause the doctor told me I'm s'posed to walk 'cause of my health—when I start walking, I got a certain place on the roadside and that's when I do what we were talking about this morning. That's when I start with the Creator, a real formal one, the long one. I start, "Mother Earth" as I'm walking, "I'm your son. I'm walking on you. Mother Earth, since the beginning of time you've been giving me food, for my Grandma, my people, and me and my kids. Mother Earth, I walk upon you today and I give you my greetings and my love."

Then as I walk, I see the grass. And I talk to the grass and I thank them too. Then I see the flowers growing in the fields and I send my words over there and I acknowledge them too. And I do all the animals: cow, horse, deer, whatever animal, domestic or wild one. And I go and I do the Opening there.

Then the next one is, if I'm gonna go in the garden . . . And it talks about that in the Karihwí:io, in all the Longhouses: where you planted, you never are to go in there, when you're mad or angry. You're not s'posed to go in that garden when you're frustrated and you don't want to be there and so you're mad now. You only go to the garden, to work in the garden, to hoe it, when ka'nikonhrí:io shá:wi, when *you're carrying a good mind.*

If you go in that garden and you're angry and you don't wanna go there, and you're mad, then that corn and those beans don't want you in there, because you don't have a good mind. And so you will stunt its growth because your mind isn't good. And you will be lucky if you get enough food outta there to help you through the winter because you stunted it. You weren't thinking with a good mind. But instead, what will grow there will be the weeds. Those are the ones who want to hear you if you are mad. So all the weeds will grow and they'll just smother all your corn and all your good food.

Member in the Creation story, when Sky Woman's daughter was laying in the ground? Corn, and beans and squash grew there from where her head was in her grave. So whenever you go to work in your garden, to weed it, you stand there, and you say,

> Takia'tíson watkonnonhwará:ton. Ó:nenhste, Áhsen Nisewatatennò: sen ne watkonnonhwará:ton.

So you direct your thankfulness to the Corn, the Beans, and the Squash 'cause they're the leaders of those potatoes and cabbage and carrots, everything growing in there. They're the leaders. So you first, you acknowledge them with love, and kindness. *Then* you can put your foot in the garden with your hoe, to hoe the garden.

And if you do that, your whole garden will grow healthy food, with love. And that's what you feed your kids, your husband and your family.

Chapter 33

The Future

The Creator made the world diverse, to be beautiful all over the universe.

The Carlisle Indian School in Reverse

As I said at the beginning, in 1995, we left the reservation and we went back to our homeland in the Mohawk Valley, in New York State. Our great-grandmothers about 230 years ago had prophesied that one day their grandchildren would return home. And that's what we have done. We have fulfilled that prophecy.

Connected to the prophecy, however, are many issues that are vital to the survival of the American Indian people. In a few minutes, I want to give you an example from my own family.

It is my belief, considering and studying the statistics on Native American people, that the Iroquois people—that is the Mohawks, the Oneida, Onondaga, Cayuga, Seneca, and the Tuscarora Indian people—will be

AND GRANDMA SAID . . . IROQUOIS TEACHINGS

extinct within five to ten years, and no more than ten years, at the rate that we are being assimilated now.[1]

In ten years, I believe our extinction will become complete. That is to say linguistically, there will be no more Iroquois dialects; spiritually, there will be no more spiritual ceremonies unique to the Iroquois; culturally and traditionally, there will be no more Iroquois. The only thing that will remain will be biological Mohawks, biological Onondagas, biological Cayugas, and so forth. And there will be no more Indians with a unique culture.

There was an intentional orchestration by different people in the United States, back in 1879. There was a school that was begun, called the Indian Industrial School, often referred to as the Carlisle Indian School, in Carlisle, Pennsylvania, about twenty or thirty miles south of Harrisburg, Pennsylvania. This school was started in 1879 and it closed up in 1918.

And this is the school that over eight thousand Indian children from the ages of four to ten were sent to, for I don't know if I could say brainwashing purposes, but for sure I could say, assimilation purposes. The founder of the school was a man named Captain Pratt. And his philosophy was "kill the Indian and save the man." That meant to deprogram all the Indians from their language, deprogram them from their spiritual orientations, deprogram them from their values or moral standards that each nation had in North America, and make them into Yankee-Doodle-went-to-town kind of people.

And he was most successful. And this attempt by Captain Pratt was sponsored in a large part by the United States government, the Department of the Interior. The reason I'm familiar with this is because my grandfather went to this school, my great-grandfather went to this school, as well as many Natives across the country. Their granddads and grandmothers went there too.

In the United States every ten years, there is a census taken. And every ten years, when this census is taken, it says that the Native Indian people have the highest alcoholism rate of any ethnic group in the entire country.

[1.] Tom made this prediction in 1999.

According to this census, we have the highest dropout rate from education, of any ethnic group. It says in this census that our teenage boys and girls from the Navajo, Mohawk, Cheyenne, Lakota, and all the other Indian nations—fourteen, sixteen, seventeen, eighteen-year-olds—have the highest suicide rate, of any ethnic group. And also our life expectancy is ten to fifteen years below the American average.

And so when one studies the statistics, it doesn't show a very favorable situation for the Native people.

But the Indian people were not born to be failures. We were survivors. We were people with dignity and honor. We were not born to be the most likely to be alcoholic people in the world. That is a new development in the last 150 years, this negativeness amongst my people.

There are reasons for this. And one of the main reasons is because our great-grandfather and grandfathers and grandmothers were forced to go to this government school, which stripped them of their language, their beliefs, their culture, and their spirituality.

And so it is that without identity and without dignity, the Indian is walking the earth, almost in a state of numbness. And almost without a goal, without the feeling of being wanted by anyone, even within our own society. Because our whole society has been broken. That is why we have the highest rate of alcoholism, why the highest rate of drug activities is amongst the Indian nations, and why there is so much hopelessness.

And so it is that there is lots of violence, family violence, and dysfunctional families. And to make this clearer, I'm gonna use my grandfather as an example. My grandfather was taken to Carlisle Indian School when he was four or five years old. And he did not return home to the Mohawk reservation until he was twenty-one. And when he arrived home, he had no more father. And he didn't have a mother anymore. And he didn't have any more aunts. And all the elders in his family were deceased.

When he arrived home, he could no longer speak Mohawk. But my grandfather was twenty-one. And like any young twenty-one-year-old man, his sex hormones kicked in. He got married. And he had twelve children. Every year he had another child.

But my grandfather never held his children. Because at the Carlisle School, you were told, "Go clean the barn. Go get water. Go pile the wood. Go scrub the floor." Everything was an order, like a sergeant gives to the soldiers in his army. That's the environment in which Carlisle taught the kids.

And so my grandfather, when he raised his twelve kids, was like an army sergeant too. "Go get wood. Go get water. Go clean the barn." It was never, "Can we clean the barn? Can we sweep the floor?" It was always an order.

And my grandfather never held his daughters or his sons, any of the twelve of them, on his lap. He'd never shake his legs and bounce them around. He never put his arm around them. Because sergeants don't do this to the people in their army.

And so my grandfather did not know how to caress his children. So my aunts and uncles grew up. My aunt had fifteen kids. My other aunt had fifteen kids. My other uncle had fourteen kids. My other aunt had ten kids. And all together, my grandmother and grandpa almost had one hundred grandchildren just between them. But none of them knew about love. Because Grandpa did not know how to show it. How could he? At Carlisle, he had no mother. He had no father. He had no uncle. And so on.

So this created a cycle of dysfunction. All the grandchildren, almost a hundred of them that they had, also were dysfunctional. And their children are now dysfunctional. And so this little story that is actually fact is almost the same story, repeated on every Indian reservation across America.

And so now the Indian people are almost all dysfunctional because of these schools.

And our language: the Tuscarora who have one thousand people, only have twelve fluent speakers left today. The Senecas who have fifteen thousand population, have fifty fluent speakers of the Seneca language. Cayugas with twelve thousand have sixty. Onondagas, one thousand population, have fourteen fluent speakers. The Oneidas, fifteen thousand population, they have 160 fluent speakers. The Mohawks who have thirty-five thousand population have five thousand. And all of those fluent speakers are my age and older. Most of them are in their seventies and eighties.

And so that's why I say in the next five to ten years we will be done, extinct.

And so what can we do about it?

The dream is a bold dream, a monumental dream, just like Harvard, Yale, Princeton, They operate on what you call donations from people throughout the country, throughout the world. And then they put this money away and the interest runs the school, from the endowments. And so what I see the dream to be is that we must start a Carlisle Indian boarding school today, except in *reverse*.

We must immerse our people, our children, and teach them how to be mothers and fathers, give them back their ceremonies, give them back their language, give them back their spiritual history and their history altogether, teach them how to be wholesome family members, ambitious, honest, and morally good. That is what Carlisle took away from the Indian nations.

And if we don't do this, then our names must be added to all the extinct species of the animal life of the world, in the next ten years.

But I believe this dream will be fulfilled. In the next years we will go the whole world over to see where we can get the endowments, just like Princeton, just like Cornell, just like Yale does, in order to stop our extinction.

And so to all of you who have listened to these few words, I want to thank you for allowing me to share this concern, this worry that I have. And I ask you to keep your eyes open for ways that we might make this school, the Carlisle Indian School in reverse, a reality.

Since Tom talked about his dream of a Carlisle School in reverse, as noted elsewhere in the book, he returned to the Mohawk Valley in 1993. He and a small group of very dedicated people began a community at Kanatsioharè:ke. The story of the journey to create a place where the traditional ways could be nurtured and revitalized has now been published in a book also by Tom Sakokwenionkwas Porter: Kanatsiohareke: Traditional Mohawk Indians Return to Their Ancestral Homeland, *(Greenfield Center, New York: Bowman Books, 2006), ISBN: 0-87886-147-5.*

Tom made the following comments about the future of the community to a group of Italian people visiting Kanatsioharè:ke in 2007.

So then we came here. And the reason why I wanted to come here, mainly, is some younger Indian people were talking about saving our language. And also they were talking about planting gardens. And they were talking about sovereignty. And they were talking about ceremonies. And to be just like a real nation again, like it used to be.

But on the reservation where we live, there are colonial governments imposed by Canada and by the United States. And they are the ones who try to destroy our traditional government. They want to eradicate it, erase it from the face of the earth. And that's where you get the Bureau of Indian Affairs in Washington, D.C. and Indian Affairs in Ottawa.

And so one of the reasons I wanted to come here is because many young people were saying that on the reservation, there was too much alcohol. Too much drinking. And it was breaking families up. Too much cocaine. Too much marijuana. Too much everything over there. There was no chance for a traditional way of life to happen because there were too many distractions. Very destructive distractions.

So that's why we came here, so that we could isolate ourselves momentarily from the distractions, like a little plant that gets transplanted into a big garden. At first, it's weak. But then it takes root. And then it makes a nice plant, if you baby it. And that's why we came here, to see if we could transplant ourselves from the environment that was distracting and harmful to us. And be able to concentrate, to get better, to get healed here. So that we could begin to focus and think clearly.

But it didn't happen like I thought it was gonna happen. I think I misjudged it. I think that we had already gone a little too far in our colonization process. Because young people were not forthcoming. The ones that said they wanted to come here, never came. They were only talking. And we did come. And it's been a hard, hard, struggle. It's fifteen years now. So this is why we came here.

So we don't know yet what's gonna happen. But, I know that I'm not getting younger. And those fields need plowing. The corn needs planting. It takes young guys to do it.

So I'm going to go, pretty soon, to all the different Mohawk reservations. And I will see if I can recruit some young families to come here, to take over. 'Cause my wife wants to go back to our home up north, on the reservation. Our children live there. And our grandchildren live there. And we're gettin' older now.

Through all the years, my wife has always done what I wanted to do, and has gone where I wanted to go. She always helps me and backs me up, in everything. Even in the little wars we had, where death was actually as close as a bullet going by our heads, she never backed down. Our children never did either.

And so in these last years of our lives, we want to have time with our family, our kids and grandchildren, to have time with each other. And let younger people, if we can find them, take over here and fulfill the vision, the dream. But we have no idea if it is possible because the young people are busy in the economic world, trying to make a living and this and that. And individualism is a priority in most people's lives now.

The community mindedness of our own ancient people has mostly been evaporated. It's not like it used to be. So there are a lot of questions as to what will happen. But, regardless of what happens to me and my family, we will always try to support the younger people if they're here, to make it work. To advise them and be a part of their journey, that's what we will try to do.

So there's a big question now, in all of Indian country, as to what will happen. But the last of the old Indian thinking, I think, is almost gone. The ones that were real Indians, I think my generation was the last to know them. Where money didn't mean anything to them. I mean *really* didn't mean anything to them. 'Cause they would drop a job, just like that, if there was a cause, or if there was a movement. Working for the American people didn't mean nothin.' They were ready to do what was needed and they were willing to live *poor*. I seen them. They were my leaders. And those ones, there aren't many, anymore.

Now everybody puts their career first. No more is there that old feeling.

I feel very privileged though, that I had a chance to rub shoulders with them, that I had a chance to listen to them, to be encouraged by them, and everything. And I feel sad that I couldn't be more respectful and do things more like they did, see? 'Cause I feel almost like I've let them down.

But we are always taught to put our nose above the water and keep on paddling! Keep going, whatever. And so, so far, we're doing all right, I guess. And so that brings you up-to-date where we're at, right now.

Our nations have been fragmented. Pieces of us are lying all over and we're not together anymore. So our society doesn't work and function like blood goes through and feeds oxygen to all parts of a body. We're operating on very small pieces of our stuff. And that's why right now we're sick and dysfunctional, most Iroquois.

And so my job is to try to get better. See if I can get that blood going and circulating again. See if I can get my psyche, who I am, to be real again. And I believe that's the same task you have too, no matter whether you're Oneida, Mohawk or Seneca, whether you're Irish, Polish, or Italian or whatever. Same thing. We want to be happy as humans here on the earth 'cause we're not gonna be here too long.

One of my uncles put it this way, one time. He said, "Now can you imagine all the flowers in the whole world, if they all turned into roses? Everybody would die of lonesomeness and boredom. That's why there's tulips and there's daffodils and there's roses. And there's morning glories and there's orchids. All different colors. Because the Creator made the world diverse, to be beautiful all over the universe."

And so that's what we follow. That's why we maintain who we are. We're trying to keep our identity. You do yours and everybody does theirs and all keep their identities going. And then together, we'll be like a bouquet of flowers, to be admired and to beautify the world.

Chapter 34

The Closing Address

And our mind is agreed.

But anyway, I'd like to thank all of you for the interest that you've had in hearing this. And again, I know that we can never cover all these topics completely, but at least it's a guideline. And so now you see that there are many other areas that require much more time in order to study them, and research them, so that one understands them better. And that way, whoever asks questions, you'll be prepared to give it a more real answer in terms of the point of view of the Native people.

So now we need to close.

At this time I am going to speak in the English language in order that our brothers and sisters who do not understand the Mohawk language, will be able to understand the way the Creator put us here and the ways that he gave us to believe in and the way we should behave on this earth, what we call Mother Earth.

First, it goes this way: Our Creator is the one that gave us the good fortune to come together here. And so we the people, send our greetings and thanksgiving and our love to our Creator because he has allowed us to assemble here together at this time. And so we say thank you to our Creator. And our mind is agreed.

(Response: "tho" or "huh.")

And then our Creator also said that when we are together, first we must give greetings and thanksgiving and express our compassion and love for one another, for those of us so assembled. And so it is to all the People who hear these words, we send to each of you our greetings, our thanksgiving and our love. And our mind is agreed.

(Response: "tho" or "huh.")

Our Creator made the earth. And when our Creator made the earth and when the world was new, our Creator said the earth would be a woman. But not just a woman, she would be a mother, and the mother of all humans, the mother of all life, the mother of all birds and animals. And our Mother, the Earth would give birth, every day, to all of the life. And when our Mother Earth has given birth, she will make the food grow that will nourish our life. And so the Creator said that will be the nature of the earth. She will be the mother of all living things and she will nourish all that she gives birth to. And that is exactly what our Mother Earth does, even to this day, since the beginning of time.

And so you who are listening to me talk today, and I, what we will do, because our Mother the Earth is ever so consistent in giving birth and life, we the people who are her children will become of one mind. And we will send our thanksgiving, greetings and love to our Mother the Earth, the foundation of our life. We say, "Thank you, Mother Earth." And our mind is agreed.

(Response: "tho" or "huh.")

Upon our Mother Earth, the Creator put the water that's in the rivers and the creeks, the ponds, the lakes and the oceans. The water is a living entity. The water is the one that quenches our thirst every single day and every night. The water is the one that bathes us and showers us so that our body will be clean and fresh, and we will have a good life. And so the water is there every day to quench our thirst. That's the way the Creator made it.

And so because of that, all the people will become of one mind. And we will send our thank you, our greetings and our love to the spirit of every kind of Water that's all over Mother Earth. And to you we say, "Thank you for quenching our thirst today." And our mind is agreed.

(Response: "tho" or "huh.")

In the water, our Creator put what we call the fish life. Some are big and small. Some are medium-sized. When anything falls into the water, the Creator told the fish that they will gobble it up and keep the water clean. When the animals and the people need nourishment, they can go to the fish. And they can take their life. And they will become food for us. So the fish who swim in the waters of the world today are continuously doing their job, the way the Creator told them to. And because of that, we have much needed help to live. We, the people, are grateful. So we become one mind. And we send our thanksgiving and our greetings and our love to the Fish Life in the waters all over the world. We say, "Thank you today." And our mind is agreed.

(Response: "tho" or "huh.")

And then our Creator planted medicinal plants next to the water, on the shores of the rivers and lakes. In the mountains, in the valleys, on the plains, all over, our Creator planted medicinal plants. Because as we the humans walk upon Mother Earth, sometimes sickness will befall us. And when sickness catches up with us, it disrupts the tranquility and the peace of our mind, and causes discomfort and dissatisfaction. And so it is for that reason that the Creator planted the multitudes of medicines everywhere in the valleys and mountains, in the big woods, and by the rivers' edges. And so we will pick these medicines which were bestowed with power by our Creator. And with this power, the medicines will take away the sickness that brings discomfort to us. And then they will restore peace and tranquility to our minds. And so the medicines every day are waiting for the privilege and the pleasure for us humans to ask them to aid us when we are sick. And so that's the way the Creator made it.

And so what we will do because of this fact, we will gather our minds as one mind. And we will send our greetings, our thankfulness and our love to every Medicinal Plant that grows in every mountain, every forest and every valley on the entire Mother Earth. And we say thank you to them. And our mind is agreed.

(Response: "tho" or "huh.")

And then our Creator, when the world was new, planted for us the gardens, and the vegetables that grow in the gardens. And the Creator chose the corn to be the leader of all the vegetables. He chose the beans to be number two. And then he chose the squashes and the pumpkin, the vines, to be a third leader of all the vegetables that grow in the gardens.

And right now it is the middle of the summer. And the gardens in my community are growing. They already are producing potatoes. They are already producing beans. They're already producing corn that we're eating. And so it is that the gardens that grow are the testimony, and we are the witnesses, of our Creator's wonderful world.

And so to the leaders, the Corn, the Beans, and the Squash, who represent all the vegetables that grow in all people's gardens, we the people today are of one mind. We send our greetings, our thankfulness and our love to the spirit of every Vegetable Plant that grows in our gardens, that brings nourishment to our bodies. We say thank you to them and to our Creator for that wonderful plan. And our mind is agreed.

(Response: "tho" or "huh.")

And then our Creator, when the world was new, he planted the berries of all kinds. When the cold winter passes, the first berry that will appear will be the strawberry. And it will be big and red, and juicy and sweet. And that is the first berry after the big snow. We call this berry "the Big Medicine." It will doctor us and it will nourish us. And when the strawberries finish, the next one in line will be the raspberry bush. And from there the blueberries and the blackberries. And the list goes right on 'til winter comes. We will be harvesting different berries all through the summer. And that is the Big Medicine for us, the people, and the animals and the birds.

And so we the people are grateful for the berries, the strawberry and the raspberry that we just finished, and the others that are yet to be harvested. And we bring our minds together as though we were all just one mind. And then we send our thank you, our greetings and our love to the Berry Plants that give us their sweet fruit all summer long. We say thank you to them. And our mind is agreed.

(Response: "tho" or "huh.")

And then what our Creator did when the world was new, our Creator made the trees. And the trees make the forests that are all over Mother Earth. The Creator chose the maple to be the leader of all of the different varieties of trees. From these trees comes the shade, where we may find comfort on a hot summer's day. From these trees come the plums and the cherries, the apples and the oranges. And the list goes on and on. From the trees, we gather the wood that has fallen to make a fire so that our families will not freeze in the cold winter months. From the trees we build small humble homes, so that when the big cold raindrops come, they won't bring discomfort to us. Grandma says that the trees make the air and the wind blow, that we may breathe and have oxygen to live. And so the trees give their life to us totally. They nourish us from birth every day.

And so to the Trees of the World, the Forests of the World, we the people will become one mind. And we send our thank you, our greetings and our love to every Tree, big and small throughout the whole Mother Earth. We say thank you to you at this time. And our mind is agreed.

(Response: "tho" or "huh.")

In amongst the trees in the forest are the animals that the Creator put there, little ones, medium-sized and big animals. And here in the northeast where we live off Mother Earth, the Creator chose the deer to be the leader. And so it is that the deer provide food for us, they provide clothing for us, and they provide medicine for us. Sometimes, when we are walking in the big woods, and we look around, we will see a deer looking at us. That means that the Creator's way continues; it is still valid. And so to all the Animals of the World, big and small, we the human relatives are of one mind. And we send our greeting and our thankfulness and our love to them. And our mind is agreed today.

(Response: "tho" or "huh.")

And then, what our Creator did is he made the birds. He made them by the hundreds of thousands. He put beautiful, colored feathers on their bodies. And then our Creator talked to the birds and gave them songs. Each variety, he gave a different rhythm, a different song. And then the Creator spoke to the birds, and he gave them a special job here on Mother Earth. He said that their job is to shake up the minds of all the human beings and the animals. They are to do that, so that boredom and lonesomeness will not find a home in our mind, so that we will have happiness and joy.

And so the Creator told the birds, as he gave them the songs of many kinds, he said, "Every morning before the sun shows his face, when only the dawn begins to show the light of a new day, all of you birds will get up and fly. And you will sing your chorus, your songs of joy, so that all life will rejoice and have a good time, as it lives upon Mother Earth."

And so it is this morning that the birds sang their songs again as they have since the beginning of time. And so again we knew joy. And so to the Birds whose leader is the Eagle we say, "Thank you for the songs of this past day. Thank you that you follow the Creator's plan for this land and life. And we say thank you again." And our mind is agreed.

(Response: "tho" or "huh.")

And then the Creator did another thing in the sky. He placed the Thunder Beings there. And those Thunder Beings are the ones who are in charge of bringing the rain to renew the rivers, the streams, the lakes and all the things in the garden. It is the Thunder Grandfathers' rain that quenches their thirst. It is they who thunder their voice across the sky and make it possible that we may have life.

And so this past summer they've been visiting us almost every day because we're their grandchildren. And they bring fresh new water, so that we may always be replenished. And so we, the people who are the grandchildren of the Thunder Beings, become one mind now at this moment. And we send our thank you, our greetings and our love to them. And our mind is agreed.

(Response: "tho" or "huh.")

Then our Creator made two suns in the sky. One sun is called the Older Brother. And he was told by the Creator to shine his light upon Mother Earth, so that we will be able to see as we walk upon her. Our Creator told the sun that he will radiate warmth so the corn will grow, and the watermelon will get big and sweet. And so it is, every day the sun does the job that the Creator instructed him to do. And that's why we have the miracle of these beautiful days.

And so we the people will become one mind. And we send our thank you, our greetings, and our love, to our Old Brother Sun who watches over us, we who are his younger sisters and brothers. And so we say a big, big "Thank you with love." And our mind is agreed in its message to our Old Brother Sun.

(Response: "tho" or "huh.")

Then the second sun of night, we call her our Grandmother the Moon. She is the one who orchestrates the women of all the nations of the world. It is she who determines when each individual woman will conceive a child, and give birth to the children who make the nations of the world. It is she, our Grandmother the Moon, who raises and lowers the saltwaters of the oceans of Mother Earth. And so it is our children are born, our grandchildren are born, our gardens grow. And the geese fly according to the moon. And so to our Grandmother, the Moon, the giver of life and birth, we say "Thank you with love." And our mind is agreed.

(Response: "tho" or "huh.")

And then, it was also when the world was new, that our Creator made the Four Winds. They bring the changing of the seasons. When our Mother Earth has become very tired from giving birth, the winds of the north and east will bring a white blanket of snow and cover her, so that she may rest. When she has sufficiently rested, the winds of the south and the west remove her blanket. And soon there is green grass, that covers our Mother Earth, like a wall-to-wall carpet. The flowers bloom in many beautiful colors. And their fragrance fills the air in every direction. Our Mother the Earth is giving birth again.

And so it is to the Four Winds that bring the changing of the seasons, we the human relatives are grateful, and we say "Thank you with love." And our mind is agreed.

(Response: "tho" or "huh.")

And then there are the stars that beautify our Grandmother Moon. When the world was new, it was the Stars who told us what was to come in the future. That is the way it was. But elders have said that a day came when all people became like small children. And we lost the knowledge of how to talk to the Stars. But one thing is for certain, even though we have lost this knowledge, we are not blind. So it is when we look into the nighttime sky, and we see the millions and millions of stars shining ever so bright, we realize there is no one that could make a more beautiful painting or creation than the Creator did when he made them. And for their awesome beauty, we say, "Thank you with love" to them. And our mind is agreed.

(Response: "tho" or "huh.")

And then when the world was new, our Creator made the Four Sacred Beings. We call them the Sky Dweller Beings, the unseen forces of the universe. They are the ones who are our Creator's helpers. And they are our human protectors. In the history of mankind, whenever there came a need that there be peace, whenever our grandfathers and grandmothers veered from their spiritual teachings, and war and discord came, one of these Four Sacred Beings was sent by the Creator to become a peace messiah, to remind us of our spiritual knowledge, and the way we should behave. And those are the great peace prophets that every race of the world has had the privilege to know. And so that's why, in the year 2008, we are still here, the human beings. And we must always remember our sacred instructions. And so to the Four Sacred Beings, who are our protectors, the messengers of our Creator, we say, "Thank you with love." And our mind is agreed.

(Response: "tho" or "huh.")

And finally, to our Creator we call Shonkwaia'tíson, the one who has no face and no body, but is the Maker of all life of the universe . . . He belongs to the humans, he belongs to the birds, and he belongs to the animals. He belongs to everything that lives. And when our Creator finished all Creation, he made us humans the very last. And then he told us, "I made one woman and one man, and from the togetherness of your bodies will be born replicas of yourselves. And they will be the future generations." And that's who we are: we are from the ones that were born when the world was new.

And the Creator did not make a museum. He did not make technological complexities or archives of philosophy or religion. When the Creator put us on the earth, he just said simply, "It's your Mother Earth. And every day, respect your Mother Earth. Love your Mother Earth. And whatever you use, whatever you eat, whatever you drink, be sure to say thank you. And when you say thank you to everything that gives you life, you are saying thank you to me." That's what the Creator said. And so it is, there's nothing complicated, nothing difficult, no big problem, just simply say thank you.

And that's what this closing is about, to say thank you for the miracle of our birth, that we're still here.

And so what we will symbolically and spiritually do, all the people who are here, we will become one mind, as if we were one person, and then we will put multitudes of layers of thankfulness, and multitudes of layers of love and greetings in a big pile. And then we will surround this mountainous pile of greetings, thank yous and love. And we will simultaneously throw it high into the universe. And we say, "Creator, our Maker, thank you for the miracle that we still live today. Thank you for all Mother Earth has." We say, "Creator, thank you with love." And our mind is agreed.

(Response: "tho" or "huh.")

Appendix A

What Grandma's Great-grandchildren Learned

The older people, they're always considered "Grandma" or "Grandpa." And it's their job; they're the ones that are s'posed to teach the young people.

At Tom's request, I interviewed some of his family, to see what impact, if any, his grandmother has had on future generations. Since his grandchildren had not met me before and felt shy, I interviewed three of his children: his son Aronienens (who's nickname is Henes) and two of his daughters, Katsitsiakwas (who's nickname is Tsiakwas) and Katsitsiahawi (who's nickname is Tsiahawi). These interviews, then, are with the great-grandchildren of Grandma.

Joint Interview
with Katsitsiakwas (Tsiakwas) and Katsitsiahawi (Tsiahawi),
June 30, 2007

Katsitsiakwas (Tsiakwas): All the things that I remember about her are from when he speaks of her. He speaks highly of her. And almost everywhere he goes, in all his speeches, and everything, it's always about his grandmother. Basically, everything he knows is what she told or taught him. So the big thing I really remember of her is his stories of her.

When I talk to my kids, I don't refer it back to grandmothers or not really to elders, I always refer things back to my father.

So the way he talks about his grandmother is the way I talk about my dad, to my kids. My mother also, but my father did most of the talking. And I learned a lot from my mother in different things, more like the women things, how to be a mom, how to do this, how to do that. I learned a lot from her that way. And I learned a lot from my father, like discipline from my father . . .

Katsitsiahawi (Tsiahawi): When I was growing up, he always says, you marry your opposite clan and you try to marry somebody that's Native. And that's what I did. And the bonus part is I found a guy that is actually the same religion—we're both Longhouse and so our children are all Longhouse.

So that's one thing I was proud of 'cause you know when you're young, you like a lotta guys and they're all different. Then he happened just to come along, and he was all the three things I was looking for, and more.

Editor: He was Onkwehón:we; he was a different clan, not Turtle; and he was "a Longhouse guy"?

Tsiahawi: Right.

I try to bring my kids up in the Longhouse way. Well, my father, his family told him, "Never use drugs. Don't drink because it changes your state of mind and your body." And so that's what stuck in my mind too, all my life, you know. So I'm trying to teach my kids too. And that you respect elders and that too.

With drugs and drinking and all that, you bring them up when they're young, keep telling them. Telling them even when they're teenagers. And you know what's funny too, was: my kids are all kind of growing. I mean they're not babies anymore. They're all older.

And to this day, my kids have never really been exposed to drinking or partying. You know, when you go places, like a graduation party or any kinda doings, people drink. It's very normal, nowadays, very open. But it's still not really something that I have exposed my kids to. If they see somebody with a beer bottle, it's like a big shock to them. "Oh my God, lookit. That guy's got a beer bottle!" You know what I mean?

Editor: Yeah.

Tsiahawi: So I was able to, with my own kids, through talking to them all the time, just like what she said about the drinking and drugs and stuff, kinda keep them . . . I can't say away from it 'cause they haven't really touched it or, you know, they're not that old yet, but . . . Do you know what I mean?

Editor: Yeah, the impression's really strong on them right now?

Tsiahawi: Yeah, yeah. Hopefully it sticks with them. I know it gets harder when they get older, but . . .

Editor: Yeah, they have to make those decisions for themselves, at that stage?

Tsiahawi: Yeah, as we were growing up, my dad used to travel all the time. We were home with my mom. But when he would come home, even though he was gone a lot, for some reason he made a great big impression . . .

Tsiakwas: 'Cause we had respect for him.

A lot of people talk about what you should be doing, what you shouldn't be doing, but he always says, "What the old people say." It's not my grandmother. He always says, "What the old people say." So he used to talk to us all the time. And I think that's the big thing. It's just talking.

So as we got older, I mean none of us drink or do drugs and stuff. But I believe it's because of everything that he used to say, as we were growing. And then when we got older, like high school age, we were never pressured into anything. And if we were, we just knew enough what to do and what not to do.

Editor: Mmhmm.

Tsiahawi: But he wasn't a real mean strict guy. He didn't have to be because . . . That's what I . . .

Editor: It's more like you both behave in a certain way out of your respect for him, than out of sort of having been forced in that direction? It's like your own free choice, but it's because you respect his views on it?

Tsiahawi: Yeah. Yeah, exactly and ah . . .

Editor: Like you look up to him, or whatever?

Tsiahawi: Yeah, and a lot of people, I think, thought that he was mean and strict with us. That's why they say we didn't get a chance to be rebellious. I know some people look at it as he didn't give us a chance to go through the bad stages that people normally go through. But, to me, I don't look at it that way at all. I just feel blessed. I just feel lucky to have a mother and father like they are . . .

Editor: Yeah

Tsiahawi: I'm gonna cry now.

But . . . yeah. I don't look at it that way at all. I just feel that we were very fortunate to have parents like that.

Tsiakwas: They weren't even strict really. They would want us to go visit or do stuff. We had our own mind, but we just had enough respect to make up our own mind, and, I mean not to—I don't know how to say it. You know what I mean? She knows what I mean.

Editor: Yeah.

Tsiakwas: Even to go places, sleep over, go away for a couple days, or with friends, we didn't want to. We always wanted to be home. I think we were so close to home that we were afraid to go away. I remember when friends wanted us to sleep over, we used to tell my mom that we have to do this or we have to do that . . .

Tsiahawi: Make up an excuse, so we don't go.

[laughing]

Editor: You didn't want your friends to think that, but you wanted . . .

Both: Yeah, yeah.

Editor: . . . to have a way out of it?

Tsiakwas: Yeah, we just loved it when they would come to our house. And they did too. Yeah, and actually a lot of my friends—one's passed away now, but she really looked up to my father. I mean she didn't have a father growing up. And she didn't really have a mom. Her mom drank a lot of stuff and she kinda left the kids a lot. So this friend became close with my mom and dad and she used to come over all the time. And I didn't even realize it until she got older, and she started having kids of her own. And she used to talk about my dad, and she said that everything she learned, like the Longhouse ways, you know, all that kinda stuff, traditional ways, she learned from coming to my house, to visit us.

She'd come over and we'd work in the garden. *That* we didn't want to do. 'Cause we wanted to play, 'cause we were kids. But my mom worked in the garden, so we had to help her, and . . . She said that she learned everything, a lot of what she knows.

Editor: She looked up to your parents almost the way one should look up to their own parents?

Tsiakwas: Yeah. But she had two kids of her own and was it four years ago, five years ago, she passed away. She had cancer.

Editor: She was your age and she's gone already!

Tsiakwas: Yeah. She was a young mother, yeah. So I think he's left a lot of the way his grandmother taught him on young people, the same thing. Except that he's not afraid to say it and speak highly of her all the time, whereas you know how people kinda keep things to themselves, nowadays.

Editor: Well, it sounds like for both of you, a big part of your lives is trying to carry on what you've learned from him?

Both: Mmhmm

Tsiahawi: We're nodding. [Laughter]

Excerpts from an Interview with Aronienens (Henes), June 30, 2007

Aronienens (Henes): My father taught us to love the Longhouse, and we're teaching our children that. That the language is real important, the culture, the way of life—that's what the Longhouse is, the way of life. And my kids are very involved.

The way that I was taught was always: work hard, and live honest. You never take anything, any kind of substance or anything that can alter the mind. We don't touch alcohol or drugs. I'm sure she taught him that and he passed that on to us. So I think our family here is pretty strong in that sense, not touching any alcohol, or any drugs.

He always taught me to work honest all the time, never to try and get rich real fast or never do anything just to make a lot of money real quick where it'll be any type of illegal activity. 'Cause there's a lot of that, that goes around at home, at Akwesasne.

What he taught us, that's gotta be coming from her. Because I've got cousins, who, when you track down the relation, it all comes down to that family, the David family. And she was a David, you know. So that family is one of the families that were still strong in the Longhouse ways, way back when Christianity took over. And they were really going down on the Longhouse, so they had to kind of stay underground.

So I guess the best thing for the future children is always to have a clear mind, think about everything that lives in the world—and just live with nature. That's the best thing you can do.

But "Grandma's" teachings, you know, that's always the way it's been in the Mohawks. The older people, they're always considered "Grandma" or "Grandpa." And it's their job; they're the ones that are s'posed to teach the young people. Even if they don't know them, they're considered Grandma and Grandpa, you know. And you're always to listen to what they say. You're never s'posed to disrespect them. You're never s'posed to talk back, or anything. That's their job. They see somethin' going on, and they go there and try to correct it.

That's the way it's s'posed to be. But today, it's not like that anymore. There are too many people that get mad right away now. And they don't want you talking to their kids that way, or anything like that. They're too much in today's society. They lost their connection, I guess . . . I don't know if they lost their connection, but maybe they were never taught.

Editor: I get a sense, when I hear you sing that song—"When the Lilacs Bloom,"* that Roy Hurd wrote for Tom's grandmother—it's like I hear his love for her repeated in your voice, as if you've picked up some of that same emotion towards her . . .

Henes: Uh-huh. It doesn't only have that effect on him. It's all the grandchildren—my father's sisters, and even their aunts, which would be Hattie's kids—they really like that song. They're always asking me to sing it.

*   Editor's note: The lyrics are reproduced in the dedication of the book (with kind permission from Roy Hurd).

Appendix B

Directions for Atenaha, the Seed Game

Atenaha is pronounced Ahh-day-nah-ha.

Six to twenty players can play. Someone is chosen to pick up the dice first and throw them.

The game will go in a counterclockwise direction (unless the game is being played to honor someone who has died—in that case the dice are passed clockwise).

The player throwing the dice continues to throw as long as s/he is winning corn from the pot, or unless s/he accidentally drops one or more of the dice while attempting to pick them up, or if s/he drops the dice while shaking them.

The pot consists of forty kernels of corn, which can be won by throwing the following combinations of eight dice:

- All eight black = twenty corn
- All eight white = ten corn
- One white and seven black or one black and seven white = four corn
- Two white and six black or two black and six white = two corn
- Combinations of 3 and 5 or 4 and 4 are no good and end a player's turn.

As a player wins corn, the player uses one hand to conceal their winnings and the other hand to pick up the dice.

Play continues until the pot is empty. At this point, any player who has not won any corn is out of the game. That is called "skunked."

Play continues as before, but now as a player throws winning combinations of the dice, s/he collects from the remaining players in the following manner:

> When a player's turn ends, the total amount of corn won is divided by the number of other players still in the game. (Example: If a player threw combinations which added up to six corn, then the three other players give two corn each. If ten corn are won and there are three other players, then each of those players must give four corn because giving three would not be enough to equal ten. Since that winner ends up with twelve kernels instead of ten, it is called a "windfall.")

Players remain in the game as long as they do not owe any corn. Players can play without any corn until they are unable to pay a winner. Then they're out. The game continues until one player has all the corn.

Corn is not collected after each throw of the dice. Rather, the player tries to maintain his/her luck by picking up and throwing the dice as quickly as possible. Only when their turn ends should they collect their winnings.

Other players may shout "shaa" (as in the Shah of Iran) as a player throws, which means to wish bad luck.

A player rolling may wish to shout "kahonta" (gah-hoon-dah) which means to make all one color, like a field.

This game is sometimes played to help settle family disagreements, by putting the decision making in the hands of the Creator.

Good luck and have fun!

Mohawk	Alternate Contemporary Linguistic Spelling	Meaning (Comments)
ahoti'nikonhrakétsko		to raise their mind up or they should/ought to raise their mind up (Tom and other ceremonial speakers often drop the "ra" syllable)
áhsen		three
ahsén:nen		in the middle or in the center of
ahsén:nen tsi nón:we		the middle of that
Áhsen Nikontatenò:sen		the Three Sisters
ahsonhthenhnéhkha		in the nighttime
Ahsontowanenkó:wa		the great, great night (the being rather than the time of day)
Ahswé:katsi		Ogdensburg (lit. the source of the spring)
Aionwahta	Ayonwahta	he always wakes up (English: Hiawatha)
akhsótha		my grandmother

MOHAWK	ALTERNATE CONTEMPORARY LINGUISTIC SPELLING	MEANING (COMMENTS)
akoià:ta	akoyà:ta	her body
Akwesasne	Ahkwesáhshne/ Ahkwesáhsne	where the partridge lives/drums
anò:kien	anókyen	muskrat
a'nó:wara		turtle
atátken		mirror (lit. to see yourself)
atenaha	atenénha	the seed game (lit. seed)
Atón:wa		Men's Chant/Thanksgiving Song/Spirit Song
Atotáhrho		he arranges, tidies up, puts things away, he hooks/blocks (contraction of tehatohtahrho) (Onondaga: Thatotáhrho)
Atsi'tsiaká:ion	Atsytsyakayon	old/mature flower, Sky Woman's name (Note: many of the old names began with an "a.")

MOHAWK	ALTERNATE CONTEMPORARY LINGUISTIC SPELLING	MEANING (COMMENTS)
eh kati tho		so be it
enska	enhskat	one
Haudenosaunee		People of the Longhouse (Seneca/Onondaga for Rotinonhsón:ni)
ià:ia'k	yayak	six, cross over
Iakoiá:nehr	Oyá:ner/Yakoyaner	Clan Mother (she's of goodness, righteousness)
Iakokweniensta	Iakokwenienhstha/ yakokwenyenhstha	she's respected/respectful (name of Tom's granddaughter)
Iensta	Ienhstha/Yenhstha	(abbreviated form of Tom's grandaughter's name)
í:iah thaón:ton	yah thaón:ton	it's not possible
í:iah thaetewanákere onwe	yah tha'tewanakerenenwe	we're not living forever, (lit. as people we won't be occupying this area any more)
í:iah thakionnheke	yah thakyonnheke	we're not alive forever (root: onnhe)

Mohawk	Alternate Contemporary Linguistic Spelling	Meaning (Comments)
í:iah teió:ri.	yah teyori	they weren't cooked right, not all the way cooked
iokahrón:ton	yokahron:ton	holes in there
ionkhihsótha	yonkhisotha/ yethihsotha	our grandmother (Speakers, including Tom, often use iethi rather than ionkhi. According to David Maracle, the pronoun yethi is often used in situations of ceremonial reference or importance. For example "Our Grandmother Moon," (lit. she is to us grandmother.) According to other contemporary linguists, the latter form would mean "we are grandmother to her.")
Ionkhihsótha Ahsonhthenhnéhkha Karáhkwa	Yethihsótha Ahsonhthenhnéhkha Karáhkwa	Our Grandmother, the Nighttime Sun (See note above re iethi/ionkhi.)
Ionkhi'nisténha Ohónstia	Yethi'nihsténha Onhwenstya	Our Mother Earth (Speakers, including Tom, often use iethi rather than ionkhi. According to David Maracle, the term "Yethi'nihstenha Onhwenstya" is often used in situations of ceremonial reference or importance for "Our Mother Earth," (lit. she is to us mother of the earth). According to other contemporary linguists, the latter form would mean "we are mother to her.")

MOHAWK	ALTERNATE CONTEMPORARY LINGUISTIC SPELLING	MEANING (COMMENTS)
ionkhisothokón:'a	yethihsothokonha/	our grandfathers yonkhisothokonha (See notes for "our grandmother" and "our mother" above.)
Ionkhisothokon:'a Ratiwé:ras	Yethihsothokonha Ratiwé:ras	Our Grandfathers, the Thunderers (See notes for "our grandmother" and "Our Mother Earth" above.)
istén:'a	ihsta'a	mother, aunt (mother's sisters)
Istén:'a tsi Iohontsiá:te	Ihsta'a tsi Yonhwenstyate	Mother Earth (lit. Mother Earth, it exists)
kahstówa		feather hat, headdress
Kaianere'kó:wa	Kayanerehkowa	the Great Law, the Constitution (lit. the great good)
kaia'ton:ni	kaya'tonni	doll
Kaientowá:nen	Kayentowanen	Peach Stone Game (lit. the big wood)
kaié:ri	kayeri	four

Mohawk	Alternate Contemporary Linguistic Spelling	Meaning (Comments)
Kaié:ri Niionkwè:take	Kayeri Niyonkwetake	the Four Beings (lit. the amount of four beings)
Kaié:ri Niiori:wake	Kayeri Niyoriwake	the Four Sacred Rituals/Ceremonies (lit. the amount of four sacred rituals)
Kaié:ri Niiori:wake Iakoterihonton	Kayeri Niyoriwake Yakoterihonton	Faithkeeper (lit. female caretaker of the amount of four sacred rituals)
Kaié:ri Niiori:wake Roterihonton	Kayeri Niyoriwake Roterihonton	Faithkeeper (lit. male caretaker of the amount of four sacred rituals)
Kaié:ri Nikawerá:ke	Kayeri Nikawerake	Four Winds (lit. the amount of four winds)
Kanakare	Kanákere	lit. it is plentiful (name of creek at Kanatsioharè:ke)
kanata		village, community
kanàtarokhón:we	kana'taronkhonwe	corn bread (lit. it is real bread food)
Kanatsioharè:ke		the place of the clean pot

MOHAWK	ALTERNATE CONTEMPORARY LINGUISTIC SPELLING	MEANING (COMMENTS)
Kaniatarí:io	Kanyatariyo	Lake Ontario (lit. nice/beautiful lake/river)
ka'nikonhrí:io shá:wi	ka'nikonhriyo shawi	you carry a good mind
kanonronkhwáhtshera		compassion and love
karáhkwa		sun
karihw—		matter, issue, business (root word: ori:wa)
Karihwí:io	Karihwiyo	lit. good business/matter (or positive subject)
Karonhià:ke	Karonhyake	the place in the sky, Sky World
Katsísta		Wampum fire
Kawenní:io School	Kawenniyo	lit. it is a good word
Kenkiohkwahnhákstha	Kentyohkwanhakstha	Circle Wampum (lit. it links the group together)
kiohkehnékha		in the daytime

Mohawk	Alternate Contemporary Linguistic Spelling	Meaning (Comments)
kiohkehnékha karáhkwa		(daytime) sun
kióhton/tióhton	tyohton	nine
konnorónhkhwa		I love you (lit. you are precious to me)
Konwanataha	Konwanatáhrha	carrier of the village (Grandma's Mohawk name)
kwé kwé		good morning, hello (probably of Algonquin origin)
Mi'kmaq		(formerly spelled Micmac)
ne		the, a, an
niá:wen	nyá:wen, niaweh	thank you
niá:wen 'kó:wa		thank you very much
niá:wen 'kó:wa tekahna'netarion		layers and layers of thank-yous

MOHAWK	ALTERNATE CONTEMPORARY LINGUISTIC SPELLING	MEANING (COMMENTS)
ohén:ton		in the front of it, in front or before
Ohén:ton Karihwatéhkwen		Opening Address (lit. what we say before we do anything important)
Ohkí:we	Okhi:we/Ohkiwe	ceremony for the dead (lit. it is just roaming around)
ohné:kanos		(drinking) water
ohóntsia	onhwéntsia/onhwentsya	earth
oià:ta	oyà:ta	body
oien'kwa'ón:we	oyènkwa onwe	real/first/Indian tobacco
oié:ri	oyeri	ten
Ojibwa		adjective describing the Ojibwa people
Ojibway		noun for the Ojibwa people

MOHAWK	ALTERNATE CONTEMPORARY LINGUISTIC SPELLING	MEANING (COMMENTS)
o'kèn:ra		soil, dirt, ashes
Onehó:ron		Drum Dance (lit. the tanned/finished hide covers this)
ó:nenhste		corn
Onenio'tehá:ka	Onenyo'tehá:ka	Oneida (lit. the ones that live around the stone that stands up)
onennó:ron	onennoron	sweet flag
onennoron'kó:wa		big sweet flag/big white pond lily
onén:tsha		arm
onkwaià:ta	onkwayà:ta	our body
onkwatsísta		our fire, our nation's fire
Onkwehón:we		Indian, First Nations people (lit. the real people)
Ononta'kehá:ka		Onondaga (lit. the people of the hills)

MOHAWK	ALTERNATE CONTEMPORARY LINGUISTIC SPELLING	MEANING (COMMENTS)
onón:wara	onònwara	brain
Oronhiatá:kon	Oronhyatakwen	the sky that bursts (Mohawk name of Paul Bero)
Ostowa kó:wa (Cayuga)	Ostor'a kó:wa (Mohawk)	Great Feather Dance
o'tónhkwa		fire or flame
otsionehskwén:rie	otsinenhskwenrye	wild ginger
Otsiskanie	ehsganye (Onondaga)	women's songs
otsiskwa		woman's reproductive organ
ó:wise		ice
Ráke'ni		Father
Rákhso		Grandfather
Raterontanónhnha	Raterontahnónhnha	Sub-Chief (lit. he's the caretaker of the big tree)

MOHAWK	ALTERNATE CONTEMPORARY LINGUISTIC SPELLING	MEANING (COMMENTS)
Ratinien'kehá:ka	Ratinyenkehaka	Mohawk (lit. the people who live where the flint stones are)
Ratironhiakehró:non	Ratironhyakehronon	the Sky Dweller Beings
Ratiwé:ras		the Thunderers
Roiá:nehr	Royá:ner	Chief (lit. he's of the good, he's good)
Ro'nikonhrowá:nen		he who has great ideas/his understanding is great
rontenentshanawá:kon		circle wampum (lit. they are holding arms up together/they are holding each others' arms up)
Rotihshennakéhte		they carry/lug the name (of whichever clan adopts them)
Rotiianéhshon	Rotiyanérhshon	Chiefs (lit. they of the good) (masculine)
Rotikwáho		Wolf Clan
Roti'nehsí:io	Roti'nehsiyo	Snipe Clan

MOHAWK	ALTERNATE CONTEMPORARY LINGUISTIC SPELLING	MEANING (COMMENTS)
Rotinenio'thró:non	Rotinenyo'thró:non	Deer Clan
Roti'nikonhrakwenhtará:'on		they whose minds have fallen to the ground (Ceremonial speakers including Tom frequently drop the "ra" and say: Roti'nikonhkwenhtará:'on.)
Roti'nikonhrakáhte		they whose minds are strong (Ceremonial speakers including Tom frequently drop the "ra" and say: Roti'nikonhkáhte.)
Rotinonhsón:ni		the People of the Longhouse
Rotiskaré:wake		Bear Clan
saià:ta	sayà:ta	your body
Sakokweniónkwas	Shakokweniónkwas	he who wins them over/enables them to do something
sanón:wara	sanònwara	your brains

Mohawk	Alternate Contemporary Linguistic Spelling	Meaning (Comments)
sewa'nikonhrakwenhtará:'on	sewa'nikonhkwenhtará:'on	your minds are on the ground (Ceremonial speakers including Tom frequently drop the "ra" and say: sewa'nikonhkwenhtará:'on.)
Shakorihonnién:ni	Shakorihonnyenni	The Teacher (lit. he is the teacher)
sha'té:ioht	sha'teyoht	it is the same on one side as the other side
sha'té:kon		eight
Shawískara		for possible meanings, see Chapter 7 re wisk (five)
shé:kon		hello (lit. still)
Shonkwahtsí:'a.	Shonkwahtsya	Our Eldest Brother (lit. our elder brother)
Shonkwaia'tíson	Shonkwaya'tihson	Creator (lit. he made/finished our bodies)
ska	ska'	one (in Seneca, Onondaga, Cayuga)
Skahnéhtati	Skanehtati	Albany
skanáhkwa		only one partner/marriage

MOHAWK	ALTERNATE CONTEMPORARY LINGUISTIC SPELLING	MEANING (COMMENTS)
skanonhsakará:ti	skanónhsati	one side of the house
Takia'tíson	Takya'tihson	my Creator
Teharonhiawá:kon	Tharonhyawá:kon	he holds up the sky
-téhkwen		acknowledgement
tehnikhen	tehníkhon	twins
teieia'taréhtha	teyeya'taréhtha	seer (lit. makes a decision on your behalf/deliberates for you)
Tekáhstia'ks	tekáhskia'ks/ tekahstyaks	it talks a lot (Tom's parrot's name)
tékeni		two
tenkatsienhi:ia'ke	tenkatsienhiya'ke	it will cross over the fire
tenthsenentsha	tenthsenentshahn	handshake (lit. wrap his arm)

MOHAWK	ALTERNATE CONTEMPORARY LINGUISTIC SPELLING	MEANING (COMMENTS)
tenthshenentshakarén:ron		handshake (lit. shake/rock his arm)
tho		so be it, that's it
tkaié:ri	tkayeri	it is correct
tóta		grandpa, grandma
tsià:ta	tsyàtak	seven
Tsikónhsase		she has a new face (name of the first Clan Mother)
tsi nikiohtón:ne	tsi niyohtón:ne	the way it was
wáhta		maple tree
wa'kieià:ia'ke	wa'tyeyaya'ke	she crossed over

MOHAWK	ALTERNATE CONTEMPORARY LINGUISTIC SPELLING	MEANING (COMMENTS)
Wakskaré:wake	Wakhskarewake	I am Bear Clan.
wa'onkkaré:wahte		they hurt me
wa'onthahará:ko		they have gone away from their spirituality (lit. removed themselves from the path)
-watéhkwen		of the nature of, of that nature or of that environment (lit. the words/business that acknowledge)
watkonnonhwará:ton	wa'tkonnonweraton	I give you my greetings and thankfulness together with love, I greet you, I acknowledge you
wísk		five

PAGE #	MOHAWK	TYENDINAGA DIALECT/SPELLING (IF IT DIFFERS FROM THE TEXT)	TOM'S LOOSE TRANSLATION
9	Ne ká:ti Takia'tíson entehsatahonhsiiohste. Ne ká:ti wi wahi kenh niionkwè:take. Kenh nón:wa iakwaia'taié:ri nón:wa wenhniserá:te. Á:ienhre ne akwé:kon aionkwata'karí:teke ta ká:ti wi ne Takia'tíson ne ká:ti enkate'nién:ten ne enkerihwaké:ron. Ne ne wi wahi ionkwanonhsión:ni ne tsi ní:ioht kionkwehtáhkwen. Ne ká:ti wi wahi enkate'nienton enkhe'nikonhraientáhten ne ká:ti ne wi wahi tóhsa thé:nen thaiawén:' en ne sa'nikòn:ra. Ne ká:ti ne tsi nihatiwennò:ten nitenatatekon renhmarà:ken. Ne ká:ti enkatste. Ta eh ká:ti niiohtonhak onkwa'nikòn:ra.	Ne kati Takya'tihson entesatahonhsiyohste. Ne kati wi wahi kenh niyakonkwètake. Kenh nonwa yakwaya'tayeri nonwa wenhniserate. Ayenhre' akwekon ayonkwata'karite ta kati wi ne Takya'tihson ne kati enkate'nyenton ne enkerihwakeron. Ne ne wi wahi yonkwanonhsyonni ne tsi niyoht yonkwe'tahkwen. Ne kati wi wahi enkate'nyenton enkhe'nikonhrayentahten ne kati ne wi wahi tohsa ki the thaye'sa'nikonra. Ne kati ne tsi nihatiwennoten nitenatatekon rahnaraken'. Ne kati enkatste'. Ta eh kati niyohtonhak onkwa'nikonra.	I said, "Today is a special day on which I'm going to attempt to explain the spiritual worldview of the Iroquois, so that's why I'm gonna use English." So I told the Creator, "Don't run away on me, 'cause you're hearing me talk a different language!"

PAGE #	MOHAWK	TYENDINAGA DIALECT/SPELLING (IF IT DIFFERS FROM THE TEXT)	TOM'S LOOSE TRANSLATION
34	Ne ne tsi nikahá:wi "sebenteen pifty pour."		In the time 1754.
34	Né:'e onkwahsóhtshera'kénha tsi nón:we niiakwahwatsiratákie. Ne éh tho wahontkennnísa Skahnéhtati. Eh né:'e éh tho ne ratihá:wi ne Onekohrha'shón:'a akia'tahnha'shón:'a. Kwah o'tokén:'en kaienton ohswen'karà:ke tsi ní:wa thi akia'tahnha. Né:'e ne éh tho wahonwatirihónnien Ratihnarà:ken. Ne ne tsi ní:ioht ionkwe'tahkwen ionkwaianerénhsera.	Ne'e onkwahsohtshera'kenha tsi nonwe niyonkwatsiratatye. Ne etho wahontkennisa' Skanehtati. Eh ne'e etho ne ratihawi ne Onekorhashonha atyátanha'shonha. Kwah o'token'en kayenton ohswenkarake tsi niwat thi atyatanha. Ne'e ne etho wahonwatirihonnyen' Ratihnaraken. Ne ne tsi niyoht yonkwe'tahkwen yonkwayanerenhsera.	Our grandfather's time, they were gone to a meeting in Albany. And there for the first time they took the great wampum belts, they even touched the floor, how big they were. And there they were telling the white people about our Constitution, our Great Law, of how to make government.
34	Ne' éh tho théntsko:te.		They're sitting there.

Page #	Mohawk	Tyendinaga Dialect/Spelling (If It Differs from the Text)	Tom's Loose Translation
45	Enhhh tsi wa'kahskane'ke thí:ken tsi nón:we nikakwirò:ten ahsén:nen tsi nó:nwe iawanákere, ohtè:ra ni tewakatohontsión:ni tókat asekhnekónnien onerahtónmion. Ahh tsi skén:nen enkanontónnion.	Enhhh tsi wa'kahskane'ke thiken tsi nonwe nikakwiroten ahsennen tsi nonwe yonkwanakere, ohtera ni tewakatonhwentsyonni tokat asekhnekonnyen' onerahtakeri. Ahh tsi skennen enkennontonnyon.	In the middle of where we live, there's that tree. And I would have no greater pleasure, my husband, than if you were to go over to that tree, and get some of its small tender fresh roots. And its bark, its skin. Make a tea for me to drink. I would be so satisfied and I would have such great peace.
45	Sesa'nikónhrhen ken í:iah teió:wen's aiakwatsté:riste thi okwi:re?	Sesa'nikónh:ren ken iah teyowen's ayonkwaya'tsterihste thi okwi:re?	Did you forget that we're not supposed to touch that tree?
45	Hánio wá:s tsi a'é:ren niahá:se.	Hanyo wa:s tsi aé:ron wa:s thi nyahahse.	*DOGGONE IT! GET OVER THERE AND DO WHAT I SAID, INSTEAD OF TALKING ABOUT STUFF LIKE THAT.*
46	Hátskwi. Shá:wi ken thi:ken ohtè:ra? Shá:wi ken thi:ken onónhkwa?	Hatskwi. Sawi ken thi ohtera? Sawi ken thi ononhkwa?	You got that root or that medicine?

PAGE #	MOHAWK	TYENDINAGA DIALECT/SPELLING (IF IT DIFFERS FROM THE TEXT)	TOM'S LOOSE TRANSLATION
46	Í:iah teiotón:'on.	Yah teyoton'onh.	I couldn't do it. (Literally: It's not possible.)
46	Ah sháthi tsi iohá:te.	Ah sathi niyohate.	Get out of the way.
49	Né:' e wa'thohén:rehte.		He began to scream at the top of his lungs.
92	Onekwénhtara niwahsohkò:ten kí:ken akwakià:tawi.	Onekwénhtara niwahsohkò:ten kiken akwatyatawi.	This shirt is colored red (the color of the blood that flows in my body).
92	Oròn:ia niwahsohkò:ten thí:ken akokià:tawi.	Orònya niwahsohkò:ten thiken akotyatawi.	She is wearing a blouse or a shirt that is blue (the color of the sky).
92	Ne óhonte ne' niwahsohkò:ten akokià:tawi.	Ne óhonte ne niwahsohkò:ten akotyatawi.	Her blouse is green (the color of the grass that grows, that color).
92	Tentsitewahwawén:eke thi rón:kwe.		We will take his body and we will wrap it in the garden blanket of Mother Earth.

Page #	Mohawk	Tyendinaga Dialect/Spelling (If It Differs from the Text)	Tom's Loose Translation
104	Ensewarihó:wanahte sewen'tá:ra.	Ensewarihówanenhste sewen'tà:ra.	Announce proudly what clan you belong to, to your kids.
117	Grandson, tóhsa sa'nikonhraksen ia'tekaié:ri tsi ni:kon wa'konrihónnien tsi náhe í:se ia'satahsónteren ó:nen. Ó:nen ní:'i wa'kerihwaié:rite ne tsi iohontsiá:te ia'satahsónteron.	Grandson, tóhsa sa'nikonhraksen yetkayéri tsi ní:kon wa'konrihónnyen tsi náhe í:se satahsónteren ó:nen. Ó:nen ní:'i wa' kerihwayé:rite ne tsi yonhwentsyate satahsónteron.	Grandson I have done my work and my duty upon the Mother Earth. I raised all my kids and grandchildren. I taught 'em what's right. Everything I prepared for them. And now I finished all my work. Now I have to go on the road to the Spirit World. So Grandson, don't be sad. Lift up your eyes, roll up your sleeves: you must take over. Your turn now.
121	Onkwathón:te'ne.		Yeah, I did hear.

PAGE #	MOHAWK	TYENDINAGA DIALECT/SPELLING (IF IT DIFFERS FROM THE TEXT)	TOM'S LOOSE TRANSLATION
121	Grandma, aesathontá:ton ken ionkwateweienstá:non? Í:iah ni'té:kehre aesahnhó:ton tekanatá:ronhwe.	Grandma, aesathontá:ton ken akateweyenhstá:ne? Yah ni:i tekehre aesehnhó:ton tekanatá:ronhwe.	Grandma, can I go to school? Because I don't want the white people to put you in their jail in Malone, New York. You can't talk English. How you gonna talk to them? And because of me, you can go to jail.
133	Ha'o shehrón:ri. Ha'o shehrón:ri.		Cut her off, cut her off. (Editor's note: literally, "Tell her, tell her.")
154	Ahsathón:tate ken tahsewennaté:ni ahsén:nen tsi nihawennò:ten?	Hakats sathontat kenh sewennateni ha'sonni tsi nihawennò:ten?	Can you translate it into English language?
169	Tóka she ne shahoti'tá:ra. Enhotíniake í:iah ní:'i thakheiakia'táhrhahse ó:ni oh nà:ken nienhén:ke í:iah ni:'i thakheiakia'táhrhahse.	Toka se ne shahoti'tare. Ahotinya'ke yah ni:i thatekheyatharhahse oni ohnaken niyenhenke yah ni:i thatekheyatharhahse.	If the same clan marries together, I will not be a party to that. I will step back and I will not be in there, what they're doing. They will be on their own.

PAGE #	MOHAWK	TYENDINAGA DIALECT/SPELLING (IF IT DIFFERS FROM THE TEXT)	TOM'S LOOSE TRANSLATION
188	Takia'tison niá:wen. Niá:wen tsi nikari:wes wa'tkatawén:rie tsi iohontsiá:te wahskenaktothåhse takatawén:rie. Ne ká:ti ne Takia'tíson ó:nen ká:ti tkaié:ri ó:nen ká:ti enwá:ton enskahtén:ti. Ó:nen enkoniaterennotháhse.	Takya'tishon nya:wen. Nya:wen tsi nikariwes wa'katawenrye tsi yohontsyate wahskenaktothahse akatawenrye. Ne kati ne Takya'tishon ó:nen kati tkaye:ri ó:nen kati enwaton enskahtenti. Ó:nen enkonyaterennotháhse.	My Creator, thank you for the wonderful life that I lived, since I was born. My Creator, thank you for the children that were born to me and my wife. My Creator, thank you for all the grandchildren that were born, that I've seen get born. Thank you for how I was able to take care of them, all these years. And now my Creator, I know that my journey and my visit here is close to being over. And so I'm ready to come to you now. I'm ready to go home. And so I sing to you for all the wonderful gifts all these years since I was born, my song of thankfulness.
189	Kwah ratirennotákie Karonhiä:ke wahón:ne.	Kwah ratirennotatye karonhyake wahonne.	They're singing as they go to the next world, the world of our Creator.

PAGE #	MOHAWK	TYENDINAGA DIALECT/SPELLING (IF IT DIFFERS FROM THE TEXT)	TOM'S LOOSE TRANSLATION
189	Ne ne ionerákwat tsi nihonkiehrha thi:ken ratiksa'okon'a iethiatere'okón:'a ne ne ionerákwat. Í:iah nonwén:ton tesathonté:' on tsi na'teiotenonhianihton tsi niióianere nahò:ten rotitharáhkwen.	Ne ne yonerakwat tsi nihontyerha thiken ratiksa'okonha yethiyatereokon'a ne ne yonerakwat. Yah nonwenton tesathonte'onh tsi nateteyonihton tsi niyoyanere nahò:ten rotitharahkwen.	You will never believe the scope and the magnitude and the sophistication of what those kids are talking about up there. The way that they see the world, the way that the world was put together, they're putting all together. That's what he's teaching them, that boy, my grandson. Unbelievable.
196	taiotiiakenhákie ne onekwénhsa	tayoyaken'onhatye ne onekwenhsa	my feet are bleeding
196	Ionekhwá:' on kahsi'tà:ke.	Yonekwen'onh kehsi'take.	Blood all over.
196	Hé: eh [nón:we] akwahsi'ta'kéhshon.		There, all over my feet.
246	Wahshétkenhte kí:ken akenónhkwa.	Wahshetkenhte kiken akenonhkwa.	You ruined my medicine.
246	Ahhh í:iah ki' thé:nen teiokié:ren.	Ahhh yah ki the teyotyeren.	It's all right.

PAGE #	MOHAWK	TYENDINAGA DIALECT/SPELLING (IF IT DIFFERS FROM THE TEXT)	TOM'S LOOSE TRANSLATION
249	Tóhsha nonwén:ton ensewatsté:riste oh nahò:ten teka'nikonhraténies.	Tosha nonwenton aesewaterihwahsteriste nahò:ten nika'nikonhratenyons.	Don't ever touch anything that alters or changes your natural state of thinking, your mind.
254	Ó:nen ska'nikòn:ra ón:ton.	Onen ska'nikonhrat ónton.	Now there's one mind.
309	Né:'e ne katkekshón:'a tá:we awenhnísera. Ne iethíatere'okón:'a né:'e ohontsiakwé:kon enhonwatihtháhrhahse ne ahonwanatahónhsatate.	Né:'e ne katkekshonha tá:we wenhnísera. Ne yethíyatere'okón:'a né:'e ohontsiakwe:kon enhonwatitharhahse tahnon enhontahonsatate.	There is a day coming in the future when our grandchildren, our great grandchildren, they will speak to the whole world and the whole world will listen.
311	Tenwatkarén:ron tsi iohontsiá:te.	Tenwatkarenron tsi yonhwentsyate.	The earth will rock.

PAGE #	MOHAWK	TYENDINAGA DIALECT/SPELLING (IF IT DIFFERS FROM THE TEXT)	TOM'S LOOSE TRANSLATION
325	Ne Takia'tíson tahskwatahontsi:iohst ne ne sakoniatathré:wahte tókat nahò:tenk wa'konrihwàkhsa'se tsi wa'tkatawén:rie tsi iohontsiá:te. Ne tewakatahontsióhn:ni aóhskon ka'nikonhrí:io enwatstónhake ó:nen enkaien'kwarakétsko.	Ne Takya'tihson tahskwatahontsiyohst ne ne shakoyatathrewahte tókat ok nahò:ten wa'keriwaksa'se tsi wakatawenrye tsi yonhwentsyate. Ne tewakatahontsyonni aonskon ka'nikonhriyo enwatstonhake ó:nen enkayonkwaraketsko.	You who are my Creator, I ask you to listen to me. I want to ask your forgiveness, my Creator, if I did something as I'm walking this earth to offend you or hurt your feelings or anybody. My Creator I ask you to forgive me, so that when I touch my hand on my prayer tobacco or I become part of your Great Feather Dance, I carry no blemish, I carry no sin, I carry no bad things. But I come, my words come to you with complete pureness of love and compassion.
326	Ne Takia'tíson ne watkonnonhwará:ton ne ó:nen ne wa'konien'kwahshonnia'te.	Takya'tihson ne wa'tkonnonhwerá:ton ne ó:nen ne wa'kwayenkwasonnya't.	Editor's loose translation: My Creator, I greet you and thank you with love and now I am causing the tobacco to find its way to you.

Page #	Mohawk	Tyendinaga Dialect/Spelling (If It Differs from the Text)	Tom's Loose Translation
326	Ne Takia'tison ne sé:ron onkwaia'tákta enkaién:take otsísta ne sé:ron eniohsatstenhseraién:take ne ne tsi iotékha ne thí:ken otsísta enkakwé:ni enkahará:tate ne enkaronhíawe'ehste ne enien'kwa'ón:we ne enkawennahá:wihte onkwawén:na.	Ne Takya'tihson ne se ero yonkwaya'tákta enkayentake otsihste ne ne se ero enyo'shatstenhserayentak ne ne tsi yotekha ne thi otsihste enkakweni enkaharatat ne enkaronhyawe'ehste ne onkwehón:we ne onkwawennahawihte yonkwawenna.	Editor's loose translation: My Creator, indeed it's beside us now, the place where the fire is. Where it's burning is where the tobacco receives strength and it will be able to go up on the smoke. And carry the Indian (original) people's words and pierce through the sky.
326	Ne Takia'tison ne shiwá:se tsi iohontsiá:te tehseiá:wi ionkwahsatstensera'kénha ne shiwá:se tsi iohontsiá:te ne oien'kwa'ón:we ne sé:ron ne ó:nen aionkwatonhwéntsionhse kaia'takenhnháhtshera ne ká:ti eniakwawennakén:seren oien'kwa'ón:we. Ne enkakwé:ni enkahará:tate onkwawenna'shón:'a tsi nón:we tisatahonhsiióhstha.	Ne Takya'tison ni shiwase tsi yohwentsyate tesheyawi yonkwa'shatstenhsera'kénha ne shiwase tsi yonhwentsyate ne oyènkwa onwe ne se ero ne ó:nen ayonkwatonhwentsyohse kaya'takenhasera ne kati ayewennokonhseron oyènkwa onwe. Ne enkakweni akaharatate yonkwawenna'shón:'a tsi nonwe satahonhsiyohstha.	Now, my Creator, you gave this tobacco to our grandfathers long ago, when the world was new. And you told us that whenever a time comes in the future that we the humans ever need help or assistance, or we wanna talk to you, that we could use this tobacco and make a fire. And the smoke of the fire will carry the tobacco up.

PAGE #	MOHAWK	TYENDINAGA DIALECT/SPELLING (IF IT DIFFERS FROM THE TEXT)	TOM'S LOOSE TRANSLATION
			And that smoke will catch our thinking and our prayer. And it will carry it to the top of the sky, of the universe, to where you listen to all. And so now, to the power of the tobacco that's been working since the beginning of time in this world that we are still using for all this time, now we offer the tobacco to the tobacco for carrying our message.
327	Ne shiwá:se tsi iohontsiá:te ne wahsherihontónnion ne Kaié:ri Niionkwé:take Ratironhiakehró:non.	Ne shiwase tsi yonhwentsyate ne kwah sherihontonnyon ne Kayeri Niyonkwetake Ratironhyakehronon.	In the beginning when the world was new you commissioned four sacred beings.
344	Tóhsa nowén:ton ne shahoti'tá:' a enhonterihón:ten tókat tho neniá:wen'ne katkekshon'a ne ká:ti enionkhihetkénhte.	Tohsa nowén:ton ne shahoti'tara enhonterihón:ten tókat tho neniá:wen'ne katke'kshonha ne kati enyonkhihetkenhte.	Do not ever make a leader or a Chief (or positions of whatever) from somebody who's from the same clan on both sides, their mother and father.

Page #	Mohawk	Tyendinaga Dialect/Spelling (If It Differs from the Text)	Tom's Loose Translation
371	Né:'e se's ken thí:ken iotéha tsi nihotirihòten.	Ne se's ken thiken yotéhat tsi nihotirihò:ten.	Editor's translation: Isn't that shameful, the way that they are./ Their ways are shameful.
375	Niá:wen Takia'tíson ne watkonnonhwará:ton.	Nyá:wen Takya'tíson ne wa'tkonnonhwerá:ton.	Thank you, you who made me. I send you my greetings, my thankfulness and my love.
380	Shé:kon skennen'ko:wa ken?		Colloquially: hello, how are you? (lit. is it still the great peace; does it still exist?)
382	Takia'tíson ne watkonnonhwará:ton tóka senh ónhka nahò:tenk wahéthken rokion tho tsi niwahsón:tes wá:s isi tho wa'koniaté:kwahte.	Takya'tíhson ne wa'tkonnonhwerá:ton tóka senh onkha'k ok nahò:ten wahetken Rotyenh tsi niwahsontehs wahs ishi wa'koyatekwahte.	Go, anything bad. Go, anything that's gonna hurt my family. Get outta here. We chase it away.
384	Takia'tíson watkonnonhwará:ton. Ó:nenhste, Áhsen Nisewatatennò:sen watkonnonhwará:ton.	Takya'tíhson wa'tkonnonhwerá:ton Ó:nenhste, Áhsen Nisewatatennò:sen wa'tkonnonhwerá:ton.	My Creator, Corn, Three Sisters, thank you. I send you my greetings, my thankfulness and my love.

CPSIA information can be obtained
at www.ICGtesting.com
Printed in the USA
LVHW052200260622
722161LV00001B/10

9 781436 335652